"YOU'RE OKAY,
IT'S JUST A BRUISE"

"YOU'RE OKAY, IT'S JUST A BRUISE"

ROB HUIZENGA, M.D.

*A Doctor's Sideline Secrets
About Pro Football's Most
Outrageous Team*

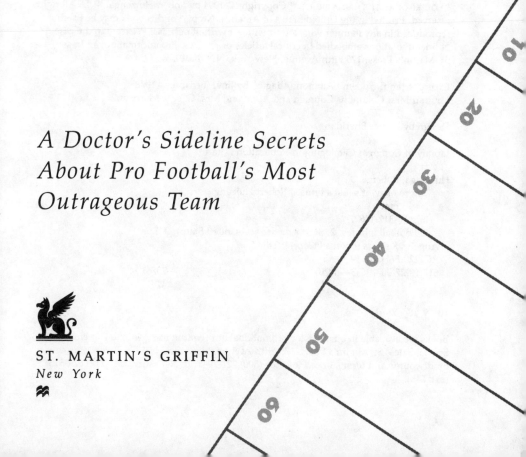

ST. MARTIN'S GRIFFIN
New York

Excerpt from the poem "Albinoni Adagio" by Jim Morrison, © 1978
Mr. and Mrs. Columbus Courson and Adm. and Mrs. George Morrison.

Design by Patrice Sheridan

Library of Congress Cataloging-in-Publication Data

Huizenga, Robert.
     You're okay, it's just a bruise / Robert Huizenga.
        p.   cm.
     ISBN 0-312-13627-7
     1. Football injuries. 2. Sports medicine—United States. 3. Los
Angeles Raiders (Football team) I. Title.
RC1220.F6H851994
617.1'027'08879633—dc20   94-20761
                                                 CIP

10 9 8 7 6 5 4

Contents

Author's Note

This is a true story, based on my firsthand experiences as team physician to the Los Angeles Raiders. I was eyewitness to most of the events portrayed. In some instances I have also relied on documentary materials and on numerous interviews with other participants or eyewitnesses.

The reader should understand that much of the dialogue in this book has necessarily been re-created from memory and is not intended to be a verbatim transcript. I did not contemporaneously record conversations or keep stenographic notes. However, I have to the best of my ability strived to achieve an accurate portrayal of both the substance and meaning of conversations and events.

It is important to note that I am a physician and the subjects of many of the events portrayed were my patients. In deference to my view of the discretion a physician should exercise, I have adhered to certain guidelines in publishing this book. Where I discuss treatment-related information or medical conditions, obtained during the course of medical evaluations or treatments, I have received permission from those treated or evaluated. I wish to convey thanks to those who granted such permission, often at the expense of a degree of privacy. Without their cooperation I could not have as fully addressed important issues concerning the medical treatment of professional athletes.

If an individual I treated or evaluated could not be located, or if permission was not received, I have either deleted mention of that individual or his treatment or condition; disguised the individual or the medically related event, at times using fictional names (indicated in italics whenever they appear), time periods, or affiliations; or excluded reference to sensitive information, reporting only so much about that person as is generally known to the public.

Finally, in certain situations I have not considered myself limited by confidentiality: for example, where information was not secured in the course of physician-patient contact, but was based solely on my general association with the Raiders, my nonmedical presence during events or conversations, or my independent research.

1

A Typical Day at the Office

The Orange Bowl was rocking! I mean actually swaying on its foundation, as 75,151 Raider-hating Dolphin fanatics stomped their feet in unison and screamed, "Beat L.A.! Beat L.A.! Beat L.A.!"

Only nine seconds remained in the opening half. We were ahead by a couple of points, but now Miami had our battered defense backed up to the one-inch line. Coach Don Shula, Miami's stoic-faced leader, waved off his field goal team. It was December 11, 1984. The Dolphins were 12–1, this year's top AFC team, and Shula wanted to beat us—the defending world champion Los Angeles Raiders—in the worst way.

Bob Zeman, the Raiders' defensive coordinator, sent in the gap goal-line smash defense. Dolphin quarterback Dan Marino handed the ball to Woody Bennett. Bam! He was immediately bent backward and dropped by Raider heavies Matt Millen and Mike Davis. The gun sounded, ending the half. Our sideline jumped in celebration.

As the reenergized Raiders jogged off toward the locker room, I ran out on the field to check one of our linebackers, who'd been stricken with a violent stomach flu. He'd started vomiting early last night, and by game time had been passing enough watery stool to qualify as a cholera patient.

"I feel like shit," he said as I threw an arm around his waist and helped him off the field.

"Are you light-headed?" I asked.

"That was two quarters ago, doc. I'm at the one-foot-in-the-coffin stage now."

"We'll pump in some intravenous fluids during half," I said.

"And I'll tell Coach Zeman you're questionable for the rest of the game."

Suddenly, just twenty yards from the visitor's locker room entrance, we were surrounded by an inebriated mob. The end-zone stands angled inward forcing us to run through a narrow alley. Red-faced, drunken Dolphin partisans—just a yard or two away from us on either side—were hurling profanities, peanuts, half-filled Cokes, and seat cushions.

Just to our right, one rowdy male fan in his mid-twenties caught Lyle Alzado right in the face with a full cup of beer, and then began to beat his chest in a drunken Tarzan impersonation. As we watched in horror, Lyle lunged over a four-foot retaining wall, grabbed the startled troublemaker's sweatshirt with one swat of his muddy left paw, and started beating the fan over the head with his helmet. Four of us rushed to grab Lyle's leg and pull him down, but he peeled us off with one torque of his hips.

Luckily, the foolhardy fan was able to stumble up several concrete stadium steps, out of Lyle's reach. Dazed and with blood dripping down his forehead, the fan was suddenly subdued. I wondered if he was sober enough to realize that he had come within a helmet hit of death.

Inside the locker room, the walking wounded congregated around four small examining tables in the cramped trainers' cubicle. It had the feel of a county emergency room on a Saturday night.

My first priority was the linebacker. A trainer had already neatly set out a large-bore intravenous needle, intravenous tubing, and several clear plastic bags of a sterile sugar-salt solution. I quickly inserted one line in his right forearm while the assistant trainer rigged a bent hanger off an overhead pipe to act as a makeshift intravenous pole. I took his blood pressure lying down, then standing up. This maneuver caused the linebacker's blood pressure to drop, confirming dehydration as a cause of his dizziness.

"You're a couple of quarts low," I said. "Maybe even a gallon."

"Pump it into me, doc," he said. "I've got a game to catch."

Replacing several quarts of fluid in a ten-minute halftime is like changing a flat tire in ten seconds in the Indy 500 pits. It can be done, but it takes know-how and teamwork. I threw in a second large-bore intravenous, and soon we had both salt-solution bags hanging, wrapped with blood pressure cuffs, which we then pumped up so the pressure would force the intravenous fluid down the tubing and into the linebacker's body faster. This was a tricky proposition, because the pressure from the blood pressure cuff could cause the plastic bag of intravenous fluid to pop and spray over the room. Worse, the vein receiving the fluid might pop. Luckily, all went well, and I was able to turn my attention to a receiver who had been patiently waiting behind me during all of this.

"My left eye's killing me, doc. I can catch a ball with one hand, but with one eye, I don't know."

"What happened?" I asked.

"I think I got swiped during a tackle."

I pulled out my medical kit and fished out a bottle of ophthalmic numbing solution as well as a strip of bright orange dye. I touched the impregnated fluorescein strip to the player's eye. A tiny bright orange line formed on the clear part of the eye, suspiciously similar in size and shape to a fingernail: a moderate-sized corneal abrasion. With his pain relieved by numbing drops, I did a rudimentary eye exam. Standing on the other side of the room, I told him to close his good eye. I held up three fingers.

"How many fingers?" I asked.

"Is that how many fingers up or how many fingers folded down?" chimed in Dave Casper, who was sitting on a nearby table getting a shot into the injured arch of his left foot.

"Five," the player said.

I was just about to respond when I looked back and saw that another player had added two more fingers behind my hand. Suddenly the linebacker screamed for me.

"Doc, get over here. Pull these pipes out. I gotta go."

"Wait! Halftime's not over for five more minutes," I replied.

"No, I gotta *go!*" the player said, pointing to his rear end and moving off the table, intravenous tubes and all.

The trainers and I quickly unhooked the hangers from the ceiling pipes and walked his double IV apparatus to the bathroom. The linebacker made it to the toilet. It was quite a sight. Two ball boys were perched atop the walls on either side of the toilet, manually squeezing the IV bags. I was pinched in between the toilet paper and the toilet bowl taking a sitting blood pressure. Then a defensive coach came by to go over the halftime changes in the defensive coverage schemes. All the while, diarrhea was hitting the bowl like a Malaysian monsoon.

As the player got up, I was faced with the final indignity of this halftime. Because I didn't want the player to bend his elbows, which might disturb the intravenous needles, he couldn't reach back and wipe himself. Enter teamwork. I obligingly wiped the patient clean after I took some stool to test for the presence of blood.

"Doc," said one of the trainers, who was standing on the adjacent toilet and looking over the stall, "if they could only see you now back at Harvard."

Out the bathroom door, I could see the team gathered around Coach Tom Flores in the main locker room area.

"I want you guys to turn up the intensity now. No stupid penalties—don't lose your heads. Just good hard Raider football for the next thirty minutes. Now get out there and get 'em!"

The players cheered approval.

The security guard at the door signaled it was time to go back out on the field, but Ted Hendricks, one tough SOB and a future Hall of Famer who had just retired the year before, stepped forward to say something to the team.

"You motherf——ers," he said, "don't embarrass me in my hometown. Get out there and hit somebody."

To demonstrate, he rammed his head into one of the metal lockers. It buckled inward. The team was hushed for a moment, half expecting his eyes to roll back or blood to gush from his mouth.

Instead he said in a psychotic snarl, "Take no prisoners, and that goes for that f——ing minister too!"

Hendricks was referring to a local pastor who had led the entire stadium in a prayer before the start of the game. Our bowed heads had jerked up in surprise and anger when he had ended his prayer by asking God to help the Miami Dolphins prevail in this game.

As the team exited, I pulled the IV lines out. On the next table, head team trainer George Anderson adjusted a large customized rubber band behind Dave Casper's thigh. One end of the two-inch-wide slab of elastic was taped just below the buttock; the other end was secured just below the knee. It was something Anderson had invented to prevent the knee from hyperextending, and of course it helped flex the knee, thereby easing the pain and minimizing further injury to Casper's ripped hamstring muscle. Dave Casper, an eleven-year veteran All-Pro tight end, was for all intents and purposes playing this game on one leg.

I went over to help the linebacker slip on his shoulder pads and jersey.

"Gee, I can't believe it," he said. "I actually feel good."

"We call this the instant man syndrome," I said. "Like instant rice. Take a pruned player, pour in a few liters of salt water, and puff!—instant man."

"Doc, you're sure these pills'll stop . . ." he began.

He was worried about an uncontrolled burst of diarrhea in front of twenty or thirty million prime-time viewers, and I assured him that the three Lomotils I had just given him would prevent that from happening.

"You know, sometimes you bear down and strain when you make a hit," he growled. "I'm warning you . . . if I get any brown stuff on the bottom of my uniform, you're fired as my doctor."

How did I ever get into this Raider team doctor thing? I guess it started on a cloudless spring afternoon in 1983. Sprinting as fast as I could, I faked right, cut hard to my left for a stride, then veered right. My defender spun about 360 degrees. By the time he reestablished his bearings, I was five yards past him. Gone.

Suddenly my right ankle exploded.

"Yeeow!"

I fell, victimized by one of the Santa Monica park system's midfield sprinkler heads. I writhed in pain, still trying to protect the rugby ball as my green-and-white-striped teammates formed overhead to ruck the ball out to the remaining running backs.

Half frustrated, half embarrassed, I waved in my replacement and hobbled toward the sidelines as the action progressed down the rugby pitch. My pregnant wife met me halfway.

"Not again!" she groaned, handing me a bag of ice. "It's time for you to start playing golf like the rest of the doctors."

"Ah, it's just a sprain," I said as the ice began to mute the jabbing pain down to an annoying throb. "I'll be okay."

"Yeah? What about me? I've got to live with your depression till you're able to run again."

I nodded in agreement, and chased four aspirin down with a glass of water. "Yeah, you're right. I probably should pop an Elavil with each aspirin."

I resolved to see somebody tomorrow at the hospital where I worked. Someone who could fix me up. I wasn't about to let this injury slow me down.

* * *

"This is classic. You see this thigh rash? Notice the redness on the outside, surrounding a central pale area."

The group of UCLA medical students inched closer. Part of my duties as chief medical resident at Cedars-Sinai Medical Center was to teach an assortment of third-year students how to spot various unusual diseases.

"You don't mind if we talk shop in front of you?" I asked the patient, a tan male in his forties.

"Nah, I can take it," the patient replied with only a little hesitation in his voice.

"Now if I tell you he's got multiple painful joints, what's the diagnosis?" I queried the group.

"Lupus?" came one response.

"Okay, that's an arthritic condition with a rash, but that rash is typically in a butterfly pattern over the cheeks and the bridge of the nose."

"Lyme disease," another answered.

"Bravo! Lyme disease, with the five-dollar medical term for the rash being erythema chronic migrans. And the fact that we're here in a monitored heart ward gives you a clue that he also suffered from a heart-conduction abnormality."

Looking at the patient, I continued. "Basically just another Beverly Hills resident who won't be doing summers in Martha's Vineyard anymore. Am I right?"

"Close," he replied. "I live in Bel Air and have a home in Nantucket that we're trying to sell."

The medical students trailed out of the patient's room after me. In the hall I spotted my chief resident counterpart in surgery. I limped out ahead of my students and caught up to him at the nurses' station.

"George, hang on a second."

"Another rugby injury?" he scoffed in disbelief as he pointed to my gimp ankle.

"Yeah." I shrugged. "But this time I've only got a week to rehab it. We've got another match this weekend. Who's the best sports orthopedist?"

He rattled off two or three names. I knew one of them, an overweight, wire-rimmed "rest it for six weeks" kind of guy. Not a doctor for me. Something about his type reminded me of my first big beef with medicine in high school. Another overweight doctor, the event doctor at a summer corn-belt wrestling tournament, had forced me to get the back of my hair cut. He claimed my barely two-inch-long hair posed a health hazard.

"How the hell is an infection going to fester up during one lousy nine-minute match?" I had complained.

With a condescending smirk he replied, "Germs can be housed in the hair and transmitted with contact to other wrestlers."

I knew even then that that was not good medicine. He was using medical mumbo-jumbo to serve his social agenda, getting me to cut my hair, and it made me furious. It was enough to drive me into medicine.

George then mentioned Dr. Robert Rosenfeld, an orthopedist who, he said, had been with the Oakland Raiders since the 1960s. I found the story fascinating. Rosenfeld was flown up by the Raiders to Oakland every Sunday, and players were flown down from Oakland to Los Angeles for orthopedic surgery! Most of the people on the ward here complained if they had to drive across town to see a specialist.

"Hey, you can try Rosenfeld," the chief surgical resident said with a noncommittal wave of his hand. "I really haven't scrubbed in with him all that much, and he *is* getting up there in age."

"Gee, I appreciate it, George," I said, figuring I had found my man. After all those years with the Raiders, Rosenfeld must have bangs and bruises down to a science.

I returned to the UCLA medical students patiently waiting for the next stop on our abnormal-body-parts rounds.

"Okay," I said, quickly scanning my three-by-five cards, on which I had listed all the ward patients with weird murmurs, recurrent tics, swollen lumps, or other student-worthy signs and symptoms.

"Okay, next case. This will be hard to guess. Here are some clues. This woman has a rash that comes out when she goes in the sun. Her teeth are crooked. She's got facial hair, and maybe even certain parts that glow in the dark. This may be the disease that inspired the werewolf mythology."

"Are you serious?" one of the students asked incredulously.

I had their attention now.

"Yup, I'm serious. Now she's been admitted to the medical ward with abdominal pain," I said as we arrived at her hospital room. "All right, get out your crosses—we're going in."

2

The Exam

I sat alone in the exam room, my bloated ankle propped up on the examining table. I'd found out that Dr. Rosenfeld had been Chief of Orthopedics at Cedars-Sinai for nine years. He also happened to have one of the largest Beverly Hills practices and took care of a veritable Who's Who of Hollywood stars. But once I stepped into his office, I could see what made him really proud. His walls were plastered with Raider memorabilia. Autographed team pictures, banners, collages of past Super Bowl victories, and multiple shots of Dr. Rosenfeld assisting dazed athletes off the field with thousands of spectators serving as a blurry backdrop.

But the real eye-opener for me was a picture of Rosenfeld next to Mr. Davis. I knew that nobody, but nobody, got close to Mr. Davis. This was the man who didn't just march to a different drummer; he heard an entirely different band. This was the man who lived the slogan "Just win, baby!"

Al Davis's career had been a football fairy tale. He never got to play college football, but upon graduating from Syracuse University, while his football-playing friends looked for high school coaching jobs, Al was talking the president of Adelphi College into hiring him as a college coach. Thirteen years and numerous coaching jobs later, at the tender age of thirty-three, he was named head coach of the Oakland Raiders. His organizational and talent-recognition skills enabled him to quickly pull a loser up to the top of the league. His aggressive football mind made him the logical choice as American Football League commissioner just three years later, in 1966. Several months after Davis took office, having openly declared war on the established National Football League, the nervous NFL owners consented to a merger with Al's upstart league. Faced with the dissolution of his job, Al's real genius emerged. He shrewdly worked a deal to return to the Raiders as general manager for one-third voting control plus 10 percent ownership of the team (which he was allowed to buy at "book value" for $17,000 and change, a sum not paid but secured through a line of credit). In 1975, Al legally finalized the coup. He won a court case which prevented Wayne Valley, the original owner who had hired Al, from, among other things, ever firing Al. Valley decided to sell rather than fight.

At the age of forty-two, Al Davis had seized total control and nearly one-third ownership of a $100 million business. This football coach had maneuvered himself into a position held elsewhere only by wildly wealthy businessmen. He had always overseen every aspect of football operations, from picking players to calling plays. Now every business decision was his too, as well as a large chunk of the profits if things went well. And when your business happens to be a monopoly, like professional football, things tend to go well. Financially, very well.

But in his crystal ball, Al Davis saw the price of top talent rising steeply. No one, not even a genius, can win with inferior talent. The extra funds needed to come from a larger stadium, which would include lucrative luxury boxes. So in 1980, Davis had taken on the Oakland city government. He demanded a stadium larger than the always-sold-out but deteriorating fifty-thousand-seat A's stadium.

His goal of getting more seats to make more money to compete more successfully for the premier players was simple. But the Oakland city officials tried to play hardball. Unfortunately for them, Al Davis was great at that game too.

It turned out the Oakland politicians were putting a lot of trust in NFL Commissioner Pete Rozelle. Rozelle assured them that league rules forbade a team from moving out of a city unless a majority of other team owners agreed. Over the years, Al Davis had alienated nearly every other owner in the league. So the chance of getting even a minority of the owners to support Davis's move to one of the most lucrative markets in the country, Los Angeles, was felt to be slim to none. It was even rumored that Rozelle himself wanted to retire and buy the L.A. franchise, further diminishing the chance Al Davis could pull off a move.

Undaunted, Al Davis attacked the NFL's authority in court. As every fan knows, he called Oakland's bluff and won a ton of money, plus the right to move to the greener pastures of L.A.'s 93,000-seat stadium and its twelve million population base.

The door opened. Dr. Rosenfeld entered and slid the X-rays up onto a light viewing box. He was a grandfatherly man in his seventies, wearing metal-rimmed glasses underneath a thick shock of white hair. He had a back-and-forth tremor of his tongue that I could see when he talked, which went along with the fine tremor of his hands.

"Rob, I think you're going to be okay. You've got a little bit of scar tissue here, but the ankle's fine. It's just a sprain. We'll get you to a physical therapist for rehab. But if you plan to play rugby on it this weekend, we could give it a little shot and strap it up real good."

I nodded. Silently I debated just how important this game was to me. And what were the merits of cortisone/Xylocaine injections? I didn't have vast experience. I'd read that cortisone shots could decrease pain and swelling but downside effects of excessive use included cartilage damage and weakening of ligaments and tendons. I knew it was standard procedure, in the few cases when cortisone was felt to be indicated, to rest the joint afterward.

What you didn't want to do was take an injured joint, numb it—in other words, disconnect its alarm system—and then overwork it. That might result in further injury that wouldn't be apparent until the cortisone and Xylocaine numbing had worn off. Still, it was worth considering because of the unproven hope that this injected concoction would speed healing.

Rosenfeld peeled back a plastic wrapper, revealing a syringe. He held a vial of Xylocaine upside down and proceeded to aspirate clear liquid from it. Then he filled a second syringe with a cloudy fluid—cortisone.

"I understand you're finishing up as the chief medical resident in internal medicine at Cedars-Sinai."

I nodded.

"What college did you go to?"

"Michigan."

"Geez—do you know Ed Muransky?"

"I've heard of him. I've never met him, though."

"That's just as well. He's been a real disappointment to Al, what with being an All-American and one of our top draft picks. He apparently doesn't have the foot speed to ever make it as a starter. Did you go to Michigan for med school too?"

"No, Harvard."

"We're low on players from there." He scrubbed my ankle down with 70 percent isopropyl alcohol. "I'm sure you know that the Raiders are moving from Oakland to Los Angeles this fall. The team internist is from up there and might not move down. So we may need somebody based here that's knowledgeable in sports medicine. Think you'd be interested?"

"Yeeow!" I got a sharp electric flash that reminded me instantly of my run-in with the sprinkler head.

Rosenfeld was probing for the tender spot with his thumb. Sweat started pouring down my chest, blotted by my shirt, leaving only my tie dry.

"Would you be interested?" he repeated. "You know, contrary to what most people think, the majority of the players' complaints are outside my department of the muscles and the joints."

"Gee, sure I'd be interested!" I brushed away some beads of sweat on my upper lip with my shirt sleeves. "I've been in athletics all my life, and well, what can I say? It'd be great!"

"Well, of course we've got five or six internists under consideration, but I'll definitely throw your name out there to Al."

He turned to pick up one of the syringes.

"I appreciate that. Um . . . you know, maybe I'll pass on the shots today. Let me try physical therapy for the next week and see where it gets me."

3

The Job Interview

The security guard waved us through. Dr. Rosenfeld pulled his black classic Mercedes 280SEL into an open spot off to the side of a modest two-story brick building. An oversized black HOME OF THE LOS ANGELES RAIDERS banner was draped over the front entrance of the converted El Segundo junior high school.

The parking lot was clunker-free. In fact, it resembled a Mercedes/BMW/Ferrari dealership. In the front two spaces sat two large black Cadillacs. "Reserved parking—Al Davis" was stenciled in white onto the asphalt.

"One thing," Dr. Rosenfeld warned as he pulled his key chain back out of his pocket to activate his convertible's alarm. "Never speak to Al Davis unless he speaks to you first. That's rule number one around here."

"Hi, doc," said a sweatshirted man in his early twenties as he jogged down a staircase toward the entry area.

"Hi, Johnny," Dr. Rosenfeld said. "Meet Dr. Huizenga."

"Another pretender to your throne?" he replied.

"He's applying for Dr. Fink's job as team internist."

"Oh," Johnny said, turning to me. "You majored in pills! Nice to meet you, doc. Got to get out to film practice."

As he left, Dr. Rosenfeld shook his head. "You know, Johnny Otten started out as a ball boy when he was eleven. Now he's a jack-of-all-trades. He's part trainer, part film guy, part computer expert. He may never get a shot at coaching because he's too damn valuable everywhere else."

Dr. Rosenfeld led me into the sprawling Raider complex. In the training room, under huge black-and-white Super Bowl photos, stacks of fresh white tape reached up toward the ceiling. There were black-upholstered treatment tables, gray carpeting, and black doors and trim. Jacuzzis were whirling. Steaming bins filled with rows of hot packs stood off to the side of the exam tables. Ultrasound and electronic stimulation machines were sitting against the back wall.

We walked into the actual locker room, lined with spacious individual lockers. What struck me immediately was that each athlete must have had twenty pairs of shoes all heaped on top of one another. Imelda Marcos probably didn't have this selection of running shoes. In front of the shower room stood a 500-pound-capacity livestock scale. In the bathroom was a large collection of deodorants, colognes, shaving creams, and mousse sprays. In bold letters, "F——You" had been scrawled across each bottle with indelible ink.

"What gives?" I asked as I picked up an industrial-size can of Arrid spray and read the obscenity.

"Hah! It's the only way Dick Romanski, the equipment manager, can keep these cheap-ass players from stealing the various toiletries and taking them home."

The medical treatment room was our next stop. It really wasn't a room, rather an unfinished eight-by-ten locked walk-in storage closet with stacks of medical supplies shelved on two sides and an exam table cramped in the middle between bundles of stored towels. On the far wall, a black skull and crossbones had been spray-painted. In smaller letters someone had printed in Magic Marker, "Dr.'s office. Enter at your own risk."

On the side table, a host of injectables and trays of hermetically sealed needles were piled next to knives, clips, suture materials, sterile towels, and umpteen vials of Xylocaine, Marcaine, and Decadron. On the back wall were slide-out shelves filled with aspirin-like medications, antibiotics, and cold pills. A large brown safe was pushed against the back corner. It housed potentially addictive prescription medications: bottles of Cheracol-X with codeine cough medicine, sleepers, and codeine pain pills. The safe door was wide open.

We exited out the back door, down a long hallway to the practice fields. Two fields were bristling with activity. Mike Ornstein, the Raider's PR guy, was the first one to greet us.

"Hey, Rosie," he called out.

Rosenfeld dutifully introduced me. "He's gonna talk to Al about Fink's job."

"You know what?" Ornstein asked. "Plunkett just threw a couple of incompletions against the scrub team, so maybe you should just walk around here for a couple of minutes. Let Mr. Davis cool off a bit."

We stood on the sideline and watched. Whap! The second-team defensive scrubs, in white, popped up against the first-team linemen, in black. Plunkett was faring better now and completed his next six in a row. I could see Mr. Davis standing alone at the far end of the field. He was intently focused on the field, frozen in thought, one hand, laden with Super Bowl rings, on his chin. He wore tinted square metal-rimmed glasses, a large black pullover sweater with decorative strips of leather and Raider insignia over the right breast, and a pair of black shiny patent-leather loafers, mostly hidden by baggy white bell-bottoms that rode low on his waist as if he'd just gotten off a liquid protein diet and hadn't seen his tailor yet.

Rosenfeld began walking slowly toward Mr. Davis, and I trailed behind like a baby duck. We stood next to the living football legend, all silent, all intently watching practice.

"Shit, he's still sailing the ball," Mr. Davis muttered, the long ends of his slicked-back hair flapping in the wind as Plunkett completed his seventh in a row.

"Get me New England," he yelled over his shoulder to an associate standing thirty yards away and off to his left. "See who else they'll consider dealing for."

"Hi, Bob."

"Hi, Al. I'd like you to meet Rob Huizenga, the general internist I was telling you about."

Al didn't take his eye off the field.

"I hear you play rugby."

"Yes, that's right," I replied.

"Did you ever play football?" he asked.

"In high school," I replied.

"And you were an All-American wrestler in college?"

"Yes, sir."

"What college?"

"University of Michigan."

Al Davis stood motionless through the next running play, absorbing every move of the twenty-two players on the field. Then he turned, looked me squarely in the eye, and asked:

"Have you ever played hurt?"

4

Auditioning for Team Doctor

"I can't believe you're going to leave me alone with your one-week-old baby!" Wanda said as our car came to an abrupt halt in front of the second-tier LAX United Airlines departure terminal.

"Oh, I'll be back before you know it. We fly home Sunday night right after the game." I hurriedly unloaded my gear from the trunk. "That's just two days."

Wanda and I had been married just over four years, spanning the up-all-night, work-all-day residency and moonlighting years. She'd been looking forward to a more normal sixty-to-seventy-hour work week and occasional free weekends now that I'd completed my training.

"Can you imagine if I hadn't delivered yet?" she said. "You wouldn't be leaving then, would you?"

"No way," I responded. "This isn't that big of a deal."

I wondered if my nose was growing longer, but I had both hands holding my luggage and was unable to check. I gave my newborn daughter, Ashley, a kiss on the cheek through the open back window.

"Be sure to call me when you get to Cincinnati," Wanda said as she kissed me goodbye.

"Okay, 'bye," I said, sprinting backward through the automatic glass doors of the terminal.

From there it was a footrace. The team plane left at three o'clock, and it was five minutes till. Luckily this was a charter, so no check-in was required. I bombed down the corridors in an ugly imitation of O.J. Simpson's Hertz ad, my suitcase in one hand and my oversize fishing tackle box in the other.

The tackle box was the product of a desperate last-minute search. Only four days ago, Dr. Rosenfeld had called and told me that the Raiders were interested in giving me a tryout as team doctor. Mini-panic had set in.

The first thing I did was call Mickey Melman, a doctor who had been my chief resident several years earlier and gone on to be the team doctor for the Los Angeles Express football team in the USFL, and later, doctor for Magic Johnson and the Los Angeles Lakers. He kindly gave me a rundown of the typical football-related medical problems.

Dr. Melman told me to keep a close eye on predicted temperatures in Cincinnati and to be prepared for lots of dehydrated players should the current heat wave in the Midwest persist. He also gave me a list of essential items—decongestants, antidiarrhea pills, antibiotics, migraine-headache medicine, aspirin and Tylenol medications, antacids, asthma medicines, and, most important, numerous bags of intravenous fluids along with the tubes, needles, and sterilizing pads needed to channel the bags of sugared salt water into a vein. Finally, he recommended an ambu bag and emergency intubation equipment (an air bag attached to a thick tube which goes down someone's throat when you totally take over his breathing), should someone decide to drop dead.

I checked the newspapers daily for the temperatures in Cincinnati. The highs were consistently over ninety, with elevated humidity. I'd spent all of last night in the medical library pulling articles about heat problems during exercise, mostly military-type studies about forced marches, but also some newer stuff from a doctor in Indiana who had studied water versus salt-and-sugar solutions in runners.

To my surprise, given all the hype surrounding Gatorade and like products, chilled water was still the expert's beverage of choice for brief stretches of strenuous activity in a hot sun. Coal miners, who worked a full shift under very hot and humid conditions, and ultramarathon runners, who also sweated during twelve-hour runs, needed salt and carbohydrate replacement. But the going theory was that football players, who eat a huge number of calories per day (up to five or six thousand), were getting more than enough salt in their diet and would not run low on salt or potassium during the course of a game—especially since their bodies had been conditioned for four to six weeks in summer camp.

Players of football size need to drink literally gallons of liquids during a game. Since water tends to quench thirst better than the sweet and salty "sports drinks," it was the logical first choice for football sideline hydration. And plenty of ice would make the drinks go down easier, get them absorbed quicker, and even help cool the athlete off a tad. I later found out that the Professional Football Athletic Trainer's Society had a deal with Gatorade. Only their beverage was allowed on the sidelines, so we had to put the ice water in large orange Gatorade buckets.

Now mercifully close to the plane's gate, I saw the airport security checkpoint ahead. I threw my bags onto the moving belt and stepped through the metal detector. When I saw the questioning look on the face of the security guard viewing the X-ray image of my luggage, I panicked. She must have seen the razor-sharp No. 11 blades, the suture-set scissors, the three-inch 12-gauge tracheostomy needle, and the packed rows of sterile needles.

"Could you open this up?" she asked.

I gingerly unsnapped the tackle box, and out accordioned four trays of ten individually labeled medications. Underneath, bundles of sterilely sealed equipment packs, a curved laryngoscope, and the remainder of the intubation equipment.

"I'm the doctor for the Raiders," I explained.

"Oh," she said, an impressed smile coming to her face. "Why didn't you say so?"

Out of the corner of my eye I saw the clock on the wall registering three o'clock. I tried to close the kit without revealing my panic, and was just about to flee when none other than Lester Hayes strolled through the metal detector. Eight-hundred-dollar black ostrich boots, black leather pants, black leather shirt, and a black leather coat. I breathed a sigh of relief. I doubted the plane would leave without the NFL's premier pass defender.

I arrived at the nearly deserted gate just ahead of Lester to find an angry Dr. Rosenfeld waiting for me.

"What do you think you're doing?" he asked. "You're two minutes late. This charter doesn't wait for doctors. If Lester Hayes hadn't been late, you'd have been left behind."

I followed Rosenfeld down the tunnel like a whipped puppy. He was right. As soon as Lester Hayes went through the boarding door, Al LoCasale, the general manager, told the attendant, "Let's go." The team as a whole was religiously on time for all practices, meetings, and flights. Fines in the thousands of dollars tended to have that effect.

There was pandemonium in the airplane galley behind the first-class section. Several large bins of iced soft drinks sat next to a rack of steaming cheeseburgers with all the fixings. An adjoining buffet was loaded with cheeses and fruit. Coaches and team members were chumming with members of the media and with a group of stewardesses who were far too good-looking to have all been assigned this flight by chance.

I found that every seat in the middle section of the plane was labeled with the name of a member of the media or some other comped traveler—typically a car dealer who in exchange for season tickets, advertising in the game day program, and a choice road trip gave a Raider staff member a free car for a year. The back section was obviously for the players, many of whom needed a minimum of two seats.

"Can I help you?" asked a pretty stewardess.

"I was just looking for a seat," I said.

"What's your name?" she asked.

"Rob Huizenga."

"Oh, okay, follow me," she said.

To my surprise, she took a left-hand turn up into first class. I stopped in my tracks when she motioned toward the aisle seat next to head trainer George Anderson, directly to the right of head coach Tom Flores and immediately in front of Al Davis. I was management now!

During warm-ups the official temperature in Cincinnati was eighty-three degrees with 65 percent humidity. The field temperature was ten to fifteen degrees warmer because of the artificial turf, which holds the sun's heat rather than reflecting it away as grass does. The temperature continued to climb. By game time, it was hotter than hell. We sprinted out of the tunnel to deafening boos in Cincinnati's Riverfront Stadium. I was dazzled at the spectacle—the frenzied crowd, the security people, the cameras. As I stood at attention, lined up on the sideline with the entire Raider team, listening to the national anthem, I felt as if I were on stage at a rock concert. Dr. Rosenfeld grabbed me as the kickoff floated up in the air.

"Just stand back today and watch me," he said. "I want you to get an idea how we do things around here. Dr. Fink will still take care of the medical things, okay?"

"Fine," I replied, instantly relieved of the mounting pressure I had been feeling.

I stood at the end of the team sideline area, next to the official timekeeper, and watched the show. The helmet-popping hits, the jaw-jarring tackles, and the thud of quarterbacks bouncing off the turf on their backs were things I'd never fully appreciated in the stands, or even when watching close-ups on television.

Early in the first quarter, Mickey Marvin, a born-again Christian, came limping out. He was cursing his fate and praying to God it wasn't serious, all in one breath. Dr. Rosenfeld put him on his stomach in front of our bench. He had him bend his knee while Rosenfeld tried to pull the foot back down. The hamstrings were okay. Rosenfeld poked his fingers into the belly of the calf muscles as the toes were forcibly pushed down. Mickey groaned in pain, sweat dripping into his eyes.

"No palpable rent in the muscle body," Rosenfeld announced. "It's just a strain."

Trainer George Anderson already had the injury covered with an ice bag and was securing it with an Ace bandage as Rosenfeld walked to a table behind the bench where a red phone sat, a direct line to the Raiders owner's box. It rang loudly before Rosenfeld even got to it.

While Mickey sat dejectedly on the bench, the Raiders, with Plunkett at the helm, played textbook football. They drove down the field, finally scoring on a spectacular one-yard Marcus Allen dive over about 3,000 pounds of flesh. Our bench let out a cheer that seemed amplified in the suddenly subdued Riverfront Stadium. However, Marcus Allen was listing dangerously to his left as he jogged off the field. As his teammates congratulated him, he grimaced in obvious pain.

"Doc, I can't feel my left arm," he told Rosenfeld as he was escorted to our bench. "It's dead."

"Squeeze my hands," said Rosenfeld.

Allen's grip was noticeably weak. He was unable to lift the arm. Dr. Rosenfeld moved Allen's neck. When convinced that the neck itself was not painful, he pushed the left side of the neck away with his straightened left arm, then pulled inward on the injured left arm with his right hand.

"It's just a stinger—you'll be fine."

Marcus didn't reply. He kept moving his shoulder as if to encourage his arm to work again. After several moments, feeling returned in the form of a painful tingling down to his fingers. Then full strength and sensation returned.

As Dr. Rosenfeld was rechecking Marcus's neurologic status, I was pulled away by a player who walked me over to a teammate sitting on the bench with a grossly deformed and swollen left ring finger. It was obviously dislocated.

"It'd be nice to get an X-ray before we put that thing back in," I told the player.

"Doc, this is the NFL," he replied. "I gotta go back in two plays."

Seeing Rosenfeld still busy with Marcus, I grabbed the lineman's wrist with my left hand, then slowly but firmly pulled the dislocated finger toward me with my right hand. Once I had good traction going, I flexed the finger forward. I felt a pop. The joint was back in place.

"Okay, grip," I said. "Now open your hand. Good."

As I taped the damaged fourth to the good third finger, I repeated, "We're still going to need some X-rays at halftime."

"Doc, there's a football game going on. Maybe sometime next week. Okay?"

"Sometime this halftime," I countered.

I couldn't get over the fact that he didn't even complain once about the pain. A normal emergency-room patient would have been screaming.

The lineman started to walk away, then came back. "Doc, does this mean I have a legitimate medical excuse not to wear my wedding ring?"

I stared back, not knowing how to take that question.

"Doc!" he said, slapping my shoulder. "That's a joke. Lighten up!"

Despite the heat, we won going away, 20–10. The players were whooping out congratulations to each other as we stormed down a walkway toward our locker room. Once inside, Coach Flores waved us together.

"You played your hearts out, men. The preparation paid off. Keep this intensity, this dedication. And nobody's going to be able to touch us."

"Nobody!" The players echoed as the happy celebration resumed.

Flores signaled the security men to let the press in. I could hear Howie Long talking to one of the local Cincinnati reporters.

"The Bengals made a mistake when they put us in black. When we're black we're bad."

Until Al Davis, every home team elected to wear all-white jerseys with just a splash of their home colors. The away jerseys were darker—the team colors offset by white numerals. The Raiders broke tradition when they went with their all-black away jerseys for home games. Other teams, hoping to throw us off our winning ways, then began requesting dark colors for their home games, forcing the Raiders to wear white uniforms with only their numbers in black. In this game, the Bengals, aware the field was practically boiling, had chosen the white, heat-reflecting, and therefore much cooler uniforms and let us use the black.

"Giving us black uniforms," Howie growled, "is like letting Samson grow back his hair."

The Raiders were the first professional sports team to have black as their color. Al Davis was the father of the black fashion craze in sports and maybe even played a role in the late-seventies and eighties fashion craze for black, when it moved out of funeral attire and into everyday life. I was told there was a simple explanation for the silver and black, the wildly popular color combination that each year puts the Raiders far in front of other teams in the $2.1 billion NFL sports merchandising business. Al Davis is color blind.

I grabbed a Coke, sat in a side room designated for the doctors and trainers, and watched Rosenfeld drain a knee, crank around a bruised shoulder, and recheck Mickey Marvin's calf. Each time he ritualistically patted the athlete on the back and authoritatively assured him, "You're okay—it's nothing serious."

I was exhausted after standing for three and a half hours in the sun. To my chagrin, the word from on top was that only the players were allowed to sit during a game. Mr. Davis felt a complacent staff might translate into complacent players. Standing for three and a half hours is no small feat. I'd had fewer muscle aches after entire rugby games.

Plus, I was bloated from a weekend eating spree. I'd started out with two cheeseburgers and a couple of pieces of fruit on the plane to Cincinnati, not realizing that the regular plane meal with unlimited refills would be served while we watched two back-to-back first-run movies.

On arriving in Cincinnati, at ten o'clock local time, we had been escorted immediately onto six buses parked next to the plane and whisked to our first-class hotel. Our keys were put in individual packets in alphabetical order over five large tables in the hotel foyer so that check-in for all forty-five players, fifteen coaches, team doctors, trainers, front office personnel, and a hundred or more journalists and other guests was accomplished within three or four minutes. In most hotels, you stay on hold longer than that to get the operator.

From there, without even checking in luggage, the team had descended on the traditional Friday-night buffet. Huge portions of fried chicken, pork, and beef ribs were laid out with a few pans of green beans, corn, and salad to color the plates. There were bowls of iced soft drinks, vanilla and chocolate Häagen-Dazs milk shakes, and three vats of Häagen-Dazs ice cream with all the trimmings for dessert.

Saturday was notable for three similarly high-calorie meals. I was shocked to see half the team order room-service food to top this off. Sunday, by contrast, was practically a fast, with only a huge break-fast four to five hours before game time, sandwiches for all the staff packed from the hotel and eaten somewhere in the hour or so before the game, and all the Coca-Cola and peanuts the stomach could hold.

Just then Charley Hannah, our starting right guard, stuck his head in the doorway.

"Hey, someone get out here quick. Killer needs some help."

I followed Rosenfeld out the door, instinctively grabbing my box of medical appliances. We found Henry Lawrence, aka Killer, the Raider's 300-pound-plus right offensive tackle, moaning incoher-ently, his six-foot-five frame sprawled in front of his locker.

"What's the matter?" Rosenfeld asked.

Killer didn't answer, instead grabbing his upper thighs and stomach and convulsing in pain.

"He's been complaining about leg and stomach cramps ever since the fourth quarter," said Hannah, a 270-pound Alabama grad whose locker was next to Killer's.

The team doctor whose spot I was auditioning for arrived with a syringe filled with Valium.

"I already gave him a ten-milligram shot for his muscle spasms ten minutes ago, but I guess it didn't do the trick," he said as he prepared to inject another bolus into Killer's upper buttock.

"Hold on," I said.

I remembered that Killer had been covered from head to toe for the entire game. Not only was he wearing a skin-tight uniform (so no defensive lineman could grab his shirt and use that "handle" to help throw him aside) and the standard helmet, shoulder pads, rib pads, hip pads, thigh pads, knee pads, and thigh-high socks, but he also was taped everywhere else. His foam-rubber forearm pads were buried somewhere underneath rolls of forearm, wrist, and finger tape. His ankles were taped over the socks and shoes, a procedure called spatting. Finally, he had neoprene sleeves over his elbows, gloves on his hands, and a protective collar around his neck. Basically, he had only a few square inches of cheek and nose to sweat freely from. I felt his forehead.

"God, he's hot," I said. "Please get me about four or five bags of ice."

As the trainer darted away for ice, I fumbled through my tackle box for a blood pressure cuff. Killer's biceps were bigger than my thighs. The usual adult blood pressure cuff was too small; the two Velcro ends didn't even touch. I had to find a thigh cuff to get an accurate pressure. His pressure was 80 over 40, consistent with shock.

"Killer! What's the matter? Do your muscles hurt?"

I wanted to make sure he was still conscious. He mumbled something unintelligible, then closed his eyes.

"Killer! What was the score of the game?"

I dumped out the contents of my kit, looking for the bags of sugar-salt solution and intravenous tubing. After quickly prepping his arm with an alcohol solution, I unwrapped a 16-gauge IV needle, really a metal pipe the size of the inside of a Bic pen, and began to insert it into his left forearm. Suddenly, just as the needle pierced the skin, his eyes opened. He let out a menacing growl as he struggled to get off the ground and come after me despite his visibly spasming abdominal rectus muscles.

"Get your f——ing hands off me," he yelled, ripping out the IV needle as he lunged forward.

Blood spurted out of his forearm. I put pressure on the wound with one hand, while leaning my body back as far away from him as I could.

"What the f—— are you trying to do to me?" He cocked his right arm, ready to turn out my lights.

I was terrified. I was convinced he was on the verge of heat stroke and was completely delirious. But there was a part of me that wasn't so sure. Maybe he was just another nasty-as-nails, street-tough psycho Raider. I wasn't certain if I wanted to bet the future of my face on the former possibility. Just then, Marcus Allen slipped behind Killer and put a full nelson on him.

"This isn't him, doc. Go ahead and do what you gotta do. Killer, it's okay, he's trying to help you."

Killer seemed to buy that and slowly laid back down. Jeff Barnes, one of our reserve linebackers, came over and helped Marcus restrain Killer's other wrist, and I threw in the IV again, securing it to the forearm with tape as fast as I could. I must have looked like Charlie Chaplin in one of those fast-forward scenes. The trainers arrived with ice, which we packed under his arms, on his chest, in his groin, and on his abdomen. That brought another howl of protest from Killer. Meanwhile a crowd had formed off to the side of the lockers. In the front was Mr. Davis.

"What's the matter?" he asked.

"Muscle cramps, severe dehydration, probable heatstroke, with hypotension and delirium."

"Is he going to be okay?"

"We'll see," I said.

By the time the paramedics arrived, I'd already pushed in a quart of liquid and his blood pressure was up. Slowly, Killer came to life. He began to move, although still with bothersome muscle cramps. I drew three vials of blood, scrawled down the blood tests I wanted the local hospital to run immediately, and handed the vials to the paramedics. I have a knack for memorization, and the entire heatstroke chapter was in front of my eyes.

"Oh, geez," I muttered.

In the middle of all the excitement, I'd forgotten to get a temperature, a critical bit of information in trying to piece the case together. Heatstroke is not much of a consideration if no fever exists. Oral temperatures are unreliable when the athlete has just drunk cold beverages. That leaves the rectal route.

It was a scene to be repeated many times in my Raider career. The cramping, overheated athlete, nearly always a 300-pound lineman, would not be pleased at the prospect of a rectal thermometer. Typically there would be insufficient lighting, and the huge size of the overlapping buttocks would obscure the rectal landmarks. I'd look to George Anderson for some help retracting a buttock. Then he'd tap the player on the back and invariably crack, "Could you fart to give us a clue?"

* * *

Killer, the trainers, and I were the last ones on the last bus to the airport. Al Davis, who always took the last bus, was seated up front. I still had the IV in Killer's forearm and was carrying his bag of fluid. We'd already given him nearly a gallon of intravenous fluids, but I figured one more quart wouldn't hurt.

"How you feeling, Killer?" he asked as we climbed aboard the bus.

"Fine, sir."

"Do we need to give him any salt or potassium?" Mr. Davis was addressing me.

"No—the blood tests show we've already done a pretty good job of replacing his electrolytes."

"His blood pressure—it's okay now?"

"Back to perfectly normal."

"He'll be able to practice?"

"For sure in a day or two, depending on how he does tomorrow and what the labs say."

We walked to the only remaining seats in the rear of the bus.

"How many cups of water did you drink during the game?" I asked Killer after I hung his IV bottle off the overhead luggage rack. "I mean, five or ten or twenty?"

It was the first time we'd really had a chance to talk.

"One or two."

"That's all? Weren't you getting thirsty?"

"A little bit, I guess."

"How much weight do you lose in a game?"

"In college I lost thirty-five pounds once."

"Henry! That's four and a half gallons of sweat. When you sweat off only two percent of your body weight, your muscles can get weak. You lost ten percent! I'm surprised you could walk off the field."

"I *did* seize up that night. I spasmed so bad in the hotel bathroom I couldn't get out for hours."

"Listen, Henry. You sweat to lose heat. Since everything except the tip of your nose is taped or padded over, your sweat has a hard time evaporating. So your body stays hot and you sweat more—and remember it's also harder for large people to lose heat."

"Isn't that why dinosaurs became extinct?" chimed in Anderson.

"Doc, tell me what to do. I don't want this to happen again."

"George," I said, "can you assign a ball boy to follow Killer around and every ten minutes force him to drink a full glass of water?"

"Sure," he replied. "Anything to keep my thermometer from being contaminated. Who's going to trust me now to put one of those things in his mouth?"

With that settled, I was curious about something else.

"Does Mr. Davis follow all the injured players this closely?" I whispered to George.

"If a player's got a medical problem, he won't sleep, or let *you* sleep, till it's under control. And believe me, he figures out exactly when the player can return to action.

"A couple of years ago, we were playing in Denver when Bobby Chandler, our wide receiver, stretched out to catch a pass and got belted on the left side over the spleen. Turns out he'd ruptured his spleen and needed emergency surgery to save his life. He was in the intensive care unit with staples in his stomach and tubes coming out of everywhere when the nurse told him there was a call from Al Davis. Since there are no phones in ICU, they had to wheel his bed out to the nurses' station and a nurse had to hold the phone for him.

"Davis told Bob he'd been up all night researching spleens. And he found out two things. First, Bob could live without it. That was lucky for Chandler, cuz the surgeons had already cut it out earlier that day. Of course, Chandler couldn't talk back, cuz he still had the tube down his throat. So then Al says, 'And second, you can be ready to play in four weeks!' "

5

Home at the Coliseum

The pregame routine became a religious ritual. All of us would breakfast with the same group at eight o'clock. Marc Wilson, Matt Millen, Chris Bahr, Ray Guy, Johnny Otten, me. We'd eat the exact hotel breakfast we'd had the week before. Then we'd catch either the early or late bus to the stadium. A large boom box was set up in the middle of the locker room, and soul music would blare. Some players would sit up against their lockers with eyes closed. Others would play cards, while others would begin rhythmically stretching to the music. If it was a particularly good song, the players would jive-walk as they went to get a cola or go to the bathroom.

The players would always get taped in the same order before every game. Each had his favorite trainer to tape him. Ankles, knees, and shoulders would usually need two layers of tape: one tape job in jocks and shorts and a second after the players had their uniforms and equipment on.

Wrists and fingers would be strengthened with tape and forearms cushioned with pads. Then the uniform sleeves were taped back tightly. Shoes and socks would also be spatted, which had a double benefit. It helped stabilize injured ankles and also allowed players who had shoe contracts but preferred wearing another brand to wear their favorite shoe. The trainer would wrap tape in a figure eight over the socks and around the shoe, hiding the logo. The trainer would then Magic Marker the "correct" logo, the one of the sponsoring shoe company, on the side of the shoe.

In a small room with lockers on one side and an X-ray machine on the other, a radiology tech would X-ray any lingering bony injuries or fractures, some of which were then taped or casted so the athlete would be able to play.

Bruce Davis, our oversized left tackle, would come in about ten minutes before warm-ups to have both his knees drained. Running back Kenny King would be close by. Either he was fascinated by medical procedures or else he just loved to see pain. Dr. Rosenfeld would test Bruce's knees beforehand, and each week it was the same: Bruce would be able to flex his knees only partway because of a large collection of fluid. Rosenfeld would clean off the side of the knee with an alcohol swab, insert a needle, and extract a Dixie cupful of straw-colored fluid. Kenny King would hold the cup and toss it into the trash when Rosenfeld was done. Then, with the needle still in place, the aspiration syringe would be screwed off. A new syringe filled with clear medication would be twisted on, and medication would be pushed back into the joint.

All the while, Dr. Rosenfeld would regale us with World War II medical stories, or with tales about famous patients he had treated.

"Strangest house call I ever made," he began one day, "was when they flew me up to the set of *Gentlemen Prefer Blondes*. Marilyn Monroe had fallen on the set, and her ankle was all blown up."

"Did you get her phone number?" kidded one of the players.

It wasn't out of the realm of reality. I'd seen pictures—Rosie had been a handsome cuss in his day, and everyone knew he had the necessary chutzpah.

"On the flight in," he said with a sly grin, "I'm relishing meeting the world's most beautiful woman. I open the dressing-room door, and there she is sitting up in bed wearing a low-cut blouse. But as I sat down on the bed to get a closer look at her ankle, I noticed her bra draped over a chair. It was filthy! I was instantly turned off. From then on it was all strictly medicine. My romantic fantasies vanished."

Eventually, Plunkett would come in after his first round of taping and tell two or three locker room jokes.

"Okay, doc, are you ready?" he would ask, standing in his silver pants, a ripped-up white T-shirt, and thigh-high socks.

"Do you know why Billy Sullivan put AstroTurf in New England's stadium?"

"No, why?" I groaned.

"To stop the Patriot cheerleaders from grazing!"

Then Lester Hayes would come in and ask for his B_{12} shot. I'd go into my regular speech—"This is just a red-colored placebo, and although B_{12} doesn't appear to have any side effects, if anybody in the universe were going to get toxic from it, it would be you, with your shot a week for your entire career, and although it's rare, intramuscular shots *have* been known to cause infections." At the end of which he'd always give me a look and I'd give him the shot.

Matt Millen heard this one day, and shaking his head and laughing, he pulled me aside.

"Doc, give it up. They're football players, not scientists. They *need* their plaque-a-bos." Matt always said it that way in honor of a rookie who had once mispronounced the word.

In the tense hour before the game, at least two players would approach me complaining of subtle throat irritation or stomach cramps. They felt like a cold or the flu was on the way. Most of the athletes had played in many high-pressure games, so these symptoms always had to be taken very seriously, but by and large, reassurance worked wonders.

Finally, at 12:03, coaches would begin to direct the various units, special teams, offense, and then defense, out to the field for the pregame warm-ups.

Once on the sideline, special teams coach Steve Ortmayer would come to me with a list of four or five numbers scrawled on a piece of paper. These would be key players on the opponent's special teams who Ortmayer had heard were injured, either through the grapevine or from the official NFL injury list that was published each Wednesday and updated on the Thursday before each regular-season game. My job was to scrutinize each player on the list for tendencies to limp or to favor one particular joint. Steve hoped to exploit this information during the game by running returns toward the injured player, or more specifically, running a return punt or kickoff to the susceptible side of the injured player.

Now some of the past Raider greats would begin to materialize on the sideline, inspiring by their presence and generally backslapping more confidence into our players. Jim Otto, George Blanda, Clarence Davis, Jack Tatum, Daryle Lamonica, Carl Weathers, Bob Chandler, Otis Sistrunk—at least two or three were always present.

Then the team would retreat to the locker room for the final twenty minutes before the game. This always seemed idiotic to me—to get the players fully warmed up and then keep them in the locker room for the twenty minutes before the game. I tried to make sure our guys stayed loose by doing floor stretches, but it wasn't quite the same as running out on the field. Pulled muscles were not uncommon in the first minutes of a game, and I was convinced this twenty-minute pause played a role.

Finally, an official would stick his head in the locker room door and say, "Two minutes." The hand-slapping, verbal pumping, and head-butting would begin, just like last week. We were still undefeated, and no one wanted to change anything we were doing. After ten or twelve guys were flushed out of the bathroom, a visit that everyone was sure would yield a quart but in fact only produced a drop or two, the team would kneel together for a silent prayer. Shouts would go up after the amen, and then quiet would reign again as Coach Flores gave a brief pregame message. His talks were always low-key.

"It'll be hot out there—I want all of you to drink a lot of fluids."

My heart skipped a beat. He had actually listened to what I had said.

"I want you to be intense," he continued, "but play controlled. Don't lose your cool. No stupid mistakes. Okay, let's go!"

It wasn't exactly a Knute Rockne type of inspirational message, but I always sensed a mix of tension and urgency in his voice. The team responded with hoots and hollers, and the cleated herd stormed out the door and down the long tunnel toward the Coliseum field.

As we emerged into daylight and an echoing chorus of cheers, we'd run through a double column of skimpily clad gorgeous Raiderette cheerleaders. On the sideline would be the celebrities. Magic Johnson, Bret Saberhagen, and George Brett were frequent visitors from the sports world. On separate sides of our bench would be the two show-business fixtures, James Garner and Lee Majors, each in his separate force field. It seemed that neither wanted to get too close to the other, for whatever reason.

One picture I would love to have is of actor Lee Majors shaking the hand of Jim Otto, the one ex-Raider who could outbionic the Six Million Dollar Man. Jim Otto, double 0, the Raiders original iron-man center, who had started a record 210 consecutive games, who had withstood up to fifteen surgeries and probably, if rumors were correct, countless shots during and after his playing years, was now a man of titanium. He had two artificial titanium knees, along with multiple other reparative surgeries, just so that he could get from his home to his Burger King franchises on his own power. I always wondered if Otto's presence, with his battered bones and painful hobbling, might alert players to the dangers of playing in the NFL and scare them rather than inspire them.

One major difference between home games in the Coliseum and games at other NFL sites was the national anthem. The singers at home games always did renditions of the national anthem you could dance to. The Pointer Sisters, adorned in black leather, would have players snapping their fingers and humming along to the music. Compare this to, say, Kansas City, where you'd get the lead tenor from a local Baptist church.

Next our team captains would go out for the pregame coin flip. When it became apparent we were kicking off and our defense would start the game, Lester Hayes would come rushing over.

"Doc, I need my pick juice." "Pick" was slang for interception.

I would then obligingly take out a bottle of stickum that he had previously shoved in my back pocket and, as discreetly as possible, spray this adhesive solution over his palms. Lester was in line to be the leading pick person in Raider history. He'd been spraying on stickum, the solution used to spray ankles before taping so that the tape would adhere absolutely to the skin, since Fred Biletnikoff introduced it to him his rookie year. This practice had been outlawed in 1981, since every time Biletnikoff touched the ball, there was so much goop on it that the ball had to be taken out of play. So Lester went underground. He was using smaller amounts and taping his wrists so that he could tell the referees that some of the stickum must have landed on his palm by mistake during his wrist tape job.

No sooner had the game started than one of our defensive linemen, Bill Pickel, lay motionless on the field. He had just taken a fierce head hit from a blocking halfback trying to clear out defenders for the ball carrier. I sprinted out with the trainers. Pickel showed the first signs of life as we were ten feet away, and by the time we knelt down had opened his eyes and was beginning to move.

"Relax, relax," I said. "How does your neck feel?"

"It's okay," he said as he tried to sit up.

That was a good sign. Anytime a player spontaneously moves his neck and gets up on his own power, it becomes less likely that he has a critical spinal cord injury. I did some quick neurologic tests.

"How many fingers?"

"Two."

"Squeeze my hands."

"Do you want me to squeeze a little, or break them?"

"What's the score of the game?"

Obviously it was still zero to zero. His eyes now opened and he just stared at me, almost in disbelief.

"Doc, I'm a defensive lineman. They don't pay me to keep score. I just hit the guy lined up across from me every play."

"He's back to normal," said Howie Long, who was hunched over his friend to make sure he was all right.

As we walked Pickel back to the sideline, Rosenfeld's beeper went off. In a selfish way, I was glad. I wanted to see whether he'd send one of his assistants to answer his phone call or go himself. I had faced a similar problem the week before.

Because I still hadn't got paid by the Raiders, not having had a chance to talk to Al Davis about my salary, I couldn't afford to pay someone to cover my private practice during home games. The previous week I had gotten an emergency beep in the middle of the third quarter. I had already spent half an hour explaining to the page operator that I would be in the middle of a football game and to page me only for life-and-death emergencies. When I got the beep, I waited until a big play occurred on the other side of the field and all attention was riveted to that corner. I then sprinted off the sideline and up the tunnel and made a mad dash into a phone booth.

You can imagine my annoyance when I found out the emergency was for a routine prescription refill for Dom DeLuise. Obviously Dom had never intended this to be an emergency, but the operators apparently got a little excited when they heard his name. Such are the special problems of practicing medicine in Hollywood.

Now I was surprised to see Rosenfeld merely press the button on his beeper numerous times, apparently reading an entire message.

"Those new message beepers must be great," I said. "You can tell right away which calls you need to return."

"Oh," he said, "I just got this for my birthday. It's got nothing to do with medicine. It beeps every time a final score comes over the wire."

Amused, I looked for myself. It was a special sports beeper—the kind of toy you'd expect a Las Vegas high-roller to own—with a continuous ticker tape of every college and pro score. It was a kick being on a team where even the doctors were a little eccentric.

6

Washington Away

The plane ride into Washington, D.C., seemed to take forever. It was 10:30 P.M. local time when we finally walked down the portable stairways that had been pushed up against the airplane doors. On the runway stood six luxury buses. By now, everyone had his own good-luck bus. It was a swelteringly hot night, and we were packed into the bus pretty tightly. Even a two-minute wait on that airport runway was deemed unacceptable.

"Bussie," someone yelled from the back of the bus.

The term "bussie" was Raider slang for bus driver.

"Bussie, turn on the air."

The bus driver obligingly switched on the air conditioning.

"Bussie, get this thing moving or we'll call a cab."

"If you do, don't let Lyle get in front," laughed Curt Marsh.

Marsh then lit into a story about a near disaster last year getting to the L.A. Coliseum from our hometown hotel the morning of a big game.

"Howie [Long], Pic [Bill Pickel], Lyle [Alzado], and I flag down a cab after the pregame meal," Marsh began. "We always shared a ride, since all of us always wanted to get to the locker room a little early. The cabbie had a really thick foreign accent, I don't know, he was from somewhere in the Middle East, and we can barely understand anything he says. Lyle climbs in the front seat while us three squeeze into the back. Lyle keeps talking to the cabbie up front while we lean back, close our eyes, and relax, kind of dozing off. All of a sudden we wake up and hear the cabbie say, 'Okay, we're here.'

"Well, Pic, Howie, and I look at each other, we see right away that the guy had stopped in the parking lot right outside of Dodger

Stadium, on the other side of town from the L.A. Coliseum. So the three of us all look over at Lyle, you know, as if to say, 'Where the hell have *you* been?'

"And Lyle, realizing that he's going to catch some shit for not recognizing the cabbie was the whole time driving in the wrong direction, turns all red, then instantly jumps over, gets his face right into the cab driver's, and screams, 'You f——ing idiot! Do we look like f——ing baseball players?'

"The driver by this time has got one foot out the door, and we're in the back desperately reaching through the partition, trying to hold Lyle back. It took about five minutes to cool Lyle down and another five to convince the driver it was safe to get back in his cab."

By the time we got to the hotel it was almost eleven at night. Somebody hadn't done his flight-time arithmetic, because curfew was at eleven. By the time we finished our evening meal and were back in the rooms, it was nearly one in the morning local time, although only ten o'clock California time.

The next morning was Saturday, and most of the players slept through an elective breakfast and looked drag-eyed as they boarded the bus at eleven-thirty for a light day-before-the-big-game practice. When we got to the field, an old city park field with rocks and potholes everywhere, the veterans scowled in disgust. Al Davis stood in the distance reaming out our advance man, Mike Ornstein.

"How can we get in a good practice on this?"

Everybody knew Al believed if you didn't have a crisp Saturday practice you wouldn't win on Sunday. Apparently we had been shut out of Robert Kennedy Stadium, where the Washington Redskins were practicing, and all the local college fields were taken because of Saturday college games.

The highlight of the practice came when Shelby Jordan's young son began crying uncontrollably as his dad's platoon went out on the field for the brief noncontact scrimmage. Shelby was a giant six-foot-seven, 300-pound offensive tackle who had just joined the Raiders in a trade from the New England Patriots. His wife and son had stayed back East, so this was really the first time he had seen them since coming to California. His son, who was only five, was nearly as big as some NFL kickers. I guess this wasn't surprising, given his dad's size and the fact that his mom was tall herself. While all the other players stirred uncomfortably at the crying child, Lyle Alzado put down his helmet, walked over, tightly tucked the child's hand in his, walked him out onto the field, and stood with him just behind his dad's unit. The young boy immediately stopped crying, now either comforted or possibly so terrified by Lyle's stern facial features and out-of-control beard that the tears froze up inside his lacrimal ducts.

The Saturday-evening meal was the most relaxing time on the trip. No one had anywhere to go, and we'd just sit back and swap stories in between courses. Last week, some of the veterans had reminisced about the 1981 preseason when wide receiver Bobby Chandler had just bought a brand-new Ferrari, a car he babied to death, getting a guy to wax it every couple of days, and somebody else to come over and clean the insides. Every night he'd put the thing to bed with a special cover right outside his hotel room. Well, Dave Dalby, Bob Nelson, Dave Humm, and Steve Sylvester were in the next room, *the* party room, the only room in camp with pinball machines, where a local beer truck made regular deliveries, backing right up to their front door to deliver kegs. They immediately ran out and chipped in for an old jalopy from Rent-A-Wreck, and had George Anderson rig up a large hood ornament in the shape of a penis that he fashioned with long bits of metal from fracture splints. Every night the foursome loudly drove back into training camp before curfew, honking the horn, and while everybody was watching, would park it right next to Chandler's car. Then they'd put their Rent-A-Wreck to bed, throwing a dirty paint tarp over the hood ornament.

Most of the players had an Al Davis story. Al Davis first approached Marc Wilson when he was still a wide-eyed rookie in 1980.

"Marc, what do you think of the philosophy 'Take what they give you'?"

Marc, like nearly every Raider player and coach, would do an Al Davis impersonation, with phonied-up Brooklyn accent, eyes squinted and fists at chest level when quoting the boss.

"Gee, coach," Marc had replied, "that worked very well for us at BYU—you know, we'd run when they were ganging up with a lot of defensive backs for the pass, and we'd throw the ball when they brought their linebackers up closer on the line to stop the run. We had a lot of success with that."

Success, hell—he had set eleven NCAA records and led the nation in total offense during his three years at BYU. But Al Davis shook his head in disgust.

"Aw, f——! I can't believe you said that! We don't do things like that around here. We take what we want! We don't let the defense dictate what we're going to do on offense!"

Several players started swapping college "money under the table" recruiting stories, each one trying to outdo the other. One vet revealed that he had made over $50,000 scalping tickets his senior year. That was a huge chunk of cash back then—in fact, in his first year as a pro he had to take a significant pay cut.

Another player shut everybody up. He told of a local college recruiter who had come to his home when he was a high school senior. In front of his parents and brothers and sisters, all living together in a tiny backwoods home, this man had opened up a suitcase full of money, packs of crisp $100 bills, and told him all this would be his if he signed with the local university. The recruiter clearly spelled out the conditions. The money could not be deposited in a bank, and was not to be spent all at once. Since this particular athlete was one of the top prospects in the country, this scene was repeated multiple times. The winning recruiter came in with *several* suitcases. "Don't sell yourself so cheap," he advised the wide-eyed teenager.

Our conversation was interrupted by the tight end coach, Bob Mischak, who doubled as a strength coach. He stuck his head into the dining area and said in a loud voice, "Last call for the movie bus."

"What's the movie bus?" I asked one of the players at the table.

"It's an old Raider tradition. The night before the game, we pile into one of our buses and go to some local theater that's showing a tough-guy movie and get in a little last-minute male bonding. We used to even have our own movie bus hats."

I grabbed a Häagen-Dazs sundae and piled into the bus. Eight blocks later we disembarked at a large suburban movie complex, which advertised *The Terminator*. About twenty or thirty of us stormed through the theater lobby. When we got to the cordoned-off area where tickets needed to be presented for the *Terminator* showing, Matt Millen merely strode by the bug-eyed 110-pound high-school-age employee, saying, "Uncle Bob's going to pay."

Similarly, as the rest of our overgrown gang stormed by the exasperated young ticket taker, we pointed back to whoever was immediately behind us and repeated, "He's got my tickets."

Finally, our uncle showed up. It was Bob Mischak, the movie bus chaperon, who dutifully counted each gate-crasher, then went to the box office and came back with the twenty-five or thirty tickets required. Meanwhile, we had converged on the concession stand, ordering several hundred dollars' worth of popcorn, colas, and bonbons.

Bob would eventually come in and tell us we were now on our own. But then the players would beg.

"Come on, Uncle Bob, use your influence with big Al to get reimbursed. We *won* last week."

Chuckling, he'd then reach into his pocket and throw several bills on the concession-stand counter. Then we'd go in and space ourselves out over the entire theater, one over here, three over there, two there. We always sat in the same seats. If one movie bus regular couldn't come, no one else could sit in his spot. And when the guys were eating their popcorn and bonbons, they would ritualistically eat some for the absent player. Everyone typically kept up a loud chatter during the movie. As the Arnold Schwarzenegger character approached the heroine, Stefon Adams might exclaim loudly, "Yo, get your sorry-ass barbell-bloated body out of my woman's face."

Back at the hotel, I put in a quick call home. "Hi, honey, what are you up to?"

"I'm just curled up in bed, watching a horror movie. I wish you were here."

"Did you have fun last night going to the bash Mrs. Flores put on for the Raider wives?"

"Oh, it was okay, I guess. All the wives and girlfriends just got up and introduced themselves. But afterward, Jerry Plunkett, Cindy Alzado, and Margaret-Ann Hannah and I all went out for a couple of drinks to Manhattan Beach. That was a lot of fun."

I was glad to hear Wanda was starting to hit it off with some of the other wives. After the excitement of my being the team doctor had worn off and reality had set in, I had sensed that she was starting to feel alone. Being on call for patients was one thing, but being away every weekend with the Raiders was starting to wear on her. She had met some of the players' wives earlier at one of Dave Dalby's Tuesday beach parties. He and his wife, Cathy, had rented a nice little house right on the beachfront strip in Manhattan Beach, and I had taken Wanda and our baby down there on several occasions. Those affairs were always wild. I remember one particular Tuesday because one of our rookie running backs, Mike Dottier, hurt his knee while diving in our beach volleyball game. All the players' kids were running in every direction, and some of the single guys, like Killer, would be over playing with them. I'll never forget him bending over to tickle our one-month-old baby, his head twice the size of her body.

Wanda struck up a friendship with Margaret-Ann Hannah, who like Wanda was an attractive blonde in her late twenties with one young daughter. Margaret-Ann also was brand new to the Raider organization, Charley Hannah having been traded from Tampa just months before. Charley was only twenty-eight, but, after seven seasons with the Tampa Bay Buccaneers, he was an aging football veteran, lucky to have survived this long in the National Football League. He half bragged about, half mourned the fact that he had failed nearly every professional football physical examination he had ever taken. When Tampa drafted him out of college, they hadn't known how loose his right knee was, and after the Tampa orthopedist flunked him, the team considered dropping him from the squad. But the general manager decided to take a chance and signed him anyway. The team doctor at that time had told him, "If I were a betting man, I'd put half of everything I owned on your needing surgery this year."

Sure enough—*snap!* The ninth game of his rookie year, Charley blew out his knee and required surgery. After that, one of the Tampa coaches encouraged him to beef up, telling him, "You've got the frame, the build, the speed. You just need some more weight. Are you sure you've done *everything*?"

Fortunately he managed to hold on to his position the following years without succumbing to anabolic steroids.

"Real nice," I told Wanda. "We're working our fingers to the bone and you girls are out flirting with the longshoremen."

"Very funny."

Just then there was a knock on my door. "Hang on, honey. Who is it?"

"It's George Anderson."

"Come on in, the door's open," I yelled with my hand over the receiver. "See you later, honey. I love you."

"Couple of things here," George said, handing me a rooming list with several names circled. "While you were at the movies I got a call from Trey Junkin—his nose is all congested. Three or four players need some sleepers, and probably a dozen more will stop you for an Indocin."

I picked up my tackle box and went out to make my evening rounds. First stop was Junkin's room.

"What's the matter?"

"My nose is completely plugged, doc. I need some more Afrin."

Afrin is a nasal decongestant that players use to treat sniffles caused by hay fever or colds.

"How many times do you take Afrin?"

"I don't know. Three or four times a day."

"How long you been doing that?"

"I don't know. Couple of months, maybe a couple of years."

"Trey, if somebody with a normal nose takes Afrin three or four times a day for a couple of weeks, he's going to have a totally blocked-up nose. There's a special name for that, rhinitis medicosum."

"I just need some Afrin, doc."

"The more Afrin you take, the more plugged-up your nose gets," I said as I quickly checked each nostril with an otoscope. "Yeah, it works for a couple of minutes, but the duration of benefit is less and less. Here—I'm going to totally switch you around. We're going to give you these antihistamine pills, and this fluorinated cortisone nose spray that won't get into your bloodstream. You'll be able to sleep a lot better."

"What if it doesn't work?"

"I'll give you some more Afrin! But you know, your adrenaline automatically gets going before a game. So allergies, runny nose, all that sort of stuff, tends to go away—right? Have you ever had problems during a game?"

"No, I guess, now that you mention it, I've never had much trouble during a game. It's just a pain in the ass trying to breathe through your mouth all the time. Especially the night before a game."

"All right. Just give this a try, and we'll talk about it tomorrow morning at the pregame meal."

"Oh, I need an Indocin too."

Indocin, an Advil-like anti-inflammatory drug, was so widely used by players for aches and pains that I was tempted to put it in the water system. I didn't think it was too dangerous—its side effects are similar to aspirin's—but I made a point of looking for stomach or kidney complaints. I'd also seen Indocin cause one player to get so foggy he had trouble remembering his plays, which way he was supposed to run and who he was supposed to block.

A call from an open door lassoed me as I was on my way to my next stop.

"Yo, doc, where are my Carbitrals?"

I had learned quickly that Carbitral had been the preferred sleeping pill of a previous team doctor. I detested the medicine, because not only did it take effect slowly, it also lingered in the body for days and could cause a nasty hangover the next morning. For a professional football player, game-time grogginess wasn't a side effect, it was an invitation to disaster. If you were a player already on the bubble, one bad game and you were out on the street.

The hollerer and his roommate were sprawled over their double beds, each reading a copy of *Sports Illustrated*.

"Doc, you've got to give us something to get us to sleep. It's hard to read this stuff about yourself in a magazine and close your eyes, much less rest your brain. This son of a bitch here," he fumed, pointing to the article, "didn't rate me in the top three for my position, and I'm pissed. If I could go out and kick some butt right now I would."

"I've got nothing against giving you sleeping pills," I answered, "but I prefer to give you one that'll start working within minutes and be out of your system by the time you wake up. I don't want to be slapping your cheeks and pouring coffee down your throat in the morning."

"Doc," he said, looking with a smile at his roommate, "I know this is going to shock you, but we've got other ways to wake up before a game."

I'd read a scientific journal three or four years before that surveyed amphetamine use in the NFL. The other medical residents didn't seem interested, but I always remembered the conclusions, that as many as 60 percent popped pregame uppers. One of the authors, Arnold Mandell, the San Diego Charger psychiatrist, had also written *The Nightmare Season* after Pete Rozelle banned him from the NFL for prescribing amphetamines to eleven players. Mandell, a substance-abuse specialist, stated he was merely trying to negotiate the doses downward in veterans with years and years of use and abuse. In an instructive postscript, Mandell made the mistake of penning unflattering remarks about powerful Charger owner Gene Klein. Klein fought (unsuccessfully) for five years to get Mandell's medical license revoked. But I wasn't going to fall into any of those traps. I wasn't going to treat the players any differently from any of my other patients. I was going to avoid the nightmares. I didn't want even one bad dream.

"You won't need them with these new sleeping pills," I said enthusiastically. "They're out of your system in a few hours, not a few days like Carbitral. Then you won't need any of that other junk to wake you up before the game."

It made eminent sense to me, but I could see he wasn't totally buying it.

"Listen," I said, "just give these a try and call me back later tonight if you want. I had the same problem when I was wrestling in college. I would just toss and turn at night, you know, running through the moves I was going to use the next day instead of sleeping. I got one of the earliest short-acting sleeping pills from our college team doctor, and though it wasn't as good as these, it made all the difference. I felt great the next day."

In fact, if sleepers were used only once or twice a week during the season, I could see little downside. More frequent usage could, of course, become addictive, and result in rebound insomnia when the pills were discontinued.

The players seemed to buy my argument, and I pulled out one of the vials from my kit and dropped a pill into each player's hand.

"Doc, give me two. I'm freakin' three hundred pounds. I've never taken only one of anything my whole life."

"You've got a point there," I said, doubling both of their doses.

As I went to close my traveling medicine cabinet, the other roommate downed his sleepers with an Indocin that had been sitting on the nightstand and asked, "Are you the one that cut us off from the candy jar?"

In the past, players had grabbed their medication out of a loosely supervised large jar of pills—everything from anti-inflammatories to cold meds to painkillers to sleepers. As a result, the players knew every capsule and tablet by size and color. I was surrounded by a bunch of pharmacists. My first official act as team doctor had been to personally distribute all prescription medicines, and some of the players didn't like listening to my sermons about why the medicine they requested might not be right for them.

"Yeah, I guess I did, but you know, we're in Washington, D.C. There's a law here prohibiting nonmedical people from distributing drugs," I joked. "Wait till we get back to California, where the laws are a lot laxer, and we can go back to the old system."

That shut them both up, and I was on my way out. It was eleven o'clock now, and security guards were outside the rooms. They were hired every time we stayed in hotels to keep out Raider fans, groupies, girlfriends, and wives, and more important, to keep players in. It was often very difficult to get to sleep at eleven or twelve local time when we'd come in late the previous night and not gotten to sleep till two or three in the morning. The tendency was to stay up late on the Saturday before the game, too. At the 8:00 A.M. (five o'clock California time) pregame meal, several players were frighteningly close to falling asleep in their breakfast bowls.

And I couldn't help thinking our pregame meal made things worse. It was common knowledge that the high-fat, high-protein items offered in our pregame breakfast, such as sausage, bacon, and hamburger-based spaghetti sauce, not to mention the Häagen-Dazs ice cream, were counterproductive for the athletes. The fat content could not be converted to usable energy by game time. It would be useless, dead weight. It might not even be out of the stomach. Additionally, some of the fruit choices and the oatmeal provided futile fiber that would only bog the athlete down.

"Kenny," I said to Ken LaRue, the man in charge of ordering the pregame meals, "I think we should make a couple of menu changes. We need high-carbohydrate items for a maximal glycogen loading. There's a consensus among doctors that this enhances athletic endurance."

"Doc," he said, "we've been doing it this way forever. We've won two Super Bowls eating this way. We're four and oh. I can guarantee you, big Al is not going to go for any changes right now."

"How about just offering more high-carbo items?"

"Good luck. Nothing changes when we're winning."

"Okay." I shrugged.

It seemed to take the players a while to wake up and get their juices flowing in pregame warm-ups. We had the same boom box cassette as at home games. We got taped the same way. We even got an energy infusion from the diehard Washington Redskins fans who were pounding their feet just above our locker room. The concrete-slab walls vibrated as the players sat on their metal folding chairs trying to get the mission in focus. We were playing the defending Super Bowl champions. We were undefeated. This was a nationally televised game.

We knelt for the pregame prayer. The nonplayers, with no knee pads to cushion the contact with the cement floor, squatted. As we rose, Coach Tom Flores slowly searched for the right words.

"This is a big game," he said. "I want you to reach down deep inside, pull out everything you got, and give it to me. We need all phases to win—offense, defense, and special teams. Use your heads out there. No stupid mistakes. Now, come on, let's go!"

We stormed out to meet our challenge. Unfortunately, we played football the first half the way the Keystone Cops did detective work. The team looked as if it were sleepwalking. The defense reacted slowly, and the offense just didn't quite click.

And when we did finally score, on a ballsy ninety-nine-yard Plunkett touchdown bomb to Cliff Branch, we paid a price. After Cliff plucked the ball out of the air fifty yards down the field, he turned on the afterburners and was jetting down the sidelines. With forty yards to go, he lurched awkwardly to his left, then slowed down to a painful lope for the remaining distance, just eluding defenders now given a second chance at him. He had shredded his hamstring muscle. After the play, on the sideline, we palpated a depression corresponding to the torn section of muscle. This signaled a severe tear.

At halftime, the team regrouped. A wild-eyed Lyle Alzado stood up just as we were about to go back out and, pounding his helmet down, challenged the team.

"I'm going to go out, and I'm going to f——ing hit somebody! If we all do it, we're going to win this goddamn game."

He grabbed his battered gray helmet, with streaks of red paint attesting to serious collisions with the Redskins' linemen in the first half, and made a beeline for the exit. Unfortunately, I was in his way and nearly got slammed into the concrete. He didn't stop, he didn't acknowledge me, he may not even have noticed me. He just forearmed me into a set of lockers and kept right on going. His piercing stare would have made Rambo cringe.

He played a great half. The offense woke up. Howie Long and the defense played superbly. We scored four unanswered touchdowns and led 35–20. But our defensive secondary was crippled when Vann McElroy got sidelined with rib pain after taking multiple helmet hits. Rosenfeld, who'd already given him numbing shots three times, was on the red phone several times trying to explain why Vann couldn't go.

With seven minutes left, Joe Theisman and his Hog teammates staged a miraculous comeback. After narrowing the score to 35–27, they prepared to kick off. We circled our team on the sideline.

"Good-hands team in there!" screamed special teams coach Steve Ortmayer, obviously prepared for a desperation onsides kick.

We kiddingly referred to them as the All-State team, the players with the surest hands to defend against a short, squibble kick.

"Six minutes left! Get out there and PLAY LIKE HELL!" implored Coach Flores.

It wasn't our day. Despite a front line of receivers and backs with great ball-catching artistry, the Redskins recovered their onsides kick. They drove down for a field goal to pull within five points of us. Then came the clincher: with thirty-three seconds left, their five-foot-nine scatback Joe Washington caught a nifty screen pass for a touchdown.

Our club was dumbfounded. *We* won games this way, never the other way around. George Anderson, the head trainer, took it hard. After a long stream of four-letter words, he turned to me and shrugged. "Hey, what did you expect? Flores told them to play like hell, and that's exactly what they did."

On the flight home, the seat belt sign went off, and I prepared for my airplane rounds. This was a slow tour around the rear section of the plane. Nearly every athlete who had seen action would request an anti-inflammatory—Indocin or maybe Naprosyn or Feldene—and sometimes a muscle-spasm medicine. Those who had an injury or had taken an especially hard pounding might request a Tylenol-and-codeine pain pill. Muscle hematomas (small collections of blood caused by a direct hit), headaches, stiff joints, and achy muscles were routine. Nausea from medication and/or the airport bar beverages was less common, but certainly not rare. Cramps were also typical several hours after the game, and the lack of leg room in the plane didn't help the situation. The stewardesses were cooperative when told that drinks in the usual airplane serving cups were worthless. They began to serve iced drinks in quart plastic containers, about the size of the ice buckets most hotels give you. And they still had to give lots of refills.

After a couple of tours around the players' section, I was drafted into the central aisle's poker game. Ted Hendricks was the commissioner of the poker league, and he and Bob Nelson, Dave Dalby, Chris Bahr, Lester Hayes, and Vann McElroy were always the core six in the game. They would try to get a seventh player, someone who had lots of money, little knowledge of cards, and a short attention span. They misjudged my financial status but hit pay dirt on the other two counts. I could barely keep track of my cards as players kept coming over with medical problems or questions. Unfazed, Commissioner Ted Hendricks enacted the no-stopping rule, which enabled the other players to ante in money from my pile when I was off doing something else.

It was hard to win money even when I was in the game and focused. I had three jacks in one hand and was betting the limits.

"You greedy money-hungry doctors are all the same," said Dave Dalby as he folded his hand.

Bob Nelson matched my bet as he waved the hex sign in front of me, a fist with the fifth and index fingers extended out.

"You're not going to tell anybody up front about this, are you?" asked Chris Bahr as he raised my raise while passing a bottle of Johnnie Walker in Ted Hendricks's direction.

"Don't tell me that's illegal," I said with feigned surprise as I reraised Chris's raise. In fact, I had heard drinking on the plane had been banned after an airline stewardess complained about a drunk player crawling down an aisle after her and biting her buttock. As the story was told to me, "Of course she was a substitute. The regulars would have just wacked him once or twice on the head with a serving tray and gone on working."

"Doc, there are only two rules on this team," Hendricks growled as he took a hit straight from the bottle. "Number one, show up on Sunday ready to play. Number two, stay out of jail. Oh . . . and number two's not all that important." Everybody laughed.

When all the cards were dealt, I was still stuck with just my three jacks, and got beat by both Nelson and Bahr.

"Doc, what was all that heavy betting for?" Nelson kidded me. "Didn't they teach you in Harvard Medical School that a flush beats three of a kind?"

Those games were played in the center aisle with four of the seats pulled down and all seven players circling this makeshift table. No one would move from the game, not even when we were making our descent to the airport. In fact, players all over the back cabin would be sprawled out sleeping on the seats, even standing in the back area talking to the stewardesses (who were strapped into their jump seats), during the landing.

It wasn't quite as bad as the story Linden King told us about the San Diego Chargers. After their wins, a group of 300-pound linemen would perch precariously on the arms of the airplane seats, and with arms outstretched would surf in on the landing, with the rest of the team placing bets on who would be the first to come crashing down if the touchdown happened to be bumpy.

As the wheels came out, instead of turning their chairs around and buckling up for the landing, the poker players would get much more intense. This time, Ted Hendricks bellowed out, "Final deal. Five dollars a bet."

I was kind of proud of myself because despite all the distractions, I had managed to stay even, somehow holding on to the $50 I had started with. However, a handful of no-luck cards later, I was down to only $25. That seemed a fair price to help pass the time on the six-hour flight home. As we taxied in to our gate, I prepared to get up and exit with the rest of the passengers.

"Hey, what the hell you doing?" asked Bob Nelson, with the others looking at me as if I had three eyes. "Sit your sorry white ass down."

"Final final!" bellowed Ted Hendricks as he prepared to deal one more hand.

Yet another hand of unlucky cards and I lost my last $25. The plane was deserted now as Dave Dalby scooped up the disheveled pot of ones and fives. Vann McElroy, who had come the closest to winning, hurled the deck of cards against the airplane windows.

It wasn't till I'd exited the plane that I realized I was in trouble. I didn't have a dime to my name, and it was going to cost at least $20 to get my car out of the airport parking structure. I went to beg a loan out of Dave Dalby, who had won the majority of my money.

"What do you mean, you don't have any money? You're a doctor. You guys are allowed to print money."

"Dave, give me twenty freakin' dollars. I'll pay you back Wednesday."

"Not so fast. How much interest?"

7

The Family That Plays Together

The team was gelling. They stuck together on and off the field. After the defensive practice on Thursday, almost all the players would attend the weekly drink-up at Stick and Steins, a bar just down the road from the El Segundo practice field.

And on Sunday nights after home games, the entire team would join family and friends at an all-you-can-eat, Davis-paid-for buffet at the Coliseum Hilton. Like each player, I got four tickets to all games as well as four buffet tickets for each home game.

My seats were at the same table as Dr. Rosenfeld's in the large banquet hall. Rosenfeld was always accompanied by his sexy young girlfriend, who caused a raised eyebrow or two with her expensive wardrobe, her sleek car, and her horses. Rosenfeld was still married. His wife remained at their Beverly Hills estate while he stayed with his girlfriend in a luxury Century City condominium. The prevailing opinion of the club was more power to him, or as he himself used to say repeatedly, "If you've still got lead in your pencil, make sure you've got someone to write to."

Even the families with kids managed to party together. On Halloween day, Janice Shell, wife of assistant offensive line coach Art Shell, hosted a bash for the young Raider offspring. Too bad nobody was there from *Psychology Today*, because it would have made one hell of an article. The players' kids were a microcosm of the NFL, each one more overgrown and more aggressive than the next. Enter our petite daughter dressed in a dainty pink-and-white ballerina outfit. But she was a quick study. By the next year she was duking it out for her share of candy.

On Halloween night, the team got together at Ray and Beverly

Guy's place for an annual shindig. For the '83 party, I wrapped my face, hands, and feet tightly in Pro-Wrap, the nylonlike material that goes directly over the skin and under tape when an athlete is allergic to tape or doesn't want to shave body hair off before being taped. Rolled over my face, it made me look like a cross between a mummy and a gas station robber with a nylon stocking over his head. I was wearing a tux, and theoretically was the invisible man.

Wanda put on a long, dark wig and came as Elvira, mistress of the night. No one recognized either of us, and it took us fifteen minutes to talk our way into the party. Charley Hannah and Ray Guy didn't want to let us in. They kept telling us it was a closed, private party.

The party was rocking. I tried to set a good example by drinking 7UP. Eventually, however, the constricting Pro-Wrap around my head caused such an excruciating headache that before long I was going for the straight tequila *with* the worm and handing the car keys over to Wanda. But the thing I remember most about this party was that the pilots and stewardesses who always traveled with us were invited. Several of the stewardesses were stunning, and one was wearing an especially sexy costume, a skimpy red devil outfit. It was a kick watching the attached players trying not to stare. A little while later, when a bunch of us married guys were off drinking at the bar, one of the vets counseled us.

"There are a couple basic rules you've got to follow if you want to keep your marriage on track," he solemnly began. "First, don't ever talk to any of the cheerleaders or stewardesses, or, God forbid, know any of them by name. And number two, never, but never, try a new sexual position on the night you come back from a road trip. Believe me on this one."

The buzz at the party was how Marc Wilson and his ballsy agent, Howard Slusher, had used the upstart football league, the USFL, as a battering ram to get a new lucrative contract. Marc was in the last year of his contract, calling for $225,000 per year. He had asked Slusher to renegotiate his salary upward to $300,000 a year, a nice little raise that would have gotten him some desperately needed cash to complete construction on his new house in Seattle. But the Raiders turned his request down flat, and he came into the 1983 training camp working off the last year of his old deal.

Then, two quirks of fate. Jim Plunkett had an off day against Seattle. Wilson replaced him for the last minutes of the game and looked like Superman, completing nearly every pass and scoring two quick touchdowns. Secondly, Donald Trump decided to court Marc Wilson. In fact, Trump wanted ten of Slusher's players. In a conference call to all ten, guys including Johnny Jefferson from San Diego and Randy White from the Dallas Cowboys, Trump made an offer to sign them en masse to the New Jersey Generals team, ensuring a huge publicity coup for the USFL. The only catch, Trump explained, was that the players had to state the salary they wanted, which was typically going to be about twice what they were currently making, and if their salary demand was met, they had to sign with the New Jersey Generals. They couldn't go back to their NFL team and barter for a better deal. The guys on the line said they had no problem with that—if their price was met they would walk from the NFL. Marc Wilson was actually anxious to leave, because he felt he had never been given a fair chance to compete for the starting job. Again this year, Wilson had outplayed Plunkett in the preseason, but Plunkett had been given the starting job because, the coaches told Wilson, Plunkett had played well against Cincinnati in past years.

Al Davis, through his network of informants, of course got wind of this offer. Just after Marc Wilson's big game in Seattle, the Raiders got very serious about signing him to a big contract. They offered him a deal averaging $800,000 over five years, a fabulous increase over what Wilson had begged for several months earlier. The New Jersey Generals offered him a contract of around $650,000 per year for three years, the one difference being that a tremendous amount of the Generals' offer was up-front cash. After they looked at the pros and cons, it was obvious to Marc and his agent that the Raiders' deal was the best. So Marc Wilson sent Slusher over to sign the Raiders' contract. But Al had already gotten wind of the smaller-than-expected numbers on the New Jersey Generals' contract. So he sat Howard Slusher down and lectured him.

"Wait a minute. It's not right that the Raiders, one of the top teams in the National Football League, should pay Marc Wilson more money than what the Generals offered. I'm ripping up this contract. I'm not going to pay him a dime more than the Generals offered."

Howard Slusher, sitting across from Al, calmly countered, "No, Al, you've got it all wrong. The New Jersey deal is actually far better! It's for *more* than what you're offering. In fact, I've got the New Jersey Generals' contract offer right here in my briefcase." He tapped his attaché case.

"Now if you want, go ahead and rip up your contract. I'll be more than happy to just cross out the New Jersey Generals in this other contract and put the Raiders in. If that's what you want. We're happy to sign the deal you've got here, but if you want I'll be happy to let you sign the Generals' deal."

Al fretted for a moment. Then he signed the Raiders' deal.

Marc Wilson was given the starting job as Raider quarterback and responded to the pressure with a personal best 318 yards passing as we edged the undefeated Dallas Cowboys 40–38 in front of a national audience. Unfortunately, he tore some ankle ligaments on the Cowboys' artificial surface and was barely able to walk for the next week. His purple, softball-size ankle slowed him down, and our most recent game before the party had been a heartbreaking loss at home to our archnemesis, the Seattle Seahawks.

Cliff Branch was at the party, but sitting through the festivities. After his hamstring pull in the Washington game, he had been cleared to resume playing last week by Rosenfeld, only to pull the muscle again running full-speed in the Seattle game. Muscle tears in elderly athletes—and elderly in sports means thirty and above—are notoriously tricky. On one hand, you want to rest them as long as you can to promote healing; on the other, you want to stretch them and resume cautious exercise to prevent excessive scarring and muscle contracture, which predisposes to future reinjury.

"Why weren't Cindy and Lyle Alzado there tonight?" Wanda asked as she drove us home.

"I don't know. Lyle's kind of a loner. Definitely not a camaraderie kind of guy. Maybe it's partly because he's only been a Raider since 1982. But I'm told he wasn't popular with his Denver teammates at the zenith of his All-Pro days with their orange crush defense. And it's one thing when you talk trash and fight against the other team, but he's got a rep for bullying teammates too, and that's not going to win you any friends."

After a pause I added, "Maybe it's all steroids. Locker room scuttle has him taking megadoses."

"I thought you always said they were just placebos," Wanda replied.

"I said most sports experts think they're placebos. But I don't think any of them have ever looked into his eyes before practice— much less before a game. He can't hold in his hostility."

Several days before, Marcus Allen and Lyle had gotten into it. Marcus had been running the ball to the left of the line in a no-contact drill when Lyle clotheslined him with an outstretched forearm, knocking him down. Marcus got up and flung the ball at him.

"You can't do that to me!" bellowed Lyle.

But as he came forward, Marcus, one of the few guys who wouldn't back down to Lyle, got in the first punch. After practice, Lyle had come into the locker room and, to everyone's shock, apologized to Marcus.

One player who had spent some time at Lyle's house was Matt Millen, whose kids used to play with Lyle's son Justin. But Lyle didn't much care for Matt now; apparently, earlier in the year when Matt was at Lyle's house getting a haircut from Lyle's wife, Cindy, Lyle had come home in a rage. He'd begun screaming and shouting at her, and then started slapping her around. Millen had jumped up, threatening to rip Lyle's face off if he so much as touched Cindy.

Just recently, though, Cindy had been roughed up pretty bad by Lyle, and had phoned me crying, begging me to do something to get him off anabolic steroids.

"I love him. He's kind and considerate. But when he starts going heavy on the pills and the shots, he flips out! He turns into a raging animal. I don't recognize him."

When Lyle had joined the Raiders it was common practice to room the cagey vets with one of the young risers who played the same position, to pass on some wisdom. Rookie Howie Long was put in with Lyle, but couldn't take his mood changes. Lyle was nicknamed Rainbow. No one ever knew what shade he'd be that day. Soon Lyle became the only guy on the team to room by himself.

The day after I got Cindy's call, I summoned Lyle into our eight-by-ten doctors' room with its spray-painted skull and crossbones.

"Lyle, you have a problem," I began.

"What are you talking about?" he said, scowling.

I thought for a moment. I had a problem, too. Unfortunately, his wife had made it clear that she did not want to press charges, and I needed a way to convince him that steroids were harming him, without putting his wife's health in further jeopardy.

"You've got a problem with anabolic steroids."

"What are you talking about? What do you know about steroids?"

I had to pause. The truth was I really didn't know much about anabolic steroids.

"All I know is this, Lyle. Steroids may make you big—I've seen your brothers, and I know how much more muscular you are. They may make you aggressive—I've seen what you do on the field, hell, even what you do in the locker room. But they may be damaging your health. They're certainly taking a toll on your personal life."

I wanted him to know I knew about his wife and what had happened.

"Look," he snapped as he stood up to leave, "I've got my own doctors. They say my body's handling the steroids just fine. You don't know what you're talking about."

"Fine," I said. "But if I were you, I'd find a new expert."

I went to the library to learn everything I could about steroids. All I found were about twenty-five articles. Some said steroids worked, some said steroids didn't. Almost all of them had major scientific flaws.

But I'd already heard way too many stories of thirty-to-forty-pound weight gains over a summer, of bench-press strength increased by fifty to a hundred pounds in already maximally trained athletes who had gotten steroids perfectly legally from their personal physicians. And Lyle was a case study of the aggressive fury that steroids seemed to unleash. So I tended not to believe the ivory-tower physicians who had never spent a day on the front lines of professional sports.

I left the library with more questions than when I'd entered. I did, however, gain a wealth of information about possible side effects of anabolic steroids, among them skin changes, including acne, which could be severe; liver abnormalities, including liver cancer reported in anemic patients given steroids; and, in anecdotal reports, enlarged prostates and later even prostate cancer.

This made sense. The prostate is a male-hormone-sensitive gland. If you jack up the testosterone level, you send a potent growth signal: the prostate is going to enlarge. And we've known for a while that sending a constant growth signal to a gland often markedly increases the risk of cancer.

There was also a wealth of data on worrisome changes in the cholesterol level of athletes taking the drugs, as well as many unexplained cases of deaths in twenty-to-thirty-year-old Russian Olympians. Sports doctors in the Soviet Union and Eastern Bloc countries had experimented heavily with anabolic steroids since the post–World War II era, perhaps intrigued by rumors that elite German troops fought more aggressively when put on testosterone-like drugs.

Word of these drugs finally surfaced in this country in 1954, when Dr. John Ziegler, the team doctor for the U.S. weight-lifting team, befriended his Russian counterpart at a meet here. He was fascinated by the Russian doctor's claims of massive strength gains— and hell, they were stronger; they easily beat the American team. Shortly thereafter, Dr. Ziegler teamed with the CIBA drug company and released Dianabol in 1956, hoping to build muscle without all those troublesome testosterone side effects like acne, balding, and prostate enlargement. It was not to be.

Ziegler had his U.S. weight lifters take one pill a day. He thought he saw strength gains, but he wanted to see if Dianabol was safe. Then he discovered that his weight lifters were taking two, five, even ten or more pills a day. Such is the mind-set of many elite athletes: If one is good, two must be better, five must be . . . Side effects became apparent. Ziegler later cursed the day he invented anabolic steroids. But the genie was out of the bottle. It was not until years later—in 1990—that federal law criminalized possession or distribution of anabolic steroids for athletic enhancement.

I would continue learning as much as I could about steroids; unfortunately, Lyle would continue his own education.

8

Still Being Tested

I faked right, then slid in left for Howie Long's right leg. I wrapped both arms around it, using all my strength. He countered by throwing all his weight on top of me and cross-facing me with his left forearm. This torqued my neck out at about a ninety-degree angle. I was dangerously close to decapitation. But I couldn't release his leg yet. Not when a group of players, circling us in the main training room, were intently taking in the action. I knew there would be some heavy razzing if a supposed All-American wrestler, even one outweighed by a hundred pounds, wimped out in a few heartbeats. Despite the mid-November cool ocean breeze outside, it seemed intolerably hot inside the training facility.

"Hey, let go of him," came a voice at the training-room door.

Mercifully, Howie released his paralyzing grip. Unfortunately, try as I might, I still couldn't straighten my neck.

"What do you think you're doing?" asked Al LoCasale, the team's general manager and, depending on who you talked to and what month it was, possibly the second guy in command. "We've got a big game in three days. Somebody could get hurt."

Astonishingly, his anger seemed to be aimed at me.

"If it makes you feel any better," I said, "the only way I would have hurt him is if he strained himself cracking me in two."

"Listen," LoCasale said, "it's a lot easier to find a team doctor than an All-Pro pass-rushing defensive lineman."

With that he abruptly turned and left.

Actually, in retrospect, going up against a guy like Howie with tree-trunk thighs and calves the size of my waist, I was lucky to be able to hang in there even for a few seconds. In fact, although my neck was kinked about twenty degrees to the left for the next four weeks, I was lucky to be alive. I found out later that Howie had been kicked off his high school wrestling team because, in a rage, he had tossed an opponent off the mat and practically into the stands.

The trainer handed me a scribbled list of players who had medical complaints. We needed to step out of his small office, which had one of the two free phones in the locker room, since Lyle Alzado was on the phone engaged in his nightly hollering match. Every night, as regular as clockwork, Lyle would be in there for a post-practice screaming session aimed at his wife, his agent, or some other unlucky associate.

Two sore throats, a hay fever attack, and an inner-ear infection later, I was answering a page in the equipment room when in strode Al Davis. Suddenly there was dead silence. I found myself whispering on the phone. Without saying a word, Romo, our equipment manager, handed Davis a small black comb as Davis, staring straight ahead into a small mirror propped up against the wall, slipped out of his white patent-leather shoes. Then, as Davis meticulously slicked his hair backward into a ducktail reminiscent of the Elvis years, Romo got down on his knees and vigorously buffed the shoes. Still without a word, or even a glance, Davis slid back into his polished shoes and exited.

I followed him to the training room, hoping to have a word regarding my salary. It was weird being in his presence. He came off larger than life. A thin, wiry man, he wore a constant pained facial expression that was at the same time intense, forceful, and condescending. And when he spoke, boy, would he make people jump to attention.

"Mr. Davis . . ."

"Goddammit," he snapped impatiently. His husky voice carried a trace of the Brooklyn neighborhood where he had grown up. "Can't you do anything about Vann McElroy?"

Vann had woken up two days before with a sensitivity to light that was unlike anything I'd seen. He couldn't open his eyes in regular room light, a problem he initially reasoned was due to staring too long at game film. He'd stay up to all hours of the night with his projector (courtesy of the Raiders), studying over and over each individual opposing offensive player on each snap of the ball. Many receivers have hidden tendencies, like clenching a fist or changing their stance or darting their eyes in a telltale direction, while certain linemen may subtly lean forward or tilt back, telegraphing either a run or a pass play. Vann—like other great defensive stars—used these tricks as well as his sixth sense to smell out the upcoming play and position himself accordingly.

Now he needed sunglasses just to sit in a dark room. That was bad enough, but his neck was stiff as a board and he had a headache that over a period of days progressed to the exploding-hand-grenade stage. It was an odd constellation of complaints, but the red dots under the right scapula in his back were the clue. Zoster meningitis. Shingles complicated by the virus spreading to the spinal fluid. In healthy folks like Vann, the disease responds nicely to rest and pain medications. He was going to be fine. Problem was, he was going to be fine in a couple of weeks and we had a game in four days.

He also happened to be All-Pro, the glue that held our treasured defensive secondary together. His absence in the second half of the Washington game had coincided with their three-touchdown rally, one of our few losses. We needed this last game to lock up home-field advantage in the playoffs.

"Can't we get him special goggles to keep light out? Can't we fit him with a special helmet?" Mr. Davis's facial grimaces underlined the urgency of this dilemma. "Can't you think of anything?"

He did not seem to believe in waiting till illnesses blew over. And he was always sure that there was a doctor or treatment somewhere that could get players back sooner. He didn't suggest that I do anything unethical. But it was obvious he wanted to push beyond the envelope of current medical knowledge.

So instead of sending Vann home to recuperate in a dark room, I had admitted him into Cedars-Sinai, called a cluster of infectious disease specialists, and begun Vann on intravenous acyclovir, a medicine that was experimental in 1983. Damn the $10,000 cost. We were going full speed ahead. I was going to try to get him healthy in days instead of letting nature do the job in weeks. Every hour, every minute, we could knock off his symptoms was vital.

"You can't win games without players." Mr. Davis was still distressed.

"Well, we're trying. But as I told you yesterday, this intravenous acyclovir is experimental. We don't have any track record with it. Not even the chief of infectious diseases is willing to predict when Vann's meningitis will respond."

"Oh, f——! Then find somebody in New York, Boston, London . . . anywhere, who understands this disease," he barked.

I was silent for a moment. It hadn't occurred to me to go beyond the local university experts. I wasn't used to his game. Outside of football, Al Davis's playing field had no boundaries.

"I've got a recent article on this new drug. I'll call the authors first thing tomorrow and see if they've got any new information."

"Why not tonight?"

"Okay . . . I'll try to call them tonight."

"Don't you understand? We're fighting for our f——ing *lives!*" He was obviously concerned that my outwardly calm demeanor might mean I hadn't grasped the enormity of the problem.

"We're giving him an incredibly aggressive treatment. I mean, to even be able to give him that experimental drug I had to go in front of the hospital pharmacy and therapeutics board!"

"Can he at least sit in the film meeting tomorrow?"

"If his headache improves a bit, in between doses of acyclovir, that's something that may be possible."

I knew, however, that unless he was much better, I'd give Vann a full medical excuse. There was a fuzzy boundary between good medicine and good team doctoring, but this one was easy. I also suspected that if I gave him a four-hour pass to watch film, he'd somehow end up in a helmet on the field.

"But," I cautioned, "even with the best of care, it could take weeks."

"Weeks! F——! What'd you tell Vann?"

"Same thing the infectious disease consultants said: that we'll follow it day to day."

"Bah. Those doctor experts," he said with disdain. "They don't know. My wife was in the intensive care unit in a coma for weeks. All these fancy neurologists came in, said there was no hope. I *know* that doctors are not the final word."

I nodded cautiously. "No, they don't know everything."

I wasn't sure where he was going, but that particular story was legend. His wife had had some sort of heart-rhythm problem that caused her heart to stop. Dr. Bob Albo, a surgeon who lived next door, gave her CPR and brought her back from death. She was taken to an Oakland hospital unconscious but still alive. The length of time her brain had been without oxygen resulted in her being in a prolonged coma.

As she lay motionless on her hospital bed, a string of neurologists came by, all with dismal prognostications. But Al Davis stayed by her side talking to her night and day, vowing to beat death and telling the doctors they were wrong.

Something worked, and against the odds, Carol Davis awoke on the thirteenth day. After intensive speech therapy and physical therapy, she slowly regained her faculties and relearned how to walk. The day she left the hospital, "Dr." Al Davis magnanimously bought each nurse in the intensive care unit a color TV. The doubting neurologists got his unending wrath. So I could understand some of his contempt for doctors.

"I don't know about you, Huizenga," Davis continued.

"Sir?" I asked.

"You're too soft, too soft with the players." He abruptly turned and exited, leaving me alone with Rosenfeld.

"I think he's warming up to you a little bit," said Rosenfeld.

"Gee, what gives you that impression?"

"If he talks to you, if he talks to you and doesn't fire you, that's a good sign. Just be careful not to tell the players anything. I heard you tell Vann McElroy that shingles with meningitis might keep him out for weeks. That doesn't work with these athletes. You've got to treat them differently from your office patients. You tell them two weeks and their mind locks into that. And then what if it turns out they're really ready in a week? They'll be nervous they're not fully healed. They won't be mentally ready to play. Never put a date in their head. That way, if they happen to get better sooner than expected, they won't have any hang-ups. At least not any that we put in their head."

I nodded politely. But even though on the surface that theory sort of made sense, the condescending approach to these athletes made my stomach turn. In fact, in my brief tour of duty, I'd never seen an instance where an athlete with enough drive to make it in the professional ranks didn't desperately want to play. So I was inclined to believe that if you gave them a date, they'd want to play a week or two early just to show how macho they were. This advice also bothered me on an ethical level. It seemed in direct conflict with my duty as a doctor. I was supposed to keep players informed of their health status, not to hide things from them. And every doctor knows that his legal and ethical responsibility is to the patient, regardless of who pays the bill.

"I talked to him a little bit yesterday about your salary," Rosenfeld continued. "Maybe next time you talk you could discuss it more, but I was kind of thinking maybe you could ask for around twenty thousand."

My heart dropped. I obviously needed the money, being fresh

from my medical training program. I'd made a pinch under $25,000 as chief medical resident and moonlighted nights at emergency rooms for $15,000 or $20,000 more. I'd hoped, even with my private practice still losing money at this point, that I could stop moonlighting. But $20,000 minus my private practice start-up cost was not going to go very far in Los Angeles.

I sat down late that night and calculated what my salary would be per hour. I had to be at camp in Santa Rosa for most of the six-week preseason. During the season, I had to be at the practice facility in El Segundo Monday noon for a few hours to evaluate the walking wounded after a game, Wednesday for three hours after the defensive day practice, and Thursday for three hours after the offensive day practice. Plus two to three travel days for the ten away games. And Saturday practice for home games, and overnight at the team hotel Saturday evening—I needed to be on hand should, God forbid, one of the athletes develop a cold or diarrhea the night before a game.

I figured that with this schedule in season, plus other duties off-season, such as flying out each February to Indianapolis for three days to evaluate four hundred prospects for the college draft, the salary was in the range of $8 an hour, much less than I was paying my office nurse or even my receptionist. On the other hand, my office employees didn't have a shot at an all-expense-paid trip to the Super Bowl . . . and a Super Bowl ring.

9

The Super Bowl: Around Here, We Don't Lose Games Like That

December 18, 1983. Our last regular-season game, and it was against the San Diego Chargers. It was scary how everything fell into place. McElroy's meningitis had improved in just four days with the experimental medicine. Barely twenty-four hours after being discharged from the hospital, he played the entire game. And he played superbly! He teamed with newly acquired Mike Haynes and stalwart Lester Hayes to shut out Charger quarterback Dan Fouts, maybe pro football's all-time greatest passer.

We could do no wrong. Jim Plunkett came off his three-game benching and played flawlessly. He had replaced Marc Wilson with six games to go in the season, after Marc went down in Kansas City with a broken shoulder. After repeatedly reinjuring his hamstring, Cliff Branch was finally whole, and again able to accelerate to world-class speed. Marcus Allen's hip pointer had mended. Killer was no longer cramping in the fourth quarter. We won the game, and clinched home-field advantage for the play-offs.

Sure we had backups bitching about not being able to play and starters bitching about life in L.A. Sure the players were complaining about underwhelming fan support and the lousy Coliseum locker room facilities. And no one could buy a house, because with the Oakland eminent domain suit, we might be back in Oakland soon. And the team was battling with the Olympic committee about building luxury boxes, and with the Coliseum commission regarding a long-term lease.

It seemed like the distractions just helped the players, coaches, and owners keep some of the rough edges and maintain the "eleven angry men" tradition of the Raiders. This was a fraternity of guys camped out at the edge of reality. Our leader never accepted convention as the final answer. Our soldiers never accepted convention, period.

Our first play-off game was against the Pittsburgh Steelers. We jumped off to a large lead so fast that I never got a chance to get nervous. It was the first time we sold out the Coliseum, and hearing the roar of 92,434 fans as we came out of the tunnel was almost unreal. It got the heart pumping and pulled out an addicting mixture of energizing brain chemicals. I couldn't believe my good fortune.

The next week I got my chance to be nervous. We had the home-field advantage in the AFC championship game, but our opponent was the Seattle Seahawks, a team that had beaten us twice during the regular season. For the first time since I'd been on board, the team seemed tight. Recognizing this, Coach Flores settled the guys down with his pregame talk.

"Men, we're going to play Seattle basic. We're not going to go out there and try to out-fancy them. Let's just keep our composure and play hard, and I guarantee you our talent will prevail. If we get by these guys, we'll be in the Super Bowl," he continued, "and around here, we don't lose games like that."

The players ate it up. They believed.

My boyhood dream of playing in a Super Bowl seemed to vanish when on our first possession Plunkett threw an interception in front of our bench. As Plunk came to the sideline, Matt Millen, in the heat of the moment, started screaming and yelling at him, really getting in his face, upset that Plunkett had forced that throw into coverage. Then the Seattle players jumped in.

"You can't win this game. There's too much pressure with the home crowd. You won three years ago, but now you're too old!"

We had another scare when Charley Hannah violently collided with a Seattle defender, Hannah's mid-chest taking a spearing blow from the helmet of the Seattle player. Both athletes fell backward groaning on the grass field. Each was rolling back and forth like an upside down turtle on its shell, desperately trying to get to his feet before his felled opponent. The injury happened next to the Seattle bench, so their trainers arrived at the scene immediately. We were still about twenty or thirty yards away when their assistant trainer, seeing that Charley was still fighting to get up, put a reassuring hand on his chest and told him not to move, the Raider staff was on the way.

There was an earsplitting howl. "Owww! Get your mother-f——ing hand off me!"

The exam and locker room X-rays explained why his chest was so sensitive. He had torn some cartilage away from his breastbone. Just moving his arms upward to pull off his uniform turned into ten minutes of excruciating torture.

After that, the game turned in our direction as if scripted by Al Davis. We stuck to the basics, we didn't make mistakes, we didn't try to out-fancy them. We eventually prevailed by more than two touchdowns. As we beamed our way back up the tunnel, walking side by side with the dejected Seattle players, free safety Mike Davis observed half in jest, half seriously, "They tried to use that Psychology 101 stuff on us today, doc. What they didn't know is that pretty much all of us flunked that course in college."

We were in the Super Bowl. Our opponents would be the previous year's Super Bowl champs, the Washington Redskins. The Super Bowl was the single biggest American sporting event, but the fact that the Raider-Redskin game earlier that year had been such a barn burner helped push the ticket frenzy to new heights.

I received calls from every deadbeat friend, enemy, relative, or casual acquaintance asking for tickets. I even got a barrage of requests from doctors in the hospital where I worked. Everybody, it seemed, wanted Super Bowl tickets. Everyone on the team was allotted up to twenty tickets, but we had to pay for them. At $60 a ticket, that was a not inconsequential $1,200 I had to come up with.

Money was especially tight. Four months after my first game in Cincinnati, I still hadn't received a dime from the Raiders. I finally had a meeting with Al Davis, which, in my mind anyway, I had shrewdly arranged late in November after a four-game winning streak. Dr. Rosenfeld had told me he'd been hoping I'd be able to get $20,000, tops $24,000, a year, although I was never able to get out of him exactly what the previous internist, Dr. Fink, had been making, or for that matter what Rosenfeld himself was making. I approached Mr. Davis as he was leaving the field after the Wednes-day-afternoon defensive day practice.

"Ah, um, Mr. Davis . . . we really never decided on my salary," I said apologetically.

Actually, we had never even decided on my hiring, but Dr. Fink had disappeared from the landscape after the first couple of games, and that seemed to indicate that I was the guy. He gave me an exasperated "I've got more important things on my mind" look, and then, after reflecting for half a moment, said, "Do you want this job?"

"Absolutely," I replied, trying all the while to figure out where he was trying to lead me. I desperately wanted to avoid stepping into one of his verbal land mines.

"Are you tough enough for this job?"

I hesitated, trying futilely to think through the possible consequences of my answer.

"I think so."

I'd never really thought of medicine and toughness in the same sentence. What was he talking about? What did toughness have to do with being a good doctor? Why was toughness a criterion for the job of team doctor? Even when I had been involved in athletics, during my heyday as a Michigan All-American wrestler, I don't think anyone had accused me of being overly tough. I was referred to as a crafty or a smart wrestler. So how tough could I be now after eight years in the library and an internal medicine degree?

"I'll give you $16,000 a year," he said. "Eight thousand dollars after the first game, and $8,000 at the end of the season."

I was still taken aback by the "tough enough" question, and the take-it-or-leave-it tone of the offer didn't seem to leave much room for negotiation. Besides, since it was near the end of the year, this meant I would get $16,000 over the next couple of weeks. I needed it right away to pay bills.

"Okay," I less than enthusiastically agreed.

As luck would have it, by the time I figured out who the Raider financial people were in the adjacent building and had requested my initial $8,000 check, we got upset by a relatively weak St. Louis team. As he was known to do, Al Davis went into a "football only, no business" mode, which meant any check larger than $2,000 could not go out. Al Davis had to authorize or sign each such check, and if he was devoting 100 percent of his attention to football, that part of the world came to a screeching halt. My $8,000 check was frozen.

Consequently, two weeks before the Super Bowl, I hadn't gotten one penny. Counting my expenses for away games—cabs, meals, my $20-to-$40 donations to poker games—I was probably down $1,000 or so. I was just squeaking by on my weeknight emergency-room earnings and a part-time job doing medical news for an afternoon TV show called Breakaway. I was still six months away from making a profit in my growing private practice. I had been in much better financial shape as a low-paid medical resident.

When I heard of the money that could be made from Super Bowl tickets, I was sorely tempted. The tickets were going for more than $600 apiece to ticket brokers. At a profit of more than $500 per ticket, my twenty tickets could translate into a quick $10,000. By the time I realized their true value, I had already promised them all out to family and friends. Everyone seemed to have the impression that I had gotten them for free, so instead of making $10,000, I ended up minus another $1,200, at a time when I was borrowing money from my credit cards to pay my mortgage. The Raiders were becoming a very expensive hobby.

After a week's practice in the El Segundo facility, the entire team flew east to Tampa Bay for a week of media hype before the big game. Reporters from papers all over the country would be desperately looking for stories, and although the players always denied it to me, it seemed as if some of them sat home nights with their agents trying to think of ways to hype themselves, maybe trying to amp up their chances for good post-football careers. The winner this year was the extremely smart—maybe "cagey" is a better word—Lester Hayes, who deplaned with his fishing pole in hand. That picture, with an accompanying article about how he was going to catch the big fish, was the lead story on our arrival, plastered over every sports page in the country.

Several days later, two more 747s packed full of wives, kids, girlfriends, ex-players, and VIPs arrived. Al was very generous compared to other owners and picked up the tab for the whole affair.

The first three days were loose. There was a party every night, and lots of great meals. One of them, at a local restaurant, started out as hometown boy Charley Hannah's dinner for his fellow linemen. But when word got out that he knew the owner, suddenly forty more players and spouses piled along for a free beef-and-booze bonanza. After a couple of courses, the mandatory football war stories emerged. My favorite, from the prior season, was a Steve Sylvester tirade. Sylvester, a nine-year vet, now a utility backup, was at the end of an exhausting practice early in the season when decisions were still being made about who was going to stay on the team and who was going to go. Sam Boghosian, the strict offensive line coach, had been screaming at him during target practice, a drill in which a man out front would take a step and the entire offensive line would have to react as if they were blocking a defensive lineman who was stunting in that direction. Often the player out front would help his teammates by pointing with an index finger on his thigh or over his stomach in the direction he was about to step so his teammates could look better in the drill. But today Boghosian had moved parallel to the player out front, so the linemen were on their own. Sylvester, not exactly gifted with the fastest foot speed, kept getting chewed out by Boghosian.

"You're sloppy," he screamed. "Move your feet, react!"

Everyone got yelled at; it was for motivation, and to improve skills. The guys didn't necessarily like it, but they'd plug along in silence. But today, the exhausted Sylvester lost it.

"I'm in this league nine years," he screamed. "This is as good as I'm gonna get. If it ain't good enough, cut me now."

Nobody, but nobody, in a backup role dared jeopardize his $15,000-a-week game check. Coach Boghosian wanted to get mad, but this time he couldn't. He and the rest of the offensive line were laughing too hard. They were all exhausted. It was one of those awkward "could have been taken either way" outbursts.

By the end, the meal turned into a gluttony clinic. Players were ordering entrees for appetizers, then thirty-ounce chateaubriands for the main course. Suddenly the tab was nearly $10,000. Hannah's sternum was better but now his wallet was hurting. To this day he claims he's still trying to pay his friend off.

"If you're writing a book," he told me, "be sure to give Bern's Restaurant a plug. I can use that to weasel my debt down a little more."

But in between the press and the parties, our mission was made clear. One of the team officials came around to everyone's room five days before the game to take measurements for Super Bowl rings.

The press was a constant fixture. When I'd get up to run at six in the morning, the *Good Morning America* or *Today* show crews would be set up in the lobby ready to interview players from both sides. Before practices there were more press briefings, and up until bedtime there were reporters milling around in the lobby looking for a scoop. One of the better media moments came from Joe Jacoby, the Redskins' grizzled veteran offensive lineman, a guy who the players joked had donated his pockmarked cheeks to a local TV station so they wouldn't have to pay for actual NASA moon surface footage. In the major briefing session, Jacoby said that if it meant winning the Super Bowl, he'd run over his grandmother. The entire news corps then turned to Matt Millen, our better-looking down in the trenches equivalent, who quickly responded, "Yeah, I agree. If it meant winning the Super Bowl, sure, I'd run over his grandmother too!"

The next day, things heated up when Lyle Alzado was asked about John Matuszak. Matuszak, who had retired the year before I came aboard, had been Alzado's defensive end counterpart on the Raiders, not to mention the zaniest of the Raider characters at the 1981 Raider Super Bowl. The zenith of his notoriety had come at the press briefing the Thursday morning before that big game. On Wednesday, Matuszak had announced to the press that his wild days were through, that he'd keep the young guys out of trouble. Then on Thursday he showed up forty minutes late, disheveled and obviously reeling from the effects of an all-night bender.

"Gentlemen, I'm hurting!" he said to a salivating mob of reporters wanting to know why after his reformation of the day before he had been caught out after curfew last night. "I am the enforcer—that's why I was out on the streets, to make sure no one else was!"

Now Lyle was telling the reporters, "John has never played a good day of football in his life. He was never a force. Howie Long is nine thousand billion times the football player John Matuszak has ever dreamed of being." Lyle paused and searched for a positive thought. "I like John, I just never thought he was a good football player."

But as Scott Osler, an L.A. sportswriter, later noted, a mental fog seemed to descend on most of the players after endless hours of disconnected questions by reporters ten deep. Lyle, while discussing plans to stop defensive Redskin running back John Riggins, suddenly stopped in confusion.

"What the f—— am I talking about?" he asked himself aloud. "Listen to this bullshit."

The previous day, Redskin defensive end Dexter Manley addressed the subject of intimidation and was quoted saying, "I think they [the Raiders] think they have the battle won . . . but," Manley warned, "it'll be vice versa for them."

Howie Long, spacing out on some basic math concepts, was quoted as saying, "Intimidation is eighty percent of the game . . . half the game is mental, the other half is conditioning."

We got a medical scare on Wednesday, four days before the big game, when one of our players, Kenny Hill, a reserve defensive back and a key player on the special teams, developed a nasty infection. He had a temperature of 104 and a terrible sore throat, was unable to eat anything, and was having trouble keeping down fluids. He could barely make it out of bed.

It was mid-January, and the seasonal influenza bug was on the loose. I considered putting him in the hospital. Fortunately he responded to aggressive fluids and oral amantadine, a specific anti-influenza antibiotic.

The possibility of losing a player like Kenny Hill was bad, but there was a worse catastrophe lurking. Influenza is an extremely contagious disease. The players live practically on top of one another. They share equipment and sometimes drink out of the same cups. They sweat on each other. Even the hand-held fluid squirt bottles that players drink out of have been shown to pass germs. Saliva-contaminated water can bounce out of a player's mouth onto the fountain handle and be picked up by the next athlete in line.

Since influenza has a three-or-four-day incubation period, I was faced with a potential disaster. Would a whole new round of players come down with influenza in the next several days? Right before the biggest game of their collective careers?

It was too late for flu shots, something that experts generally frown on giving healthy young subjects. Another option was giving the anti-influenza antibiotic amantadine to everyone. It might prevent the spread of the disease. But drugs are never a free lunch. Amantadine can make the user light-headed or, very rarely, throw his balance off kilter. What if it had an effect, obvious or otherwise, on Marcus Allen's God-given three-dimensional navigational skills? What if it ever so minutely affected the position sense and the brain's black-box timing mechanisms? I must have spent hundreds of dollars phoning every expert I knew for advice.

The decision—no amantadine. Just an old-fashioned quarantine. I held my breath hoping that the bug hadn't already been spread. I got only a couple of calls about it from Al. He must have been really preoccupied, because he almost made it sound as if he was going to trust my call on this one.

As I walked through the lobby to tell one of the assistant coaches about the defensive back's questionable prognosis, I was stopped by a reporter who asked an unrelated question about Charley Hannah's chest injury. I shrugged my shoulders and told him to ask Dr. Rosenfeld, the team orthopedist. I'd been told in no uncertain terms to zip it up when it came to the press. The press was our enemy. No information was to be given unless cleared by Mr. Davis.

But suddenly it dawned on me. For the first time in my life I had information that people would pay money for. Big money. A player was very sick, and there was a chance many other players would be very sick in a few days. Right before the Super Bowl, *a game that billions would be bet on*. It was a very strange feeling indeed . . . to have inside information.

It was also strange when a Puma representative sought me out that night. He handed me a pair of beautiful all-leather tennis shoes and even hinted that money might follow if I would wear them for the game. I was surprised at first. But I soon realized that when I run onto the field and crouch down, my shoes are featured very prominently. They are close to the face of the fallen athlete. One such TV shot, in front of 125 million viewers, was worth beaucoup advertising bucks. My ethics were saved by the fact that our equipment manager gave us our entire outfit every Sunday and these new shoes would stand out like a sore thumb. I also really didn't need shoes, because whenever my tennis shoes wore out or I needed new rugby cleats, I'd simply go to Jim Plunkett, who would order me a new pair from his Nike shoe guy. He had a big contract with Nike, and when a shoe company services a Super Bowl quarterback, "no" is not in its vocabulary. Better yet, Malcolm Barnwell, our speedy wideout, had the same size feet as mine and would give me some of his castaways, already comfortably worn in.

The town was absolutely jammed toward the end of the week. Fans swarmed outside our hotel, and we had to fight our way onto and off the bus to practice. This still didn't prepare me for game day. We arrived at the stadium our usual two and a half hours before the game, and there was a mob scene outside. Fans crowded around us as we exited the bus, and people on every side of me were shoving pen and paper in my face asking for autographs. During the season I would say, "I'm only the team doctor," and most of them would vanish, but not today.

"Here you are on the team picture," they'd say. "Sign over here."

"Go get 'em today," they'd say, patting me on the back as if somehow I might have a chance to win it in the final moments.

In the locker room there was an enormous collective tension. It overflowed during the pregame warm-ups when sports announcer Irv Cross, live on CBS, tried to walk with his camera crew into the Raider sideline area where I was standing, busy with my pregame scouting of injured Redskin special teams players. Mike Ornstein, the Raiders' PR guy, told Cross he couldn't go inside our sideline area for an interview, and when Cross persisted walking in that direction, Ornstein shoved him live in front of 125 million people.

Irv Cross stammered, "I, I, I . . . we're on national television here."

"I don't care," said Orny. "You've gotta move now."

Finally Cross composed himself, smiled, and said, "I'm sorry, we've got a lot of confusion down here! Back to you, Brent."

The jive music in the locker room had loosened up the players somewhat. But what really helped were two critical plays in the first half. On the first, the Redskins mixed up on a blocking scheme when they were punting, which allowed our reserve halfback Derrick Jensen to get in and block the punt, and then beat teammate Lester Hayes to the ball in the end zone for an easy seven points. Derrick wasn't exactly a world-class sprinter, and everybody was laughing on the sidelines that that was the first time he'd ever defeated Lester Hayes in his life.

The other play was probably even more crucial. With time running out in the first half and the Raiders holding on to a very slim lead, the Redskins were working with their backs to their end zone. Johnny Otten ran up to defensive coordinator Charlie Sumner with a computer printout detailing Redskin tendencies when they had more than eighty yards to go for a touchdown. Based on computer statistics, the Redskins favored a particular screen pass in just such situations. When Sumner saw Joe Washington, their speedy back, who had caught a screen to beat us in our earlier game, replace John Riggins, he immediately pulled Matt Millen, our "all-world stop-any-run" guy, and inserted backup Jack Squirek, known for great hands and great speed.

"I don't give a shit where Washington goes—follow him!" Sumner hollered as he waved Squirek in with the defensive call.

Matt Millen grudgingly came out of the game, loudly cussing, frustrated at being yanked at such a critical juncture. Sure enough, Theisman dropped back to pass, turned to his left and saw Alzado charging arms up in his face, then lofted a screen pass to Joe Washington. Standing in the ball's path, obstructed from Theisman's view by a charging Alzado, was none other than Jack Squirek, who got the pick and pranced the remaining twelve yards into the end zone for the decisive touchdown. Our sideline went berserk. Matt Millen instantly ran to Charlie Sumner and in jubilation bear-hugged him high in the air. Johnny Otten probably deserved a little lift too.

The Raider fans were in a frenzy, and we hourly wage earners on the sideline were beyond bliss. The players were battling for pride, for the chance to fulfill their personal dream, and for a chance to show their wares in front of 125 million fans. Money really wasn't that much of a motivating factor. In fact, if you took the $64,000 Super Bowl player's check and divided it by the three or four games it took to win a Super Bowl, the winning share came to $15,000 or $20,000 per game. This was a sharp pay cut for many of the players. In fact, players like Mike Haynes, Marcus Allen, and Jim Plunkett might make two or three times that per game during the regular season.

Contrast that with the plight of the lowly salaried employees. The trainers, video people, and equipment people, who made $20,000 or $30,000 per year, stood to gain a half share, or possibly a whole share if they had been on staff long enough. They could essentially match or double their yearly salary in one fell swoop. That's why these employees would die a thousand deaths on the sideline as the team's fortunes rose and fell during the course of the play-offs.

Even the coaches couldn't help but think of the sizable Super Bowl paycheck during the game. While the head coach typically pulled down a six-figure income, the assistant coaches might make $50,000 to $60,000, with some going as low as $30,000. Figure in working hours from seven in the morning to midnight during the season, and you had another group not much above the minimum hourly wage. So the Super Bowl check was a huge motivator for them as well. Many of the longtime coaches and other staff members would make this evident when referring to their homes or various investments—"Yeah, my house is Super Bowl Fifteen," one might say, or "That Popeye chicken franchise is Super Bowl Nine."

I was very curious whether I was in line for a share of the Super Bowl bounty. On the one hand, it seemed blatantly unethical for a team doctor to have a financial stake in whether the team won or lost. There could be a lot of questioning of motives if particular players were allowed to play despite injuries, or were given painkilling shots to play despite injuries. But given my financial situation, I couldn't help but pray that I would qualify. A full share would be four times my yearly earnings.

By the second half it was obvious that we were going to walk away with this game. Millen and the D-line stuffed Riggins. McElroy, Haynes, and Hayes grounded Theisman's passing attack. Plunkett and his veteran offensive line played flawlessly. Marcus Allen, who had run wild through the Redskin defense all day, took himself out in the fourth quarter even though he was just shy of breaking an all-time Super Bowl rushing record. He let in Greg Pruitt, his veteran backup, so that Greg could get a taste of running in the greatest show on earth. Marcus, in the league for only two years, had no doubt he'd be back many times and would get plenty of chances in the future to break the Super Bowl record. The rest of us were even more cocky. With a team this talented, it was just a question of whether we'd have enough fingers for all the Super Bowl rings.

When the whistle blew for the two-minute warning, I looked up at the scoreboard. We had an invincible 38–9 lead. The emotion of the Super Bowl victory suddenly enveloped me. The chanting Raider fans were on their feet. Mickey Marvin had his arms raised to the sky in prayer. Matt Millen was bear-hugging everyone in sight. Lyle Alzado started to cry.

We sailed into our locker room and amid a crush of reporters we sprayed and gulped champagne in glee. Then, as if this were some surreal sports version of a Captain Hook story, we cheered while Al Davis, our proud rebel leader, made archvillain Pete Rozelle hand over the Lombardi trophy. I was proud to be a black-shirted Raider outlaw.

10

The NFL Combine: Human Meat Market

It was three in the morning and bitter cold. I stood alone on a curb outside the New Orleans airport, an arrival sign overhead. As I climbed into a cab, I realized I hadn't really been able to savor the old-fashioned whopping we'd given the Redskins in the Super Bowl. I'd barely had time to wonder about whether I'd get a share of the Super Bowl money, or even a Super Bowl ring.

In the nine days since returning home from Tampa, I'd been too busy catching up with my private practice, sprinting between patients at the hospital and returning phone calls, not to mention churning out extra TV medical news stories at night to make time for my present four-day trip to the National Football League combine.

The combine system had just recently been enacted. It replaced an absolutely insane system—each NFL team would separately fly in all the top recruits for physicals with that team's doctors and for running drills and workouts with that team's scouts and coaches. Most of the top players would fly to twenty or more cities, sometimes back to back, sleep in airports, and, obviously, miss a ton of school. Not that anybody really cared. Although colleges put pressure on the NFL to change this system, when it was finally canned by the NFL the reason was probably that it cost each team a fortune.

Now twenty-six of the twenty-eight teams combined to pay common scouts to handpick the top three or four hundred prospects and fly them all to a central city like New Orleans or Indianapolis several weeks after the Super Bowl. Of course, the Raiders were one of the teams that didn't join. Al was never big on group efforts. But Al did decide to pay a fee, nearly $50,000, to allow Tom Flores and his twelve assistant coaches, plus Ron Wolf and his six assistant scouts, along with Dr. Rosenfeld and two of his associates, myself, two trainers, and the general manager, to participate. Al Davis and several gofers (who set up his phone banks and the Nautilus gym equipment in his hotel suite) were also in attendance.

Everybody had a job. I was being flown down specifically to make sure there were no medical problems (muscle and bone problems were for the orthopedists) in any of these four hundred All-Americans. More specifically, I was to do detailed examinations of about fifty of the athletes who were on my "eyes only/top secret" list, which had been generated by our highly touted scouting department. These were the players we hoped would be available when our draft picks came up. Since we were Super Bowl champs, our draft position was twenty-eighth, dead last, unless we elected to trade up and give away a player or future draft choice.

I glanced down at my itinerary. I wasn't going to be able to get much sleep. The first batch of All-Star offensive linemen were already in town and would hit the Mayhorner Clinic at seven in the morning for their medical and orthopedic exams.

After their exams they would go to the Cybex station. The Cybex machine measures strength in the quadriceps and the hamstring muscles. Even minor knee injury can cause an athlete to favor that leg, resulting in subtle muscle atrophy. So a Cybex may pick up a knee injury the athlete could otherwise hide. In the past, the strenuous Cybex tests had been done just before the sprinting part of the evaluation, resulting in burned-out athletes with pulled muscles and slow times. Now the Cybex and sprint testing were on separate days.

Another station was the bench press, where a 225-pound weight was set up on a rack between two spotters. The athlete would do as many lifts as he could. A trainer would make sure the buttocks never came up off the bench. Arching up was not only very bad for the lower back, it was considered cheating.

At the last station, a crowd of scouts watched as the athletes, now stripped down to their shorts, were weighed, measured, and had full-body front and back photographs taken.

The next day we'd start in with a new batch of eighty All-Stars, the defensive linemen. The offensive linemen would move to the second day of their marathon, which would include the forty-yard sprint, flexibility tests, the short shuttle, the long shuttle, the vertical jump, and the standing broad jump.

"Here's the Hyatt, sir," the cabbie said without turning around.

I handed him a twenty and asked for a receipt. The Hyatt dominated the skyline and stood next to the majestic Superdome.

I was fading, but still awake enough to be impressed when I opened my room door and entered a huge three-room suite on the penthouse level, with a breathtaking night view of the entire French Quarter. I walked around the place for about ten minutes looking out all the windows. I mean, this Raider doctor thing, I could get used to it!

This was before the days of computerized wake-up calls, and my six-thirty call didn't come in until seven o'clock. The operator apologized and said that they were a little overwhelmed by the number of six-thirty wake-ups. I quickly took a shower and got downstairs, but our trainers and Rosenfeld and his associates had all gone. The Mayhorner Clinic, where all the examinations were going to be held, was some distance away. By the time I gave up on the courtesy bus and found a cab, it was already eight o'clock.

As I walked into the auditorium where the medical examinations were taking place, I saw twenty or so other doctors, mostly dressed in short-sleeved team logo shirts. They were standing in bunches examining players behind flimsy partitions. Several of them looked up to see me in shirt and tie, identified as the Raider doctor by name tag.

"Hey, Al Davis is gonna be upset at you for coming in late," a physician in an orange Tampa Bay shirt called out across the room. "I just examined that pulling guard from Oklahoma. Good blocking technique, great foot speed, tough as nails, and a recent arrest for assault and battery."

"Nope," I said, looking at my secret cheat list to make sure I hadn't really missed something. "Mr. Davis instructed me to only consider two-time felons or anyone pardoned from death row."

A round of handshakes and a chuckle or two later, I was part of the club, a fraternity of doctors who in many cases were national experts, or at the very least highly respected physicians in their particular community. And these were just the team doctors, typically internists. Down the hall, in an adjacent amphitheater, were the team orthopedists, the real heavy hitters. Not only respected but rich.

The orthopedists, unlike the internists, could use their esteemed position as team doctor to get almost unlimited referrals for joint or muscle problems. For example, if little Johnny got hurt playing high school football or basketball somewhere out in the suburbs, his concerned parents would certainly want the best doctor, and wouldn't that be the team orthopedist for the local NFL team? Figure $3,000 to $4,000 per average orthopedic surgery times hundreds of self-referrals. Not exactly chump change. No wonder rumors floated, and *Sports Illustrated* reported that at least one NFL physician was paying the team for the privilege of being team doctor!

On the other hand, the team internist typically had little to gain in his private practice. If your mother had a stroke or developed diabetes, you wouldn't instinctively run to the nearest NFL city and look up the team internist. Sure, I got a few calls, but it was usually either a professional wrestler looking for anabolic steroids (his face very upset when I stepped up onto my anti-steroid soapbox and sent him home empty-handed) or somebody with a hurt knee who mistakenly thought I was the team orthopedist.

But team internist was still a plum job, and there were doctors lining up in every NFL city for it. More than ten L.A. doctors had thrown their hats in the ring and asked Rosenfeld to consider them for my job. Rosenfeld told me later that several doctors had even referred him large numbers of patients in a vain attempt to win his favor. He kiddingly, or maybe not so kiddingly, indicated that the strategy was unsuccessful for one doctor, whose referrals generally had Medicare for insurance. Medicare pays less than $1,000 for a forty-five-to-sixty-minute knee scope surgery, whereas good private insurance will pay $3,000 to $4,000.

I pulled out my tools. Otoscope, ophthalmoscope, stethoscope, sphygmomanometer, reflex hammer, and a vibrating tuning fork, along with a box of rubber gloves. There was a line of athletes winding out the auditorium door. I motioned over the first in line.

"Hi. My name is Dr. Huizenga, Los Angeles Raiders."

"Nice to meet you, sir. Trevor Hall. Penn State." He was a huge specimen.

"Any medical complaints?"

"No."

"Any past medical problems?"

"No."

"Any past surgeries?"

"No."

"Says here on your form you don't smoke, you don't drink."

"No, sir."

"And you've never had any skin rashes, any problems with your eyes, hearing, sense of smell, no allergies?"

"All no, sir."

"No breathing problems? No fast heartbeat? No stomach nausea, vomiting, diarrhea problems? No blood in the urine, no urinary infection, no muscle aches and pains, no numbness or weakness, no anxiety, depression, suicidal thoughts?"

"No, sir."

"All right. Let's take a look." As I prepared to put the otoscope in his external ear canal, I realized I had set a record of sorts. I'd done a complete medical history in all of one or two minutes.

When I was a medical student, a complete history would have taken me a minimum of three hours. Even now in my private practice, a history never takes me less than thirty minutes.

But patients come to my office because they have problems. They want to talk about them. Here, after another couple of complaint-free histories, I recognized the pattern. No matter what the question, the player would answer no. I didn't meet one who admitted to even a hangnail.

The players were suspicious of the doctors. The doctor was the enemy. Even a minor medical flaw might lower their stock. If a player was a marginal prospect, it might keep him out of the National Football League altogether. If a player here ever had a heart attack, he'd deny he felt any chest pain.

Toward the end of the morning, one player was just about ready to leave our station, where one of us would do the exam while three other team doctors closely looked on. This particular player was claiming to have no medical problems when a Pittsburgh trainer, assigned to help keep our station moving, quietly informed us that the player had gone into heart failure after an orthopedic surgery in college.

The Pittsburgh team, like every other team, sent out questionnaires to each school on its top prospects and got the college trainer to record all previous injuries as well as answer routine questions such as "What's his true height, weight, and growth potential?"

The Raider questionnaire was much more to the point: "Is the athlete injury-prone?" "Does he recover quickly?" "Will he play when he's ailing?" I wondered how the NFL got trainers at state-run institutions to spend hours fattening up the NFL intelligence archives.

"Come back here," I called. "It says here you had surgery last year complicated by a heart rhythm problem of sorts, and heart failure."

"Oh, that was checked out, and my doctors told me that all the tests showed my heart was fine."

The doctors gave each other knowing glances. Healthy twenty-year-olds don't get postoperative cardiac complications. We made a note to investigate, first by calling his home town doctor.

In the afternoon session there were less dramatic cases along the same line. One athlete with loud wheezing said he'd never before been told he had asthma. Another with a large lymph node said he had just had a recent cold and his glands always blew up like that. And an athlete with a loud heart murmur said no one else had ever heard anything abnormal when listening to his chest.

I had trouble getting over the denial. In my private practice, patients would come in with tons of complaints, and it was my job to figure out which ones were significant and which ones weren't. Here I was supposed to look at patients who uniformly said nothing was wrong and try to figure out who was lying.

In my whole life in medicine, all through medical school, through my residency, in my private practice, I had never conceived of this twist in the doctor-patient encounter. This was a whole new branch of medicine. Detective medicine. The players would categorically deny everything. It was my job to see if I could find medical diseases that might affect their ability to play football for the Raiders—namely cancer, heart disease, and internal organ or medical muscle disorders. We didn't really worry about psychiatric problems, because, well, our crazy players had just won the Super Bowl.

The athletes were on their best behavior in front of the doctors. In fact, they were overly cordial. Each one swore he'd love to come play for the Raiders. Slowly I checked off the college prospects on my secret scouting list. On the second day, in walked Sean Jones, a six-foot-ten, 280-pound defensive line prospect from Boston's Northeastern University.

"Hi, Sean, I'm Dr. Rob Huizenga. I hear you've had a hell of a year."

I figured that was a safe bet. His name was circled on my secret list.

"Thanks," he replied, "but our league's not the toughest one in the world, and who knows what the future will hold?"

His honesty was a refreshing break from the bravado I had heard all morning. He fit the mold in that he had no complaints whatsoever. However, in between his pharyngal exam and his neurologic exam, he talked to me about the Northeastern curriculum and his fifth-year work-study stockbroker job. "Hey, if I get drafted," he joked, "I'll have a shot at the highest-paying work-study job in Northeastern history. If I don't get drafted," he said and shrugged, "I'll still have a job in the stock and land market." Sean was a change of pace from most of the other players, who were focused only on sports, and some of whom had trouble even comprehending the questions on the prefab medical history form. Granted, the forms were a bit confusing, as most forms are, but some of the responses were definitely odd. One player put a yes next to "Family history of heart problems?" only to reveal on follow-up questioning that he was referring to his brother, who had been stabbed with a knife in his left chest and subsequently bled from the heart. Another wrote that an aunt had "sick as hell" anemia.

Toward the end of the morning, as the influx of new players slowed to a trickle, in strode Dr. Charles Brown, the team physician for the New Orleans Saints. A graying man in his mid-fifties, he was tall and thin, with a classic bespectacled professorial look. He was the president of the eighty-or-so-member National Football League Physicians Society, a group of the twenty-eight teams' orthopedic surgeons, internists, general surgeons, psychiatrists, and even dentists. Some teams also had two orthopedists, and almost every team had one or two junior orthopedic partners who would trail along with the head orthopedic surgeon. The junior partners were perfect for doing the scut work, like dictating the myriad of reports on the four hundred or so players and their X-rays.

Dr. Brown had been overseeing the entire health portion of the combine, making sure all the medical and orthopedic exams were going smoothly. He had also been meeting with the National Football League hierarchy about ways to stem the use and abuse of drugs and begin an educational program.

I overheard him making arrangements to go deep into the French Quarter for lunch with a group of similarly distinguished-looking team doctors. Actually, in spite of my shirt and tie, all the doctors looked distinguished compared to me. I had the longest hair and was the youngest by at least ten years. I walked over and invited myself along.

We caught a couple of cabs to an elegant New Orleans landmark. It had fans overhead, waiters scurrying around, and a very in-looking clientele. I ordered a beer and a shellfish appetizer, and in the next forty-five minutes of lunch I learned more about sports medicine than I had in the previous month or two.

I found out what the routine was in the National Football League for treating exercise-induced cramps. Fluid, quinine, and massage were used, with some teams clinging to potassium or calcium. Except for fluid replacement, there were no data on the efficacy of any of these therapies. I heard about some side effects of quinine, including a story about a player whose platelet count went down so low there was a real risk of spontaneous bleeding in the brain. The player had to be hospitalized and was sidelined from football for several weeks. I found out what teams did for postgame pain, what they did for concussions during a game, who they'd let back in, who they wouldn't.

I was struck by the fact that none of the doctors had looked into the effects of anabolic steroids, though they acknowledged their universal use in the league. They recommended that athletes not take them, but didn't have much ammunition against them to back up their counsel. Everyone seemed to agree that heavy users were big and nasty.

We talked about the players. Some of the doctors also had jobs with other professional sports teams, including hockey, basketball, and baseball, in addition to taking care of local rodeo riders, professional wrestlers, or Olympic athletes. To a man, the doctors seemed to agree that team doctoring was the best in professional football. The doctors were regarded as equals or at least as friends and were not seen as adversarial administrative types.

In basketball and baseball, the star players are treated differently, and often they choose not to associate with lesser teammates. But football players must socialize together. A baseball player can play right field, hit .350, and act like a perfect jerk to his teammates. Try that in football. No matter how great an athlete, he'd get killed. Football is brutal. You need your teammates to help you make a good play, and to protect your backside after the play is over. That's why you rarely see a football player with his nose in the air, or one openly critical of teammates.

I found out about some of the doctors. Dr. Levy, the New York Giants' team internist, was the one with the long fur coat on the sideline at those cold November and December East Coast games. Dr. Nicolas, the orthopedist for the Jets, had devised the famous Joe Namath knee stabilization brace. I had already met the New England Patriots' highly regarded orthopedist, Bert Zarins, during my orthopedic surgery rotation at Mass General Hospital. The Browns' doctor was a well-known cardiologist from the Cleveland Clinic. I found out which doctors played golf regularly with their team owners and which doctors were in hot water with their team owners.

For the most part, the team doctors got along admirably with each other, but intradivisional rivalries did exist. The Denver physicians were not talking to any of us Raider doctors, because of an incident earlier that year. At the Coliseum in Los Angeles, one of the Denver players had become injured. They had signaled over to our bench for our X-ray technician. The X-ray technician apparently never got word, however, and did not arrive at the Denver locker room to complete the X-ray of the injured player for approximately ten minutes, a lapse the Denver physicians called unconscionable and blamed on Dr. Rosenfeld. They accused him of slowing down the X-ray process on purpose to delay the possible return of their athlete onto the playing field.

After lunch, back at the Mayhorner Clinic, we methodically examined the remaining thirty offensive linemen. We then circled our chairs to compare notes. We had each examined about a fourth of the players. Some of the players, for example high draft choices that most teams were interested in, had been examined by several groups. But for the most part we had no reason to distrust the other doctors' evaluations.

Joe Diacco, Tampa's doctor, and the group's self-appointed organizer and humorist, led the discussions about today's batch of players, who were all defensive linemen.

"*Aurbauch*, that's spelled *A-U-R-B-A-U-C-H*, *Steve*. Alabama. Nose tackle."

We all checked our player printouts to see which group had examined this player.

"Mild hypertension, one-forty over ninety-two," responded the doctor from Seattle in front of the group, which now included Dr. Brown and several other physicians who had not been in attendance throughout the whole examination process.

"*Barasch, Richard*. University of Washington."

"Clear."

"*Barbanel, Jack*. Defensive end."

"Clear."

"*Benjamin, Sheldon*."

"Wolff-Parkinson-White on his electrocardiogram," chimed another doctor. "We sent him for an echocardiogram."

"*Broncato, Chris*. Boston University."

"We did this guy," Joe reported. "And I hope we draft him, too.

He's a good player and has a real nice right inguinal hernia. If we could just draft two hernias a year I'd be all set." He grinned.

We all laughed. Joe was the only team doctor who was a general surgeon. As such, in addition to taking the role of a family doctor, he would do any general surgical procedure like gallbladder, abdominal, or hernia surgery on the players.

As we finished the list of the day's eighty or so players, eyes darted to personal "eyes only" scouting lists. Every doctor had access to the results of all examinations, but it was clear by the depth to which certain doctors had worked on certain players that some information could conceivably have been withheld. Maybe a doctor might get a tip that a player had a cocaine problem, then see ulcers in the nasal lining and not report it. I never saw it happen, mind you, but I worried that if the money got big enough, even doctors might be tempted into such unethical omissions.

I walked out of our examination area with several of the internists and down to the hospital wing where athletes were being examined by the orthopedic doctors. They had it easier than we internists when it came to finding past problems. Scars don't go away, so past surgeries could not be hidden. And an abnormal joint reveals damage when it moves in a direction a normal joint won't, or when it creaks excessively. It takes a great actor to keep a straight face when a damaged joint is spun every way but loose.

But if our routine with chest X-rays, electrocardiograms, three vials of blood, eye charts, hearing tests, and several medical exams was excessive for healthy twenty-year-olds, it was nothing compared to what the bone-and-joint doctors were doing. Unlike the internists, the orthopedists showed zero trust in any other team doctor. Each of the twenty-eight doctors might decide to do his own exam. So a player, especially a blue-chipper, could have his knee yanked in six different directions by twenty-eight doctors.

For people who have not had a thorough knee exam, where the two knee bones are bent and pulled in opposite directions, just one round of this can make you a little gimpy. Five or six could keep you aching for a few days, and more than ten is practically a legitimate work excuse. Not to mention shoulders torqued in every imaginable plane, necks and backs bent at every imaginable angle. The players would literally crawl out of this station. Anyone who came in with a real orthopedic malady would need a wheelchair to get out.

The orthopedists still had a line of players winding down a long corridor needing to be seen, so my companions and I jumped in a cab and headed over to the Superdome. There the offensive linemen we had examined yesterday were doing drills in front of the coaches and scouts. I found one of our assistant coaches and sat down.

On the field, players were lining up for the forty-yard dash. The starter's hand would go up and then drop as the athlete sprinted off. A hundred clicks echoed in the stands. At the finish the scouts and coaches sitting perpendicular to the end line would click again. Everyone would compare the time he got with the official time, perhaps hoping to discover a mistake and have a find. I looked at my official list and saw one of the players I had examined, who had displayed no muscle problem, scratching on the forty-yard dash.

"What happened to him?" I asked. "Did he pull a muscle?"

"I doubt it," the coach said cynically. "You know, the turf down there is so worn that a lot of the players from bigger schools like Notre Dame, Michigan, or Tennessee fake an injury. Then we have to time them at their home school later in the spring. Those schools have newer AstroTurf, and chances of a faster time are better. I really can't blame them. A tenth of a second can translate into moving up a round or so. That translates into thousands of dollars."

That evening, still burned out from my flight several nights before, I used my NFL ID to sneak in and eat with the players at the large buffet set up in the hotel ballroom. The incoming batch of collegians were in their street clothes, while those who had been there for the first day or two of evaluations were wearing their All-American T-shirts, courtesy of the NFL combine.

The entertainment turned out to be quite interesting. First up was Charlie Jackson from NFL security, a stately-looking, well-built black man with slightly graying hair, who spoke forcefully. After touching lightly on some of the potential medical consequences of cocaine and marijuana, he hit hard into what seemed his major concern. This group of players, he said, was going to come into a lot of money very soon.

Drugs were all around, and, he claimed, if they fell into that trap they might make bad decisions, spend so much of their money that they might then need to sell their services to a gambler to fix a game. The gamblers with money in hand were on every corner, he said, but if they were allowed to compromise National Football League games, and fan confidence went by the wayside, the very game would be in jeopardy. I wasn't really sure whether the confidence he was worried about was that of those sport-lovers who sat in the stands or in the den at home with a six-pack, or of those millions of

Americans who gambled large sums of money on games and wanted a "fair" bet.

There was no mention of alcohol, driving under the influence, or driving with a teammate under the influence. There was no mention of growth hormones, anabolic steroids, or even amphetamines. Nothing about the intense pressures the players would feel to enhance their performance with these drugs during their careers, or about the depression they might fall into after being cut and unceremoniously released into the real world. Nothing about ex-player divorce rates approaching 70 percent, or of player after player left penniless after a brief career. Even the finest universities can't fully prepare the departing athlete for "football hangover."

There was, however, a phenomenal dessert selection, with pumpkin pie, Boston cream pie, chocolate cake, and Häagen-Dazs ice cream together with a huge array of toppings, and all of the home-baked New Orleans pecan pie any sweet freak could ever want.

Charlie Jackson ended with a throwaway freebie. To help unsuspecting NFL players avoid unscrupulous gamblers, underworld types, and other undesirables, the NFL offered players security reports on anyone they wanted to check out—business advisors, new friends, even renters—free of charge. Years later, I was to wonder if it might not have been better to offer NFL players free access to the surgical complication rates and the number of pending malpractice suits against their team doctors.

11

D-Day

Draft day. Just as the fate of the Allies hung in the balance during the Normandy invasion, so the future of the entire Raider organization hinged on the wisdom of the ten draft-day picks. Top players, "impact" players, don't just walk off the street and sign on. You've got to either draft them or trade for them. Certainly Al Davis was the master at plucking up presumed over-the-hill players for a song, like Jim Plunkett, Lyle Alzado, Ted Hendricks, and John Matuszak. He was also adept at seeing players with unlimited potential who'd been dropped from other teams, such as Todd Christensen, or recognizing underappreciated players, such as Mike Haynes.

But success breeds its own difficulties, and now fewer and fewer clubs were willing to deal. First, because a deal with Al Davis meant closer media scrutiny, and none of the other owners wanted to risk being hoodwinked by the villain of professional sports and then reminded of it repeatedly by local media. So although they would have loved to outsmart him, few had the guts to try. It was safest just to turn away and not get involved in trades with the Raiders.

Secondly, many owners personally disliked Al. They'd battled with Al since his days as AFL commissioner and now staunchly supported Commissioner Rozelle in his continuing battle against the Raider move to Los Angeles. So, even if they were sure a trade would help their club, they were automatically opposed to it if it would also help Al Davis's club.

In the 1983 draft the previous year, the whole team had been on the block. Al would have traded anyone to get the rights for John Elway. Al wheeled and dealed and, in fact, offered far and away the most in terms of trades and future draft picks, but the Colts didn't want to deal with Al Davis. They ended up trading him away to Denver for what amounted to a draft pick less than what the Raiders had offered. A similar situation arose years later when the owner of the Buffalo Bills refused to deal with Al regarding the rights to Jim Kelly.

Even when a deal did come down and the trade seemed finalized, there was always the Rozelle hurdle. Any trade would be scrutinized more closely because of the Davis/Rozelle personal animosity.

The Mike Haynes trade, in which we traded away our 1984 first-round draft pick to New England to acquire Haynes in the middle of the 1983 season, had been a classic example. The commissioner nixed the deal, saying that it had been finalized fifteen minutes past the October 15, 4:00 P.M. EST official trade deadline. Bam. Al Davis threw it back to the courts, and before you knew it there was an out-of-court settlement. And of course Mike Haynes stayed with the Raiders.

So the draft was becoming more and more important for the Raiders. Since pro football players last an average of 3.2 years in their rough-and-tumble world, several bad draft years could turn a Super Bowl powerhouse into a last-place dog. Here again, Al Davis's past success meant he had to be all the more crafty. Teams picked in reverse order from their last season's finish. Since the Raiders were the Super Bowl champions, we would get the twenty-eighth pick in each of the proposed ten rounds, meaning we'd get pick number twenty-eight and pick number fifty-six and so on down to pick 280, the last pick of the draft.

Players not drafted were called "free agents." They could negotiate with any team, but since they were less desirable, there was rarely any bidding between teams, and these players usually signed for small sums of money.

I pulled into the El Segundo Raider training facility's parking lot just as the sun was cracking over the horizon. There were four or five TV trucks already on hand. The parking lot was nearly full. There were reporters and camera people milling around downstairs as I entered. It was only 5:55 A.M., but the draft was scheduled to start in five minutes.

We had our representative in New York City at the Astoria Hotel ballroom, usually Al's brother Jerry, while the remainder of our force, our six or seven scouts, our thirteen or fourteen coaches, and of course Al Davis, were ensconced in our war room upstairs.

As I passed security and headed upstairs, I figured I had already done my part. Besides going to New Orleans and personally examining the greater part of the four hundred college All-Americans, I had also spent several afternoons going over all of the laboratory and X-ray results, not to mention reviewing additional history gleaned from college trainers, which included the infamous will-they-play-ailing form.

After four days, forty hours of exams, and four early wake-up calls in New Orleans, I had come up with only four players who had major problems, medical conditions that might limit their desirability as draft picks. One had an abnormal chest X-ray that was suspicious for lymphoma, a type of cancer of the lymph cells. Two had abnormal electrocardiograms suggesting a condition called Wolff-Parkinson-White syndrome, in which electrical current goes around the heart in an abnormal way, predisposing the patient to spurts of very fast heartbeats. These two players had had problems in the past. The fourth player had a bleb, a pocket of air, in his right lung that might predispose him to a collapsed lung after a helmet hit him in the ribs. I didn't even count the post-op heart-failure athlete since we weren't at all interested in drafting him.

Add to this scores of players with minor medical nuances: hernias, asthma, high blood pressure, benign heart murmurs, testicular atrophy or undescended testicles, past concussions, and in one case a scarred iris. These players were considered entirely cleared after further discussions with their local physicians or further review of their records.

So only the four players were medically graded down, meaning simply that if the Raiders wanted to take any of these players, it was my opinion that, given their medical conditions, they should be entirely passed over or taken several rounds lower in the draft than originally planned.

Most of the downgrading of players was due to orthopedic problems. Dr. Rosenfeld had worked out a system from five to zero, five meaning perfectly fit orthopedically, and zero meaning the player could make it on the football field only in a wheelchair. This system was a painstaking and tricky undertaking, as many of the premier football players had had prior knee or shoulder surgery that would make them slightly less effective and slightly more injury-prone in the future. On the other hand, if you only took players with no history of injury, you'd have a hell of a time filling up your roster.

Down the second-floor hall and to the right was the war room. It was a large conference room with a loudspeaker system and seating for about thirty around the room's two centerpieces. The first of these, a large board, held tags of all the available players by position, and the second, another large board, matched the players as they were drafted to the teams that chose them. There was also a large blackboard.

Each team had up to fifteen minutes to make its first-round pick, so the first round alone could conceivably take more than six hours. We had already traded away our first-round pick to the New England Patriots for Mike Haynes. I had expected calm.

There was a frantic bustle of activity, however, and I soon understood why. Even though only four or five teams would deal with us, the phone banks in the next room were constantly lit. Assistant coach Steve Ortmayer would work the phones and come in with an offer for a trade. A few names would be thrown around, and Davis would either busily pace while talking about pros and cons of the possible trade or simply say, "Tell him we don't want it," sending Ortmayer back to the phone.

Al was pacing again.

"Put these four players on the board," he directed an assistant coach. "Put the last two in capital letters."

He pointed to one of the assistant coaches.

"Who would you pick?"

"Well, I'd pick the running back," the coach responded. "He ran a four-point-two-five-second forty. I timed him twice. You can't teach speed."

Another coach disagreed. "I'm tired of speedy players. This guy can't play football."

"Yeah, he's not exactly a racehorse when he runs laterally," chimed in another coach. "More like a Clydesdale."

Al pointed to a scout.

"Yeah, he's fast, but we'll have to view him as a project. He's a good kid, he might make it. Or"—the scout shrugged—"maybe he won't."

"Way to put your balls on the table," Al Davis snapped contemptuously.

The first round came and went. No deal materialized despite our burning up four or five phone lines, despite the list of players we were anxious to get, despite another list of our players we would sacrifice. We had just won the Super Bowl and had some high-profile players to offer, but there were no takers.

"Gee, I'm sure glad we didn't take that big stiff running back. I'm tired of track guys who can't play football," said one of the assistant coaches over coffee in an adjoining room while out of Al Davis's hearing.

"Yeah," another assistant coach sarcastically replied. "All it takes is a couple of players like that on the team and pretty soon we'll find ourselves fired."

The Raiders were known for not being afraid to dispense with big-name stars if it was felt they were on the downslope of their careers, especially if they had rubbed Al Davis the wrong way by committing the cardinal sin of bad-mouthing out loud, as had Ken Stabler, or holding out for what Al felt was unreasonable money, as had Dave Casper.

Rumor had it that when Casper was traded, it had something to do with a characteristically flip remark he made to Al Davis after the loss to Denver in the AFC championship game on New Year's Day in 1978. The Raiders had won the Super Bowl the previous year and had appeared to be on their way to a repeat. Instead, they had lost a heartbreaking battle to Denver. Later in the locker room, Ghost had thrown his arm around Al and in his own inimitable way tried to comfort him. "Don't take it so hard—you're still the Super Bowl champ for another two weeks."

Keep in mind he said this to someone who threw a fit if he saw someone laughing on the team plane coming home after a preseason loss. For Al Davis the sun doesn't come up, the birds don't sing, and certainly there's no humor for months, if not years, after a critical play-off loss.

A new list went up of the players we were looking to get in the second round. The room buzzed with excitement and activity; it was like a bull run on Wall Street. All the while, H. Rod Martin, the assistant trainer, zipped back and forth between Rosenfeld and me with the medical reports on the players being considered, to see if any of the players the Raiders were hot on presented extra medical risk.

The board, listing players being drafted and their new teams, slowly began to take form. The blow-by-blow of the draft picks and the minutes remaining kept coming over the loudspeaker from the back of the room. Ortmayer shuttled back and forth from the adjoining phone room, receiving trade offers or calling teams with our offers.

Finally it was our turn. We had five minutes to make the pick.

Three names remained in capital letters. Al Davis quickly went around the room asking for thumbs up or thumbs down. The consensus—go with Sean Jones.

"Is he really that good?" Davis muttered half to himself, half to Earl Leggett, who had been heavily pushing the pick. Davis shook his head very uncertainly. "I don't know . . . I . . ."

One of the coaches pointed out that Sean hadn't played in a top-caliber college league and it was hard to evaluate how good he was. The final opinion Al sought was from head scout Ron Wolf, generally regarded as the only man Al would take absolutely seriously about personnel decisions. Ron nodded affirmatively.

"All right, take Sean," Davis said, biting a thumbnail.

Once he heard the name announced on the loudspeaker from New York, he brightened noticeably.

"Yeah, I think I've got a great pick. Yeah."

Then Al turned to Rosenfeld, who was standing next to me in the doorway, and said, "You're absolutely sure he's all right?"

Rosenfeld nodded affirmatively.

But Al persisted, "This time you're sure?"

That brought some snickering from the coaches and made Rosenfeld blush. We all knew what that cut was about. Last year, Rosenfeld had thoroughly evaluated first-round pick Don Mosebar at the combine. Bob, like all the other team doctors, concluded that Don, one of the best offensive linemen ever to come out of the University of Southern California, was entirely healthy. We had then gone ahead and drafted him.

After our pick came in, after it was totally irrevocable, we found out the unthinkable. A reporter phoned and asked if we were aware that just days before Don had left the hospital where he had had major back surgery, a hemilaminectomy, to correct a pinched nerve that was causing a foot drop, meaning he couldn't lift up his toes.

It was unthinkable. First-round draft picks get more medical attention than some entire Third World countries. Our scouts knew more about the first-round draft picks than they did about their own families.

Dr. Rosenfeld took immediate heat from a livid Al Davis and was ordered to drive to Don's house and evaluate him pronto. Apparently Don Mosebar had been feeling fine during the winter combine examinations, but several weeks before the draft had noticed foot numbness after throwing the shotput. The numbness had quickly progressed to foot weakness. His doctors elected to operate the week before the draft to prevent further nerve damage, which if left untreated could become permanent.

Once Don was drafted, he and his agent, Howard Slusher, let word of the surgery leak out to the press. Don really wanted to play for the Raiders, and his agent feared that if the Raiders alone found out about the surgery, they'd try to trade him to another unsuspecting club. Slusher then scored a PR coup by telling the press that he could have had Don hold out with unreasonably high salary demands until his back was totally healed so that the Raiders and the NFL would never have known about the back injury. But he had taken the high road. All the while, Slusher knew word of the surgery would almost certainly leak out, and when Don signed, his medical records would have to go to the Raiders. Plus there's no denying a surgical scar.

Would the Raiders have drafted somebody else if they had known these medical facts about Don? Absolutely yes. In hindsight, that would have been a terrible mistake. There are a lot of intangibles that don't come out in a simple medical report. Over the next ten years, Don Mosebar went on to be one of the most productive players on the Raider team, a bona fide All-Pro. Plus he was a fiery team leader, and a general all-around great guy, qualities hard to rate by flexion testing or back X-rays.

After the pick, there was a mass exit from the war room as the coaches and scouts headed to visit the bathroom or take a look at the catered buffet set up in another room with ESPN draft-day coverage blaring from a big-screen TV in the background. But there was no highlight film of Sean running over a ball carrier or manhandling a quarterback. This choice was unexpected and film clips are not generally available from small-time football schools.

One ESPN analyst berated the pick. "There the Raiders go again—reaching. Jones would have still been on the board in the fourth or fifth round. Why draft him now?"

"That guy's really full of shit," said one of our defensive assistants. "Sean's a dominant player. He'll be big. Mark my words."

After a morning of brass-knuckled negotiations, player evaluations, and fidgeting, the coaches munched on cream-filled doughnuts and recharged with more coffee.

Then they headed back to command central and on to round three. With each round, another list of names went up, some written in capital letters and some not. The same question always arose: was it worthwhile to give up future draft choices to trade up for one of these projected future stars? Of course, if a player that we had predicted would go in the second round was still available in the third round, things would intensify. Our desire to find a way to draft the player would take on the urgency of a full-fledged emergency. The Sunday ended when we finished the third round.

A second grueling day was needed for the last seven rounds of the draft. I stayed at my office with phone contact for those rounds. By late Monday afternoon, it was finished. After tens of thousands of dollars spent on medical evaluations and medical input, not to mention hundreds of thousands of dollars on scouting and player personnel input, we had our catch.

Nine players, none of whom had any serious orthopedic problems, but two of them with potentially severe medical problems. One had an asthmatic reaction to multiple things, including grass, which could make playing football a little tricky. One of our last picks was the real medical challenge. A player from a major college powerhouse, he hadn't been on the list of four hundred players invited to the combine, so I had never gone over any of his medical history.

A phone call back to his college trainer revealed he had Von Willebrand's disease, a hemophilia-like condition in which the clotting system doesn't work properly. It had been diagnosed after he took a helmet blow to his arm during a game. Two days later he had a black-and-blue bruise the size of Rhode Island. I could just imagine him dropping back to throw a pass, then realizing the blitz was on and stepping forward, only to be sandwiched between 600 pounds of defensive ends. What if he got driven back onto his head? What if he collided helmets with another player? What would the risk be of bleeding in the brain? I left the El Segundo complex and headed for the library.

12

Santa Rosa Training Camp

My plane touched down at the Oakland International Airport in the mid-July heat. I was met by a driver, a high school kid, one of the handful of bright-eyed Johnny Otten wannabes who faithfully ran errands during the entire six-week summer camp, maybe hoping someday to have their very own Super Bowl rings. Six weeks earlier, in an elaborate ring ceremony at the Beverly Hills Hilton, I had gotten mine: a mammoth block of white gold studded with three large diamonds, each representing a Raider world championship, surrounded by many smaller diamonds. I hadn't gotten any of the Super Bowl money, but this ring was definitely worth a chunk of cash. A jeweler friend of mine had squinted professionally and told me, somewhat to my surprise, that these diamonds were top-quality. Still, it was hard to imagine wearing a ring this ostentatious on a daily basis.

Ninety minutes and ninety miles north, we finally turned in to the fabled Santa Rosa El Rancho, a funky one-story motel complex with two well-groomed football fields and a custom-built locker room behind it.

The veterans were obliged to report to camp by one o'clock this afternoon or face a stiff fine. I was here to clear them with their preseason physicals. I'd already been down a week and a half ago when the rookies and free agents had reported. Those examinations had gone flawlessly. The players had lined up in an orderly fashion while Johnny Otten took blood pressures on both arms, H. Rod Martin checked their vision, and an assistant trainer processed their history forms. They had waited patiently in line, and, given the fact that I had to do over fifty evaluations, I had just enough time to make sure there were no medical disasters waiting to happen.

As the veterans came lumbering into the training room after lunch, it was clear to me that these exams would not go nearly as smoothly. The atmosphere was festive as the players hugged each other; they hadn't seen their teammates for several months. My exam was all that stood in the way of their reconvening at the local watering hole, the Bombay Room, before tonight's team meeting. Try as I might to maintain some sense of order and professionalism, I could barely hear a heart sound in the bedlam. It reminded me of working the emergency room at Massachusetts General Hospital on a Saturday night after a Boston Celtic play-off victory in the nearby Boston Garden. That had been one part celebration, one part M.A.S.H. unit, one part riot.

I was searching for Greg Pruitt's heartbeat and could hear only about thirty beats per minute. It made me very nervous, although he looked fine. Most of us have a heart rate of about seventy or eighty beats a minute, but trained athletes have lower heartbeats, sometimes in the sixties, the fifties, and occasionally the forties. Interestingly, as recently as World War II and the Korean War, athletes with heart rates below sixty were considered 4F, not fit for war duty. In those days, a heart rate that low was erroneously felt to be a sign of heart disease. Now we recognize that it can also be a sign of exceptional conditioning. A more detailed evaluation of Greg revealed that his low heart rate was just that.

Kicker Chris Bahr was next. I went through a rapid-fire list of questions about current and past health and was just beginning my evaluation of his ears, eyes, nose, and throat when he stopped me.

"Doc, why are you doing all this? Last year Doc Fink just asked me how I felt. I told him, 'Fine,' then he shook my hand and said, 'You pass.' Actually, on my way out I ran into him again in the hall and he shook my hand goodbye. 'Hey, you know what?' he said with a grin, 'That's your second normal physical!' "

"I don't work like that. I don't know you from Adam," I replied, "but I know you can't find anything wrong if you don't look. That's what I'm supposedly here for."

"What're you going to find," Howie Long challenged from the front of the line, a twinkle in his eye, "that's gonna convince me to sit out? I don't know any other way to make this kind of living. And Al, what about Al? What could you possibly find that could convince Al Davis to keep an All-Pro defensive lineman off the team?"

He had a point. Still, anyone sustaining professional football levels of trauma required a thorough yearly physical exam. And this examination and the blood tests tomorrow were perks for the players that had been negotiated by the NFL Players Association.

"Hey, go on the Donahue show if you wanna gab about that stuff," shot Dave Dalby, who was about four or five places back in the line. "You guys are cutting in on my time at the Bombay Room. And if I'm not outta here in another ten or fifteen minutes, I'm gonna steal your stethoscope and your rubber gloves."

That got a laughing round of applause, but I was speeding too intently through the remainder of Howie Long's exam to take much notice. I waved on the next patient, Lyle Alzado, as I peeled off my gloves and washed my hands.

"Wait a minute," he growled. "No way you're doing a rectal—no one's ever been in there and no one's ever gonna go in there."

Actually, I had not done any rectal exams so far. They generally are not needed in this age group, although Lyle was one of the few that I felt needed one. Individuals using anabolic steroids get prostatic hypertrophy at a very early age, and prostate cancer was a legitimate fear. But to perform a portion of the medical examination against a patient's will is assault and battery. In this instance, performing an unwanted rectal exam would have been suicide.

Fortunately, I had a little bit of extra time to do a more thorough exam on Lyle, as trainer H. Rod Martin and Johnny Otten arrived to assist me. Over only mild protestations, I gave Lyle a hernia check. This involved putting my fifth finger up the side of the scrotum and into the inguinal ring, a cylinder-shaped region lined by muscle that serves to pass the testicle from inside the body to the scrotum just before birth. I had him turn his head to the left while I checked his left inguinal ring for hernia.

"Cough, please."

Then I checked his right inguinal ring. He instinctively wanted to turn his head to the right.

"Keep your head to the left, please," I said.

"Wait a minute," he said. "Isn't this some kind of reflex? Don't you want me to look to the other side?"

"No," I said as I sat just off to his right side. "The object is to keep the patient's head pointing to the left at all times so he doesn't cough in the doctor's face."

I finished with the testicular cancer evaluation.

"Doc, what the hell are you doing?" he said, now getting a bit exasperated.

"Testicular cancer is one of the most common tumors in young men," I replied. "It's one of the most important things I'll do today."

"Sure, doc," he said. "Don't throw out medical statistics to justify your fetishes."

The impatient line of players embellished this witticism with comments of their own.

"If you've gotta be *this* thorough, couldn't you at least put on some makeup or hire a better-looking assistant?"

Matt Millen was next, and checked out perfectly. I sped through his exam, then stepped behind the flimsy three-by-four-foot screen to perform the hernia and testicular evaluation. As my head disappeared below the screen, he exclaimed in a loud excited voice, "Gee, doc, your nose is cold!"

That brought a howl from the room. I stood up, blushing.

"Sorry, doc," he said. "At least you didn't slug me like the doctor in high school who I pulled that on."

At 7:00 P.M. sharp the year's first mandatory full team meeting began.

"I want to welcome you men back," began Tom Flores. "We're going to work our tails off here. We're going to prepare ourselves for the long season ahead. Everybody's going to be gunning for us. We are the world champions. But if we work our tails off, if we get the desire, then with our talent we're going to march through this season and repeat as Super Bowl champions!"

After he finished his brief inspirational opening, he introduced the front-office and medical personnel to the new players, and then it was on to the rules. Bed check was at eleven, lights out at eleven-thirty. He gave the two-a-day practice schedule and the schedule for taping ankles and injuries.

Then he explained the fines, what it would cost to show up late at practices, or miss curfew, or even sprain an ankle if you hadn't taken the time to go in and get it taped before practice. The veterans, however, were already smiling at each other, waiting for the traditional last warning.

"And I don't want to catch anyone messing around with the maids," ended Tom Flores.

A cheer went up, and then the team, almost en masse, headed

over to the Bombay Room, to, as Dave Dalby put it, try to study for the blood and urine tests scheduled for early the next morning.

I had learned from the camaraderie sessions that followed the Sunday games and Thursday practices last year that there was an advantage to playing hard and partying hard together, and it made sense that forcing grown men to leave their families and bunk together in close quarters would pay dividends by bringing the team closer together. If you're friends with the guy next to you on the line, if you're really close, you'll be more apt to sacrifice self for team.

Compared to my day of frantic physicals, my evening initiation at the Bombay Room was a breeze. The veterans were very generous. They'd never let the trainers or other hourly wage earners pay a food or a bar bill. They also would not let me pay, but they would give me a hard time. For instance, Jim Plunkett, probably the most generous of the vets, after paying a bill would always say, "Geez, doc. You're printing bills in Beverly Hills with all your high-priced patients. Come on. Get out your cash and quit stiffing us guys who'll be jobless in a year or two. You better pay for the next round."

Then when the time would come and I'd pull out my money, of course I'd find out he had already paid for it.

A couple of beers into the night and I felt I knew most of what had gone on for the last ten training camps. There was a circuit of about three bars the players would hit, then they would just barely make it back for their eleven-o'clock curfew.

I heard all the Dave Casper stories, including the time he paid someone else to sleep in his bed in a dark room to beat the curfew check so that he could go to his good friend Willie Nelson's concert back in San Francisco, only to be caught when the coaches, watching the concert live on TV, saw him in the front row. When I talked to Dave later, the story was a little different, but the idea was the same. He was holding out of summer camp, and the Raiders wanted to sign him and get him back in camp as quickly as possible, but no one could locate him. Then they saw him on the front page of the daily newspaper in a celebrity softball game with Willie Nelson.

I heard the Jeff Barnes stories. How one time when there was a power outage and all the lights at the training facility went out, he said to a teammate, "Gee, I hope my car starts."

Or the time the chartered plane's wing bumped into a luggage truck, slightly jarring the plane, and Barnes exclaimed, "Gee, I'm glad we didn't hit that in the air!"

Or the time a teammate's wife said she was due in September and he said, "This year or next?"

Or the time Chris Bahr had just joined the team and needed to get to Sausalito and someone said, "Well, ask Jeff Barnes—he grew up in Hayward, which is right outside of Oakland, so he must know the way."

"Hey, Barnesy, do you know where I can find Sausalito?" Bahr had asked him.

And Barnesy kind of looked at him and said, "You know, I don't bother him, and he doesn't bother me."

Barnesy denied most of these stories, but not too vigorously. They gave him a piece of Raider immortality.

I heard Charles Philyaw stories. He apparently came to camp one year riding in his car, which was being towed. It had supposedly been towed over a hundred miles."

"Charles, what happened?" someone asked.

"Oh, I ran out of gas. And I wanted to get here on time," Philyaw replied.

And teammates asked, "What's with the tow truck?"

"Well, I didn't have any money for gas."

They looked at him and asked, "Well, how'd you get the tow truck?"

"Oh, I had a credit card," he replied.

Or the time Philyaw stepped on the scale with all his clothes on, including a floor-length fur coat, and, seeing his weight, bitched, "No way I'm this heavy!"

George Anderson sighed and reminded him, "Charles, take off your coat. It probably weighs twenty pounds."

"Oh, okay," said Philyaw, and proceeded to take off the coat, put it over his arm, then step back on the scale.

And, of course, there was an assortment of John Matuszak stories, including one infamous abduction of a low-level Raider staffer to chauffeur him around town, while Tooz reclined with a local girlfriend in the passenger seat of her cherry-red Vega.

At every stop sign, he ordered his victim to put a hand in his girlfriend's crotch and tell him what it smelled like. After what seemed like an hour of wandering, they arrived at a mansion full of nude women, where Tooz met several other Raider vets and soon disappeared. It took the young Raider staffer several hours to convince two sisters, both stark naked, to give him a ride back to the El Rancho hotel.

And then came stories about Matuszak's use of large quantities of drugs. Some guys took low levels of amphetamines and got off a bit for games. They were called cropdusters. Others indulged more heavily. They were called 747s. Tooz was called John Glenn. The Raiders finally had to assign someone twenty-four hours a day to try to keep him clean.

Another story was told about a promising defensive lineman who got so strung out freebasing cocaine he mindlessly put his shoulder pads and rib protectors over his suit and tie in the locker room before a game. He was put in an ambulance outside the Oakland locker room and sent directly to a drug rehab hospital.

"Gee," I said nervously. For the first time I wondered if I really knew what I was getting myself into.

"Don't worry, doc," another player said. "We got rid of all the big-time druggies."

I breathed a sigh of relief. I didn't want this job to turn me into a high school principal.

"What about that maid thing everybody was laughing about at the meeting tonight?" I asked.

A vet laughed. "Yeah, I remember my first camp. I heard this don't-mess-with-the-maid stuff and I'm looking around goin', what? Who's he talking to? The maids? Me? Not likely! But you know, after about two weeks in this godforsaken place, even those short hundred-and-eighty-pound maids, they really start looking good!"

Another player added, "That's the Tennessee ho rule. About five years ago, there was a line of players going out the door of one of the hotel rooms waiting for their turn with one of the maids, who all the while was screaming, 'Bring on more! I'm just a Tennessee ho!'

"When she asked one of the guys for cocaine, he turned around and pulled an Indocin out of his pocket, then opened the capsule and shook out the white powder stuff inside. She eagerly snorted it, sighing blissfully, 'Oh, this is great stuff.' "

The entire team got a wake-up call at six the next morning. We boarded several buses to the local hospital, where fasting blood tests, urine tests, electrocardiograms, and X-rays were done.

The usual camp routine started with a wake-up call around six-thirty. The rookies would hustle to breakfast and then begin their taping at about seven-fifteen. The veterans could sleep a bit later, since they were taped last, right before the eight-forty-five morning practice.

Morning practice would go to eleven-thirty. Then the players would break for lunch and get a chance to rest for a couple of hours before they had to be taped again from one to two-thirty, preparing them for the two-forty-five–to–five afternoon practice.

After dinner the players had two hours of lectures and film review from seven to nine. They would break into small groups and study film clips and book upon book of plays. They'd be tested frequently. They had to know where to line up and what direction to run when the ball was snapped, which would depend on the play that was called and how the opposition was lined up. From nine o'clock to eleven, the players were on their own. Who knows? The male bonding at local watering holes like the Bombay Room may have accounted for as many wins as any other part of the day's schedule.

I attended the practices and, in between, pored over the returning test results. Besides showing amazingly slow heart rates, the ECG results showed downsloping waves on about ten players, results that in a sixty-year-old man complaining of left chest pain would be diagnostic of a heart attack. Athletes have stronger, thicker heart muscle. Electric impulses travel through this thicker muscle in unusual ways, ways you'd never see in the typical out-of-shape 150-pound American. Before long I was almost an expert—no longer alarmed by the players' ECG oddities.

I was sitting in the training room at about one o'clock the next day, collating the final blood test results, when Don Kimball, a quiet, likable rookie free agent, came in with some scary complaints. Severe stomach pains, total body tingling, a feeling that his body was tied down by weights, and progressive weakness in his legs, associated with some twitching. Progressive weakness in the legs is one of those flashing-red-light medical complaints. I ran a quick mental check on possible emergencies such as a dissecting aneurysm of the aorta, a spinal cord problem, a major blood electrolyte or mineral problem, or even a drug reaction.

His blood pressure was fine. He claimed he had been drinking a lot of liquids, so I didn't think he was dehydrated. However, he did have signs of leg paralysis. I quickly drew some blood and called an ambulance while the blood samples were hand-carried to the lab for immediate tests. Before the ambulance arrived to haul him away to the local emergency room, I got a phone call from the lab. Don's potassium level was 8.1. Levels of potassium in the 6's and certainly in the 7's have been known to kill persons because of heart rhythm disorders; 8.1 was a code-blue alert.

I dumped out the contents of my kit, looking for my crash-cart meds while a trainer dialed 911. I injected Kimble with a lifesaving mixture of bicarbonate, calcium chloride, glucose, and saline. The paramedics came soon thereafter, and en route to the ER I finally figured it out. Don, apparently, was under the impression that potassium pills helped treat cramps. Later I found out this belief was widespread, even among veteran teammates.

Don, like the other rookies, was doing a tremendous amount of running in the two-a-day practices, and understandably getting what we call "overuse" leg cramps at the end of the day. Unbeknownst to me, he had been taking pills of K-Lyte—you put it in water and it fizzes and releases a ton of potassium—in an ill-advised attempt to treat his muscle cramps.

He took one K-Lyte the first day, then the next day, when he got more cramps plus twitching, he took three pills. The day I saw him, he had increased his dose to ten pills of K-Lyte. About an hour later his legs were nearly paralyzed. Months later, I presented this case to the head kidney and potassium expert at Yale University. He was incredulous. He'd never seen a case of a healthy individual with no kidney disease reaching such a lethal level of potassium with oral pills.

His level soared because of several factors. Kimball was also taking Indocin, an Advil-like medicine that decreases the kidneys' ability to get rid of potassium. Second, he was somewhat dehydrated from practicing in a very hot and humid environment. Third, and most important, he was working out hard and getting hit on his muscles, which, although many football players and other athletes don't realize it, tends to make your potassium level go *higher*, not lower.

After this incident, Don Kimball became known as K-Lyte Kimball. He probably helped his teammates more than he ever realized. I went room to room that evening relating Kimball's story, with his blessing, and I was shocked at how much potassium I was able to get players to dump.

Tom Flores was receptive to these medical points, and he helped me emphasize to the players that cramps were to be treated with more water. I was grateful, for I knew that other coaches of that era were not nearly so enlightened.

I remembered some of the stories I had heard at the New Orleans combine. During one doctor-trainer get-together, sponsored by—you guessed it—Gatorade, I was recounting my experience with Killer's Cincinnati dehydration episode in 1983, and all the fluid we had poured in to revive him, when one of the trainers stopped me cold.

"That's nothing. A few years back our head coach wouldn't let any player touch a drop of water. Our summer camp was located in the Mid-Atlantic region, and every day the temperature would be about ninety-five and the humidity would be about ninety-five. There'd be a couple guys a day that just keeled over with rigor mortis–like cramps. You could practically pick them up by their feet and shoulders and they'd stay as stiff as a board. We had a guy who would back the team van down to the field, we'd slam the doors shut and off he'd go. He basically worked full time running these guys back and forth to the emergency room."

"You're kidding me," I said. "You couldn't do anything about it?"

"No. We used to beg him to let the players drink water," he said, "but he was convinced this was going to toughen up our players. It did smarten them up, I have to say," he added. "The veterans would sneak out before practice or the night before and hide bottles of water under the cones that served as yard markers. Then every twenty minutes or so, they'd run a sweep and everybody would fake a fight and push each other way out of bounds, and while they were rolling around, they'd find their hidden water jugs."

Other coaches did allow water but were under the misconception that practicing in outrageously hot and humid conditions somehow prepared a team for the hot games in the early fall. The problem is that when a player's body temperature heats up too much, because of either an inability to expel heat in the hot humid conditions or an insufficient intake of water or both, then the muscle function goes down. And if your muscles are complaining, it's going to be hard to get in good shape or practice technical skills like blocking and catching. Plus, hyperthermia, with muscle, kidney, and brain damage, is always a risk.

Summer workouts should be scheduled for the coolest times of the day. If a game has to be played in a hot, humid midday time slot—good scheduling could prevent this—then the team in the best shape with the best technical skills will have the advantage if aggressive fluid replacement and cooling measures are employed.

That night I put together all the lab results, and during the next afternoon break in the action, I was ready to make my rounds and talk to the players. The blood tests were not easy to interpret. The kidney, liver, and muscle tests were set up with the average 150-pound out-of-condition American male in mind. However, when I factored in the muscle mass of each particular player, I was convinced I could identify some abnormal tests which were really normal.

There was the expected mix of medical problems for young men—increased cholesterol, a couple of subtle thyroid problems, urine abnormalities indicating nonspecific urethritis.

I was particularly relieved to see that the urine drug screens revealed a smaller percent of positives than I had feared, even taking into account certain urine samples that were room-temperature, an impossibility for any body fluid moments after exiting a 98.6-degree body. Even the number of positive alcohol urine screens, indicating typically more than four or five drinks, was relatively low, a miracle given that the night before the test was a bar night for the players.

The percentage of players dabbling in cocaine also appeared definitely less than the estimated 17 percent of regular cocaine users among college students. It was also less than the approximately 10 percent of cocaine users that I had seen among the doctors in my medical training program in Los Angeles.

The percentage testing positive for marijuana was also less than the estimated 36 percent of regular marijuana users in college. The effect of marijuana on athletes has never been rigorously studied, although it's known to decrease short-term memory and could make it harder for a player to learn a complicated new offensive scheme. In terms of effects on longevity and medical consequences, I put it somewhere behind cocaine, cigarettes, alcohol, anabolic steroids, and amphetamines on the list of drugs sometimes abused by young athletes.

I started making my "abnormal result" rounds after lunch, when the players were relaxing in their rooms. But I soon found out that even those with no abnormals wanted to find out what their results were. This included the athletes who had been so impatient with my exam several days ago.

When I got to Lyle Alzado's room, I was startled to see several uncapped needles carelessly placed in a bag outside his door. That upset me. I took him a little bit by surprise when I said sternly, "Lyle, sit down. Your insides are revolting. Your liver tests are way out of whack. Your cholesterol is in the three hundreds, and your

HDL, the good-guy fraction of your cholesterol, is eight. Nobody has an HDL that low. You're a heart attack waiting to happen. I've had patients with cholesterols twice as good who dropped dead of plugged heart arteries in their forties. Plus, your thyroid's all screwed up and you've got blood in your urine. Do you have any idea what all the shit you take is doing to your insides?"

"Hey, you don't know how to read my tests," he said, clearly on the defensive. "I've got two different experts checking me. They know what steroid side effects to look for. And they told me I'm handling them fine."

"Come on, Lyle," I said. "Last year I admitted I didn't know much about steroids. Well, now I've read every article there is. Steroids work. I'm convinced of that. 'Roids make you bigger. They make you stronger. They make you mean and nasty. And maybe you even play football better if you can stay healthy and out of jail when you're not on the field."

"Doc, I don't want to talk about it," he said. "Get out of here."

"Listen, I told you those so-called sports doctors who say anabolic steroids are just placebos are dead wrong. But if these blood tests are any indication," I said, waving the reports, "you're going to be dead right."

I left without saying another word. A week later, we spoke again when his wife, Cindy, was present and he was in a softer mood of his "rainbow." Despite our combined pleas, he reiterated his pro-steroid position.

"Doc, I've been taking steroids since college. I wish I didn't have to. But it's a decision I've made, something I've gotta do to stay competitive. I've only got one or two years left. When I quit, I'll walk away from steroids. But until then, it's something I gotta do to play. It's a risk I've gotta take."

I flew up north again for our first preseason game in San Francisco. The low draft pick player with the rare bleeding disorder was penciled in to play during the fourth quarter. With the aid of a USC hematologist, we'd figured out that a newly available but very expensive brain hormone called DDVAP could help him. It came in white powder form and needed to be taken intranasally half an hour before game time.

The DDVAP would increase a clotting factor and, according to our tests, essentially remove any bleeding tendency from the player. In my mind, that made him no more likely than the next guy to get bleeding in the brain. However, to make sure he understood the risks, and to protect the Raiders, I had him sign a statement saying we had thoroughly discussed this issue and that he was perfectly willing to take an increased risk of bleeding, including bleeding in the brain, in order to play in the National Football League. He snorted the valuable white powder in the locker room at halftime in anticipation of his first NFL appearance.

"Wow!" said a teammate in mock disbelief. "Huizenga, you're not that bad after all. You took away our candy jar, but letting us snort this white powder stuff at halftime—hey, it pulls you even in my book!"

The Tuesday following the second preseason game was the date for the traditional Raider rookie party. Dave Dalby was the perennial organizer and rules maven. Every year he would go to head coach Tom Flores and negotiate as late a curfew and as easy a morning practice as possible. The party was to be paid for in full by millionaires, the year's top rookie draft picks. They had to pay or face very upset vets in practice. Teams of two had signed up long in advance for the sacred air hockey tournament, and Dalby would scribble a cynical comment or two next to each pair.

I was considered a rookie, as this was my first training camp, and no rookie was allowed to team with a veteran Raider player. My teammate was Don Hasselbeck, a backup tight end from New England whom we'd traded for in the middle of the 1983 season. Since rookies were prohibited from cheating, Dalby only gave us a one-in-five-thousand chance to win the coveted air hockey tournament crown. Since cheating was encouraged for veterans—indeed, this was air hockey rule number one—we were definitely at a disadvantage. Dalby also claimed we had no talent. He went on to suggest that Hasselbeck change his name to Casselbeck, since every other great Raider tight end had a name starting with C—namely Chester, Casper, and Christensen.

Rule number two was to teach your body who's boss—attendance mandatory—after an old Dave Casper line. Several training camps ago, on the night of the air hockey tournament he had looked terrible. He had bags under his eyes and was in a listless fog after having been out after curfew several nights in a row. The afternoon practice finished, he came shuffling toward his hotel room and related his late-night exploits to a couple of bemused players.

"Well, I guess at least you're going to get a good night's sleep tonight, Ghost," Marc Wilson observed.

"Nope," replied Casper. "I've got to go out tonight and teach my body who's boss."

The single women of Santa Rosa would inevitably try to crash the party, despite a warning that had once been printed in a local newspaper: "The Raiders are back in town. Lock up your wives, daughters, and house pets." The single players gave the women some halfhearted attention, maybe three-quarters attention to a set of attractive twins, but the married players, as a rule, remained in it only for the show. Sure, several of the married players were known to remove child seats from their cars and securely lock them in the trunk just in case the right opportunity came along, but for the most part the married players were saints compared to your average American traveling salesman.

The party centered around the air hockey table, trucked in from Oakland specifically for this party, the same table reputed to have been involved in the Dan Pastorini box lunch incident. That incident had inspired air hockey rule number three, no eating on the table during tournament play. The air hockey tournament was wildly competitive, and the veterans played a no-holds-barred, frenzied version of the game. They grabbed opponents and pushed and shoved, sitting all over the table. It was all-out war. This year, rule number four—you must be legally drunk—wasn't enforced. In the past, participants would blow into a Breathalyzer, secured from the chief of police, a yearly attendee. If the numbers were too low, you had to chug a beer or two. This was intended to keep incredibly coordinated nondrinking athletes like Todd Christensen, Marcus Allen, Odis McKinney, and Marc Wilson from repeatedly winning the tournament. Rule number five, no belliage, was enforced after George Anderson blocked a shot with a roll of his abdomen.

At one o'clock, a team bus arrived to cart back the more inebriated players who were unable to fit in the back of a nondrinking teammate's car.

Each Monday at seven in the morning, another batch of players got cut loose. We started camp with about one hundred players and ended with forty-five. There were few surprises early on, but after the final preseason game, one week before the season's opener, there were a handful of veterans who would be cut when trades couldn't be worked out. A phone ring—in the early morning of a "cut Monday"—was like the sound of death. If you picked up the dreaded receiver, you heard Don DeBaca, the head coach's aide, asking you to bring your playbook, which of course contained the entire year's offensive and defensive strategies. "Coach Flores wants to see you." You'd get dressed quickly and head into Tom Flores's office and hear the bad news in person. From there, you'd carry a pink slip of sorts to the equipment manager, who would sign off when you had returned all your uniforms, pads, and team shoes. Then it was on to the trainers, who needed to sign off on special protective equipment that might have been given to you.

Last came the doctor visit.

If the player said he was fine when he came to me, I'd get him to sign a waiver so stipulating. If the player said he had any football-related bone or muscle injuries, he'd be sent to Dr. Rosenfeld. By law, no player could get cut from the team if he had a football-related injury.

The majority of the players answered truthfully, but occasionally a player would try to scam a few extra weeks' pay by faking an injury. This was very hard to do, since all practices were filmed, and the player would have to walk through a land mine of questions explaining why the injury hadn't been reported earlier.

I always tried to pep up the crestfallen player during this last interview, but that was especially hard for me when it came to players I'd gotten to know, like the quarterback from Colorado, or Don Hasselbeck, my air hockey partner.

Don's battle was the classic football story. A talented veteran who had made some key catches in the previous year and blocked an extra point in the Super Bowl, he was beaten out by a young blue-chip rookie draft choice, Andy Parker. It would be so sad, that final handshake.

This particular camp closed out on a high note, of sorts. On the last night of camp, a number of us on the training and medical staffs hit the town with the players one final time. The players all left the bar at about three minutes to eleven, giving themselves just enough time in case any of the three red lights en route to camp didn't cooperate. The rest of us straggled back a few hours later and went to bed.

But before I drifted off to sleep, I heard a painful screeching in the distance. It was the motorized "cherry picker" that expanded from four feet to a three-story-high filming tower from which Johnny Otten filmed practice every day. Soon afterward, on-and-off pulses of light reflected against my motel walls. I walked to my window and could see police cars on our practice field with lights flashing and officers of the law pointing their spotlights at the top of the tower.

And there on top, none other than Johnny and a partially disrobed woman were trying to get out of the spotlight's glare. Possibly because of the influence of alcohol, Johnny in his haste to score must have forgotten how much noise that motor made: in fact, he had more important things on his mind. But just before the pair could get down to something serious, the police cars had silently moved in for the kill.

In a moment the creaking began again, this time bringing the guilty parties down to field level. Once on the field, Johnny, trying to talk his way out of the jam, reached into his pocket to show his Raider I.D. Wham! With guns drawn, the local police knocked him to the ground and handcuffed him.

It was two in the morning, and a handcuffed Johnny Otten, head hung low, surrounded by a contingent of local police officers, had to wake up head scout Ron Wolf, who, trying not to laugh, corroborated his identity. George Anderson and several players who had been awakened stood outside their motel rooms and, to the annoyance of the police, continuously applauded through the whole affair.

He escaped jail but not the razzing; for the rest of the year, he was "Johnny High Tower."

13

Turf Wars

It was a crisp Chicago morning, the first week of November 1984. The team was halfway through the Saturday helmets-and-sweats pregame practice, preparing for the game tomorrow against the Bears. Despite the fact that we were seven and two and only in second place, an air of confidence hung over the club. Sure we had just lost a heartbreaker to the Denver Broncos, the current first-place team, but we'd practically given them the game with a million fumbles and interceptions. And they still had only been able to beat us by a field goal in overtime after Frank Hawkins fumbled at our twenty trying to run the ball to the center of the field so we could kick the winner ourselves.

"Hey, warm me up a little bit."

It was Jim Plunkett, who had just finished slowly jogging around the field four or five times. He was on the IR (the injured reserve) list since ripping an abdominal muscle four weeks ago, which made it nearly impossible for him to move quickly.

"Sure," I responded as I backed up, careful not to go too far away for fear that I'd either throw an errant pass or, worse than that, not be able to get it all the way back to Plunkett.

He began by throwing some arcing twenty-to-thirty-yard passes along the sideline in front of the bench.

"How are those abdominal muscles doing?" I queried.

"The one good thing is that my bruises are finally disappearing," he replied. "I'd forgotten what my normal skin color looked like."

"Remember that Seattle game last year?" I asked. "When you got smacked into the turf every other play? Your entire backside was one giant black-and-blue bruise. What'd your wife say when you got home?"

"She said maybe I need a better doctor."

"Gee, I heard she said maybe you should learn to release the ball a little quicker," I responded.

Zing! He rifled a bullet about a foot directly over my head, exactly the most difficult place to catch a football. To stop a ball there, it's all hands. You can't use the basket catch and try to guide it in between your arms and body.

The ball sailed cleanly through my hands and didn't stop for another forty or fifty yards.

"I hope your hands are a bit more nimble at putting in IVs," Plunkett needled.

"That was a terrible pass," I responded. "We're going to have to work on your accuracy." I returned the ball as I asked him, "Did you see that message for you at the hotel from President Reagan?"

"What are you talking about?" he asked in a voice that indicated he might be buying this a little bit. A Super Bowl hero gets calls from everyone.

"Well," I continued, "I guess the State Department from what I hear is looking for somebody to overthrow Gorbachev."

Zing! Same pass, same location, but this time I blocked it with my right hand, causing the ball to career twenty yards off to the bleacher side. The tip of the ball caught me flush in mid-palm with the impact of a full hammer swing. My hand was throbbing and burning, and beginning to numb. I was sure I had broken it.

Back at the hotel I finally threw off the bag of ice. Everything in the hand seemed to be moving. Maybe I didn't have a workers' comp case after all. I pulled on a sweater and hurried down to the lobby.

Marcus Allen and Odis McKinney had decided to go shopping to help pass the afternoon. I was going to tag along. Our hotel was on State Street, just a few blocks from Marshall Field's and the other large Chicago department stores. We barely made it. A walk down the sidewalk quickly turned into an impromptu mob scene. Nine out of ten pedestrians recognized Marcus Allen. Their eyes would light up, and they'd call his name and reach out for a handshake. Then they'd fumble for a pen and some paper.

"Can you sign this for me?"

"Marcus! Write 'To Billy.' "

I was taken aback. Sure, Marcus was fresh from his Super Bowl,

Most Valuable Player performance in Tampa, and he was the league's leading rusher, but I just didn't think this many people in downtown Chicago would care about football, much less recognize one of our players. We had to literally run into a store and dart through several aisles to break free from the throng. Even the salespeople clamored around him. It was impossible to shop, or even browse. We finally had to give up and fast-walk back to the hotel.

Actually, Chicago gave him a better recognition than L.A. Several months before, Marcus had been driving his brand-new black Ferrari on the west side of town and was pulled over on suspicion of car theft. He tried to tell the police who he was, but they didn't believe him. Pointing guns at him, the officers had him spread-eagled facedown on the ground. It turned out they had stopped him right in front of an elementary school, and it was recess. A group of kids gathered around to take in the action.

"It's Marcus Allen," they began shouting.

The police, still not believing this or not caring, kept him down at gunpoint. It turned out that Marcus had accidentally put the license plates, sent for the car he was given as the Super Bowl's Most Valuable Player, on his new Ferrari. So there's Marcus being held down an additional ten minutes for a police radio check while a group of young kids are clamoring around him begging for autographs.

Funny thing, despite our white players' habit of breaking nearly every motor vehicle regulation in their fancy foreign sports cars, I never heard a similar story from any one of them.

After returning to the hotel, we sat down for our traditional Saturday-night fat-laden feast.

"Geez, Dave," I said to Dave Casper, our veteran tight end, back for his second tour of duty with the Raiders, "you're supposed to eat plain carbohydrates, you know, pasta, baked potato, and so on, the night before a game. Those three pieces of roast beef and buttered-up vegetables and that milk shake are going to be dead weight for tomorrow's game."

"Doc," he replied, "I've been doing everything wrong for ten years. Don't even waste your breath."

Charlie Hannah, Mickey Marvin, and two other 280-pound-plus linemen sat down with similar food choices. I decided to take Casper's advice.

Later, we were sitting around watching the college game of the night on one of the two or three TV sets that were positioned around the banquet room. Certain players, especially the "Domers," the former Notre Dame players, were walking around the room collecting their $5 bets from teammates whose college teams had lost to Notre Dame earlier that day. Fortunately there was Ed Muransky, a former University of Michigan player, who would soak up most of the Michigan bets, but I got hooked into a yearly bet on the Harvard-Yale football game by Kenny Hill, a defensive back from Yale who had been traded to the New York Giants but would call in every so often. The first year we bet a school tie, and miraculously I won, although the Yale tie was so abysmally ugly, an off-blue color with an awkwardly repeating Y, that I wasn't sure if I had won or lost that bet.

"Hi, Lyle."

"Where's the A.1. sauce?" Alzado complained without returning the greeting.

Mickey Marvin, knowing full well that Lyle never used anything except A.1. sauce, pretended he was going to pour some ketchup all over Lyle's inch-thick slab of prime rib.

Lyle glowered right through Mickey Marvin and snapped, "Get out of here with that!"

Mickey Marvin, a born-again Baptist, said in his usual cheerful voice, "C'mon, Lyle, buddy, ya know I love ya, I'm just kidding."

Then Lyle, without saying anything else, stormed off to the kitchen for his beloved A.1. sauce. Dave Casper, who had seen this running joke between Mickey Marvin and Lyle about the ketchup in the previous weeks, then grabbed the Hunt's and pounded the bottom, emptying a king-sized bottle of ketchup all over Lyle's prime rib, essentially burying it.

Mickey Marvin was the first to react.

"You asshole," he yelled at Casper, knowing full well Lyle would immediately blame him. "What did you have to go do that for?"

He abruptly pushed his chair back and, although his dinner was only half finished, threw down his napkin and made a fast exit, not looking back.

The rest of the table, several tons of linemen, quickly followed suit, fast-walking for the door. People later asked me what Lyle said when he got back to the table, but I was in the elevator before anybody else, despite the fact that I had barely eaten my salad.

As we got off the elevator on the player floor, Dr. Rosenfeld and his girlfriend entered the elevator, dressed for a night on the town, probably with Al Davis.

"Hi, Bob, hi, Christina," I said.

Rosenfeld's girlfriend had on a body-hugging black leather outfit, as usual, tonight with a diamond Raiders brooch on her lapel. With a cocky swagger, Dr. Rosenfeld greeted us.

"Goddammit, Rosie," squinted one of the players, a clenched fist in the air, in his best Al Davis impersonation. "Just sin, baby."

"Hey," Rosenfeld replied, "if you still got lead in your pencil, you might as well have somebody to write to."

It seemed like the fiftieth time he'd said that in the short time I'd known him.

"You've got to hand it to him," I said, my head shaking as we walked down the hall. "For a guy in his seventies . . ."

"He's amazing," one of the players interjected. "Women, booze, gambling. He does it all. I hope I have half that much energy when I'm old, gray, and shaky."

"What do you mean, gambling?" I inquired.

Yesterday was the first time I had seen proof positive of Rosenfeld's gambling, not just the suspicious questioning of players and coaches about upcoming college and pro games or the ever-present final-score beeper. I had been sitting in the El Segundo training room reading a medical journal, waiting for the last shuttle to ferry us to our airport charter.

Just as we were locking up the training room, in burst Rosenfeld, pale and more tremulous than usual. He always had a mild tremor, really a familial tremor, something passed down in families that gets worse when you attempt fine motor activities. When the adrenaline is pumping, the tremor can go to minor-earthquake levels.

"I lost some important papers," he said.

He was searching over the floor, apparently trying to retrace his steps. Suddenly he spotted several loose pieces of paper with a central fold, next to the training-room phone. Instantly, his whole manner changed. It was as if someone had injected him with Valium. His tremor practically disappeared, and he smiled and regained his usual cocky swagger.

Five minutes before, I had made a call from that phone and seen the list—the entire weekend of football matchups with point spreads in a Parkinsonian scribble. Seven or eight of the matchups had been circled. He refolded the papers carefully and placed them in the inside pocket of his suit jacket.

"How do you know he gambles?" I asked, returning to the present.

"Is the Pope Polish?" the player responded. "I heard him once calling in a late college game bet, when I was in the locker room getting treatment before the Saturday practice. And that guy's not doing token five-dollar bets either. Try thousands."

The game against Chicago proved to be a miniature reenactment of Custer's last stand. Players on both sides were dropping off left and right. Mostly on our side. We'd never seen Buddy Ryan's four-six defense before. Our guys never figured out where their rushing defensive linemen were coming from. And our quarterbacks didn't just get sacked. They got KO'd.

On our second possession of the game, with the injured Jim Plunkett standing and watching in street clothes, Marc Wilson dropped back and was looking downfield for one of our receivers. Suddenly the Bears' blitzing linebacker, Otis Wilson, ran into him like an out-of-control train. Marc's body arched backward and his head literally bounced two or three times off the artificial turf.

I cautiously moved onto the field, several yards over the sideline, then raced out with trainers George Anderson and Rod Martin when Marc didn't move.

I was still feeling the effects of my first chewing-out several games ago. I had instinctively sprinted onto the field to assist a fallen player with a leg injury. Trouble was, there was less than one minute left in the game, and the Raiders, up by only three points, were trying to run out the clock. When I went out on the field, the Raiders were automatically charged with a time-out. In this particular instance, it gave the Minnesota Vikings forty extra seconds to run plays, and nearly win the game. "Let the f——ing player get up and off the field by himself!" Davis had hollered, his face contorted in anger.

I couldn't imagine what he would have said if we had lost!

"Don't move, Marc," I said. "How does your neck feel?"

"Did I fumble?" Wilson asked, looking aimlessly into the sky.

"Marc, does anything hurt?" chimed in George Anderson.

"No, I'm okay," Marc said as he gingerly tried to sit up.

"Relax," I said.

All the while I could hear Dave Dalby screaming at Otis Wilson in the Bears' defensive huddle, "You cheap motherf——er!"

Otis Wilson had knocked out Archie Manning, Minnesota's quarterback, in his previous week's outing. According to the Vikings, Manning's bleeding hadn't stopped for an hour.

In trotted our third-string quarterback, David Humm, a perennial backup who hadn't thrown a Raider touchdown pass in nine years. Humm was an intensely hardworking player, well liked by his teammates, and although no one wanted to see a teammate get hurt, I could see excitement in his eyes as he trotted out to the huddle, passing us as we guided Marc Wilson off the field.

But there was no miracle for Dave Humm. On his first offensive series, although he completed one short pass, he got belted by another Bear defenseman and lost a tooth and the ball when he was thrown to the ground. He located his loose tooth, but the Bears recovered the football.

By the time the Raiders got the ball again, the cobwebs had cleared from Wilson's head and he was able to pass a complete neurologic exam. He trotted back in with a couple of seconds left in the first quarter. Five plays later, he got his right thumb pounded, possibly crushed, by a Bear helmet. When he came off the field, his thumb was already twice normal size. Good for hitchhiking, not great for gripping a football. It's hard enough to throw a pass with two or three defenders leaping in your face, ready to bend you in two, but when you're having trouble holding the ball you're in deep trouble. Wilson tried to throw a few passes on the sideline without much success. He headed off to the locker room with the assistant trainer for X-rays of the thumb. Apparently he was through for the day.

In trotted Dave Humm for a second shot at the NFL dream. He had been a winner in college, and was a take-control guy in the huddle. But things went from bad to worse. He got popped in the jaw again on his first play back, lost another tooth, and fumbled. He recovered the ball for a nine-yard loss, but this time was unable to find the tooth. Second down was an incomplete pass. Third down the ball was intercepted by Bear free safety Gary Fenik.

And then things got really bad. Two other players suffered concussions, sidelining them for several plays, and after a Vann McElroy interception, Humm came back on the field with our offense. On his first play, Humm stepped up and threw just long for Todd Christensen. As he released the ball, old friend linebacker Otis Wilson speared his helmet directly into Humm's knee while Bear tackle Jim Osborne drilled Humm high. Down went Humm screaming in agony. As we arrived on the field, Marcus Allen and Dave Dalby were screaming at the now subdued Otis Wilson.

"You're trying to maim us!"

Just a few plays earlier, Wilson had chop-blocked the back of Marcus Allen's knees, a technique guaranteed to fill an orthopedic ward. He seemed like he was going to apologize, but Dalby and Marcus wouldn't let him get a word in. Rosenfeld gripped Hummer's knee and tested the ligaments. The knee is basically a hinge joint, but Hummer's was swinging in all the wrong directions. The ligaments were definitely torn. His season was over. Humm pounded the turf with his fist. The pain was bad, the frustration worse.

Humm began to hop slowly off the field on one leg, his arms around H. Rod Martin and me, with Rosenfeld walking directly in front. Hummer was spitting blood and cursing the inglorious series of downs that had marked his brief moment out of the shadow of Jim Plunkett and Marc Wilson.

"I can't f——ing believe it," he kept repeating.

"Hey, put him down! Put that c——s——er down!"

It was one of our assistant coaches, motioning vigorously with one hand. We were still about twenty yards from the sideline.

"We've got to stall a little bit, Hummer," we cautioned as we put him down as gingerly as possible.

Rosenfeld obligingly started to test his knee again as I looked at his jaw. Since our third-string quarterback was now out, we needed extra time to figure out what we were going to do for a quarterback. Rosenfeld went through a complete knee/ankle/hip exam on the field, something we normally would do once we got the player to the bench.

On our sideline all we had was Ray Guy, a macho do-it-all punter who hadn't played quarterback since high school. He was nervously taking snaps from our second-string center, Jim Romano. One of the trainer assistants had run for the locker room, but before he could even get to the entrance, out sprinted Marc Wilson with a trainer in hot pursuit, still wrapping his thumb.

Marc had been sitting in the X-ray room watching the game on TV while waiting for his X-ray to develop. When he saw Hummer go down, he simply grabbed his helmet and screamed for the trainer to begin taping his thumb.

Now it was Hummer's turn for X-rays, and he got to watch Wilson gamely finish out the half on television.

"God, I wish I was suited up," said Plunkett, who was fidgeting on the sideline.

"You got a death wish or something?" snapped back a student trainer.

Plunkett chuckled, but I knew he was serious.

When the half finally ended, the score was Raiders: three concussions, one blown-out knee, one blown-up thumb, one chin laceration, two lost teeth, one displaced filling, and about two square yards of forearm skin lost to artificial turf, versus Chicago: one bruised foot, one twisted elbow, and one half-time hospitalization for a lacerated kidney noticed in the locker room when Bear quarterback Jim McMahon couldn't stop urinating blood.

The Soldier Field artificial turf was essentially green concrete. Compared to other stadiums' turf, it seemed much harder, either because the padding was worn out or else because somebody trying to save a couple of bucks hadn't put enough padding in. Some players even compared it unfavorably to the old beat-up turf in San Francisco, where players were regularly sliced and cut by pulverized bits of concrete which came up through the seams of the carpet.

Veteran players loathed turf games because it meant the usual post-game aches wouldn't disappear after running a lap or two on Monday morning. They might last all the way until Wednesday. God forbid you had knees which had been scoped a few times. Then, despite pre-game Indocin, the knees would swell and stiffen for days on end compared with twenty-four to forty-eight hours of soreness after a game on grass.

More ominously, the only existing study suggests that artificial turf increases serious knee injuries. Statistics reveal that an NFL offensive lineman's risk of a serious knee injury (requiring surgery or a minimum of three weeks rest) during passing plays goes up 70 percent on turf. An NFL running back's risk of a serious knee injury during rushing plays goes up a whopping 56 percent.

It's not unreasonable to wonder what turf does to footbones, ankles, and hips. And in a game known for pounding human skulls to the ground, it doesn't take a million-dollar government grant to figure out the brain is going to prefer sod over cement.

But despite the player outcry over artificial turf, despite the fact that many players rearranged their careers to try to play for clubs with home fields on grass, more and more teams went for artificial turf. It made economic sense. It's an expensive undertaking—though now technically possible—to keep grass alive in enclosed stadiums, or in good playing shape in cold and rainy climates. Owners also gravitate to turf to accommodate concerts, motor cross races, and other cash-generating events. Probably somewhere, in some dark room, an accountant had punched in all the numbers, and found that the cost of having grass surfaces was more than the extra insurance premiums and the salaries of the extra players the league would pay each year due to extra artificial turf injuries.

As we limped back into the locker room for halftime, defensive backfield coach Willie Brown, a former Raider great, was mothering our guys up and down.

"You call yourselves players? You guys are letting your quarterbacks get murdered!"

"They're playing like us," growled Lyle Alzado off to one side of me.

He acted insulted, as if they had stolen our patent.

14

Military Medicine

Our air-conditioned caravan of player buses pulled into a rickety two-story circa-1960s motel called the San Diego Stardust. I automatically faded back to my first visit here in 1983. I was hardly a veteran in the big leagues, but this still represented a bit of a culture shock. I'd stayed at Marriotts in Washington, Houston, and Denver and at the Hyatt Regency in Kansas City (albeit the one where the gracefully suspended catwalks had collapsed years before, a source of mordant humor to our players, who examined the lobby walls for splattered blood).

A motel with an actual vacancy sign in the window and a registration office didn't seem to fit our style.

"The last time we were here, I found this motel was stealing *my* towels," said Matt Millen, who disembarked as usual with no luggage, no carry-ons, just a toothbrush sticking out of his right rear pocket. His austere travel kit had a colorful beginning. Millen broke into the league in 1981, and the day before the first away game, Flores sat the team down and gave them guidelines, saying that sure the Raiders didn't travel formal like other teams, but he was at least expecting the players to show up in a presentable sports shirt. The plane was full and the players were milling around the trays of food in the galleys when in walked Matt Millen. He wore a beat-up old John Deere hat that he had found in some barn, a tattered flannel shirt with half of it hanging out the back, and some old jeans with his hunting boots. Everyone stopped talking and stared in disbelief. Then Gene Upshaw broke the silence.

"When Flores said he wanted you to wear a sports shirt, he didn't mean hunting."

Flores, who was looking on incredulously, asked, "Matt, where's your overnight bag?"

Matt Millen pointed to his back pocket. "Gee, all I need is my toothbrush. We're only going to San Francisco for two nights. I can borrow toothpaste from my roommate, and on the second night I'll just turn my underwear inside out."

"What gives?" I now asked Millen, as I looked again at the quite modest motel in front of us.

"One of the front office people screwed up back in the '81 play-offs and didn't get our hotel reservation in on time, and every hotel in the whole town was filled up except for this one. We won the game, and now we're stuck here. It'll take a loss to get us out of here, so learn to like it," he advised.

The hotel was hooked to a full eighteen-hole golf course, but that was off-limits for the players, so it didn't lessen the bitching.

It was only Wednesday night. We were here for a special nationally televised Thursday-night game. We were being served our usual Saturday-night "before the game" meal: the infamous fried chicken, prime ribs, vegetables dripping with butter, and rich ice cream. It was almost as if we were thumbing our nose at the scientific community, as if we were so good we could do all the wrong things and still win.

I was sitting down with Matt Millen, Marc Wilson, Chris Bahr, and Johnny Otten. Every time someone would get up to get something to drink, Matt Millen would reach over, empty the absent man's plate onto his, and pretty much have it eaten by the time the man got back.

"Hey ex*cuuuse me*," he'd say. "So they didn't teach manners at Penn State."

"Manners!" Johnny Otten laughed, turning toward me. "Did you ever hear about when Marc and his wife first ate over at Matt's house?"

For a pro ballplayer, Marc Wilson was relatively quiet and very polite. He was unusual in that along with his wife, he had continued to stay faithful to the Mormon lifestyle.

"Have you ever met Coleen, Marc's wife?" Johnny asked.

"No," I answered.

"Very proper, prim, you know. She's there in the middle of dinner with Matt and his wife, and she asks where the bathroom is. She's already a little uneasy cuz, you know, Matt eats so much he has to open up his belt buckle during dinner, and belch once or twice, so anyway, she asks, 'Where's the bathroom?' Matt says, 'There's one right across the hall there,' then after she takes a step or two he says, "But if you really have to blow it out, I'd advise going up the stairs and using the bathroom in the bedroom there.' "

"She was pretty shocked by it all," Marc said. "At least I had some idea of what to expect. I'd eaten out with him at camp. We went to a Kentucky Fried Chicken one night, got a bucket of chicken, and we're both sitting there taking pieces out and eating them, when Millen starts throwing the dirty bones right back in the bucket."

"Hey, that's nothing," chimed in Johnny. "Frank Hawkins was over there for dinner one night, and afterward he's walking to the bathroom and in the hallway he saw Marcus, Matt's two-year-old, who'd pulled off his diaper and was playing with chunks of his own stool."

Hawkins came back to the table and told Matt, "You'd better go get Marcus. He's just about ready to eat his own poop."

So Millen got up to check it out, but came back only seconds later, totally unconcerned, and sat down. "He's just picking out the pieces of corn."

After that story, somehow my vegetables didn't look so appetizing.

As I got up to leave, I was called over to look at a tiny bald spot on Frank Hawkins's scalp, and a rash on Charley Hannah's arm. I ended up with another dessert, immersed in a roundtable gripe session about the pressures some of the guys were feeling. There was no job security; one bad game and they could be gone. There was always somebody on your shoulder. The vets had to hold off the rookies, and the young guys had to fight for playing time to prove their worth. When you did play, you were almost always going to end up playing hurt. If you didn't play hurt, you risked going on Al Davis's shit list. If you got a reputation as a wuss around the league, nobody else would ever even trade for you, or pick you up if you got cut.

And the money wasn't even all that it was cracked up to be.

"Seven hundred and fifty thousand dollars over three years," said one of the players. "People think you're bringing all of that home in a wheelbarrow. Shit, after taxes, agents, lawyers, business advisors, it's not that much, especially considering you can only count on being in the league for a couple of years."

"Still," I said, "it's funny how we all grow up wanting to be major leaguers. I know I used to dream sports every night, pray for the talent to make it in baseball or football."

"You're the lucky one," Hannah stated, pointing at me. "You're a doctor, you've got security, you'll make a good living for the next fifty years, you don't have to beat up your body, you can hang around sports for as long as you want with this team doctor job, you've even got that TV show. You've got it made. I'd trade places with you in a second."

For the first time I realized that while Charley was younger than I, his career was nearly over. Mine had just begun. "It's weird," I said with a frown. "I've always wanted to trade places with you."

I walked out of the clubhouse lounge alone, deep in thought. There was a stone pathway from the golf course running between the two-story extensions of the motel. The full moon was out, and up ahead a group of players had stopped and were looking up. My first thought was that they were checking out the moon. I was partly right.

"She's built like a brick shithouse," said a player.

It was Rosenfeld's girlfriend. She was standing in her birthday suit, toweling off her hair in front of the mirror. The drapes were completely open, and every light in the room was on. She finally pulled out some clothes and went into the bathroom. The crowd of players moved on at the apparent conclusion of the show.

"I've been on three different teams," said one of the players, "and I'll tell you one thing. There ain't no doctor in this league that can keep up with old Rosie."

I stopped briefly in my hotel room for my medical kit, and after glancing down at my two-page list of players' rooms, headed over to room 17.

"Hey, how you doing?"

"Good."

"How're those stitches?"

"No problem, doc, no problem."

He had about a one-inch stab wound on the back of his thigh. He claimed he had backed into a knife in his kitchen. It wasn't the most convincing story I had ever heard, but gentle probing had not revealed anything more.

"We're going to leave these in for another three or four days," I said. "It shouldn't affect you at all during the game tomorrow."

"All right, doc, whatever you say."

I picked up my kit and headed for the door. Sometimes I felt as if I were in my county hospital days. I remembered a young woman who'd come in with a gaping bullet hole through the center of her palm. When I asked her what happened, her six-foot-five street-tough companion snarled, "That's none of your f——ing business."

I was getting similar vibes in this case.

"Doc, what's going on here?" It was Lyle. I walked into his room.

He pulled off his shirt and pointed to a misshapen "Popeye"-looking muscle on his right upper arm.

"You ruptured your biceps," I said, astonished that he was just complaining about it now.

"Yeah, I know, that's what Rosenfeld told me," he said. "But it looks terrible, and I can't be weak."

"What did Rosenfeld say?"

"He told me I don't need this muscle, that there's no reason to sew it up in the middle of the season."

"Well, true, you don't need your biceps to play defensive line—your biceps are for pulling in, and you mainly need your push muscles. But if you want the muscle to look better, and be one hundred percent for weight lifting, you'd better have it operated on now—before the muscle scars up."

"Doc, you know, I'm in the movies. They expect me to do shots with my shirt off."

"All right, get it operated on."

Then practically without hesitating he said, "Nah, I don't want to miss any games. We're going to win the Super Bowl this year, and I want to be there."

I shrugged my shoulders.

"You're the boss, Lyle. But just remember our little talks about steroids. I wouldn't be surprised if they caused that muscle to rupture."

San Diego's Jack Murphy Stadium was alive. Any night game due to be televised for a national audience with the ABC *Monday Night Football* crew had an extra jolt of energy. Prime-time TV was like tonic to the Raiders. They had twenty-two wins in that slot over the years, versus only two losses. Also, there was a long feud with the San Diego club, especially in the Dan Fouts years when the teams were closely matched.

This game began as intensely as any other. Lots of helmet and shoulder-pad popping. A player came out who had been punched in the cheek through his face guard. Another had his arm bitten. Human bites can be dangerous. Luckily here, no skin was broken. I told the player not to worry, the teeth marks would fade by halftime.

For most of the first half, San Diego got the best of us. Then with just a few seconds on the clock and us down 10–7, Plunkett overthrew Todd Christensen down the middle. But Todd reached out, tipped the ball up in the air, and ran under to claim it against his chest and glide untouched into the end zone.

It was a huge lift. We stormed back after halftime and took control of the game. With our offense on a roll, Plunkett called a counter trap play to Marcus Allen, who veered left after Kenny King hit a Charger lineback crossways. No gain. But when the players untangled, Kenny King, a star running back in his own right, now demoted to blocking fullback, lay on the ground motionless. I arrived at his side just after H. Rod Martin and George Anderson.

"My neck, my neck!" cried Kenny in pain.

"Can you feel your hands?" I asked, examining his arm under the sleeves of his uniform down to his fingertips.

"The left arm is numb," he responded. "I can't feel my left arm. It's dead. Am I okay?"

"Yes, yes, don't worry. Squeeze my fingers." He was unable to squeeze his left hand. "Don't move," I said. "You're going to be fine. Just relax."

"My neck, it's my neck, it's a terrible burning pain!"

I motioned to the paramedics in the corner of the stadium to bring out a stretcher. Just then, Dr. Rosenfeld made it to the middle of the field and knelt down. He had tried to run, but was pretty much reduced to a fast walk. The players used to joke that he needed a TV time-out to get out on the field and examine an injured player.

"What's he got?" Rosenfeld barked.

"Severe neck pain, spontaneous lack of motion, numbness, weakness of the left upper extremity," I replied.

"Okay," he said, pushing me aside. "Can you grip my fingers?" he asked as he had Kenny grip.

Then he took Kenny's head between his hands as he knelt behind his head and ever so gently moved his neck from right to left and then from left to right. My heart stood still. I couldn't believe my eyes! Even a third-year medical student knew that severe neck pain and a motionless patient were bad signs. Odds were it was a benign stinger injury of the arm nerves that would be fine in minutes, but, until proven otherwise, it was a neck fracture. And any first-year medical student knew that in some unlucky instances, moving a fractured neck could lead to permanent paralysis.

"You're okay—it's just a bruise," Rosenfeld said as he tapped Kenny's helmet.

"It's still dead, doc," King anxiously replied.

"Here's the stretcher," I said, as the paramedics moved toward us.

"He doesn't need the stretcher," Rosenfeld replied firmly.

"Let's just be on the safe side," I pleaded, realizing Rosenfeld was totally convinced that the left-side-only symptoms meant it was a benign stinger. "Let the paramedics bring him into the locker room for neck X-rays."

After what seemed like hours of Kenny lying perfectly still on the field, Rosenfeld agreed to go with a stretcher. Killer started to cry when Kenny remained unable to make a fist after repeated requests. Then Kenny started to panic. Tears of fear rolled down his cheeks as he was strapped onto the stretcher, his neck immobilized by one of Rosenfeld's associates. As I walked with Dr. Rosenfeld behind the stretcher, I could feel my blood pressure rising.

"What was that all about?" I questioned as Kenny's stretcher pulled out ahead, just out of earshot. "You should never move a player's neck when he's not moving."

Angered, Rosenfeld turned and said, "I've been doing this forty years longer than you. I know when there's a severe neck injury. I'm the expert here."

I knew there was no way he could know for sure whether there was a severe neck injury—he didn't have X-ray vision. But his arrogance stunned me. I desperately tried to search my medical memory. Was I missing something? Was I off-base and ignorant? If not, why would Rosenfeld risk his own neck and the player's? What possible reasons could he have? I tried to remain calm.

"What's wrong with just being on the safe side and keeping the neck immobilized until we get a precautionary X-ray?"

"Al doesn't like us to use stretchers," he said, with no hint of apology. "The team gets demoralized and plays less aggressively when they see a teammate geting carted off the field on a stretcher."

"What?" I exploded. "Is this military medicine? The health of the individual soldier subordinated for the benefit of the combat mission? It may be okay to let a soldier die if keeping him alive would endanger the remainder of the troops in combat. But this is not war! It's football!"

Now he was really red-faced.

"I've been doing this since before you were born. Believe me, if he had had a neck fracture I would have known it. And from now on, stay out of the orthopedic injuries. Stick to the colds and cramps you were hired to treat!"

We won the football game, but I felt defeated. I sat alone in the corner of the locker room, wondering what the right thing was for me to do. Fortunately, Kenny King's X-rays had come back entirely negative. There was no fracture. His neck still hurt like hell, but he was moving it on his own now. The ice therapy was even beginning to knock down the discomfort.

One of the players came over to ask how King was doing. Then he took a look at me.

"What's the matter, doc?"

"I can't fight this. I quit."

"What do you mean, you quit? What's up?"

I vaguely alluded to the day's events with Kenny King and explained how, medically speaking, Rosenfeld had just played Russian roulette with Kenny King's spinal system and happened to have been lucky this time.

"Great—you quit and we get some stoolie M.D. Shit, if I'm laying out there half paralyzed I'd like somebody with at least a little bit of my interests at heart coming out there."

"It's not ethical for me to stay here. I can't be associated with this kind of medicine."

"Wait a minute. Don't you care about the players? You can't change Rome in a day. Don't you think we deserve a real doctor?"

"Well, maybe I can't even help. I couldn't stop Rosenfeld from moving Kenny's head, could I?"

"Stop feeling sorry for yourself. Why don't you use that fancy Ivy League diploma to figure out a real way to help us get some legitimate medical care?"

"I appreciate your support," I said quietly as I walked over to talk to Kenny King, who had just exited the shower. "How you feeling, Kenny?"

"Good, good. Pain's almost all gone, and I can move my arm."

"Tremendous," I said. "Squeeze, keep your arms out, put your fingers apart, lift up your wrists. Okay, keep your elbows bent."

His neurologic status tested out fine.

"Hey, Kenny," a teammate called in an annoyed tone. "Because of you I won't be able to watch my moves at the end of the game. I set my VCR at home for a four-hour game, and with you lying out there so long, the game ran over four and a half hours, you son of a bitch."

Kenny smiled and shrugged his shoulders.

"Sorry."

"I mean, it'd be okay, I could forgive you, if you were in the hospital at least."

Kenny laughed.

"You know, doc," he said as I was about to walk away, "you made me kind of nervous out there. You know, telling me absolutely not to move, arguing about the stretcher."

"Well, I was concerned," I responded.

"Well, Rosenfeld told me you overreacted. He said it was an obvious stinger and that I shouldn't have been carried off on a stretcher. He said you scared me for no reason."

I felt my blood pressure skyrocket again, this time higher than before. God, that made me angry! Angry enough to stay on as the team doctor.

15

Losing Ain't Easy

The end of the '84 season brought a spate of oddball injuries. Killer began vomiting up blood after the Detroit game, when he decided to quadruple his Indocin dose. Ray Guy suffered a foot drop on his kicking leg when he decided to insert a can of Red Man chewing tobacco under his knee-high white socks and then tape around the top of the sock to keep the can in place, handy for a mid-practice chew. Unfortunately this sandwiched the peroneal nerve, the major nerve to the foot, between the can and the head of the fibula bone. The irritated nerve decided to go to sleep for weeks. We taped the partially paralyzed left foot so tight that it was like a piece of wood. And we bumped up security to Cold War levels so no opponents would hear about it. Miraculously he peg legged out onto the field and still managed to get off a few forty-plus-yard punts the following week against the Broncos.

This was the most dramatic tobacco-related disease I saw at the Raiders, but I was always disturbed by the popularity of chewing tobacco. It was the in thing for players to do, and the accommodating Red Man, Skoal, and Kodiak chewing tobacco and dip companies filled up huge lockers with free chewing tobacco every month. They knew the value of those TV shots of athletes with bulging cheeks. Meanwhile, studies are showing a rise in mouth cancer in athletes who use chewing tobacco.

Lyle Alzado had a painful foot—plantar fasciitis, which makes every step you take like a knife jabbed in your arch. In order to play, he needed an injection before each game. Shots hurt, but shots in the foot are probably the worst. One home game, as the shot went in, Lyle began howling in pain. When the shot continued, he completely lost it and started sitting up, reaching out with his arms as if to strangle Dr. Rosenfeld, yelling, "You motherf——er, take it out now!"

Rosenfeld quickly withdrew the needle in self-defense. Just then the numbing medicine took effect. Lyle relaxed, just slightly, and, daring Rosie to answer, growled, "I'm not a bad patient, am I?"

Shelby Jordan, who had just broken into the starting lineup, was blocking Seattle's defensive end Jeff Bryant behind and around Wilson. Just as that battle passed our quarterback, Jordan's left knee took a direct helmet hit from a diving Seahawk. The knee bent the wrong way. On the trip home, he had to be taken off the plane in a wheelchair. Outside the airport, a team aide was pushing Shelby to the team buses when he miscalculated a curb. Splat. Out fell Shelby, his six-foot-seven frame sprawled all over the traffic lane right in front of the United arrivals sign. Al Davis looked on in horror as his prize offensive lineman was unceremoniously dumped to the pavement. Shelby's teammates, by now fully loaded on the team buses on the other side of the roadway, were holding their breath, hoping that Shelby wouldn't be run over by a car. Luckily it was three in the morning or he might well have been. Shelby slowly collected himself, and with aid slowly got up on his one good leg and managed a faint smile. Davis got in his limo and slammed the door. The team began to hoot and holler for a new team wheelchair operator.

Later in the hospital it became apparent that Shelby was one of those unfortunate rare cases where leg veins behind the knee get damaged at the same time the knee ligaments are torn. That led to phlebitis, which had to be treated with blood thinners and weeks of hospitalization.

Chris Bahr had a stomach muscle pull that wouldn't go away, and his kicking was off. We couldn't do much about his muscles, but the coaches requested a sports shrink on the off chance he could blow up Chris's confidence and help him better aim that ball between the uprights.

And finally Don Mosebar, after playing brilliantly in his first year as a starter, and taking umpteen game-day blows, managed to reinjure his back by merely bending over at practice. Suddenly he felt lacerating left-leg pain down to his foot. I was elected to cart him to the hospital for an immediate icing of his lower back area and the required twice-daily exams to make sure that the pinched lumbar nerve wouldn't deteriorate and sap Don's leg strength.

"It's the blue Oldsmobile with the peeling paint," I said as Don limped alongside me to the parking lot.

"Gee, great car, doc!" the twenty-two-year-old football million-aire said, winking at me as he hunched his six-foot-six frame into the front seat of the seven-year-old sedan I had bought off my parents.

"I wish I'd stayed in school for an extra ten years, gone to Harvard Med School, and become a doctor. Then I could own a car like this."

I had to laugh. It was just too true. Although my TV job had ended, my practice was just building to the point that I was now looking around for a nicer car. Plunk was trying to talk me into buying his kelly-green Mercedes 280SL sports coupe. But either he just didn't get it or he was dogging me, because the $30,000 price was way out of my reach. So for now it was my clunker, Hannah's Honda, and Dalby's van that stood out like sore thumbs in the players' parking lot.

"What are they going to do for me in the hospital?" he asked.

"Well, we're going to ice the back down all night—traction's kinda fallen out of favor. And then tomorrow we're going to go right to the gold standard and do a myelogram—you know, we'll inject dye into your spinal canal, and then do a CAT scan of your back to see if a disc or any scar tissue is pushing on your nerve. Normally there's a smooth sleeve of spinal fluid around the nerves, so we'll be looking to see if that liquid's been displaced."

"Just promise me one thing."

"What's that, Don?"

"If I need surgery, make sure I get sent over to USC. I've got a lot of faith in my back surgeon there."

I breathed a sigh of relief. Don was a local with his own set of doctors from his USC playing days. I wouldn't have to go "under-ground" and recommend other second opinions. Rosenfeld made it tough on the players—and me—by insisting on doing all orthopedic surgeries, even tricky hand, foot, and back operations that many general orthopedists referred to specialists.

"I think you're definitely better off getting your surgery there."

"I hope the Raiders won't be unhappy. I don't want to hurt anyone's feelings."

"Don't worry," I reassured him. "The only feelings we have to worry about are the ones from your back to your toes. Well, actually, you could have been a little easier on my old Oldsmobile . . ."

* * *

The season ended on a flat note. The replacements for our hospitalized offensive linemen couldn't keep out the attacking defensemen, and we dropped our final game to Pittsburgh, meaning we were in the play-offs, but had to play on the road in the domed Seattle sound box.

The season had been tough. Trying to repeat as Super Bowl champions was grueling. Every other team came at us with both six-guns blazing. Teams felt it would make their season if they beat the Raiders, just one game. Fending off opponents that psyched-up, that possessed, week after week required maintaining our health and our intensity. Given the physical and mental battering of pro football, that was a tall order.

We were off to Seattle for the first play-off game. Pro football teams lose 6 percent more games on the road than they do at home, maybe because of fans, maybe because of referees, maybe because of travel and jet lag, or maybe because of something nebulously called familiarity with the field. Seattle's Kingdome was particularly tough on us. Maybe it was just a Seahawk hex.

Tom got everybody together for the game and read us the riot act—Tom Flores–style.

"Now men, I don't have to tell you what this game means. It's going to be very loud out there, and I don't want anyone getting rattled. It's going to take all phases of the game to win this one. Offense, defense, and special teams."

"I hope he doesn't tell them to play like hell," George Anderson whispered to me.

"No mistakes, nothing stupid, just good solid Raider football. Now let's go!"

The guys put on their helmets and, amid much backslapping and loud banter, charged out the side door to the field. Coach Flores went back to the small coaches' room and took a long drag on a cigarette he had left lit. He'd come a long way for a farm boy from Fresno. One Super Bowl ring as a quarterback for Kansas City, one as an assistant coach for the Raiders, and two more as head coach. But that was ancient history. He needed this game. The pressure was etched in every crevice of his face.

He'd done everything he could. He'd put in sixteen-hour days in the spring viewing film and helping to select players for the draft. Worked sometimes twenty-hour days in training camp, molding young players and whipping the veterans back into shape. Then, with every other team in the league plotting to stop him, he tried to rework successful play schemes and keep the team on track for another Super Bowl assault.

He and his group of assistant coaches would formulate a game plan over the first two or three days of the week and refine it during the key offensive and defensive practices Wednesday and Thursday, after which he'd watch films of the practice till one o'clock to check for flaws. Finally, on Friday, he allowed the coaching staff to get out at five so they could rest before the stress hormones started really kicking up for the game on Sunday.

Jim Plunkett and Tom called every play on the field. But afterward, win or lose, Al would second-guess every failed play. He'd corner Tom in the locker room after a game. Then he'd corner him again in the first-class galley during the plane ride home.

At least Tom earned a reasonable salary. The assistant coaches worked those same ragged hours but in some instances brought home as little as $30,000 a year. And while other teams generally let coaches know a week or two after the season whether they have a job the following year, Al Davis worked it differently. The assistant coaches never knew if their contract was being picked up until the very end of January, when they would either receive a secret list of draft favorites or not receive it. But by that time the other clubs would have filled their vacant coaching slots and the let-go Raider coaches would be out in the cold. If word slipped out in early January that they were looking for other jobs, Al would fire them. And there wasn't exactly a huge market for Raider assistant coaches. Al had the fear factor working with the other clubs. Owners were afraid to pick up Al's ex-coaches, afraid that these apparent castaways were really well-paid moles. Everybody knew Al was willing to spend whatever it took to get whatever edge he could. So the suspicion was that Al would pick up the phone, cash in his marker, and pick the brain of his former coach. In fact, over the years very few assistant coaches had left the Raiders and signed on with another team, the notable exceptions being John Robinson and Bill Walsh. Non-Raider coaches seemed to move more freely from team to team.

Tom Flores took another slow drag of his cigarette. He'd gone all out this past week. The indoor Seattle Kingdome, known for tremendously high-decibel sound from the fans, put visiting teams at a real disadvantage.

When the quarterback went to the line of scrimmage, occasionally the play that was called was totally inappropriate based on the defensive scheme. In most games the quarterback simply checked off verbally with a not so complicated series of code words. So if you called a running play to the right where four players were now stacked up, you could easily change it to a pass or a sweep the other way. But in Seattle the noise was so loud that you had to call your audibles with hand signals or you were out of luck. Additionally, since the offensive line charges out on the snap count and the D-line moves when the ball moves, loud noise can potentially affect blocking more than the defensive rush.

We had considered practicing with loudspeakers and earplugs to simulate the experience. After hearing this idea, several players jokingly suggested that if we won and came back to the Coliseum, with its laid-back fans and its architecture that put the fans miles away from the field and damped almost all crowd noise, maybe we should prepare for that game in a library.

Tom Flores took one last drag and then snuffed out the cigarette with his foot. He slowly walked toward the exit to the field. He had done everything he could to win this game. No, he hadn't put $64,000 in dollar bills, the play-off prize, in a shopping bag and emptied it all over the locker room floor and screamed to the players, "How much do you want it?" as another coach had. That wasn't his style, and besides, this was the same team that had cashed that $64,000 check last year.

He hadn't punched his hand through the chalkboard or waited until the very last second and entered the room screaming a string of four-letter words. He wasn't into gimmicks and he wasn't into cursing. He hadn't taken the opponents' mascot, live or otherwise, and castrated it in front of the team. That was college sports.

Sometimes even well-thought-out fire-and-brimstone tirades can backfire. During the Chicago Bears' Super Bowl season, they found their undefeated season record in jeopardy when they were losing to Miami. At halftime, Mike Ditka, the mad maven of motivational tricks, sat the entire team down, then paced in front of them, veins popping out, face an angry red, screaming, "You're playing like pussies and assholes! Is that what you are? Pussies and assholes? Well, that's what you're playing like!"

The team was frozen in front of him, heads bowed, so silent you could hear a pin drop.

"Well, I wanna know," he hollered. "If that's what you are,

if you're a pussy, or if you're an asshole, then just stand up. Stand up."

Again, absolute silence. Then looking to his left, he saw his star running back, Hall of Famer–to-be Walter Payton, getting up out of his folding chair.

"What are you doing?" Ditka screeched, his neck veins again bulging over his sweat-drenched pullover.

"Coach," responded Payton slowly, "I didn't want you to be the only one standing up."

The team busted up laughing. So did Ditka. They played better the second half, but still couldn't win.

What Coach Flores hadn't prepared for was Seahawks defensive lineman Jacob Green, who had lost his dad days before. His father's funeral was being held up until after the game. Jacob was playing on a whole other level and he buzz-sawed through our entire offensive line.

Plunk, just back from being sidelined for ten weeks with an abdominal muscle injury, was harassed, hooked, harried, and humbled. We lost the game. Seattle gave the game ball to Kenny Easly, who had played flawlessly with a cast over a serious hand fracture.

Our team retreated hurriedly to the locker room. We sat in solemn silence, heads hung, with that helpless, hopeless knot in the pit of the stomach. I could remember feeling pretty despondent after tough wrestling losses in college, but I had no idea I'd feel this bad now. I was only the doctor, but I had an incredible urge to punch the wall. George Anderson was kicking a can of stickum around the training room. Throwing a roll of tape off the rear wall, he cussed the officials. "Those motherf——ers, did they call one holding call? Did you see Howie getting hooked and held every other play?"

Finally Al Davis sulked in. He stepped into our training room. He looked nowhere in particular. He just kept repeating the F word.

"Goddammit, we didn't challenge them!"

Then he moved out to the main locker area, where he would typically go to console someone who had made a particularly bone-head play or congratulate someone who had played solidly. He stood motionless as he looked around for someone he could congratulate. Finally he went to say a few quiet words to Ray Guy, the punter, maybe the only guy who had outplayed his opponent. After four or five minutes of near-total silence, forty-five or fifty members of the press burst in. The rows of desolate players were now forced to respond to the outside world.

16

Raider Ups and Downs: 1985

The promising 1984 season wilted and died in the din of the Seattle Kingdome. But like a perennial seed, the 1985 team slowly came to life. The Raider staff went to Phoenix for a new combine, four hundred new physicals and workouts. We came home again for a new draft, and new spring tryouts, then went to Oxnard for a new summer camp. A new home opener was just six weeks away.

The repetition of these sacred football rituals, each year with a sprinkle of new players, was rejuvenating. It gave promise and hope for an undefeated Super Bowl season.

Our offensive line was healed. Don Mosebar's back was as good as new—as new as you can be after two back surgeries. Shelby Jordan's knee and leg veins were healed now, nine months after he ripped his posterior cruciate and got phlebitis. Curt Marsh's fractured left hand and twice-operated-on back were better. Marc Wilson's ankle finally shrank, a year after being rudely twisted, and more importantly his thumb had almost healed and he could grip a football again.

My dad happened to be visiting, and given the up mood at the camp I figured this might be one of those relatively rare chances a son had to make his dad proud. What better way to strut my stuff than to bring him by one of our inner squad scrimmages, let him see his son in action, as well as Al Davis and all the Raider bad boys up close and in person. Even though my father, the chairman of physics and chemistry at the University of Rochester and co-discoverer of elements 99 and 100, Einsteinium and Fermium, essentially lives and thinks several planes over my head, he seemed to be genuinely enjoying himself. Then we went into the locker room. He looked a little startled when a grinning George Anderson inquired, "Hey doc, build any bombs lately?"

He had heard my dad had spent time in Oak Ridge involved in the Manhattan Project during World War II.

Then Jerry Robinson called out from one of the iced Jacuzzis where he was freezing down a hamstring. "Whoa, nice designer tweeds," nodding approval at my dad's East Coast wardrobe. "If I would have known nuclear physicists make that kind of money, I would have studied harder in school."

This year, I wasn't quite as naive about the preseason urine drug tests I was supervising. Through the rumor mill I had heard who the abusers were and how their straight teammates gave them "clean" urine. It wasn't too hard to catch the several abusers. I merely demanded to see the urine actually leaving the body. Even so, there were some clever schemes. We had one player who ran a catheter from a bag of clean urine under his arm through a tube on the lateral side of his penis. That urine just wasn't hitting the toilet bowl like I thought it should. Another tried to dip down and dilute the urine with water from the toilet bowl. A lame attempt at sleight of hand.

Basically there wasn't much of a problem with recreational drugs. The percentage of players using cocaine and marijuana was about the same as the year before, lower than expected for men this age, especially considering their income brackets.

Anabolic steroids were a different matter. Sometimes it seemed that the NFL players were split into two groups, players who were taking steroids and players who were thinking about taking steroids. Intelligence I heard from players traded from other teams suggested that in terms of guys using steroids, we were in the lower half of the league. Word was there were three or four teams where steroid use was especially heavy, where small, fast players were drafted and then later chemically beefed up.

My problem with steroid use came down to a couple of major users and a handful of moderate users and occasional dabblers. Since we weren't testing for anabolic steroids, I had to piece my information together in other ways.

The major users had the stuff coming out of their pores and showed all the signs—the massive size, the bulging muscles, the acne, the hair loss, the shrunken testicles, the aggression and rage attacks. These guys were all self-accredited endocrinologists, hormone specialists, and generally weren't impressed by my soap-box steroid sermonettes. The prototype, of course, was none other than Lyle Alzado. The list of drugs he ingested was so outlandish that teammates used it to goof on rookies. When Lyle started a new injected steroid called Blasterol, several teammates saw a bottle of the stuff. The name was so fitting they made up a story for the rookies that Blasterol had toxic madness as a unique side effect. In would walk Lyle, pulling his hair out, shaking uncontrollably, and faking drool coming out of the side of his mouth, while cursing and randomly kicking equipment out of teammates' lockers. Then Lyle would go around the corner and laugh his guts out while the vets, trying to keep straight faces, would watch the rookie defensive linemen stare in white-faced horror.

"Holy mackerel," rookie Mitch Willis gasped. "He's *really* dangerous."

Lyle would take tamoxifen, an anti-estrogen hormone women take to ward off breast cancer, to prevent "bitch tits," the breast nodules and swelling that come as a side effect of the estrogenlike breakdown products of many of the anabolic steroids. He would take beta-HCG, a hormone that's purified from pregnant women's urine and that in men can prevent the testicles from shrinking as a side effect of anabolic steroids. He would mix and match as many as five or six different types of male hormones. Then he'd cycle the doses in the unproven hope of preventing side effects. Maybe even worse, he wasn't afraid to recommend this poly-pharmacy to teammates who would ask for strength tips. He even went so far as to offer free steroids to Johnny Otten, who was getting quite serious about weight lifting. I nearly freaked when hearing about that irresponsible recommendation. Fortunately, Johnny decided to do his muscle building naturally.

The moderate users might exhibit some effects, but it varied greatly from player to player. They tended to be secretive about their drug use. They seemed embarrassed, even guilty, about being associated with anabolic steroids. But occasionally, their bodies and their blood counts gave them away. Elevated liver functions, depressed HDL cholesterol, and altered thyroid and sex hormone levels would make me suspicious.

The dabblers were about evenly split between the secretive and those who were nervous enough about potential side effects to come up and question me. These players typically showed no side effects whatsoever of the anabolic steroids. Sometimes the only clue might be their interest in Bob Goldman's book *Death in the Locker Room*, which I passed around. It was a composite of the medical megaproblems like heart attacks and strokes experienced by Communist Bloc Olympic athletes and others who had for years pumped down large doses of steroids. As a matter of fact, I never did get my copy of the book back. At this very moment it's sitting in some ex-Raider's library.

I did my annual painful yet necessary march into Lyle's room to report that his blood tests again showed cholesterol ratios beyond the high-risk range and into the may-as-well-put-on-the-toe-tag area. In fact, every time Lyle went down on the field, as the trainers and I were running out there, we'd wonder, "Oh God, is it a muscle pull—or a heart attack?"

During my career with the Raiders, a Kansas City Chief running back and a Chicago Bear center, both in their thirties, had heart attacks—so, believe me, this is something that can happen even when steroids are not involved. And if anybody in the league had the numbers for a heart attack, it was Lyle. My big pitch to him every year was to have a thallium stress test done on his heart, so that we could see what kind of shape it was in. And every year he would adamantly refuse. I think he was as worried as I was.

I went into his room with all this bad news, and sitting with him was a beautiful dark-haired woman, soon to be the new Mrs. Alzado. Apparently some contractor had come to redo the whole Raiders camp and had made the mistake of bringing his beautiful wife along—so Lyle stole her. She was a knockout. Lyle just waved me off with a flap of his paw, and that was that; I never had the chance to get into my pitch. But I remember his look, as if to say, "Stop intruding on our private time."

Training camp entertainment was provided by Vann McElroy and rookie Steve Strahan. Vann, son of a Texas preacher, had a bad habit—incessant nose-picking. Vann figured the best defense for the razzing he took was to go on the offensive, so he began each day by sticking the biggest booger he could retrieve on a piece of white paper and taping it to the locker room wall. Soon Strahan, the recipient of numerous college academic awards, took the challenge. Now two signed and dated sheets of white paper—with chocolate-chip-size nasal masses—appeared daily. Even the hardened Raider vets gagged as they passed the sheets on their way out onto the practice field.

One day, the hotel maid was cleaning Vann's room while a

couple of the other players relaxed between practices. As she picked up a bowl of leftover guacamole, she chucked and said, "Gee, just like a couple of little boys—look at the guacamole all over the wall."

The players burst into hysterics. They knew the green goop stuck to the wall was from Vann's nose.

One player stopped laughing long enough to phone Vann's beautiful wife, a very proper Southern belle, and tattle about her husband's hobby.

"Gee, that's nothing," she calmly replied. "At home he wipes them on the headboard."

One of our suave single guys provided the R-rated locker room juice. He'd hooked up with the most attractive Raiderette, a tall, well-built blond beauty he'd met at the Family Day ceremony, the annual summer camp ritual that brought the cheerleaders down to Oxnard to help introduce the players to a stadium full of local families.

"You won't believe this," he said to a packed locker room several weeks later, shaking his head. "She invites me back to her place and takes me down the basement, and there's one of the other Raiderettes down there who's got bandages all over her face—she's there recovering from a nose job. So we go into this little bathroom, and we're rolling and groping around—clothes are being flung everywhere. All of a sudden, upstairs, I hear the doorbell, I freeze. 'Who's that?'

" 'Don't worry,' " she whispers, 'it's probably my husband. I'll take care of it.'

" 'Your husband?'

" 'I'll explain later.' She throws on her clothes and pushes me into the shower. 'Wait right here.'

"All of a sudden I hear some arguing, and the husband saying in a loud, sarcastic voice, 'Honey, it's your Raider friend at the door!'

"She comes back and starts to go at it again in the bathroom, smooching. I'm saying, 'Who is it up there?'

" 'Oh, one of your teammates. But I like you best.'

"And I say, 'Whoa—what about your husband?'

" 'I'm breaking up with him.'

"Then all of a sudden I hear, 'Come up here!' It was the husband, obviously not finished with the argument. She goes, 'Oh, shit! Don't move.' Then she runs upstairs again. I'm down there hearing this loud screaming, glass breaking. So I stick my head out of the bathroom and beg her Raiderette friend, 'How do I get out of here?'

" 'You've got two choices. Up the stairs—right past him—or out the bathroom window.' Then I heard these men's shoes coming down the stairs. I'm jumping up trying to get out of this tiny little crawl-space window and I'm stuck at my shoulders. I had to rip the screen out to get through, and finally I squeezed out. Then I'm putting my shoes on behind a bush in the yard and I'm hearing the husband screaming out, 'I'm going to kill you!'

"Boy," he concluded, "I'm lucky I'm alive."

Al Davis had a real thing about players' weights. Everyone on the team was weighed in each day, and Al would study the numbers like a crazed commodity broker. He would somehow calculate a perfect playing weight for every player, and woe to the player who didn't get down to that weight by the season opener. It was no fun being on Al's shit list.

Sometimes Al's perfect playing weight scheme didn't make too much sense. For instance, Mike Haynes was an All-Pro speedster with less than 2 percent body fat, but Al decided he wanted him down ten pounds! That had to come from either muscle (not desirable), bone (really a bad idea), or dehydration (a sure way to be weak for games). I remember him on some cockamamie diet before our big game with Miami in 1984, about ready to faint. In the first quarter, he picked off a Dan Marino pass and ran it back 101 yards to keep us in the game. But then, despite the fact he was one of our best conditioned players, he sat on the bench sucking on the oxygen-mask, unable to return for the rest of the half. But sideline oxygen is just a stylish placebo: he wasn't low on oxygen. His mandated pre-game weight loss had left him dehydrated and glycogen depleted. Mike Haynes, regarded by many as the greatest defensive back ever, deserves to get into the Hall of Fame just for having had to compete under these circumstances.

One not-so-skinny player particularly under the gun in every summer camp was Bruce Davis. Bruce was a good-natured, almost jolly kind of player who never took Al Davis's pronouncements all that seriously. He hadn't been below 330 since his days in high school, but this year Davis was adamant about having him play at 281. Well, Bruce had come into camp weighing about 340 or 350 pounds, and like most of the other players, lost a handful of pounds each week during the two-a-day practices. He slowly fell into the 320–330 range.

But here is where Bruce's smarts came in. Knowing that he was never going to make it under 310, he, like a number of other veterans in similar circumstances, would jam a popsicle stick with a predetermined amount of tape wrapped around it just under the scale. The scale would then miraculously never go above the desired weight. Sometimes it was necessary to bribe the person doing the weigh-in to tack on an extra three or four pounds of weight loss every week. Bottom line, come the start of the season, Bruce was down to 281, right where his boss wanted him. After the regular-season opener, Al Davis came up to him in the locker room, shook his hand, and gave him a sincere compliment.

"Bruce, you played great out there. You had phenomenal foot speed. You were really moving well laterally. I'll tell you, you play so much better at two eighty-one compared to the three hundreds."

Of course, when Al walked away, the offensive linemen with lockers adjacent to Bruce's fought to control their laugher. Bruce had admitted to them he was about 310. And they figured he was lying about that number too.

In the summer of 1985, I got an education about the rookie scholarship program. Toward the end of a summer camp practice, Plunkett stepped back and fired an up-and-out to rookie find Rod Barksdale. Rod went up, caught the ball, and cleanly evaded defender Lester Hayes.

"Nice catch, Rod," yelled one of his teammates on the sideline. Word had already spread that Rod was one of Al's guys, a group of probably ten or fifteen players whom Al Davis had either drafted for, traded for, or found on the streets and then nurtured into stardom, undeterred by the negative assessments of so-called football experts. Or at least he tried to nurture them into stardom.

Rod had never played football in college, but had been a world-class sprinter at the University of Arizona. The Raiders wanted to make sure they got him, but didn't want to waste a draft pick on someone who was untested in football. Come draft day, they hid him in a "safe" place, so any team calling to inquire about his rights, any team calling to make sure he was healthy, would not be able to reach him.

Then immediately after the draft was over, after it was legal to sign a free agent, they gave him a contract. If you could take a player that raw, who wasn't drafted, whom other team scouts didn't know, and turn him into a starter, that was a coup. Al Davis lived for stuff like that.

On the next play, Plunkett was instructed to throw at Rod again. Rod ran an out-and-up, the very same play, and Lester missed him again. Now George Anderson seemed to be getting agitated on the sidelines. "Lester, what the . . ."

Lester made a calming gesture with his hands and with his broad stutter tried to reassure him. "I, I, I got it. It'll be fine."

Again, Plunkett to Rod Barksdale. Same play, but this time Plunk overthrew him. The players sitting on the sideline were now starting to catch on. They began yelling, "Take three . . . take four."

Finally when it became obvious that everybody knew what was going on, George Anderson screamed to Rod Barksdale, "Just fall down, you idiot!"

On the next play, Lester hit him low just as the ball arrived, and Rod went down clutching his leg. Johnny Otten, filming the sequence from his tower, zoomed in on the injured player.

There was a round of applause on the sidelines as the players sarcastically shouted comments.

"Yeah, yeah, that's good. Nice grunt when he hit you!"

"Yeah, yeah, that looked real."

George ran out on the field to help Rod limp off while the other players continued their running commentary.

"People have gotten their SAG cards for less."

"Do you use the Stanislavsky method?"

I quickly learned that most teams would fake injuries, hiding talented but green prospects on the injured reserve list. One Super Bowl team supposedly had nearly thirty people on injured reserve one year. Most of them were "rookie scholarships." They were given to players with immense promise who still didn't possess the skills necessary to make the active forty-five-man roster. They were given two or at the most three years to mature in this manner. I remembered a group of doctors at our last NFL Physicians Society meeting arguing about injured reserve, how the rules could be changed so that the team doctor was not thrown right in the middle. Now I understood what they were talking about.

According to NFL rules, after players had been on injured reserve for a couple of weeks they could come back and practice with the team the remainder of the year. During this time they would try to hone their skills by watching the vets and learning from the coaches. Although every team did it, it was still illegal to fake these injuries, and teams had to make sure a player's injuries looked legitimate, since the NFL had a system of neutral doctors who were supposed to make sure no cheating occurred.

Most of the time the injuries were reported as back injuries, since these are the easiest to fake. A person can point to the lower back and go "Ow, it hurts" and still have a normal X-ray.

But with coaching from a doctor, of all people, a player could come up with an even better story, could say exactly where the pain seemed to radiate to and what areas of the leg were numb. Better yet, if a player knew exactly when during a physical exam to scream in pain there would be no way an independent doctor could refute the low-back story.

But ten back injuries on the IR list would raise suspicions.

Since the league was cracking down, the club would ask the player to go down during a game or during practice, and then you could go to the league's independent doctor with a reel of film and say, "This is how it happened."

The rookie scholarships had worked well for Al in previous years. Cliff Branch had hidden for several years on injured reserve while he worked on his ability to catch a football. Rumor was that in Cliff's first year, he couldn't catch a cold. Al Davis shrewdly continued to recognize players who needed a little time to mature, and that was one expense he didn't hesitate to pay.

There wasn't room for everybody, though. The Monday morning before the home opener was especially brutal. It was the last cut down from fifty to forty-five guys. I was sitting in the training room reading a medical journal and waiting for players who had been cut to come by for their exit physical. Through the door strode Odis McKinney. With a powerfully proportioned six-foot-three frame, Odis was your throwback player—tough as nails, a team player, a well-liked sociable guy. But now his eyes were puffed and his nose stuffed.

"You got cut?" I said, trying to keep from gasping.

"Yup," he gulped.

"I can't believe it!" I said.

Odis was the first key member of our 1983 Super Bowl team to get released.

"It's like a bad dream. I got the six-thirty phone call. I didn't want to answer it, I wish I could just have let it ring. It was DeBaca. My heart stood still. He told me to take my playbook and that Tom wanted to talk to me. But I told myself I was going to take it like a man, I wasn't going to cry. I went into Tom's office, and I did all right. He gave me the usual—'It's a numbers game,' 'too many defensive backs,' I was odd man out. He shook my hand, that was it.

"I walked out. Then there was a note that Al wanted to talk to me. He started talking about the 1981 Cleveland ice bowl game—you know, the one where Mike Davis got that interception in the end zone with a couple seconds left. That won us the game and got us into the Super Bowl that year, and Al said if Mike Davis had run for governor that year he would have won, but that the play that set it up, the play that kept us in the game, was when I was covering Ozzy Newsome and he did an out, caught the ball, and had a wide-open field, could have run sixty yards for a touchdown. I was coming in to cover him but I slipped on a patch of ice, so with my last effort I dove, caught him by a shoelace, and tripped him up—keeping it to a nine-yard gain. Al looked at me and I could see tears welling up in his eyes. He said, 'I'll never forget you for that play.' Of course, then I start blubbering like a little baby, and hug him and say I want to thank you for all you've done for me. He's crying and says, 'Don't worry, I'll always take care of you.' "

His voice trailed off as he tried to stop the tears again.

"It's probably not in your medical books," he sniffed. "But you die a kinda death when you leave football."

The opening kickoff soared up near the stadium lights. The 1985 season was underway. It had more ups and downs than the Himalayan skyline.

UP: We kicked the Jets' tails 31–0 in front of sixty thousand of our own fans and tens of thousands of additional green-shirted New York partisans.

DOWN: I got to see Mark Gastineau up close, and I visually confirmed what three independent sources had already told me: he was a big-time anabolic steroid user, the Lyle Alzado of the Jets. He had the look, the stare, the reckless abandon. Like Lyle, he was not popular with his teammates.

After he became an item with Brigitte Nielsen, word quickly spread among his teammates that he had gone out and gotten a "Brigitte" tattoo on his right buttock. Mark was taking a shower after the next practice when in walked the rest of the team, anxious to bust his chops, all with a "Brigitte" fake tattoo on the buttock.

Besides the rumor mill, and the fact that our players had seen him at the Pro Bowl with one of the telltale signs, a large lump from repeated steroid injections into his upper buttocks (a lump our guys affectionately called a "Lylie"), the newspaper stories gave him away. Anyone can be in one barroom brawl—just in the wrong place at the wrong time—but when you're in multiple altercations, when there's girlfriend beating, the big A for anabolic steroids leaps off the printed page.

DOWN: Something about the stress of the profession, the time spent away from home, or the sudden glare of the limelight led to a high divorce rate. Fully 40 percent of the married players from our 1983 Super Bowl team were involved in divorce proceedings over the next several years.

One player who had gotten caught running around and been thrown out of the house by his wife finally got his act together and seemed to be putting things back on track.

"How's it going with your wife?" I asked.

"Well, things are going okay, I guess," he replied. "But, well, it was kind of hard because I had to tell her I got herpes, which didn't sit too well with her, so obviously things are still a little rocky."

"That's too bad," I sympathized.

We both sat in silence for a while. Finally he continued, "Well, you know, I really didn't get herpes, I just told her that just in case in the future somebody else happens along and, y'know, really does give it to me! I just wanted to be on the safe side."

UP: Odis McKinney signed on with the Kansas City Chiefs and got his full salary. It was a bit of a culture shock for him. They all had to wear the same color blazers on plane flights, and they all had to go to church together before games. Wisecracking was not tolerated. "Hey," he told me, "sometimes you gotta bend your principles if it means keeping those game checks coming in."

DOWN: Plunkett, after being brilliant in the home opener against the Jets, was maliciously sacked by Jeff Stover, a headhunting San Francisco 49er defensive tackle, and not just tackled but grabbed around the torso, flung in the air, then driven headfirst into the ground. Result: a shoulder that was miles out of joint. So far out of joint, in fact, that it was obvious even through the bulky shoulder pads.

"You'll be okay, Plunk, don't worry," I said as he screamed in pain.

With a serious shoulder injury, you may damage the brachial plexus nerves, so you always want to check sensation downstream.

That was okay. I felt his wrist, and his radial pulse was bounding, ruling out a weird fracture compromising blood flow.

Just then the panting Dr. Rosenfeld arrived. He put his hand up the uniform sleeve to the shoulder and palpated the dislocation. Plunk grabbed his bad arm out in front of his waist, something people do instinctively, since it's the most tolerable position for an out-of-socket shoulder. Twisting the forearm while pulling down on the shoulder, Rosenfeld tried to pop the shoulder back in joint right there on the field. This elicited a painful scream as muscle spasm and bleeding into the joint sent electrical jolts back to Plunk's brain. It didn't pop back.

This shoulder was no virgin to football injuries. Plunkett had had three surgeries back in 1975 and a rotator cuff repair in 1981. The surgeries in 1975 had sent shock waves through the Harvard orthopedic community. I was doing orthopedics at Massachusetts General Hospital at the time. There was great gnashing of teeth when this premier athlete turned down the advice of surgeons at Harvard and went with his college orthopedist from Stanford, who recommended screwing the distal end of Plunk's clavicle to the top of his wing bone.

On the sideline, Rosenfeld finally reduced the shoulder back in. He then walked Plunkett to a waiting golf cart, piloted by Al Degler, our seventy-year-old equipment assistant. Plunk needed to go back to the locker room for some X-rays to make absolutely sure we weren't dealing with a fracture.

Degler, a sweet Norman Rockwell kind of grandfather figure, was a Raider story himself. He'd come down from Oakland with the team but couldn't afford housing, so for the entire season he lived in a camper truck out in the parking lot. Off-season he went back to his wife and home in Oakland.

Unfortunately, Degler was unfamiliar with the workings of this particular cart and couldn't quite get the gearshift from reverse into forward. So with Plunkett propped precariously in the back, the cart jerked backward, only to be braked suddenly as Degler tried again to slip the gear into forward. The jolt had popped Plunkett's shoulder out again!

In terrible pain, Plunk let out a scream, "You f——er, put this thing in forward!"

He was dying a thousand deaths, his shoulder popping in and out with each jerk of the cart. Degler remained oblivious to it all, calmly turning around with his standard line, "Don't worry, honey, I'll get it."

To which Plunkett screamed, "Get Romanski to drive this thing!"

And Degler, still madly trying to figure out the gears, sincerely tried to soothe him: "It's okay, honey, don't worry, I've got it."

Meanwhile the shoulder continued popping in and out . . .

UP: Plunkett and his wife, Jerry, not only persuaded the nervous ambulance driver to jump out and get them a six-pack on the way to Cedars-Sinai, they also talked him into pulling the ambulance into the drive-through at McDonald's for burgers and fries.

UP: Marc Wilson replaced Plunk in the next game, and we beat New England on their home turf in Foxboro despite practically declining a free touchdown. We were behind late in the game and the Patriot crowd was really on us. But Marcus Allen had just ripped off about a forty-yard run, and we were poised on New England's thirty-yard line—in striking distance of the enemy's goal line. Their nose guard, who had gotten his chops popped pretty good in the previous play, just crawled off the field in agony. The Patriots, who either hadn't had time or hadn't seem him leave, didn't replace him, leaving a gaping hole right in the middle of their line. Recognizing this, Wilson discarded the play sent in from the sideline and audibled a Frank Hawkins run right up their gut. We had three huge linemen ready to scream right through the middle with nary a soul there for New England. It was going to look like an autobahn for our powerful fullback to run through. All of a sudden, just as Wilson was shouting out the snap count, just as we were ready to hike the ball, Mickey Marvin, our North Carolina guard, stood up and in his inimitable Southern drawl informed the Patriot players, "Yawl know you don't have a nose?"

The Pats immediately called a time-out. Our team began mothering Mickey up and down. Marc Wilson grabbed him aside.

"Mickey, what the hell are you thinking?"

"But Marc," Mickey said, "my assignment was to double-team the noseguard. They didn't have anybody playing there. What was I supposed to do?"

DOWN: Marc Wilson now got laryngitis and was nearly unable to speak on the Saturday morning before a big home game. If he had no voice, our entire audible system, where he changed plays at the line of scrimmage by screaming out a series of code words loud enough so that even the split ends could hear, would collapse. I recommended voice rest, steam, and gallons of fluid.

DOWN: I was afraid that Marc might need cortisone pills the day of the game if he didn't improve. I had to do some soul-searching after being so critical of cortisone shots for muscle and joint problems right before a game, but was assured by multiple ear, nose, and throat specialists that rock stars and opera stars routinely take cortisone for severe hoarseness, then go out and perform, and there is zero chance of long-term vocal-cord damage.

UP: Marc was speaking better at game time, so I didn't have to give him cortisone.

UP: The players heard his signal counts and audibles and we won the game 19–10.

DOWN: With a two-game win streak under Marc Wilson's belt, we were preparing for our next game with the tough New Orleans Saints. Before the game, Wilson's roommate, Matt Millen, was visiting his good friend Bruce Clark, the star defensive end for the New Orleans Saints. Clark told Millen that his coach, Bum Phillips, had guaranteed the defense that if they could get Wilson out, New Orleans would win the game. So in the third play of the game, a player blindsided Wilson, legally, but then picked him up and just flung him to the ground, on his shoulder. Gritting his teeth in pain, Wilson rolled over. Standing directly over him was none other than Bruce Clark. Wilson was having trouble moving his left arm, the same one he had fractured in 1983. So Rosenfeld took him to the locker room for X-rays in the middle of the game. A little while later, a somber Rosenfeld walked in with the developed X-rays.

"Marc, I've got bad news for you. Your shoulder's completely blown out. You've got a shoulder separation as bad as they can get. It could only possibly be worse if that bone was sticking out through your skin."

As Wilson related later, he just sat there thinking, "Oh, geez, this is going to take forever to recover."

But Rosenfeld continued, "So you really can't hurt the joint any more. We may as well just shoot it up and let you go back out there and play."

After I heard this story, I wondered if the recommendation would have been the same if Plunkett hadn't been out for the year with his dislocated shoulder and if we had a quarterback other than untested, untried rookie Rusty Hilger. Rosenfeld shot up the shoulder, and Wilson went back out and played. We won the game 23–13.

UP: Rosenfeld decided that Marc Wilson's severe third-degree AC joint separation deserved a couple of weeks to get better and recommended that he not play in the next week's Cleveland game. A decision was made to start Rusty Hilger.

DOWN, THEN UP: We went to Cleveland the next week, and starting at about four Sunday morning, I got serial phone calls from Todd Christensen, Chris Bahr, Rusty Hilger, Marc Wilson, and two linemen, who all simultaneously came down with fever, vomiting, nausea, and profuse diarrhea. I finally alerted Al at 6:00 A.M. It was suspicious to me that this large number of players had all come down with the same symptoms within an hour or two of each other. At that moment we even imagined some kind of sinister poisoning plot.

The previous night's dinner had been prepared by the local Cleveland hotel, and there had been over thirty different cooks and waiters involved in serving our meal. I went through each player's food choices as carefully as I could, but since every player had pretty much eaten everything, I had a hard time narrowing down one potentially poisoned dish. As I sat in my room, I didn't know whether to recommend to Davis that we call the Center for Disease Control or the FBI, but we knew we were in trouble.

I decided on anti-nausea medicines and intravenous fluids before the game. We hooked up the IVs in the shower. That's how cramped the locker room facilities were at the antiquated Cleveland Stadium. Rusty Hilger was too sick to play. You guessed it: "Marc Wilson, please report to Dr. Rosenfeld for a shot." But despite the prophecies of doom, despite the rabid bone-throwing dog fans, we managed to hang in the game. With just seconds remaining, and down by six points, we had first and goal at the nine-yard line. The first three plays were all incomplete passes. Sensing victory, the stomping crowd notched up the end-zone noise to a collective past fire-truck howl. But on fourth and nine, we scored on a pass from the only good shoulder of a dehydrated Marc Wilson to a febrile Todd Christensen. The kick was good, thanks to a nauseated Chris Bahr. With no time left, L.A. Raiders 21, Cleveland Browns 20.

DOWN: Just before we left the Cleveland locker room to get onto the bus, after I had pulled out my last IV needle and taken down my last hanger-held bottle of normal saline, Rosenfeld was busy on the other side of the locker room draining the knee of a big defensive lineman named Elvis Franks, who made his home in the Cleveland area. He'd been working on Franks for about ten minutes when I came by to pack some of my equipment. As Rosenfeld withdrew the needle from his knee, Franks merely grunted and walked away.

At that point, Rosenfeld looked up at me, and in a tone that caught me totally by surprise, asked quizzically, "Who is that guy?"

Elvis had been on our team for weeks and weeks, and Rosie had no idea who he was. He wasn't just asking as if he'd momentarily forgotten this player's name. It was more like where did that guy come from? Is he a security guard or does he play on our team? Rosenfeld was really spacing out.

I had thought of him as an ornery over-the-hill orthopedist, a guy with oodles of experience that compensated for his deteriorating skills. But now I wondered—had he seen enough fading doctors to now recognize it was his time to retire?

UP: As the three trainers and I wearily got onto the bus at the end of the game, Al Davis turned in his seat and remarked to all on this last bus to the airport, "The medical staff deserves the game ball for this game." It was the first compliment I ever got from Al Davis.

DOWN: It was the last compliment I ever got from Al Davis.

DOWN: After rationalizing Lyle's steroid use as the work of a semilunatic whom I had counseled to the best of my ability, I was stopped by Marc Wilson the next week.

"Do you think I should take these, doc?"

He handed me a prescription in his name for anabolic steroids. It was signed by Dr. Rosenfeld.

I was speechless. If you had a health-be-damned attitude, Marc was probably the world's best candidate for anabolic steroids. Immensely motivated and phenomenally talented, Marc had one giant hurdle on his road to football success. He was basically just all skin and bones, and his six-foot-five-inch toothpick frame had difficulty withstanding the NFL beating week after week.

Marc played extremely well when he was healthy. He was a world-beater. But then some disaster would inevitably strike. A fractured shoulder, a wide-open shoulder separation, a nasty ankle sprain, torn knee ligaments, ripped thumb ligaments, concussions. He wouldn't complain; he was way too tough for that. He wouldn't make excuses; he was way too proud for that. But his football skills would deteriorate noticeably while he was injured, from those of a world-beater to those of a middle-of-the-pack journeyman.

He had tried to gain weight, he'd lifted weights, he'd bulked up his diet, but his genetic envelope was only slightly larger than that of a beanpole.

"Marc," I stammered, "what do you want to accomplish by taking these drugs?"

"Rosenfeld said it'll make my shoulder heal quicker."

"That's not true," I said with a sigh. "He's giving you these to try to bulk you up. Maybe if you did put on some extra muscle it would help you prevent injury in the future. But you've also got a son, and you've got to think of that future too. Nobody knows how much these steroids can help you in your football days. My guess is that they definitely would help you for a while, but it doesn't take a very deep reading of that *Death in the Locker Room* book to realize that, at least at very high doses, steroids are trouble. Even at low doses, which maybe aren't so dangerous medically, there might be mood changes that affect your relations with your wife and kids, even if they're not as drastic as Lyle's nightly screaming matches."

UP: Wilson ripped up the prescription.

DOWN: Shelby Jordan, who had fought back from last year's spill into traffic and a life-threatening phlebitis episode, was unable to shake the muscle tear in his groin suffered in preseason, and after waiting so patiently for so many seasons and working so hard to make the starting eleven, was now facing injured reserve, essentially being frozen out of the action for the rest of the season. It'd be like making an undercover detective work a desk job.

He got called into Al Davis's office before the decision was made. Shelby Jordan pleaded his case.

"Mr. Davis, I'm going to physical therapy twice a day, doing all the stretching and strengthening exercises that have been recommended, taking anti-inflammatory pills every day. I'm doing everything they tell me."

"You haven't done everything," shot back Al Davis.

"What do you mean?"

"You haven't taken a shot, a little shot," Davis replied, holding his forefinger and thumb a fraction of an inch apart in the air as if to measure how small it would be. "I've talked it over with the doctors—it won't hurt you in any way."

Jordan had repeatedly refused the shot from Dr. Rosenfeld. The shot could be novocaine, which numbs, or cortisone, a potent antiswelling, anti-inflammation agent, or both.

But there is much controversy about their use in athletes, especially when injecting a newly damaged muscle or joint, and then sending the player back on the field without the normally protective pain system in place. In other words, while anti-inflammatories of some sort plus appropriate physical therapy and rest may be medi-

A typical Sunday at the office meant my patients would be involved in hundreds of violent collisions. Here linebacker Rod Martin and teammate Lyle Alzado have a painful tête-à-tête.

All photographs are reproduced courtesy of Greg Cava, © 1994, except where otherwise indicated.

Players/patients would frequently go down...

often needing assistance to make it off the field. Here safety Mike Davis uses trainer H. Rod Martin and me as crutches.

Cornerback Lester Hayes sits in my sideline consultation room at the Pontiac Silverdome and complains of right shoulder pain. (*Los Angeles Times*/Joyce Kamin)

Dr. Robert Rosenfeld, a former USC team doctor and former chief of orthopedics at one of LA's most prestigious hospitals, was team doctor for the Raiders since 1968...

and he was one of Al Davis's few confidants.

Accompanying receiver Mark Pattison to the Candlestick Stadium locker rooms, I toted my infamous fishing tackle box which housed a veritable emergency room.

Massive Henry "Killer" Lawrence looks on as George Anderson applies Pro Wrap to his wrist—the first step of his taping odyssey.

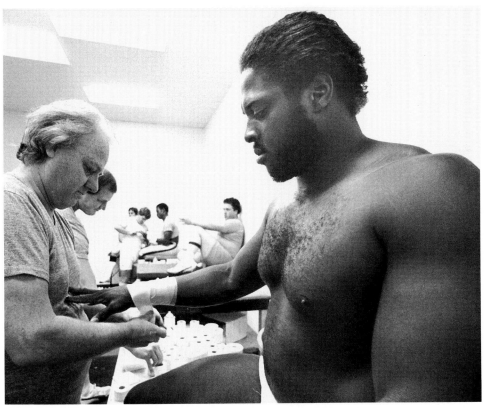

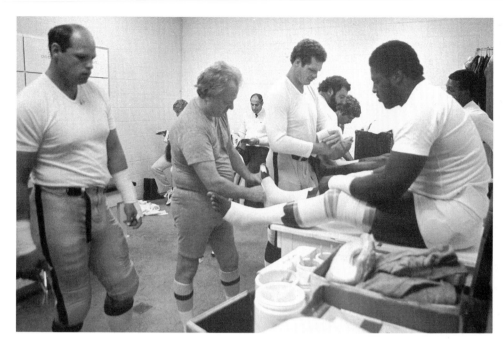

The thighs, knees, ankles, toes, and wrists get the first coat of tape. (Left to right: Steve Sylvester, Anderson, Dr. Robert Albo, Ted "Mad Stork" Hendricks, and Lyle Alzado)

H. Rod Martin applies the finishing touches: elbow guard, forearm shield, and padded gloves are firmly taped on. Only the nose and cheeks will be left uncovered—unless they're smeared with shoe polish to decrease the sun's glare.

Tom Flores claps encouragement as his team emerges from the Coliseum tunnel for the 1/1/84 division championship game vs. Pittsburgh, flanked on either side by the Raiderettes. (Don Hasselbeck–87, Marc Wilson–6, Malcolm Barnwell–90, Frank Hawkins–27, Cliff Branch–21, Mike Haynes–22)

Cliff Branch is sidelined with a hamstring tear. It ripped as he accelerated down the left sideline at RFK stadium, en route to a 99-yard pass reception. It's still an NFL record.

Pre-game, Al schmoozes with James Garner.

Tom Flores congratulates the team on another huge win. Behind him, from left to right, are Al Degler, Coach Art Shell (obscured), Coach Franklin, Mike Ornstein (in tie), and General Manager Al LoCasale (in suit).

Charlie Hannah got his sternum smashed in the following week's AFL championship game vs. Seattle.

During a quiet pre-game moment, Lyle Alzado surveys Bronco stadium, his former home in the Orange Crush years.

But nothing could keep us from our destiny: a victory in Super Bowl XVIII. Here Lyle Alzado, after wiping away his tears, kisses the Lombardi trophy.

The rock-hard Soldiers Field turf took its toll. First, Marc Wilson got KO'd. Here, I check out his cranial nerves—and the rest of his brain.

Back-up QB David Humm came off on his own power after a jarring head hit that knocked out several of his teeth. Moments later, after Wilson returned only to injure his throwing thumb, Humm took a career-ending blow.

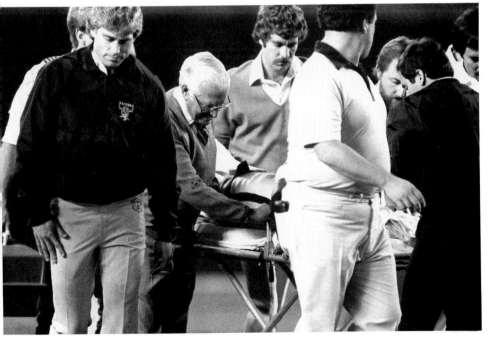

It was a painful moment for all: Kenny King, his injured neck firmly secured, gets carried off the field on a stretcher—finally.

Being head coach under Al Davis is no picnic. Tom Flores was calm on the outside but...

Vann McElroy confers with the defensive coach Willie Brown as Johnny Otten looks on. Vann returned to the line-up just days after being discharged from Cedars hospital with meningitis and helped the Raiders clinch home field advantage for the 1984 playoffs.

An injury forces Marcus Allen out early in the 1986 New York Giants game, ending his streak of 13 consecutive games rushing more than 100 yards. A tell-tale sign was there from the start—Marcus grabs high on the injured ankle.

Al Davis wanted Marcus Allen back playing. "Goddammit, we gotta have you!"

Curt Marsh confers with Gene Upshaw, the last rookie lineman before Curt to start for the Raiders.

Strike 1987! I massage a cramp from replacement (league term)/scab (NF Player's Association term) player Eddie Anderson. Sunglasses were needed to protect against the glare of 85,000 empty seats.

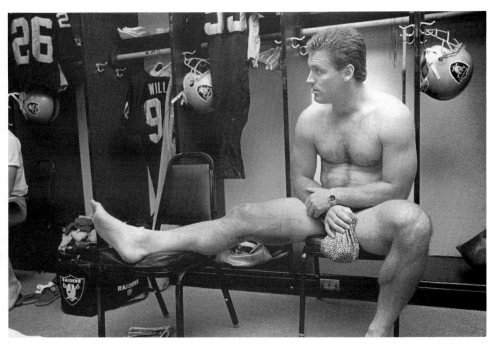

Howie Long, holding an ice bag, models one of his war wounds: an ever expanding right leg hematoma.

Stacey Toran puts a hit on Denver's John Elway just months before Stacey's tragic death.

Steve Beurelein, wearing a number 30 waist patch in Stacey's honor, comes out with strained knee ligaments. (*Los Angeles Times*/Michael Edwards)

Off the field, Matt Millen was relaxed, intelligent, and down-to-earth. On the field, he could get quite emotional...

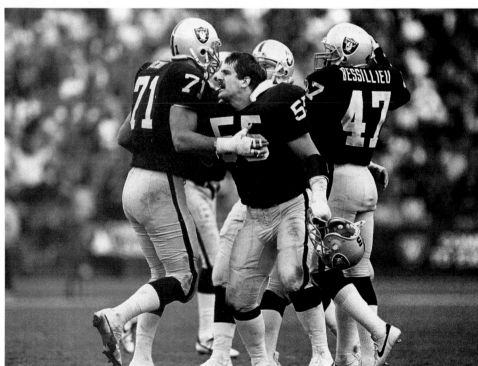

cine at its best, a shot followed by the most violent of physical activity may be medicine at its worst.

Some players were very reluctant to take a shot. They'd heard hallway talk that cortisone was bad for you. Otherwise, why was the team pushing it so hard? Players seemed to regard it as something that one would do to please the owner. It was part of collecting the paycheck. Of course, Shelby Jordan also wondered if jamming a shot into his groin would affect his sexual function. Or his fertility.

"I feel humiliated," Shelby told me. "If I don't take a shot, I'm not a team guy. But my common sense tells me not to take a shot directly into my genital area. I think I'm a pretty level-headed guy, but you get this craziness from playing. You want to play so bad. Just one more game."

DOWN: Shelby elected to take a series of three cortisone shots with novocaine from Dr. Rosenfeld. His pain continued, and he was still unable to play with full strength.

Somewhere down into the season, Shelby's plight came up in conversation, and Matt Millen, out of the blue, agreed, "Yeah, the shot I got in my groin didn't help me much either."

I had known Matt was having problems with recurring groin muscle pulls, one of which actually filled up with calcium, causing him severe pain at the line separating the leg coming up from the abdomen going down. Unbeknownst to me, he talked this over with Dr. Rosenfeld, who suggested a shot. Millen couldn't decide and asked George Anderson for advice.

"Well, if you do decide to do it, just make sure he infiltrates it right where it hurts the most."

So later that day, Millen went in and had Rosenfeld look at it again. Millen showed him right where it hurt, and then Rosenfeld poked around with his thumb and meandered down a bit.

"No, no, it doesn't hurt there, it's hurting right up at this crease here," Millen reminded him.

"Fine, okay, fine, I'm going to inject it," replied Rosenfeld.

He turned around and filled a syringe with cortisone and novocaine, spurted a bit in the air to clear out the bubbles at the top of the syringe, then turned back to Millen and, much to Millen's surprise, gave him a shot practically in the middle of his thigh, a foot or more away from the spot that was hurting. Millen scratched his head, wondering what was going on. Was the medicine going to get to the injury by diffusion? He knew gravity wasn't going to get it there.

Millen walked back into the training room and told George he had decided to take a shot, but that Dr. Rosenfeld had given it in the middle of the thigh, even though his pain was a foot higher in the crease of his groin. George hit the roof, ranting and raving. He grabbed a felt pen and put a giant X right on Matt's groin, then turned him around and sent him back to Rosenfeld. Rosenfeld then gave him another shot, this time in the center of the X.

Of course, in the tradition of football war stories, even this shot story was topped. Dave Casper estimated that he had had over forty shots in his career, especially toward the end, when he was having troubles with his back, left hip, hamstrings, arch—nothing seemed to want to work. On a Thursday in 1978, before a critical offensive day practice, he was unable to move because of severe arch pain. None of the orthopedists were on hand, so Casper quietly snuck into the training room, drew up a syringe full of Xylocaine and cortisone, and gave himself a shot into his own heel. When I heard that one, I asked him incredulously, "Ghost, what the hell were you thinking?"

To which he responded, "Doc, normal people do normal things."

DOWN: Al Davis was hot! He was not speaking to Dr. Rosenfeld. Instead, Davis got all the orthopedic and medical scoop via the trainers, calling them every day to discuss the status of each injured player. He was quite upset that our team had scored more the night before the New England game than we had that Sunday afternoon. And we scored a lot of points that Sunday afternoon.

Depending on whose story you believed, Dr. Rosenfeld's girlfriend had slept with one or even more players that night, and word spread that it hadn't been the first time, either. Davis forbade Rosenfeld from taking his girlfriend on any more road trips, and his job was rumored to be on the line.

Rosenfeld and Al Davis had been quite close. They would have dinner together frequently at Davis's favorite Los Angeles restaurant, Matteos, or on the road. Then all of a sudden not only did they not go out to dinner, but Al wouldn't even talk to Rosenfeld.

The part that bothered me was seeing Rosenfeld tend to players who had purportedly been with his girlfriend. I didn't know if Rosenfeld had heard the same rumors I had and also had no idea whether the players knew that Rosenfeld knew. But he could easily affect their careers by altering the amount of medication they got, or worse yet, out of spite, altering key decisions about whether they should play or not.

UP: Marc Wilson gained five pounds by eating more.

UP or DOWN: Rosenfeld won big money going both ways. All week before the Cincinnati game, he was nervous. He'd bet heavy on LSU, a two-point underdog to the favorite Alabama. Toward the end of the week he got cold feet. It seemed like the preponderance of people in the locker room were telling him Alabama was going to walk away with it. So he placed an equally large bet on Alabama, so that he only stood to lose the several percent bookie's commission. But the spread had moved a few points, so when he placed his second large bet, LSU was favored by one. You can imagine his reaction when the game ended up tied and he won both of his substantial bets. That was bragging rights for a couple of months.

UP: I was running back up the tunnel during halftime of the Cincinnati game when the suave single player jogged over and pointed out his "dangerous liaison" Raiderette. The scrapes on his shoulders from squeezing through the window had pretty much healed.

DOWN: Later that game, Lyle Alzado heard a loud pop, almost like a muffled gunshot. He was trying to stand up, but couldn't do it on his own power. When we arrived on the field, it seemed a mystery, because he wasn't in much pain. But on the other hand, he couldn't flex his toes down either.

He'd blown out his right Achilles tendon. As can happen with major knee injuries, when a tendon or ligament is totally torn, the immediate pain is substantially less than when there's only a partial tear. So when a player walks off and says the joint doesn't hurt much, an exam can still show bad news.

Lyle needed surgery. His Achilles tendon was frayed beyond recognition. What had started as a solid rope was now reduced to tiny bits of frayed spaghetti. It was way more than the typical Achilles tendon rupture. It had the smell of steroids.

I sat with Lyle and his agent, Greg Campbell, in his room after the surgery trying to persuade Lyle that this would be the perfect opportunity to work up his heart, considering his horrific cholesterol panel. The perfect opportunity to work up his kidneys, considering his continued blood in the urine. And a perfect time to get him to withdraw from steroids and allow me to monitor for depression, given the fact that he had announced his retirement. I went zero for three.

Unlike other veteran players who would continue to see me as their private doctor, Lyle was followed by his steroid "experts," and

I never heard another word from him until his ill-fated comeback in 1990. I did hear that he made several honest attempts to get off steroids. In each instance, some fake friend, airhead fan, or fawning date would speak the fatal phrase—"Gee, Lyle, you're not nearly as big as I thought you'd be." Boom. He'd be back shooting 'roids and popping pills before the echo of the words died down in his brain.

DOWN: George Anderson got the team penalized fifteen yards in a key situation. We were fighting for a touchdown against the archrival Broncos when Dokie Williams went up for a pass and got hit well before the ball arrived. An interference penalty. When nothing was called, George went ballistic on the sideline, screaming at the five-foot-four referee, "You little blind c——s——er! That was interference all the way!"

The short ref, who had his back to our sideline, quickly turned around and, staring at George, H. Rod Martin, and me, demanded, "Who said that?"

No answer. We all stood like statues in denial. But the ref kept staring in our direction.

"If you were a man you'd admit you said it," he challenged us.

After a momentary pause, George glowered and said, "Okay, I said it!"

Wham. The referee whipped out his yellow penalty flag and tossed it high in the air.

"Raider sideline is penalized fifteen yards," he yelled, pointing at George as he signaled unsportsmanlike conduct to the TV audience.

The 75,101 Denver fans screamed in delight. George stood numbly on the sideline, hands at his side. He had just committed a grievous error. For all we knew, despite his nearly thirty years of service, Al Davis would summarily fire him. I felt terrible for him but really didn't know what to say. Finally, still a bit pale, George broke the silence.

"That was stupid," he said to me as he slowly shook his head. "I should never have called him *little!*"

UP: We won the game in overtime, and Al Davis even managed a wan smile afterward as George explained how the ref had baited him into confessing.

UP: We went 12–4, ended up in first place, and had only to defeat the New England Patriots, a team we had beaten earlier in the season, to make it to the AFC championship game.

DOWN: A beat-up Marc Wilson had a subpar day. A few untimely interceptions and we lost. The fans turned on Wilson and heartily jeered him, not knowing or caring that he had donated his body for the team all year. He hadn't played hurt. He'd played injured.

UP: Patrick Sullivan, son of the New England Patriots' owner, who had been hollering at Howie Long and several other players from the sideline all through the game, rushed excitedly up to Howie Long as we walked into the Coliseum tunnel, wanting to razz this Boston-born-and-raised Raider, who had had the nerve to criticize the Pats in the hometown Boston papers. Matt Millen, walking with me about ten yards behind Howie, saw this little man in street clothes with his face up near Howie's and, assuming it was a drunken fan who had jumped over the wall and eluded police, quickly ran up behind him and belted him over the head with his helmet.

UP or DOWN: When asked about it later, Millen stated he should have hit Sullivan harder—it might have knocked the silver spoon out of his mouth.

WINDING DOWN: The following Thursday was the year-end Pancho's Bar camaraderie session. Most of the players were flying to their homes around the country, while a handful were staying back for end-of-the-year tune-up surgery. A tune-up surgery was surgery that a player needed but that was not urgent enough to keep him from playing. Kind of like a lube job on a car. Bob Nelson was scheduled for knee surgery number six. He was optimistic. His shoulder, which Rosenfeld had reconstructed, was as good as new, and he figured this knee scope was comparatively minor. Hannah was more nervous about his upcoming fourth knee surgery. I had to assure him again that I had spoken to Fred Nicola and he would be doing his entire surgery, not Rosenfeld. Nicola, a young associate of Rosenfeld's, had a steady hand and, in my eyes, a good track record, especially with his knee surgeries. On the other hand, it was outright scary thinking what Rosenfeld, with his pronounced tremor on good days, could do to a star athlete's knee during arthroscopy, which required exceptional hand-eye coordination and three-dimensional visual skills.

Dalby, Kimmel, Van Pelt, Rod Martin, Plunkett, Bahr, the sauve single guy, and a handful of others were also in attendance, mourning the season's failures, vowing not to let it happen again, all the while knowing their sports career clocks were ticking down. There was only so much time left to catch another pass, make another tackle, win another ring, or even drink another beer as a full-fledged Raider.

The New England Patriots had a psychiatrist who'd actually published his approach to winning in the *New England Journal of Medicine*, the contemporary bible of medicine. He wrote that their success, the success that took them to the 1985 Super Bowl (where, incidentally, they were shellacked), was in part due to his regular player/player and player/coach therapy sessions.

The Raiders had developed their own brand of outpatient therapy and had used it quite effectively over the last twenty years. It was held at least once a week in a bar and was called camaraderie. Camaraderie spawned togetherness. It hatched hundreds of pranks and running jokes. It kept practice fun. It prevented burnout. A woman or two might try to butt in, but it was pretty much a player-bonding thing; wives, girlfriends, and significant others were discouraged.

I felt a tap on my shoulder.

"Do you want to dance?"

I couldn't believe it! It was the tall blond dangerous liaison Raiderette.

Before I had time to make some excuse, I heard laughter coming from behind me. Hey, it's a tough job being the butt of childish professional football pranks, but somebody's got to do it.

17

Marcus Allen: Fall from Grace

Preseason camp 1986 brought the traditional ringing in of the new and disposal of the old. At the top of the new list was Bob Buczkowski, our first-round draft pick out of the University of Pittsburgh. Before the first day of summer camp he already had the accessories: a brand-new Corvette (which he'd already bottomed out by making an illegal U-turn over an eight-inch-high median strip full of plants), a diamond earring, and a Raiderette live-in.

He had even the veterans shaking their heads during his locker room descriptions of the morning massages she'd give him immediately after cooking him a gourmet breakfast and serving it to him in bed. She did everything to make him feel at home short of putting AstroTurf in their bed. Unknown to the rookie, her last several exploits with veteran players had come up empty-handed. He wasn't suspicious of her motives . . . yet.

Chris Riehm was another newcomer, a highly touted guard we had lured from the rival United States Football League. He signed approximately three weeks into summer camp for a hefty pile of cash. To make up for lost time he not only had to do the vigorous twice-a-day workouts, but had to stay and run through plays afterward so that he would be up to speed by the season opener. But several days into this exhausting routine, while Al Davis watched him hustle through his third workout of the day, Chris began gasping for air. He was heaving like a fish out of water. He was too weak even to get down in his stance. I walked him over for a short water break. But his huffing didn't stop. Then he began to cramp up. His stomach muscles involuntarily pulled him forward, his hamstring cramps pulled him the other way. As Dalby used to say, "It's IV time."

It never ceased to amaze me how promptly a muscle cramp responded to an intravenous fluid push. Riehm also was quite impressed—he felt as good as new. He begged to attend that night's rookie party, paid for by Bob Buczkowski. But Riehm's blood tests, sent off to the hospital via one of our runners, returned a tick out of whack. His kidneys were functioning at less than a fourth of normal, and he showed evidence of a severe breakdown of muscle protein.

Ordinarily this sort of patient would be put in the hospital for lots of IV fluids and daily kidney tests. But Chris had already gotten some IV fluid, was drinking tons of liquid without difficulty, and felt well. I opted to follow him myself with daily blood tests. The easy part was explaining it to his wife, who happened to be a doctor. The hard part was explaining it to Al Davis, who seemed incredulous when I tried to explain why Chris might be out for a day or two.

"Acute tubular necrosis? High potassium? Early rhabdomyolysis? Shit, how come we never had any of these problems before you came?"

"I think you probably did, sir."

"Oh, shit, you don't know," he scowled.

I didn't bother to argue the point with Al. Problems like this resolve on their own most of the time. I would have liked to please my boss, but not at Chris's expense. If he was the rare unlucky one, watch out!

That evening was the big party, and it was easy for me to rationalize my presence. Somebody had to make sure that Chris Riehm didn't drink any alcohol. My air hockey tournament partner was Marc Wilson, a bad sign for him, since my previous two partners, Don Hasselbeck and Dave Casper, had been cut or retired soon thereafter.

In addition to Lyle Alzado, who couldn't make it back from his nasty Achilles tendon rupture, a whole list of our Super Bowl starters were on their way out—Cliff Branch, Tony Caldwell, Mike Davis, Bob Nelson, Jack Squirek, and Dave Dalby. Dalby knew he was on the ropes despite 205 consecutive games down and dirty in the trenches. But he got one last hurrah as air hockey tournament chairman. In fact, it had to be. Dalby had a clause in his contract that he couldn't be cut before the air hockey tournament. After the next preseason game on Monday morning, he got the call from Don DeBaca.

"Bring in your playbook—Tom wants to talk to you."

This cut went especially deep for Tom Flores. It was the height of camp; the preseason juices and jitters were beginning despite the physically draining twenty-hour coaching days. But when a guy like Dalby walked in, a guy who had faithfully gone to battle for him for the last fourteen years, a guy who had left a lot of blood on the field, it really affected Tom. He tried to handle it with humor.

"Actually, Dave, you've played a long time for somebody who runs a five-point-four forty," Tom began, alluding to a recurring gag about Dave's slow sprint speed.

The fallout was worse for Dave Dalby. Soon after being released, in a post-football funk, he ballooned up into the three hundreds, saw his marriage dissolve and his money evaporate. His wife got the kids, the house, and what cash he had. Dave had put all his investment eggs in Technical Equities, a real estate investment firm that he had heard of from numerous other professional athletes who had invested in it. It had toppled because of a large embezzlement scam and his $700,000 investment was worth nothing.

Word filtered back within a period of months that Dave was literally out on the street. After fourteen consecutive seasons, numerous Pro Bowl appearances, three Super Bowl rings, and his ironman streak of 205 consecutive games played, Dave was bedding down in the back of his van.

He had little cartilage and less cash. He was dying his football death in a way not terribly dissimilar from others, but was dangerously close to dying his real death too. Dave had always quoted a small study which purported to show that the average National Football League lineman only lived to age fifty-two. He used to refer to that repeatedly when I'd chide him about his weight.

"It's no use, doc—we're all going to die by fifty, so I might as well have fun."

But now at age thirty-six he seemed intent on lowering that statistical number even further.

The new 1986 NFL league-wide drug-testing program turned out to be a bust, at least on our team. Out of about a hundred players reporting, only two were positive for cocaine, and they were both walk-ons, cut by the time the test results returned. A handful of other players came back with codeine in their urine, which was not a giant surprise, since they had been prescribed Tylenol and codeine for various orthopedic injuries. We had a positive phenobarbital on one player (he was on it legitimately for seizures), and one player had moderately elevated marijuana levels.

For the last one, I caught holy hell. First I got the call that Al wanted to meet with me. I went into his office, a large room decorated totally in silver, black, white, and mirrors. He had a huge desk but instead sat in a chair behind a TV tray as he motioned me to sit down on a black leather couch. On the wall above Davis was a blown-up picture of him, his head buried in his hands, deep in thought, during his last days as AFL commissioner. I realized I had really never sat down and talked one-on-one with him before. It had always been while he was running from one place to the other, or in passing on the plane or the locker room. But now he was giving me his undivided attention.

"What's happening with this test?" he asked.

I explained to him again the new 1986 National Football League drug policy formulated by the new drug czar, Forrest Tennant. It was a once-a-year announced test at the beginning of summer camp for all drugs, with the exception of anabolic steroids. Recreational drugs were the first to be attacked, as they had a worse PR rap, with the recent cocaine deaths of star athletes, and were in terms of numbers a more manageable problem. They were also testing for alcohol, but league officials still hadn't decided what to do about positives. A positive urine for narcotics, cocaine, or marijuana would constitute one strike. Any outside-football court convictions for a drug-related offense would constitute one strike. Any suspicious behavior by the player during the year would constitute "reasonable cause" for testing, and if a positive was found, that would constitute one strike. The first strike was kept confidential and no penalty was assessed, but the player had to be intensively counseled. Two strikes and the player was to be suspended for a minimum of four weeks and might be sent to a drug rehab center. Three strikes and the NFL bounced the player for life. Al was furious that one of our starters had even one strike.

"Why the hell didn't we test all our guys earlier in the summer so we could have prevented this?" he asked.

I was getting the distinct impression that it was my fault the player had tested positive. So I explained that I had tested everyone the previous year, had counseled this particular player, who had tested positive for marijuana, and had sent him and every other player a letter during the spring telling them what to expect and what the penalty was should the urine test turn up positive.

"So why the hell didn't you test him earlier this summer so we knew where we were?"

I was smart enough not to open my mouth and argue. I probably should have tested everybody a month before the NFL's test. I had assumed the very rare positives from the prior year had taken my warnings seriously. My personal opinion regarding marijuana—that it was not in a league with cocaine, alcohol, speed, and steroids—made the "rehab" phase a bit tougher. This athlete had done well in school, he'd been a stand-out athlete, he'd never been in trouble with the law, he never missed meetings, and he was, from all outward appearances, an exemplary citizen.

I was down on marijuana use because I knew one joint equaled the dangers of approximately five cigarettes, and cigarettes, like chewing tobacco, could kill you through heart disease or cancer. I was also down on marijuana because I knew it definitely affected the short-term memory and was not conducive to maximal learning, especially in a school situation. Although I found most of the Raiders surprisingly smart, there were a few who needed every neuronal synapse to remember which direction to run when the ball got snapped.

I probably hadn't pushed as hard as I could have to get this particular player off marijuana. Years later I would find, to my chagrin, that some team doctors were drug-testing all their athletes before the official NFL test—and keeping positives out of camp in phony contract holdouts until their urine was clean.

"What happens to this kid now?" Al said.

"The league will test him at its discretion, which for marijuana will probably be at most once per week. When his urine's clean, he'll be tested less often."

"This is insanity," he replied. "He could be suspended for smoking marijuana again?"

"It's the league's new policy," I said, shrugging my shoulders, not trying to defend it.

"The league," he said disrespectfully, "the league that every year makes us start on the road, this year against two of the best teams, then we come home for the third week against *the* best team. Well," he said, shaking his head as if I couldn't understand the complexities of the league's plot against him, "that's not something you need to be concerned with. Just tell me—can you figure out how to get this kid through? You know, you take away this kid, we're not competitive. We're out of the race. D'ya understand what we're fighting for?"

"Yes."

Really, I had no idea just what he was driving at. I figured I'd respond to the heart of the most sinister interpretation of his words.

"For your information, there are a million ways to phony up the urine. You can lower the levels way down with water pills or block it with other agents. When the money gets high enough, I'm sure somebody will just take clean urine and have a urology technician push it into the dirty player's bladder—then he can stand in front of the drug counselor and pee right in front of him, and it will come out clean every time. But I'm telling you, if we cheat for the kid, it'll come back to haunt us. Even if we don't mind the kid staying on something as innocuous as marijuana, word's definitely going to leak out. And you're sending a strong message to other players. I personally think you're better off having a player suspended. Even if it's a key player. If it means making sure that the rest of the players stay off drugs, and maybe that even means amphetamines and steroids."

"What are you talking about? What do you know about amphetamines?"

"They can cause serious heart rhythm problems and severe withdrawal reactions."

"You don't know what you're talking about." He scowled and disgustedly waved an end to our meeting.

I stopped off at the library on my way home and rummaged through several texts. I finally photocopied several pages from Goodman and Gilman, the standard pharmacology reference book, and circled the section on common side effects of amphetamines, including rapid heart rhythms, anxieties, post-use depression and withdrawal symptoms, seizures, and death. I put the sheets in an envelope and mailed them to him that very afternoon.

True to Al Davis's worst nightmare, we lost our first two games. Marcus Allen rushed for over a hundred yards in both games, continuing his blistering 1985 Most Valuable Player rushing pace. But Denver and Washington, two of the top teams, edged us by two and four points respectively, essentially one bad bounce of the ball. Marc Wilson, after playing superbly, got flung down on the

Washington turf one time too many and separated his shoulder again.

In Al Davis's off-season strategy session he'd decided to do anything he could to keep our best players on the field. Curt Marsh was one player who had been hurt for most of the last three seasons. Davis figured he'd hold out an extra carrot. He promised Marsh $20,000 cash—on top of his regular salary—merely for staying healthy enough to play the first three games. In the opener, Marsh played a fabulous game, but his back kicked up in the second half, and it started hurting him so bad that he could barely bend over enough to get into his stance at the end of the game. He decided not to tell anybody, and in order to practice the next week, he had to show up at the training facility an hour and a half early and sit in a hot sauna just so he could bend over and put on his shoes. When the second game came, he tried new shoes he hoped would be better for his back, and in the first quarter he got blisters the size of small pancakes. He had to come out for a series while George cut off the blister tops, slapped on a skin replacement wound dressing, and taped it securely in place. Then he went back in and got smashed in his knee the second quarter. Rosenfeld came out on the field to test it and saw it swinging sideways, but Rosenfeld told him it was okay, since he had some instability in his knee to begin with. Then, just before the half, his ankle was stomped on and blew up like a beach ball. At halftime, George taped up the knee and Rosenfeld gave him a shot in the ankle. Marsh trotted back out. Then on the first series of downs, he snapped his fourth finger; the thing was pointing toward his thumb. Curt popped it back in joint himself. But every time he forearm-blocked somebody, the finger slipped over to the side again. So now he was popping it back after nearly every play as he limped back to the huddle. Marsh couldn't see leaving the field with a lousy finger dislocation, not after they'd had to attend to his feet, his ankle, his knee, and his back. After the game he collapsed and told George, "Just tell Davis about the finger—don't mention my knee, or my back."

He just had one more game to go to get his $20,000 bonus. But despite taping up his knee so tight his circulation was practically cut off, it was wobbling more and more during the next week's practices. His ankle was down to a soggy softball, but he still was going to Rosenfeld to get shot up just to make it through practice. The Friday before the game, the coaches were reviewing the practice film.

"Hey, what the hell is wrong with Curt Marsh? He can barely move!"

Marsh practically cried when he was put on IR two days before the third game. Two days before collecting his $20,000. The $20,000 he had hypnotized himself with to deaden his pain.

The third game, our home opener, was against the eventual Super Bowl champion New York Giants. We were playing them even, with Jim Plunkett in for the injured Wilson; we just needed a break to beat them. Then with the Raiders down by just a couple of points, Marcus Allen darted up the middle, cut sharply to his left, and was slammed to the ground by three defenders.

A warm wind blew through the peristyles of the famed eastern end of the Coliseum as the layers of bodies peeled off the pile. Marcus was now standing but couldn't go anywhere. He finally began to hop on one leg toward the sideline, motioning in his replacement, Vance Mueller.

On the sideline, Rosenfeld cranked around Marcus's ankle. Marcus had pain on the outside and high up the ankle to his shin but not much swelling to speak of, not unusual for the first few minutes of an ankle injury.

"See if you can walk on it," Rosenfeld said.

Marcus took one step and winced in agony.

"Let's take him up for X-rays," said Rosenfeld, himself getting on the motorized golf cart with Marcus.

Marcus, along with Howie Long, Jim Plunkett, and Marc Wilson, was a star. Rosenfeld would accompany the stars to the locker room during a game. Otherwise, one of his assistants would be sent along to read the films for players needing X-rays in the middle of a game. With TV cameramen jogging behind, the cart motored off toward the locker room.

"It's a good thing Rosie wore his blue shirt," said one of the assistant equipment guys.

While everyone else, including me and Rosenfeld's two orthopedic associates, wore the traditional white Raider shirt with the gray Raider pants and tennis shoes, Rosenfeld rotated outfits for good luck, often choosing a coat and tie, always with a blue shirt, which someone had once told him makes you look better on TV.

If you looked around the league, it was the same. Low-key team doctors would blend in on the sideline wearing the same garb as the assistant coaches. There were four or five prima donna doctors in the league, however, who would walk onto the field with coats and ties, or even suits. I used to relish seeing those doctors kneel down to check out a player on days when the field was nice and muddy, or seeing a player throw an arm dripping with blood and sweat around their expensively clothed shoulders as they helped the player limp off the field.

We eventually lost a four-point heartbreaker to the Giants. We were 0–3, our backs through the wall, with the Raiders' and the league's most valuable player sitting in the locker room under ice.

About five minutes after the end of the game, in strode Al Davis, as was his habit. He stayed to himself, muttering while he walked slowly through the locker room and into the training room. He strode up to Marcus Allen and with a tightly clenched fist, one of his nervous habits, asked, "How you feeling, Marcus?"

"It's okay, Mr. Davis."

"Goddammit, Marcus," he said with his fist at chest level, "we really need ya back, we gotta have you.

"What did the X-rays show?" he asked Rosenfeld as he walked him away into a corner.

"There's no fracture," replied Rosenfeld. "The ankle joint is tight. He's got just a small amount of arthritis in there, but that's always been there. If we strap him up good and George gives him good physical therapy, he'll be ready for next week."

But he wasn't ready for next week. Even though the ankle was only modestly swollen, the pain was too much to play. He couldn't cut, he couldn't dig his foot and get support to dart laterally, without getting tell-tale shooting shin pain.

This injury was a tough one to comprehend. We had ankle injuries on almost a weekly basis, and the majority of players were able to play to near full capacity in one or two weeks. Even the classic cantaloupe-size ankle sprains of Marc Wilson, Dave Dalby, and Derrick Jensen, to name a few, didn't keep them out of the lineup the next week. But after three or four weeks, Marcus's ankle showed no progress, despite weekly pronouncements by Rosenfeld that Marcus was going to be able to play. The pressure on Marcus mounted.

A repeat X-ray, looking for a stress fracture à la Bill Walton, was negative. The ankle now was essentially down to normal size, with no evident bruising. Rosenfeld was starting to look at Marcus funny when Marcus said the pain was too severe to play. Nobody in his right mind thought Marcus was milking the injury, not given his past history of playing despite repeated episodes of numbness and weakness in his right arm (an injury Rosenfeld had worked up in 1983, my first year, with a CAT scan), a painful shoulder separation in 1982, and surgery on his elbow in 1981, plus the usual assortment of sprains, strains, cuts, and bruises over his body. He had never missed a play with those injuries. Of course, his contract was almost up. And he was acknowledged to be the league's best player. Was there a mental element in all this?

Finally after three weeks he made it back in the lineup. But he was a step slow, not the old Marcus. We had strung together a number of wins against weaker opponents and were back in the playoff picture with a 7–4 record, and the pressure kept mounting to get Marcus back in 100 percent running form. In San Diego, in the locker room before a huge Monday-night matchup, someone from management came to Marcus with a message from Al.

"You're still favoring that ankle. Take a shot."

He had been resisting a shot from Rosenfeld for all these weeks, but it was hard to refuse the guy who signed your checks. He took the shot. The game was a back-and-forth classic, with Marcus's open-field running and darting pass receptions single-handedly keeping us in the game. With less than sixty seconds left, we were losing 31–28, but Wilson was driving the team, using the hurry-up offense, desperately trying to move into field goal range. After an incomplete pass, Wilson saw Charley Hannah rolling around on the ground hurt. Wilson realized the Raiders had only one time-out and needed to save it for the field goal kicker, if we got close enough. If a guy on your team gets injured in the last two minutes of a game and you have to call an injury time-out, it automatically counts as your regular time-out. So Wilson ran over, leaned down, and said, "Charley, are you hurt?"

There was no answer; Charley was just rolling around, grabbing his knee and moaning. Then the referee ran over.

"Captain, do you want to take a time-out?"

"No, sir, Charley's going to get up and walk off the field on his own. We don't need a time-out," replied Wilson.

To which Hannah now responded. "F—— you, I'm really hurt!"

A time-out was called.

We finally managed to get the ball into field goal range, and enough time remained for Wilson to throw an intentional incompletion to stop the clock and let Chris Bahr come out and attempt to tie the game. Bahr's kick was good. We then went on to win on a goose-bump Marcus Allen zigzag run which ended spectacularly when he dragged six Charger defenders into the far corner of the end zone.

Marcus was the man of the hour. He was a hero in the executive box as well as on the streets of L.A. But his place in the sun was short-lived. Only one game later, he fell into Al Davis's doghouse.

Our record was now 8–4, not a bad turnaround from our 0–3 start. We were playing the hapless Philadelphia Eagles, a team with a lot of potential but not many wins that season. We toyed with winning, but a key fumble by Rod Barksdale, the inexperienced phenom we'd hidden on injured reserve the year before, sent the game into overtime.

In overtime, Bill Pickel quickly sacked Randall Cunningham, who coughed the ball into the arms of the onrushing Howie Long. Then Plunkett hit Allen crossing to the right of the field for a nifty twenty-seven-yard gain. We were on the twenty and just needed to line the ball between the goalposts to get the winning field goal and lock up a play-off berth. But sometimes football isn't that easy. Marcus took the handoff, saw a crease, and instinctively cut for it, as he had the week before for the winning touchdown. This time he bobbled the handoff. Defender Seth Joyner batted the protruding pigskin and, almost as if a string were tied to it, it leaped into the arms of oncoming Eagle defender Andre Waters. While the stadium stood in shocked horror, Waters ran eighty-one yards for the win. The Eagles had landed.

In the locker room afterward, the players were cursing, throwing their equipment into walls, smashing their lockers, overturning the benches, and generally moving anything that wasn't bolted into concrete.

Al Davis was furious. He was flinging four-letter words to no one in particular and just fuming at Flores, fuming at Allen. Everywhere he walked, players and coaches would clear out a fifteen-foot circle. He finally trapped George Anderson.

"He just had to hold on to the ball. Why did we call a run?"

He didn't give George Anderson a chance to respond before he bubbled out his next expletive and walked away, only to return thirty seconds later with another unanswerable question.

Even after that ill-fated outing, when we had plucked defeat out of the jaws of victory, we still had three tries for a play-off berth. But maybe once you're good enough to make it in the pros, the rest is really nine-tenths mental. And this mental mistake sapped our lifeblood. We lost each of the next three games, including a game

"YOU'RE OKAY, IT'S JUST A BRUISE"

168

against the inept 2–13 Colts. For the first time since I'd become a Raider, we were out of the play-off hunt.

For Al Davis, that was a fate worse than death. Despite knowingly risking the health of his ankle with a shot, despite playing all year on a bum ankle and still making it to the Pro Bowl (a Pro Bowl he was unable to play in, incidentally, because the doctor there flunked him based on his ankle exam), Marcus Allen took a lot of heat, even blame, from Al Davis for our dismal season.

Rod Barksdale, who also had a costly fumble in the Philadelphia debacle, was dealt with in a different way. During the last game of the season, a game that didn't have much meaning to us, Rod Barksdale was inserted into the game and showcased—in other words, everything was done in the play-calling scheme to enable him to have a big game. He did have a big game, so big he accumulated more yardage for one game than almost all of the former Raider greats, including Cliff Branch, Fred Biletnikoff, and Todd Christensen. With that highlight film in hand, Al was able to trade him. He got Ron Fellows, a highly regarded Dallas Cowboy defensive back, in return. Quite a coup for an inexperienced free agent. As for Tom Flores, the man who called the fatal overtime run, it was also the beginning of the end.

A week and a half after the Super Bowl, all the team doctors were huddled together at a medical symposium after the first long day of examining the college All-Americans in the predraft combine of 1987. One of the young postdoctorate fellows working with the Indianapolis Colts was giving a ten-minute presentation.

"Usual ankle sprains occur either here, in the lateral malleolus, or here, in the medial malleolus," he said, pointing to a diagram, "and have pain over the protruding bony part of the ankle associated with a lot of swelling. And on the average, in my study of National Football League players, they tend to return to action within one to two weeks. Compare that with tib/fib ankle sprains. The amount of swelling tends to be much less impressive, and at least some component of the ankle pain tends to radiate up the shin."

My ears picked up. This was exactly the picture Marcus Allen presented. The young doctor concluded, "This less common form of ankle injury tends to take a full six weeks until the player is able to return to action."

I looked over in Rosenfeld's direction to see if any of this was registering, or if he was showing any external signs of remorse for having contributed to Al Davis's suspicion that Marcus Allen was milking his ankle injury and not returning as soon as most other players would have. Rosenfeld had his eyes half shut. He wasn't finding it particularly stimulating.

18

Don't Bet Against Bo

I knew a man Bo Jackson and he runs for you
In Nike shoes
Silver hat, blackened shirt, and football pants
He runs right through
Mr. Bo Jackson . . . Mr. Bo Jackson
Run.

—Adapted from Mike Downey
(*L.A. Times* sportswriter),
parodying Jerry Jeff Walker's *Mr. Bojangles*

"It's deadly. It could be lying next to you tonight. The more partners, the higher the risk. Vaginal sex. Rectal sex. Probably oral sex too. It can be passed via blood. Via shared needles. AIDS is a fact of the eighties. There's already a reported case of a weight lifter who made two bad decisions. One, to use anabolic steroids, and two, to share needles while he was injecting. Turned out his weight-lifting partner was HIV-positive. Wham, he contracted it as well."

There was dead silence. I'd never seen the entire team so quiet. No jokes, no titters, nothing. I was doing the little medical talk that for the last several years had been a fixture at the season-opening team meeting. It was the beginning of summer camp 1987, and the veterans had just finished their physicals. Following this meeting, one of the big bar nights of the year would start. I was nearing the end of my ten-minute slide show, having already explained what AIDS was and how you tested for it.

"Now rumor has it, no names mentioned, some of you were taking home women from Nude, Nude, Nude."

Nude, Nude, Nude was a strip joint only a mile or two away from our El Segundo facility.

"That's scary."

Now the comments began to fly from the back of the room. I continued.

"Five percent of local prostitutes, maybe more, test positive for the HIV virus. I'd like to urge you guys to use better judgment than that. And even when you *do* use better judgment, be sure to wear a condom.

"I'm also going to recommend that none of you share any razors or other equipment in the locker room. We're going to ask the trainers to wear gloves when they handle any cuts and the equipment guys to glove up when handling towels or uniforms that have bloody secretions on them. As I think most of you know, we're offering confidential HIV testing of the blood samples we drew today. All you have to do is call me up at the office or grab me in the hall. We drew enough extra blood on everyone. I want to make it clear, though, we're not going to do an HIV test on anyone who doesn't request it. By law that would be assault and battery."

I flashed my last slide onto the overhead. It showed a well-dressed man in a coat and tie sitting in his favorite armchair, his feet up on a footstool, a beer in his hand, watching an X-rated movie on TV.

"What we'd prefer is absolutely safe sex, and, uh, unfortunately I guess this is it."

I left the stage without having time to get into some other worrisome items. I'd heard rumors that Alzado and one other player had taken black-market growth hormone, a blood product sometimes taken by strength and speed athletes trying to put on muscle. No one knew if it worked. But in the past it had been made from pooled cadaver brains, and therefore it carried a risk of AIDS. Also, some of the players in the league were gay. While the percentages may not have been as high as in activities like figure skating or dance, there was no reason to think the percentage of gay men in football was lower than in the armed forces, another macho field where gay men of necessity kept their sexual preference a secret.

Blood was part of football. Often games degenerated into veritable bloodbaths, with bloodstained uniforms up and down the line of scrimmage. The cover shot on last year's NFL program, *GameDay*, was a classic close-up of Matt Millen's hand, his fingers curled in the face mask of his battered helmet, with a blood-and-sweat-soaked hand and wrist guard dripping down to stain the tape that held his scraped knuckles in place.

In 1987, no one really knew what the chance was of passing the

AIDS virus from a blood-spurting gash. Particularly worrisome was the fact that nearly every player up and down the line had open turf burns on fingers, wrists, or elbows from the day-in, day-out beating their extremities took. These abrasions were literally an open door through the body's protective skin layer, a possible conduit for infected blood to enter.

Acting on the HIV tests was going to be tough. First, any player who already knew or suspected he had AIDS might not take the test for fear of losing his job. And what would the players who did request an HIV test do if a positive appeared? There were confidentiality problems. Doctor-patient confidentiality would forbid my revealing a player who tested positive. What if that player refused to retire voluntarily? Would I side with the HIV-positive player's decision, or would possible but unproven risks to teammates be an overriding concern? Fortunately, all the players tested negative.

Two years later, in 1989, the first case of an AIDS infection via a sports injury was reported. A twenty-five-year-old soccer player in Italy collided with another player, and both sustained large bloody gashes over the eyebrow. One player was known to be HIV-positive; he had supposedly contracted the virus via a dirty needle used while he was addicted to IV drugs. Two months later, the second soccer player was found to be HIV-positive. He had been in the Italian army just a year prior and had tested negative. He was married and had no known risk factors.

Because of the importance of this case to football, not to mention contact sports throughout the world, I phoned the reporting doctor in Italy. I had learned from an old Harvard Medical School classmate, Dr. David Ho, now at Cornell Medical Center heading one of the country's largest AIDS research teams, that because of constant small mutations, the HIV virus in different patients typically has minor differences. I proposed that the Italian doctor send the two HIV viruses from the colliding players to New York City so they could be tested to see if these two players did in fact have an exactly similar virus, which would prove beyond any doubt that contact sports could spread the HIV virus. Unfortunately, the Italian researcher was unable to get both patients to cooperate with this request. The case was sobering, even though scientific doubt remained.

Also worrisome were seven other cases of AIDS contracted via blood being splashed on mucous membranes or on skin with open cuts. These occurred in hospital settings, but the significance to scraped-up football players was evident.

There were several known cases of full-fledged AIDS infection in former NFL players, but in each instance the player was gay, and so the route of infection was almost certainly sexual contact. AIDS had to be reckoned with in professional football, the same as in other "blood sports" like boxing and wrestling. Fortunately, the worst-case risk estimates were very small, probably significantly less than the football risks of quadriplegia from a neck injury. But, understandably, the players were more terrified of an unusual, unknown disease than of familiar risks, such as their chance of becoming paralyzed in a football collision. Doctors have known for years that people feel more comfortable with risks that they undertake voluntarily than with lesser risks that they feel are imposed on them from outside.

I took a deep breath. There was something very comforting in the stale-sweat-sock locker room aroma. A lab courier had dropped off a four-inch stack of blood tests, and I was racing to review and alphabetize the results before the afternoon practice ended. A number of the players wanted to laminate a xeroxed miniature of their HIV test results for their wallets, as a future barroom gag.

As was true every year, there was an infusion of forty or fifty new names. At the head of that class was John Clay, this year's 360-pound, somewhat roly-poly first-round draft pick. The hope was that he was Art Shell's heir apparent. Art, the Raiders' homegrown all-superlative tackle, had been similarly roly-poly coming out of college. Clay was nimble for a man of his size. He could dart the one or two yards across the line of scrimmage to head-butt an opponent. But for him a hundred yards was a marathon. He could barely make it nonstop around the football field. The veterans began to joke about it. The morning after my AIDS talk, the entire team lined up for the NFL drug tests, now administered by a handful of off-duty policemen, who stood and watched the urine come out (no more urine bag under the arm with tubing running down and held next to the penis to make it all sound real from behind). As Clay stepped forward to pee, one vet yelled, "I don't know what they'll find in your urine, but they won't find speed."

Suddenly the tranquillity of the locker room, with the periodic dropping of ice cubes from the ice maker, was punctured by cleats on concrete and curses. It was Curt Marsh. Six feet six, 290 pounds, All-World tough, Eastern European aggressive, Barnum and Bailey agile. He'd recently been in a melee in a local bar. Four weight-lifter types had been staring him up and down.

"What are you looking at?" he demanded.

One of them threw him the finger. Curt attacked, knocking the whole bunch over like so many bowling pins. Jamie Kimmel, an aggressive 260-pound linebacker who also happened to be a former Syracuse All-American wrestler, jumped in and tried to pull Curt back so he wouldn't maim anyone.

Afterward as they were walking back to camp, Marsh complained, "Geez, here I am in a major barroom brawl against four guys and you don't even help."

"If I'd been on your side," Kimmel replied, "it wouldn't have been a fair fight."

Marsh had been the team's first-round pick in 1981 and was good enough to be the first rookie lineman to start since Gene Upshaw in 1967. It seemed just a question of time before he followed Upshaw and Shell through the doors of the Canton, Ohio, Hall of Fame. But after seven years in the professional ranks, he'd started less than four games per year. Only his medical stats were impressive. Eighteen hospitalizations, thirteen surgeries (an average of two per year during his career), and suspicious liver and cholesterol tests.

To the outside world he was a hard-luck lineman. To me he was a disastrous dictionary of football side effects. Sure, his steroid use was minimal on the Lyle Alzado dose scale, but it still may have tipped the scales of his health. His muscles were too strong for his tendons, his body too powerful for his bones, his desire too charged up to handle everyday life or tolerate his medical setbacks. He began his pro career by ripping out a hernia in 1981, and two in 1982. In 1979 and 1983 he slipped some discs and required two major back surgeries. He snapped his right arm in two at the beginning of the 1985 season, when he forearmed Vann McElroy's helmet (Vann's head was inside at the time), then on returning to action he broke his left hand. Then the disastrous first two games of 1986 and IR with knee, ankle, back, and finger injuries plus repeat knee arthroscopy. In between were hospital visits for atrial fibrillation, an erratic heart rhythm, maybe related to alcohol, steroids, or pre-game coffee and uptime. Most recently he had gone under the knife three times for his battered right ankle: the first in 1986 to clean out chips of bone, the second in 1987 to clean out a reactive bony spur, and the last, just three months previously, to clean out a joint-threatening infection.

Curt rehabbed aggressively and had been going full out in the drills for the first two days of camp, but something had happened, and now the ankle hurt so much he couldn't walk. Rosenfeld placed him up on one of the training tables and with his thumb probed around the ankle bones for pain.

"F——, doc!" Curt yelled as he quickly yanked back his leg. "I already told you on the field that it hurt there."

"It's just a sprain," said Rosenfeld. "I think you just irritated one of your ankle ligaments. A shot will make you a lot better."

Marsh scowled. "Come on, doc, I've taken a million shots. I can't walk on the f——ing thing. Let's at least do an X-ray."

Without missing a beat, Rosenfeld responded, "Sure, I've got no objection to that. I'll call in the order now and we can have one of the runners take you down there."

When Curt returned, practice had ended and the other players had showered and gone to dinner. Rosenfeld held up the X-rays against the ceiling light in the training room office.

"I don't see anything," he said.

Curt Marsh stood behind him.

"What are these, doc?" he asked, pointing to several pebble-size white spots.

"Ah, they're just loose bodies," replied Rosenfeld. "Don't worry, they're not the problem. There's no broken bone. It's a ligament. I'm telling you, a shot's the best thing to get you back."

But Curt knew he couldn't walk. He was at the end of his rope.

"I want to see a second doctor," he demanded.

"You don't need to see another doctor," Rosenfeld said. "It's just a sprained ligament. Ligaments hurt like crazy. A shot will cool all that down."

"No," Marsh persisted, "I'm going to get a second opinion."

He then rattled off a list of orthopedists, several of whom he'd run by me a bit earlier.

"Well, I can tell you what they're going to say." Rosenfeld shrugged matter-of-factly. "They're going to tell you that you need surgery for those loose bodies."

"Wait a minute!" replied Marsh in an exasperated tone. "If all these doctors are going to tell me to have surgery for the loose bodies, why are you telling me not to have surgery?"

"They all want to say they operated on a Raider. They'll take out the loose bodies, but that won't help you. The ligament strain can heal as I told you, without surgery."

"Fine," said Marsh. "I still don't understand how these doctors would all say something different, though, if all I really have is a ligament sprain."

He got up to leave.

"Well, I'll tell you what," Rosenfeld said, in his own way trying to be accommodating. "I'll write you a letter explaining your condition to these doctors, or else, you know, I'll do surgery too if you want those loose bodies removed."

Curt Marsh's eyes nearly ballooned out of his head.

"Now you're recommending surgery?"

It turned out Curt Marsh's foot did need surgery. He went for a second opinion in Los Angeles the next day, and the orthopedic surgeon realized that given Curt's history, the X-ray, which didn't show a fracture, wasn't enough. A CAT scan showed a fracture that the routine X-ray had been unable to detect. Metal pins were surgically placed to stabilize the break.

Curt Marsh shook his head in frustration. He was twenty-eight. He had the skills, he had the desire, but his body was trashed. His days as a pro were numbered. His contract was up at the end of 1987 and his luck was running out. Maybe he had pushed his luck with the anabolic steroids he had taken. Or maybe it was just football.

As Curt Marsh's career faded into eternal injured reserve, we acquired another steroid user whose medical history was outright scary. Dean Miraldi wouldn't just get more aggressive, more testy, and more combative when he put on the pads. At times he would out-and-out lose it. When he was a rookie with the Philadelphia Eagles in 1981, his muscles started twitching and cramping during a sweltering summer practice session. He drank water and popped salt tablets, to no avail. His muscles continued to jump in pain. Then he began to gush sweat, as if someone had switched open floodgates. Then he blanked out. Only later, when he woke up in the hospital, being treated for severe dehydration, did he learn that he had turned into a wild banshee, attacking the coaches, including head coach Dick Vermeil, pummeling them with his fists until teammates pulled him off.

Understandably, Dean was panicky about the prospects of having another outburst. So when he got muscle cramps and twitching he would become incredibly apprehensive and essentially tune out, obviously making him very hard to coach. He was labeled a head case and, in spite of his exceptional physical skills, sequentially discarded from the Philadelphia Eagles and the Denver Broncos. His stock plummeted to zero. But he was still one of the fastest, strongest, most physically capable linemen in the National Football League. Al Davis picked him off the waiver wire for a dime phone call, and Dean Miraldi became another Al Davis reclamation project.

"Doc, help me!" Miraldi begged, a faraway look in his eyes. "I'm starting to cramp up."

I was standing right behind our offensive unit, in the middle of the field, as five thousand fans in the Cowboys' Thousand Oaks, California, training camp stadium watched our summer scrimmage with Dallas. After each play, our offense would come back and huddle with the offensive coaches, who would call the next play of the scrimmage. I was with the coaches, functioning as Dean's personal water boy, making him drink eight ounces every five to ten minutes. I had been weighing him before and after practice to make absolutely sure we were pushing enough liquids.

Finally, Coach Flores waved off the offensive unit and brought the Raiders' defensive unit in against the Dallas offense.

"You did great," I said, handing him another drink as we walked off the field.

"I'm feeling edgy. My muscles are twitching like there's worms in them. If I'd played any longer I would have lost control."

"Are you taking amphetamines?" I asked point-blank.

"No."

"Did you stop the anabolic steroids like I told you?"

"I'm thinking about it," he said. "This is my last chance in the pros, and I've got to be ready."

"Geez, don't you get it? Strength is not your problem. You're the King of the Jungle out there. You're getting cut because of your muscle cramps, your spacing out, your panic attacks. Believe me— I've seen it before, players freaking out on anabolic steroids. It could be the steroids standing between you and All-Pro."

Dean took off his helmet, revealing a cherubic face that seemed oddly out of place on top of his chiseled granite 310-pound physique.

"I don't know, doc. I felt this way a couple of years before I started taking anabolic steroids."

"Yes," I responded, "people who have claustrophobic panic-anxiety complaints get more edgy when they're packed underneath a helmet, shoulder pads, ribbies, and a uniform laced down tighter than a straitjacket. But the steroids amp up the panic. Not to mention the out-of-control rages that you seem to be the poster child for. Hell, the steroids may even be responsible for your muscle twitching."

I got a phone call sometime after midnight. I rolled over and punched the second line. It was usually my service, which woke me out of a sound sleep every three or four nights to patch in a private patient, or more typically a nurse with questions about a hospitalized patient. But not this time.

"Hello?" I mumbled.

"I didn't wake you up, did I?"

It was Al Davis!

"No, no, I was just about ready to go to sleep," I lied, still fighting to clear the intraneuronal cobwebs.

"How do you think Dean Miraldi did in today's scrimmage?" he asked.

"Okay from my angle," I replied.

Usually I took these nighttime calls lying on my back in the dark, but I realized I was sitting bolt upright.

"He had some cramps and he started getting a little bit edgy," I continued, "but I think he's gaining some confidence. He's taking high-dose calcium and the Inderal, as I told you yesterday, and I think his seeing that top muscle expert at USC the other day was very reassuring. He was telling me that none of the other teams had ever paid any attention to his muscle problems and he was very grateful for the thorough workup we did on him."

"Good, good," responded Davis. "He was drive blocking better than anybody else we have out there today. A couple of plays he absolutely dominated."

"Well, there's a chance that if he stops the steroids and the anticramp muscle stuff we're doing kicks in, it will help relieve some of his panicky symptoms and let him focus on football for a change."

"Okay. Call when the rest of his muscle tests return."

"Sure."

Click. "Goodbye" was not part of an Al Davis phone call.

"Was that a real emergency?" Wanda groaned as she rolled over and tried to get back to sleep.

I was wide awake now. To get a nighttime call from Al Davis was practically an invitation to his inner circle. After attending practice and viewing film all day, Al would meet with the coaches from about nine, when the coaches would finish their position meetings with the players, until about midnight or one. After that, Al would retreat to his hotel room and place his intelligence calls.

The entire team was lined up outside my cramped doctor quarters just off the entry of the El Segundo facility. Fifty physical giants with their pants down to their knees. It must have been quite a sight for the female Federal Express employee who happened to walk into the lobby unannounced. The guys at the back of the line were laughing, the guys at the front were whining. They were bad-mouthing Bob Buczkowski and Mike Wise even more than me.

Four weeks ago, just before the summer camp Family Day, when all the wives and kids would visit to attend a special practice that was open to the public, Bob Buczkowski had come down with hepatitis A, presumably from a Maryland raw oyster binge he'd gone on two months before. At that time I'd given gamma globulin shots to his roommates, the two player wives and player kids he had kissed, his girlfriend, and assorted extras. But the nasty hepatitis bug didn't want to fade that easily. Two days ago, nearly four weeks after Buczkowski's eyes had turned yellow, Mike Wise got feverish and achy and noticed his urine was looking more like Lipton's tea than lemonade. Now, a month too late, he came to me recalling that he had taken a sip out of Buczkowski's beer just before Buczkowski turned yellow. Now Wise was yellow too. That's why hepatitis A is called an infectious disease.

The Raiders were looking down the barrel of a decimating epidemic. There was a chance that a slew of cases would turn up in the next few weeks, since hepatitis A has an incubation period of two to six weeks, or maybe there'd be a big outbreak some weeks farther along as a result of Mike Wise's unknowingly spraying the virus around.

The team gamma globulin shot was the first step. Like any good general, Coach Flores stood at the head of the line and took the first shot. He was easy. Some of the nervous players with huge gluteus muscles were tough. When they tensed their buttocks, they'd bend the needle.

The second step was getting Wise out of the locker room. He

would be quarantined for at least a couple of weeks. The third step was an end to all communal drinking. No more shared spray bottles or hose gizmos. I'd seen two or three epidemics already—a stomach flu several years before, and an eye virus last year that had a third of the team red-eyed. But hepatitis A was in a different, more dangerous league. Fortunately, unlike hepatitis B, this wasn't one that tended to progress to chronic liver disease, but Mike wasn't going to get back in pads for a long time, no matter how many world experts Al Davis called and no matter how many experimental remedies were tried.

Maybe it was sheer coincidence, or maybe Davis had seen Wise slacking off for three or four days during the prodrome of his hepatitis illness, but the day before I made the diagnosis, Mike Wise was traded to the San Francisco 49ers for future draft picks.

"Mr. Davis," I said, "I understand Mike Wise has been traded, but you've got a problem. He's got hepatitis A."

"What?" Davis replied. "What are you telling me?"

"Well, he's got hepatitis, sir. Either it's a sheer coincidence or else he was exposed to Bob Buczkowski last month, and after five weeks of incubating in his body, the virus has now come out."

"Isn't there anything you can do?"

"There's no way to treat hepatitis A at this stage of the game. It's just a watch-and-wait thing. We watch his liver tests, we wait till his energy level allows him to exercise again."

"How would another team know he has it?"

"He's yellow, sir."

I would have repeated George Anderson's recent wisecrack about how he now confused Mike Wise with a former player, Louis Wong, but it was racially insensitive, and besides, you never crack jokes with Al.

In the library that night I found a very worrisome precedent. In the 1960s, the entire Holy Cross football season was canceled when a hepatitis A virus swept through the whole team. Football players live, breathe, and sweat on top of one another. They eat each other's food, they bleed over each other, they sit on the same toilets, they cut their toenails with the same clippers, they sometimes go out with the same women. So when a contagious disease steps into the locker room, look out.

* * *

On the plane ride home from the season opener in Green Bay, Al Davis was in an uncharacteristically good mood, even considering we'd won.

"How'd we do?" he asked.

"Couple dings and scrapes," I replied. "Miraldi had no cramps and felt good despite the heat."

He let a thin smile come through. Miraldi had indeed started and had given up no sacks. A minor miracle for a castaway who hadn't started for the last several years. But he was still driving the coaches a little bit nuts. They swore that in game situations he couldn't remember the snap count from the huddle to the line of scrimmage. And so, as the other offensive linemen began to crouch down in their three point stance, Dean would sometimes still be asking Don Mosebar, the center next to him, questions about his blocking assignment. Years later I found out why. Dean had dyslexia with marked right-left confusion. If a new play was called, mini-panic would set in as he raced to decipher which direction he should block. No wonder he occasionally forgot the snap count.

Bo Jackson was another reason for Al's uncharacteristic up mood. He represented a major personal triumph. Bo had won the Heisman Trophy as best college player and was quickly snapped up as the number-one pick by the Tampa Bay Buccaneers in 1986. But Bo elected to turn his back on football and signed a lucrative contract with baseball's Kansas City Royals.

After a year, the Buccaneers lost their claim to him and his name was thrown back into the draft. Bo repeatedly stated he'd never play football, so no one wanted to waste a draft pick. Al gambled anyway in the seventh round of the '87 draft, then dangled a carrot so large that Bo couldn't refuse. Play baseball. When the season's done, then come play football. And get a whole year's salary. The Buccaneers had demanded he play only football. Well, now Bo's baseball team was out of the play-off hunt. In a few short weeks he'd be in El Segundo to begin moonlighting as a running back.

I stood my ground through the conversation about Mike Wise's progress, and about a flu that was going around the team, keeping on my stern game face. I might have overdone the scowl a little bit, because "Dr." Davis actually asked me if I was okay.

"Gee," I said, totally taken aback, "I'm fine. A little nervous about my wife—her due date for our second kid is in three weeks, the same weekend we're away in Denver."

"Ah, don't worry if you're out on the road. Same thing happened to me," he said. "I missed my son's birth. First responsibility always is your job. Everything else'll fall in place."

I assumed that meant that his son, Mark, had been born in the fall, during the football season. But later, talking about my son, who was born in October, I commented to Mark Davis that he too must have been born in the fall.

"No, in May. Why?"

Geez, I thought, as I made some excuse to mask my incorrect assumption, what the hell was Al talking about? They weren't playing spring ball in the fifties. What did he do? Miss the birth of his only son on a recruiting trip or something? I was dying to ask Mrs. Davis about it but didn't have the chutzpah to do it.

We won our first two regular-season games. Then the season came to a screeching halt. The team went on strike, demanding free agency, among other things, or a percentage of the owner's profits.

"It's a joke," Plunkett said to me as he walked out to his car after the second game against Detroit. "I've got a zero chance of benefiting from free agency if it comes to pass from this strike, and this strike has about a zero percent chance of working now. So I'm giving up seventy thousand dollars a week in money I'll never make back to help a bunch of kids that are still in college, and maybe a couple of our first- and second-year players."

"Well, don't go on strike, then."

"No," he said, shaking his head. "This is a team sport."

The strike was no picnic for the team doctors either. We had to cross out an office day and come to camp to work up forty-five nonunion, strike-breaking replacement players.

As I slowly drove into the El Segundo camp, I saw the parking lot entrance was blocked by picketing team members.

"Scab doctor!"

It was Bill Pickel. I was shaken by the venomous tone of his voice. I took care of his wife! His son! Someone else was banging on the back of my car. How could this thing have gotten so ugly so fast? Then the players in front of my car parted and I saw Bill wink and flash a smile.

"Scared ya, huh?" he laughed.

After only a one-weekend layoff, Sunday football resumed. The nonunion version. I jogged down the storied tunnel and into the light of the historic L.A. Coliseum with our merry band of forty-five soon-to-be-ex-Raiders, guys who just a week ago were working civilian jobs, guys who basically showed up at a football fantasy camp and got paid $6,000 a game to boot. Most of them were training camp fodder, guys who had basically served as bodies for the real players to beat up on, and then been dropped weeks before the season started. Some players did have NFL experience and had been cut loose in past years. But as we emerged into the sunshine and sprinted toward the field, their collective adrenaline began flowing like a river. They wanted to win so bad I don't think they even noticed the Raiderettes, who lined them on both sides. The lack of sleep didn't seem to affect them. Half the team had been up till the wee hours the night before with nerves. Twelve others had gathered outside the Hyatt lobby fully dressed with suitcases in hand at four in the morning, after a Richter five-point-something earthquake rocked the hotel. A couple of the guys had never been west of the Mississippi and were absolutely freaked by the sixty-second bucking bronco ride. The others weren't sure whether it was an act of nature or a dynamiting job by some of the striking Raider vets.

I came out on the sideline, rather blasé. George Anderson put on his sunglasses.

"The glare off the backs of those eighty-five thousand empty seats is blinding me," he deadpanned.

"It's going to take pinpoint accuracy for the fans to keep that beach ball they always toss around up for more than one hit, considering how far apart they're sprinkled," I observed.

"Yeah," H. Rod Martin agreed. "It's going to be hard for the gang members too. They're going to have to walk across a whole section just to get close enough to another ticket holder to start a fight."

Scott Osler, of the *L.A. Times*, summed it up best: "Let's just say the crowd was forty thousand shy of a wave."

But a funny thing happened as we patiently waited for halftime. Our quarterback, Vince Evans, who had several years of professional football under his belt but had been a car dealer for the last three years, started running around a lot in the backfield and was completing some pretty nice passes to a couple of receivers who suddenly looked pretty legit. The anemic high-school-size turnout didn't seem to matter. Our team was up on their feet, crowding the sideline, screaming encouragement at the top of their lungs. For all they knew, the vets were returning to work for the second half. This was their moment in history.

When the final gun sounded, we'd won 37–17. Our guys jumped, gyrated, and gestured in glee. Defensive end Phil Grimes sprinted in front of the bleachers with index fingers spiked high in the air, screaming, "We're number one!"

And you know what? The ten thousand diehards who actually showed up stayed the duration and screamed their approval. They were loving it, too. They didn't care that the striking players' union had vowed to have the game results blotted from the record books, or at the very least followed by an eternal asterisk.

The euphoria flowed into the locker room. It dissolved back to grim reality only when we had to board a row of buses back to El Segundo. The buses had been backed down the tunnel adjacent to our locker room, behind fences and security guards. Always before, team buses had been left outside the gates. A bevy of motorcycle cops escorted the caravan. Instead of the usual parade atmosphere, when we'd be waved through red lights and crowded intersections to get to stadiums on time, this was more of a prison guard motif. A few of the vets pounded on the bus as it emerged through the chainlink fence and hurled curses at the scab players.

"Put your picket signs back in your Mercedes and leave us alone," sighed one of our no-name players.

Just before the second scab football game, Rosenfeld fell ill and was hospitalized. I'll never forget dropping by his room and seeing three women all outdoing each other in an effort to take care of him. His live-in girlfriend had the cool compresses on his forehead, his wife was jealously gripping his hand, and his personal secretary paced nervously back and forth.

We traveled to Denver for our next replacement game. Rosenfeld, for the first time in the four years that I had been involved with the Raiders, did not make the trip. We were the pregame favorite, mainly because Howie Long and Bill Pickel had signed on. Howie Long was especially frustrated at the strike, saying the $84,000 game check he had forfeited the previous week was enough of a donation to a lost cause.

"When you've got to choose between Gene Upshaw and your wife and kids, it's not a hard decision," he'd said.

But his teammates weren't so sure. Greg Townsend, among others, called him "Gone Hollywood," and the screaming would intensify outside the camp when the scabs drove through to get to practice.

The flight to Denver was somewhat subdued. The replacement

players were still in awe of the trappings that went along with professional football—the charter, the nonstop first-class meals, the luxury hotel. They also had very few requests for the medical staff. Their legs were fresh, they didn't need Indocin, there were no veterans who had taken a whole decade of cutback blocks. (In one well-known San Diego lawsuit, it was estimated that seven-year veterans might absorb over 130,000 full-speed blows. That's definitely more than an Advil ache.) Also, because they were injury-free, these players could use their own juices to get up for a game. They didn't have to rely on pills, sports hypnotists, massage therapists, manipulation, acupuncture, ginseng, whacked-out amino acids, or caffeine cocktails.

When the game started, all the attention was on the crossover vets. But our two starters never really figured in the game, and the Denver first-stringers who suited up ended up being injured by halftime. It was our soon-to-be-ex-Raiders versus their soon-to-be-ex-Broncos. And this time it was Denver's no-names' turn. The outcome had Davis chewing his lower lip on the long plane flight home.

When Al Davis got the game films hand-delivered to him at his home late that Sunday night, he must have seen something that made him panic. He didn't know how many more scab games were on tap, and he probably realized, correctly in this instance, that the scab games were going to end up counting in the final standings. Rumors flew that he was pulling out his brass knuckles, putting every ounce of pressure he had to bear on our first-string players to cross the picket lines. Unsubstantiated tales quickly spread about Al's offering contracts and future jobs, as well as calling in personal markers. The team knew Al would do whatever it took to stud his lineup with ringers.

He knew he was taking a calculated risk, a risk of creating a civil war between those he'd induced to break the strike and those who continued to forgo their sizable game checks to support the strike. Al rationalized his move by convincing himself that talent won games. He was quoted in the newspaper saying that camaraderie was overrated. This from the lips of a guy who had always bent over backward to foster camaraderie by encouraging the guys to hang together at preseason training camp, by sanctioning the air hockey and rookie preseason parties, by fostering the Thursday-night camaraderie sessions, by getting families together every week after the games, by having a movie bus for the guys before the games, and by sponsoring Saturday tours on away games.

But now, his replacement players having been shellacked by over two touchdowns, he decided to play hardball. Twenty-six players crossed the picket line, a phenomenal number, considering that the next week's opponent, the San Diego Chargers, had only coerced three regulars back inside their locker room. Greg Townsend decided to cross despite his critical comments about Howie Long only a week before, perhaps because Al's persuasive tone had convinced him Hollywood and a fat game check were better than anything Upshaw could deliver.

One notable exception was Marcus Allen, who, despite intense pressure in giving up $70,000 to $80,000 each week, elected to stay out on the picket lines. If his Philadelphia overtime fumble in 1986 was his first sin against Al Davis, this was surely the second. Maybe the third was the fact that year after year, Marcus remained the best-liked, most recognized Raider in Los Angeles.

I got a call on Friday afternoon before the San Diego game from the training room.

"Doc, it doesn't matter who or what you've got on the books at your office. Cross it out, you've got to be here at four o'clock."

"What do you mean?" I asked. "I never come over there on Friday. That's just a short walk-through practice."

I was irritated because I had been sprinting around my office trying to finish up with the last of the afternoon patients so I could zip home and pick up my wife and bring her to the hospital. She was a week overdue, and her doctor had kindly agreed to start the induced labor at seven o'clock that night so that I could still get through a regular workday. It'd definitely be pushing my luck if I asked her doctor to push the time back again, especially since it was already a Friday night.

"Bo Jackson has landed," he exclaimed. "Johnny Otten's picking him up at the airport at exactly three-thirty, so we need you here by four. Mr. Davis doesn't want him waiting around."

I began some mad mental arithmetic. I had half an hour to finish up in the office, I could make it down there in half an hour, and if the workup took less than half an hour, I had a shot at getting back home and getting my wife to the hospital somewhere near seven. Hell, maybe I could make up for some of the lost time by throwing in her IV and starting the Pitressin drip myself.

Bo looked the part of a sports god. He had a build that would put a Greek statue to shame, a build that stood out even in a room of muscular professional football players. If there was any fat in his body, it would have to have been attached to a recent meal and not yet absorbed into his system, because it was pretty obvious from looking at him that his system took every bit of food out of the GI tract and instantly turned it into muscle.

Bo passed the physical. He was officially a Raider.

I made it to the hospital in time to be with my wife. We had an eight-pound-six-ounce bouncing boy, and I was euphoric. Even the fact that I got no sleep that night couldn't bring me down.

Two days later, our twenty-six strike-breaking veterans plus a few replacement hangers-on, the closest thing the league had to a real NFL football team, strutted out onto the field against San Diego's team of only three veteran players and forty-two replacement hangers-on. Something very strange happened on the way to putting a notch in our win column. We lost. Our demoralized talent got whipped by their enthusiastic journeymen. Al Davis had outfoxed himself. Camaraderie was not overrated.

The strike ended, but our troubles were just beginning. The disharmony was at active-volcano proportions. There was no kidding, no razzing, no gags, pretty much no talking between players. The tension during the first post-strike practice was especially high. The veterans who had held out were looking to pop teammates who had crossed the picket lines and were especially incensed that a number of players, such as Vince Evans, the replacement quarterback, and Eddie Anderson, one of the replacement safeties, had been kept on the team. In one of the first blocking and hands-only drills, the second-string offense was going against the black-shirted first-team defense. Anybody our defense didn't recognize was presumed to be a holdover scab now trying to make the regular roster, and was going to get a violent baptism into the pros. On about the third play from scrimmage, the second-team quarterback flipped the ball to his running back. Defensive linebacker Matt Millen saw the guy's unfamiliar face and sprinted over with a maniacal look on his face, ready to powder him off. The ball carrier was Bo Jackson. But Matt Millen had never met him and had no idea what he looked like. When Bo saw this 250-pound linebacker hurtling toward him with a crazed look in his eye, he wisely accelerated in a blaze for the sideline, leaving the diving Millen lying on his grass-stained jersey grasping nothing but air. A demoralized Millen walked slowly back to the defensive huddle.

"Shit, this layoff has really affected me," he moaned as he dejectedly shook his head. "I've got absolutely no pursuit speed anymore."

"You idiot," said fellow linebacker Rod Martin, "that's Bo Jackson."

"Oh, thank God," said the suddenly relieved Millen. "I thought I'd really lost it!"

The players never came together. Backstabbing replaced brotherhood. One of the coaches used to say, "I want you guys to think about this. If you were hanging off a cliff, all you had was a rope to hold on to, no chance to get a toehold anywhere, the rope is your only hope for survival, who would you want to be on top holding that rope? When we get done with preseason, when we gel as a unit, I think most of you, if you had to come up with five people, all five of those people would be guys you play with on this team."

During every other year, that was true. But not now. Too many of the guys had cut their own deal, and, unfortunately, the owner had cut his own throat. We lost seven games in a row. A dubious distinction, the longest losing streak of the Al Davis–era Raiders. The fun totally dried up, and football became drudgery. Bo provided a few brief glimmers of fun when he'd call a few of us over during pregame warm-ups in Minnesota, then later in Seattle and Kansas City, point far up over the scoreboard in center field or maybe the upper deck in left field, and kiddingly boast, "I hit one right there."

But he was also going through some torment, mostly because the press hounded him constantly about his infamous "football is just a hobby" quote and asked him repeatedly when he was going to decide whether he would quit football and concentrate full-time on baseball. I could see that Bo was burned out on the press. He was a national figure since winning the Heisman and still trying to manage a love/hate relationship with a very powerful press that had welcomed him with open arms at first, and then blasted him when his average dropped and he was benched by his Kansas City baseball team.

I got to know him a little, since he would avoid reporters by dressing in the training room, which was off-limits to them. I would occasionally go out and get his clothes from his other lockers when he wanted to duck the repetitive and leading questions that were getting under his skin. Once dressed, Bo would have to bowl his way from the training room out onto the team bus to minimize his contact with the fifty or so reporters camped out for a quote, a word, or even a mannerism.

Several games after the strike ended, Dr. Rosenfeld came back on the travel squad and slowly resumed his duties, although he still pretty much needed a golf cart to make it out to the center of the field. It looked as if he would phase out his Raider orthopedic duties and hand the baton over to his associates. I thought this would be a perfect situation, since after Rosenfeld's life-threatening infection I questioned his competence more and more. He was getting hard of hearing and his sight was going south, and then there were his tremor and periodic memory brown-outs. I was sure his three-dimensional hand-eye operative skills were down a dimension or two, even with a surgical nurse steadying his hand. But after our seventh consecutive loss, I saw his mean streak flare and wondered if his imminent retirement was only wishful thinking on my part. Rosenfeld's partner made the mistake of telling one of our younger linebackers that a muscle pull was probably going to keep him out for three weeks.

"You idiot!" Rosenfeld nearly screamed, in full hearing range of some of the players and the training staff. "I'll tell the players what they should and should not expect. You do the exams and report back to me."

I was taken aback. I couldn't believe the guy had that much breath left in him, let alone that type of venom. According to all accounts, he was getting back into his weekly football betting routine and starting to see more patients in his office, so for the first time, I realized I might have to campaign actively to have him put out to pasture. But that wasn't going to be easy. Number one, he was back in Al Davis's good graces—they apparently were going out to dinner again—and number two, I felt uneasy trying to can the man who had gotten me my job. But I felt I had to do the right thing, and I was moving closer to both the general manager and Al Davis. In the meantime, when I heard about serious orthopedic problems, I'd try to go to the players and counsel them about seeking second opinions.

I was still getting regular calls about Dean Miraldi, who during the course of the year had already resigned because of near cramp/panic attacks. I did everything I could think of to treat his attacks and work back his confidence so he could climb into a football uniform again. We were flying back from New England when Dean got that look in his eye, a look that said he just had to jump out of his skin or something would explode. He felt his muscles twitch and cramp. He was visibly mortified when he started shaking so bad he spilled his drink over a teammate sitting next to him. He tensed up like a 310-pound stick of dynamite. He was teetering on the edge of a full-blown attack. The team of neurologists, psychiatrists, and rheumatologists I'd consulted were still trying to figure out how best to treat him. I tried a STAT double dose of Ativan in his gluteus. It worked. When he'd settled down, his teammates began kidding that Tom Flores, after hearing about the Coach Vermil beating, had requested I purchase one of those wild game tranquilizer dart guns . . . just in case.

Curt Marsh, ten weeks into his injured reserve sentence, nearly freaked out. His career was ending, quite unhappily. He had head-aches, numbness, and his joints hurt so much he needed help getting out of bed. He found, after umpteen back-to-back surgeries, it was tough getting off pain pills and sleeping pills. Lump on top of all that the possible need for more ankle surgery and two more episodes of atrial fibrillation and you had a scared, sick, unprepared, soon-to-be ex-football player. What saved him was his family, his dedication to kids in general, and his unflagging sense of humor.

"Honey," he instructed his wife Pamela, "if I even *mention* returning to football, just get a gun and shoot me!"

We had just dropped seven games in a row. We were the pits. We were out of the play-offs, practically in midseason, and the remaining morale was zero. Starting quarterback Rusty Hilger had just been yanked two weeks ago in the middle of a game after an irate call from Mr. Davis in the owner's box via the red telephone. Plunkett, who had retired from the Raiders the previous year, used to talk about some of the dark days of playing for the loss-a-week Boston Patriot franchise back in the seventies—his coaching staff, after hand-signaling plays to him on the field, would then flash a "Hail Mary" sign. It seemed we were past that stage. Our patched-together offensive line couldn't stay healthy and couldn't block, our young receivers were having trouble hanging on to the ball, and our defense in general was having trouble defending. The coaches were second-guessing themselves on every play. It'd take forever to get the plays signaled in, and we were repeatedly assessed rally-snuffing delay-of-game penalties.

Into this turmoil stepped Marc Wilson to take over for Hilger and shoulder the inebriated wrath of the fickle L.A. fans. From the instant he stepped out of the tunnel, the stadium would swell with catcalls and boos. The negative volume would increase when he ran out to take the first snap and crescendo after every incomplete pass. The boos wouldn't stop until the team ran back up into the tunnel and into the locker room at the end of the game. Nothing went right when you lost seven in a row, and Marc Wilson, like everyone else, was an absolute head case.

Marc was in the last year of his five-year contract, a contract that had paid him $3 million in his first four years and now $1 million in his final contract year. He was a soft-spoken, religious family man. He was a spotlight-avoider. He had played hurt, he was unbelievably tough, and he was used to succeeding, but success had suddenly and inexplicably been pulled out from underneath him. Now before every home game, as he stood at the tunnel ready to sprint out to the field with his teammates for the opening kickoff, he would close his eyes and try to prepare himself, try to insulate himself from the jeers, the helplessness, the loss of self-esteem. He wanted to quit, but with eyes still closed he'd tell himself, "Marc, if you can just make it for five minutes, then you can quit." He'd calculated that at his 1987 rate, five minutes netted him about $5,000. He'd promise himself that if he could just make it five minutes and earn a quick $5,000, then he could quit. As the game wore on, he'd look up at the scoreboard and see he was five minutes into the game and counsel himself, "Now, that wasn't so bad. Okay, just hang in for five more minutes. May as well make another five thousand."

Wilson probably would have quit if not for the support of trainer George Anderson, whose humor gave him perspective and kept him aware of the absurdity of the whole situation.

"You f——ing Mormon," George would tease him, "you make more per interception than any other quarterback in the league. What are you complaining about?"

At halftime of another game, after Marc had struggled and thrown three interceptions, George pulled him aside in the locker room.

"Marc, you've got it all wrong," he deadpanned. "We're wearing the black jerseys. Those are the *good* luck ones."

Our next stop was Seattle, an away game with the Seahawks. The media already had us forfeiting this game. Several weeks before, we had lost to Seattle on Raider home turf, a humiliating 13–35 blowout.

From the 1983 season on, we'd had six straight losses in the Seattle dome of doom. In the last two seasons, with relatively good Raider teams, we had been slaughtered by a combined 3–70 score. We changed hotels in every away city after each loss, so after this many losses, we'd run out of first-class hotels in downtown Seattle.

"Boys," kidded lineman Bill Pickel as he stood up on the bus driving us from the airport, "if we lose this game we'll be staying in Tacoma next year."

"No, there's still a youth hostel and a YMCA downtown we haven't stayed in yet," chimed in another player.

It was a nationally televised Monday-night game, and early on it looked as though we were falling into our old pattern. Marc Wilson got sacked all the way back to the nine-yard line. It was third and about a mile to go, and Seattle brought in six or seven defensive backs from their sideline against our offense, which had a formation with one wide receiver and two tight ends. One of the tight ends brought in a play from Flores calling for a long pass. Wilson said to himself, "Screw this." He'd read the Kingdome script one too many times. The Raiders control the ball early, then fumble, get sacked or intercepted. The crowd noise jumps to front-row Van Halen concert levels, and the Raiders self-destruct.

"I'm not going to risk an interception by throwing into this coverage." So he nixed the coaches' play and barked out his own call. "Tight, Near Right, 17 Bob Trey '0.' " Translation: Bo runs left.

Surprise! Bo Jackson grabbed the ball and just sprinted around the whole Seattle team, streaking the ninety-one yards downfield in a blur, still picking up so much speed by the end zone that it took him fifty yards up the Seadome tunnel to decelerate. It was like all of a sudden rocket engines went on, and he just had a couple of extra afterburners; it was like watching a moon shot or some new scientific discovery. This was a whole new level of sports, to see a guy weighing 230 pounds who was that fast. There were very few times short of the Super Bowl when forty-five veterans were off the bench hooting in glee on the sideline. This was one of them. Everyone wanted to see what this guy would do next. Something very special was in the air.

As the jubilant offense bounded off the field, Tom Flores came halfway onto the field to meet the celebrating Wilson.

"What was that play?" he screamed over the din of the crowd. "What was that play?"

And Wilson, who had forgotten he had changed his coach's play in the huddle, said to himself, "Oh shit." He figured he was going to be chewed out.

"Tight, Near Right, 17 Bob Trey '0,' " he replied hesitantly.

"Great call!" said Flores as he patted Wilson on the back.

Seattle's Brian Bosworth, a big-mouthed, anabolic-steroid-using rookie sensation, had complained after the Seahawks crushed us earlier in the year at the L.A. Coliseum that he had been looking forward to playing the Raiders his whole life, and had been really disappointed when we just rolled over and died. After his touchdown, Bo broke loose again, up the middle of the line, eluding everyone except Bosworth, who was in a perfect position to stop Bo at the three-yard line. But Bo planted his head right in Bosworth's gut and bowled over this 260-pound man of steel, as if he were just one of those big Styrofoam fake rocks you see in B monster movies. The hometown Seahawk fans were riveted. There was dead silence. People had never witnessed this type of force before, a force that could move a linebacker of this size. A running back is supposed to be a small, shifty, fast guy. But Bo was an Olympic-speed athlete, as fast as anybody in the world, and he weighed 230 pounds with 2 percent body fat. It was an unbelievable combination in an athlete. Bosworth looked like a stalled car getting pulverized by a runaway train. Our sideline just went berserk; we couldn't believe it. The defensive guys forgot about their tired legs—no one wanted to sit down and rest for fear he'd miss part of this once-in-a-lifetime show.

In the middle of all this bedlam, all this excitement, there was Rosenfeld about five yards back with a bewildered look on his face. All of us were whooping and cheering in unbridled celebration, and he was standing alone in the middle of all this, subdued. He had a thin smile on his face and was clapping mildly, but he didn't seem to be into it. I felt sympathy for him, assuming that his recent splenectomy, the travel, and the excitement of everything were wearing him down. Then one of the staff came over and excitedly whispered, "Look back there—you see Rosie?"

"Yeah."

"Look at him, look at that expression. He doesn't know whether to laugh or to cry. His team won, but he bet a bundle on Seattle."

I figured that was just a vicious joke that was actually funny because, like a lot of good jokes, it could have been true. I wrote it off as that, but then another Raider came running over to me and grinned.

"Hey, I hear your medical buddy found out the hard way. You don't bet against Bo."

19

Do You Want to Be President?

The humidity of a June 1988 Maryland morning engulfed me as I exited the airport, luggage in hand. I was late for the NFL Physicians Society meeting. My connecting flight had been thirty minutes late, and my luggage the last to drop onto the conveyor belt.

I hurriedly flagged down a cabbie and headed for the Baltimore Omni Hotel; only ten minutes later, luggage still in hand, I found the conference room. The doctors were milling around, but the meeting hadn't begun yet. I dumped my luggage in the back of the conference room and headed over to a table stacked with soft drinks and fruit. I was just about to pop open a 7UP when I was surrounded by three of the ranking doctors in the society. Startled, I wondered what was up. What were they going to tell me? To get a haircut or something?

"Do you want to be president?"

It was Charlie Brown, the stately internist for the New Orleans Saints, the society's equivalent of Franklin D. Roosevelt. He had had his term as president extended two or three times. In the eighties he had been the NFL's go-to guy on drug matters, and no one in the Physicians Society wanted to shut down his established lines of communication. It was true that to date the National Football League regarded the drug problem as merely a public relations snafu, but should the league decide to get serious in the future, we wanted to be in a position to help chart the course. With him now were doctors from the Indianapolis Colts and the Houston Oilers.

"Gee," I said, caught totally off guard and just now realizing that these three doctors formed the nominating committee. "Sure."

"Do you have the time to commit to it?"

"I'll make time," I responded, slowly absorbing the magnitude of this offer.

I knew it wouldn't be easy. My practice was booming. Internal medical practices grow based on patient referrals, and I had reached a critical mass several years ago. I was booked solid in the office and usually had three or four hours of phone calls and hospital work tacked on at the end of the day.

The NFL Physicians Society meeting was called to order, and after only slightly botching my name (which is pronounced *Hize-inga*), they nominated me for president, the motion was seconded, and my nomination was approved by acclamation. I felt a rush of adrenaline. I was being given a chance to make a difference, to address the public relations approach to eliminating drugs, the ambivalent position on anabolic steroids, the lack of a position on amphetamines, the precarious malpractice position of doctors, the hypocritical rules that encouraged faking of injuries. I was being given a chance over the next several years, a chance to try to separate the business of football from the practice of medicine.

The first order of business today was the Krueger case, a precedent-setting legal decision. An ex-49er had sued the team orthopedist and the team for malpractice. He claimed he had received countless cortisone and novocaine injections in his knee, never being told of the possible consequences. He testified that in one game he got a piece of knee bone chipped off in a collision, was given a codeine pill on the sideline, and sent back in. When he retired in 1973 he was completely disabled, unable to ride a bike or even walk without pain. A judge ruled in his favor and awarded him $2.37 million. But the kicker was that the judge ruled it was not medical malpractice but medical fraud.

The distinctions, as I understood them, went like this. If a doctor gave knee injections and the player understood the risks and benefits and agreed, that would be good medicine. If a doctor gave knee injections, explained the risks and benefits, but mistakenly stuck the needle into the cartilage and damaged it, that would be malpractice. If the doctor, however, recommended knee injections and knowingly withheld possible future risks from the player, or went on giving injections even when complications became apparent, that would be fraud. Your basic doctor's malpractice insurance does not cover fraud. So in this type of judgment, the doctor pays with his car, his house, his wife, his firstborn kid, whatever.

This case had the team doctors in a tizzy. Already a number of other cases had turned up where an injured player had claimed the team doctor hadn't warned him of possible long-term arthritic complications. What would this do to the already high malpractice premiums that we had to pay? Would any malpractice carrier be stupid enough to let an NFL team doctor pay only the already outrageously high standard premium? Rumors swept around the room that in some instances the malpractice carriers were coming to team doctors and asking them to pay an additional $20,000 to $30,000 per year. Even considering a bump in my Raider salary to $24,000 a year, the job of team internist was now an out-and-out financial joke.

To make matters worse, as a result of this Krueger case, the Raiders several months earlier had sent me a document essentially asking me to hang myself out to dry. Their legal staff had decided their best defense against medical fraud cases was to make me walk the malpractice plank alone. I had to sign a statement saying I was not a team employee, merely an independent contractor. In fourteen years of medicine, I'd never had a malpractice claim filed against me, but if I now admitted I was an NFL team doctor my insurance company might double my premium. On the other hand, if I didn't and later got sued, the company might decline to cover me on the ground that I hadn't fully disclosed this risky activity I was engaged in.

The consensus among the doctors about this issue was that the best defense was good doctoring, full disclosure of risks to players, impeccable record-keeping, and constant finger-crossing.

Next up at the Physicians Society meeting was Forrest Tennant, Commissioner Roselle's newly appointed drug consultant for the National Football League. He ran a group of drug rehab facilities just east of Los Angeles. Tennant gave us some rosy figures on the declining number of drug positives in the four hundred college All-American players evaluated each February. In 1986, 17 percent had tested positive for either marijuana or cocaine or alcohol, but the figure had dropped to 8 or 9 percent in 1987 and then to only 0.4 percent in the recent winter 1988 All-American testing combine. Tennant implied that these glowing stats signified increased awareness of the dangers of drugs, and also the decline of drug abuse at the college level. I viewed the stats somewhat differently. I figured word was just now getting from the drafted college players to their underclassmen teammates: if you want to sign a big fat contract, don't screw it up by doing drugs in the weeks before the physicals. A positive urine drug test would drop a player down in the draft, and the lower the draft pick, the lower the contract. The use of drugs hadn't changed much in college in the previous three years, and there was no reason to suspect that use had changed much on college football teams.

Forrest then walked us through one of the more murky areas of his new drug program—alcohol. The league had endured a rash of bad publicity surrounding arrests of inebriated players involved in bar fights, domestic quarrels, auto accidents, and the like. He proposed that a player get a strike in the three-strikes-you're-out drug program if elevated alcohol levels were detected in his urine.

"Wait a minute," said one of the doctors. "How can you ban a substance that is legal in this country? Unless you can show the player was driving a car while under the influence, he really hasn't broken any law. I think that one's going to be tough to defend in court."

Another stood and shook his head.

"Isn't this a bit hypocritical? How are you going to ban alcohol when every stadium has alcohol ads plastered all over it? Alcohol is the biggest sponsor for NFL football on TV. What kind of mixed message are you trying to send?"

We also battled over the best way to approach the anabolic steroid problem. In 1987, 8 percent of players had tested positive on an announced "no penalty" steroid test given the first day of camp. This suggested either that players could get off the stuff if you announced the testing date, or that anabolic steroids were not being used as much as the underground would have you believe. This year, positives were going to result in suspensions. Strangely enough, the plan was to kick players out for a month if they tested positive for steroids the first time, although if they tested positive for cocaine a first time they would merely receive a warning slap on the wrist. The steroid user with a second positive test would be banned for life. Since many injectable steroids stay in the system for up to nine months, the question was raised whether there would be legal liability if a player was allowed to return in four weeks when steroids were still in his blood. What if, for instance, a player with steroids still in his blood injured another player? That player might be able to claim in court that the team doctor and club had allowed a player known to be illegally more aggressive and vicious to play against him, thus increasing the first player's chance of injury.

Maybe the most ludicrous suggestion regarding anabolic steroids was a request by league officials that team doctors do reasonable-cause testing. Who in the world would you do reasonable-cause testing on? The biggest guy? The fastest guy? The guy who hit the hardest in the game? The guy who had the most tackles?

So while with cocaine the NFL found cooperation by teams that wanted to turn in the troublemakers, it was definitely going to hit a roadblock with performance-enhancing drugs. Like game-day amphetamines (which the league didn't test for), steroids were vocational—not recreational—drugs. A doctor stood up.

"What do you want us to do? Maybe we can take the heroes of the game as they're getting ready for the postgame interviews and get their urine before they're allowed on TV."

Back at summer camp, my new friends in high places and I had our first disagreement. I bitterly protested what I felt was a senseless quirk in the drug program's step-two penalty phase. One of our players, Greg Townsend, tested positive for marijuana. This was his second offense, so the test results were made public and he was suspended for four weeks. Although I didn't view smoking marijuana as a threat to modern society or the integrity of the NFL, the rules had been clearly stated. Our player had been counseled and should not have used the drug. The player openly admitted he'd made a mistake. But I vehemently disagreed with where the four-week suspension should be served. If you honestly thought marijuana was a problem—or any drug, for that matter—I reasoned that what you'd want to do is keep that person around the football camp, let him get razzed a little by the other players, let him get counseling, let him work out so he can have an outlet for his frustration. Don't make him go back to his hometown, God knows not back to a drug-infested city. Don't let him get out of shape, because if he's not in good shape he's going to be much more prone to an injury when he comes back. Injuries lead to player depression. Depression is one precipitating factor for drug use. So what's the penalty recommended? They tell Greg Townsend to leave camp and all the people who would watch him and give support, and put him back in his home in the middle of Compton, where he had smoked marijuana, as he admitted in the newspapers, since he was in sixth grade. Oh yeah, and don't penalize the player in terms of pay. That had to be the most ass-backward penalty scheme I could have imagined. I let the NFL know, but they didn't buy my line of reasoning. The minute

Greg's four weeks were up, he was back in a game two days later. Luckily he didn't get hurt.

The second problem in this case was that no one had ever studied the disappearance of marijuana from the system of an individual this large who had smoked marijuana for this long. It turned out that although he didn't get near a burning weed, his levels stayed the same or decreased only very marginally over many months. No one could have known, but the more marijuana Townsend smoked, the less his liver was able to break it down. Because of his large size, the active ingredient of marijuana, tetrahydrocannabinol, hung out in his body fat and muscle stores and was in no hurry to exit. We were essentially doing research as we went along, but unfortunately, because of NFL politics, were unable to do legitimate research protocols.

Summer camp ended with the usual last-minute holdouts coming back into the fold. This year it was Matt Millen. He signed a $750,000 two-year contract and immediately addressed curious reporters' questions about whether he would be sleeping in Al Davis's doghouse now.

"Hell, no," said the off-season carpenter. "This summer I built a doghouse for myself. I don't need to crawl into his."

Probably the most bizarre incident of the year occurred in one of our last preseason games. We had a great offensive line prospect from West Texas, 330 pounds, six feet six—Newt Harrell. Right before the game, one of the coaches came up to him and told him the man upstairs wanted him to go down. Newt, fresh out of college, hadn't heard about the "rookie scholarships." He stared back with no idea what the coach was talking about.

"You've had some neck problems before. When I tell you when, just hit the guy and lay there. You'll get your full salary this year and get a chance to make the team next year."

So came the third quarter, Newt got the signal. Word had spread up and down the sideline, so everybody was standing around watching to see how he would do it. I was wondering why I was part of this ridiculous situation, comforted only a little by the fact that discussions with other doctors revealed this practice was widespread throughout the league. Our wide receiver, Mike Alexander from Penn State, was given the signal to go down with a leg injury on the same play, so I decided to walk out to him. It somehow didn't seem as offensive as faking a neck injury.

The quarterback dropped back, and there went Newt, gunning

at a linebacker, diving and driving his helmet between the defender's pecs. Then he just lay motionless. On the other side of the field, Mike Alexander was groaning with a leg injury, and I jogged over to help bring him back. I had to laugh to myself, because two opposing defenders also went down. Four players injured on the same play late in the game. What a coincidence.

As I was coming back to the sideline, I looked over and was shocked to see big Newt getting the whole treatment—the neck immobilizer, four guys straining to get him up on a stretcher, the cart coming out, the whole nine yards. The game was held up for quite a while as all this commotion was going on. Other teammates also seemed amazed and anxious, wondering if something had really happened. As they slowly drove him up in the cart on a stretcher, through the tunnel toward the locker room for X-rays, one of the players next to me asked, "Gee, I wonder what the hell his wife is thinking up there, or his parents at home watching this thing on TV."

Meanwhile, a drunken fan with a big gut leaned over the tunnel railing, cupped his hands, and screamed at Newt, who was strapped down motionless on his back, "You big pussy!"

The whole thing was surreal. For all the fan knew, Newt was paralyzed for life. Finally, in the fourth quarter, George came back from the locker room. The first-string players, now standing on the sideline, huddled around George expressing concern. We knew it was okay when George cracked a big smile.

"I almost broke my back lifting that mother up," he groaned. "The next time they have a three-hundred-and-thirty-pounder fake an injury, you can bet your sweet ass he's going to be able to walk off the field."

20

I Never Thought It Would End This Way

Steve Beuerlein was hot. It was Saturday afternoon, we had less than twenty-four hours before the second game of our 1988 season against the Oilers in the Houston Astrodome, and he was lying listless in the hotel room, his cheeks rosy red as if he'd just been slapped. Six days before, he'd had his first start as a professional quarterback, and had guided the Raiders to an impressive win over the San Diego Chargers, our always pesky cross-county rivals.

Then that very night, Al Davis dropped a bomb. He announced an ill-fated trade, the fallout from which was to burn the team for years to come. The trade, born in the desperation of the disastrous 1987 strike season, sent stalwart lineman Jim Lachey plus draft choices to the Washington Redskins for Jay Schroeder, the strong-armed Redskin quarterback. Jim Lachey was practically a Don Mosebar equivalent. He was a sure thing when it came to keeping opposing linemen off his quarterback, plus he was a team leader, motivating the younger players and giving last-second instructions to the "head cases," players who had trouble remembering directions in the heat of battle. The new quarterback was now busily studying the complicated offense of our new coach Mike Shanahan, and given the high price we had paid for him, it seemed that it was just a matter of time before Beuerlein was relegated to a spot on the end of the bench. I took the thermometer out of his mouth.

"It's a hundred and two point four," I said as I otoscoped his ears and got ready to look down his throat. "So besides the nausea, aches, and diarrhea, anything else bothering you?"

"No, it's just a little flu."

"I think you're right," I said as I probed deeply into his right lower abdomen, then withdrew my fingers quickly, like a pianist arching up off the keys after finishing the final chord. There was no recoil pain. The rebound test was negative. So the stomach pain and fever probably didn't mean an inflamed appendix or a ruptured ulcer.

"It probably is just a little flu," I continued, "but I want to be extra cautious here. Remember Bill Lewis last year?"

I flashed back to the locker room before that game when Bill and I were talking about whether he should even bother to suit up. He didn't have any rebound and his temperature was down to a hundred, so I told him the decision was basically his. If he didn't want to suit up I'd tell the coaches that I had specifically told him not to suit up. If he felt he had enough strength to contribute should the first-team player go down—Bill Lewis was second-string—then we'd watch him on a play-by-play basis. Well, Lewis, like almost all of the guys, was determined to do whatever it took to get out on the field, and so I gave him a liter of fluid to make up his diarrhea losses and out he marched. Fortunately he didn't have to play a down. Toward the end of the game it was obvious that he wouldn't be able to play even if he had to. The pain was getting worse, and I told the coach to cross him out of any potential plans. It turned out he had a retroflexed, ready-to-burst appendix, something that's frequently misdiagnosed, since it occurs in only one of a hundred cases of appendicitis. Few of these can be diagnosed early, since the abdominal pain can be relatively modest and does not localize in the right lower abdomen as in most appendicitis attacks, and early on the rebound sign may be absent. Still, I was upset, since he was under my care. Even if it was an unusual presentation, I would have liked to have picked it up earlier. The very fact Lewis had a uniform on was tacit acknowledgment that should push come to shove, I had at least initially approved him to play.

"I'm going to play no matter what," stated Beuerlein, "so don't tell me any different."

"I could let you play, but if your temperature stays up you'll be a real setup for dehydration and heat cramps or even heatstroke. Let's just be on the safe side. Let's hope it's just a twenty-four- or forty-eight-hour thing. We're going to have to reevaluate it in the morning and make a decision then."

The medical jury is still out about strenuous exercise when you have a viral infection. Doctors used to advise not working out, whether or not you had a fever, mainly out of fear that you were the very rare case with a virus that, besides causing the usual flu symptoms, was also infecting your heart, and that strenuous exercise could bring on a life-threatening rhythm disturbance. There's really no hard evidence, though, to support that stance, and many doctors are swinging toward the other end of the spectrum, especially since some studies are now showing that people with the HIV virus do better, maybe even live longer, when they work out on a regular basis.

I knocked on Beuerlein's door early the next day, game-day Sunday, just after the seven-thirty wake-up call. His temperature was down below one hundred. His stomach felt better, and he swore up and down he felt fine. But it was obvious that he was still dragging. It was also obvious that he was going to do whatever it took to keep Jay Schroeder out of the starting lineup. Since his temperature was down to near normal, I felt justified in clearing him, but under no circumstances did I feel that he was 100 percent, and I told him and the coaches so.

Amazingly enough, he played with a lot of spunk. He put thirty-five points up on the scoreboard, an impressive number for any quarterback. Problem was, Houston's versatile quarterback, Warren Moon, did just a little more, putting up thirty-seven points against our defense which at times played as if they were the ones who were ill.

After three games, we were a lethargic 1–2, and despite the fact that Beuerlein played solidly, he was benched in favor of the new kid in town, Jay Schroeder. Schroeder had exactly three weeks to cram. That wasn't much compared to the usual seven weeks of preseason, not to mention all of the summer months after the spring camps, to learn the two-inch-thick playbook. The offense was simplified a little, and on paper, anyway, Schroeder knew where all his receivers were heading on each call. However, it didn't look that way in the first half of his debut against the Denver Broncos in Mile High Stadium. In front of a national Monday-night TV audience we had ineptly stumbled to a 27–0 deficit by the early third quarter.

But the football gods can give as easily as they take away. The heavens opened and showered us with some of the early-eighties Raiders karma. Steve Smith scored on a long run after grabbing a Schroeder swing pass. Then the defense finally figured out how to stop the Broncos. We got confident. We knew no matter what the score, we could win this game. Schroeder's passes were suddenly sticking in our receiver's hands as if magnetized. The defense was getting in John Elway's face. We marched up and down the field, and with just seconds remaining, were down by only three points, 27–24.

Enter Chris Bahr, who had been faltering for the past several weeks. His makable misses had cost us the Rams game. It didn't matter a lick that he had been the Raiders' Mr. Reliable for the past nine years. Three or four other kickers had been brought into the El Segundo facility in the last week for tryouts. It was a foregone conclusion that Bahr would be unceremoniously booted out of the pros should he miss this game-tying kick. Given his salary multiplied by the number of years he could stay in the league, he had about $1 million riding on the trajectory of the stupid little pigskin ball. He glanced over to the sideline with a look that seemed to say this whole thing had to be a joke, then blasted a kick so perfect that if there had been a target exactly between the goalposts this ball would have hit it. And just to prove it was no fluke, he came back moments later in overtime and kicked the winning field goal in front of a disbelieving national audience.

Wow! Personal redemption for Bahr. The record books for the Raiders. We had just staged the biggest comeback ever in professional football. From the sideline, the second half had been absolutely exhausting. Everyone was hoarse. The emotion, the joy, when that last field goal sailed slowly through the uprights! We were lifted halfway to heaven.

Coach Shanahan was in tears in the locker room after getting this kind of win, and against his ex-teammates and his former head coach. Hollywood couldn't concoct an ending like this. We were just two and two, but the season was very young, and we were going to get much, much better.

In the old days, one of the vets like Ted Hendricks or Marcus Allen or Rod Martin would quiet down the clubhouse bedlam and, after a short two-or-three-sentence summary of the game, give the game ball to a key player who had sparked the victory. This time the overcome Shanahan quieted us down as he waved the ball in the air and said simply, "Men, this is the gutsiest victory, the wildest finger-scratching comeback, in football history. Everybody in this locker room deserves a game ball."

I still have mine. Hand-painted in black and silver over a quarter of a Wilson-brand, Made in America NFL official ball: "Dr. Rob

Huizenga, 9/6/88, 30–27 Los Angeles Raiders over Denver." Hell, who cares if there are sixty other copies?

Two and a half weeks later, in the training room after the Wednesday-afternoon practice, faces were not quite so happy. The magic of new coach Mike Shanahan and new quarterback Jay Schroeder had been short-lived. We had lost the next two games and were sitting a dismal two and four near the bottom of our division. Adding insult to injury, Howie Long, our defensive line stalwart, had been kicked, cleated, and leg-whipped in his right calf. He felt an electric jolt every time he tried to accelerate out of his three-point stance, making his chance of contributing during this week's Kansas City game iffy at best.

We'd called Cedars-Sinai's bone-and-muscle guru, radiologist Dr. Jerry Mink, immediately after last Sunday's loss. Dr. Mink agreed to come into the hospital from home to do a magnetic resonance imaging scan of Howie Long's calf muscle. We needed an immediate contingency plan if his muscle was torn, because a torn muscle would take four to six weeks to heal. The MRI showed slight calf muscle swelling with a tiny bleed, par for the course when someone tees off and kicks your calf in. There was no muscle tear evident.

"You're okay," said Rosenfeld, grabbing Howie's toes and bending the foot back upward toward the body as he probed the calf of his outstretched leg. "It's just a bruise. The MRI is normal."

Howie got off the table and bent into a three-point stance on the carpeted training room floor. He took a quick step—as if to veer around an opposing tackle—then abruptly stopped. The stabbing, icepick-like pain had returned. No way he'd be able to accelerate hari-kari through a three-hundred-plus-pound genetic freak of nature.

"Don't worry," Rosenfeld said reassuringly. There's no evidence of a muscle tear, so it's just a matter of days. It's a bruise. You've got to expect a little soreness."

A bruise in football terms means it's not a ripped muscle, not a fractured bone, not a skin gash. Just a drop or two of blood and saltwater swelling under the skin or inside a superficial muscle. The typical black-and-blue patch is quickly reabsorbed into the body. In other words, the player is fine. A muscle bruise will hurt, yes, especially in the morning when the muscles are stiff, but once you get them moving much of the pain and tightness disappears. Once you stop, of course, the banged-up muscle will freeze again, and you've got to walk like a wooden soldier for a couple of minutes until you get it warmed up again.

The trainers were working the franchise leg like crazy. Howie had gigantic blue-ribbon-size calves to begin with, and the right one was slightly enlarged. The trainers were trying massage, electric stimulation, and repeated icing. But the next game came and went and then the next one, and still no Howie.

Every day the same sad scene was repeated. Long would come in for treatment with the trainers, Rosenfeld would feel that calf for evidence of a muscle tear or defect.

"You're okay, it's just a bruise."

Long would counter that the cattle-prod zap inside his calf told him something was wrong. Meanwhile, the pressure to play was mounting. Howie had just signed a $1-million-a-year multi-year contract, and the whispers started that maybe Howie had gone soft, maybe the internal fire that set him apart and had made him such an achiever had finally blown out. He started getting looks from players. The press was questioning him. Rosenfeld was telling Al each week there was no reason he wouldn't be able to go the next week. But the next week he couldn't go. Howie was putting pressure on himself. He became visibly depressed. His only consolation was the fact that a prominent crosstown orthopedist—Howie was a major star, and unlike many other players was not afraid of recriminations for openly insisting on outside consultations—felt he had a partial calf muscle tear and should not be playing.

The calf swelling didn't go down. It increased. And the pain increased. I told him that the original MRI had shown a pinch of blood, which could be interpreted any number of ways, that the MRI could be consistent with your usual kick, bang, and bruise, but that when the patient's complaints don't fit with the test results, sometimes you have to repeat the tests. Finally the MRI was repeated. It showed why Howie was having so much trouble. He had developed a pear-shaped collection of blood deep in his calf muscle. When he was told about the results, his calf discomfort remained, but a layer of pain in his face quickly slipped away.

He almost had been believing there was nothing wrong—but he couldn't walk, much less run. Now the MRI images explained it all. He wasn't okay; it wasn't just a bruise. He had a gigantic hematoma.

Rosenfeld was intent on draining the body fluid through a tiny puncture, then trying to apply a pressure wrap so that the hematoma would not reaccumulate. But it was for naught. Six weeks after the original injury, after blood tests for different hemophilia-like conditions turned up negative, after Howie felt a sudden snap and more swelling when he was told before the San Diego game to practice take-offs from his three-point stance, it became painfully obvious that an open incision was needed to find the tiny bleeder responsible for the calf hemorrhage. A third MRI was done because, again, the crosstown orthopedist suspected this latest event was in part due to a continuing muscle tear. The MRI showed only an expanding clot of blood. After much discussion, Howie agreed to have the thing surgically opened up and drained. But he had no faith left in Rosenfeld. So he cornered Rosenfeld's associate Dr. Fred Nicola, whom he trusted, held him by the throat in the training room, and made him swear he'd do the entire procedure himself.

The surgery proceeded flawlessly. A large congealed mass of blood was removed, finally putting an end to Howie's calf problems. The small calf incision was extended a full ten inches so the doctors could run their fingers up and down the actual calf muscle. It was smooth—there was no tear. The theory of Dr. Rosenfeld's rival had been disproved.

I didn't realize until much later how terrified Howie was about his surgery, when I heard a telling story during one of the Saturday night on the road, post-meal player talk-a-thons.

"On the big day," a fellow lineman began, "Howie's in the operating room, feeling confident, cracking jokes with Nicola and the anesthesiologist. Then the anesthesiologist puts the intravenous in, injects a fast-acting sedative, and tells Howie, 'Okay, we're ready to go. Have a good sleep. Start counting backward from twenty.'

"So Howie starts counting, 'twenty, nineteen, eighteen . . .'

"Then in walks an old guy who Howie assumes is an orderly.

" 'Hi Howie,' the guy says. Now all of a sudden Howie realizes it's Rosenfeld with his surgical mask on!

"The anesthesiologist is holding a face mask over Howie's mouth but Howie reflexively screams. 'Don't . . . let . . . him . . . touch . . .' And then boom, he's out.

"When Howie wakes up still in the surgical suite, he flashes back to his last conscious thought and goes, 'Oh shit!'

"He immediately looks at his calf as the nurses bandage a long gash, not the short one he had expected, and in his half-drugged mind he moans, 'Oh, my God. Rosenfeld operated on me with a broken beer bottle!' "

* * *

"Rob, we have problems. We could use your help," said Forrest Tennant, the NFL drug czar. His trademark baritone voice resonated through the dimly lit penthouse restaurant of the Pasadena Hilton. "Now, you're going to be president until when? How long's your term?"

"Well, this is my second year as vice-president. Next year I'll start a two-year term as president. Dr. Ellfelt, the orthopedist from Kansas City, is the current president. We switch off between having a team internist and a team orthopedist as president. When an orthopedist is president, the president-elect takes over the drug problems—as you can well understand, that's more an internist's area. And any league policy dealing with bones and joints gets turfed to the orthopedist."

"Well, the first problem we have," Tennant said, "is our alcohol policy. Right now, we have the ability to suspend players who are arrested in alcohol-related crimes, but we still don't know what to do when our drug screens turn up with alcohol in them."

"I know," I said, shaking my head. "On the one hand, alcohol is definitely the most abused drug among pro athletes. On the other hand, your people come in and do the urine tests the day after all of our players arrive in camp, and of course the first night everybody gets back is an automatic three-deep-at-the-bar party night. So handing out penalties based on these results really isn't fair—and probably not legal either. We really need to get information from family and friends to find the problem drinkers early. But getting cooperation—in the current player-management adversarial relationship—is going to be next to impossible.

"But I'll tell you what I'm having a bigger problem with," I said as we finished our salads. "I'm getting complaints from doctors because none of us were informed about the new wrinkle in your drug policy. All of a sudden players with low levels of drugs are not being penalized."

"Well, Rob, we had some legal problems. Some of the players ran and got lawyers. With the low levels found, they claimed they got the cocaine from a spiked drink, or they got it having oral sex with a girlfriend who was using cocaine, or they swear the traces of marijuana found were taken in passively—they were in a room where people were smoking it. And it turns out, at this time anyway, the only legal proof of drug use the court's going to accept are the same levels as the U.S. government uses to suspend its employees. The U.S. government can't afford the gas-chromatography-mass-spectrometry method that we use. So while we accurately detect cocaine at five or ten nanograms, their old technology is only accurate above three hundred nanograms."

I figured something like this must have happened. One of Forrest Tennant's good qualities was that he was straightforward and open, but sometimes he was too open. He had told me several weeks earlier, in one of our frequent phone conversations, that a particular Bronco first-stringer was going to be suspended because of a second positive urine drug test.

I had been very happy to hear this bit of news, since we were going to play Denver in a week and this was one of their key players. They didn't have much of a backup, and so they would really be hurting. At first I was tempted to run out and announce this great news to the coach, or maybe even Al Davis himself, but I controlled that impulse. I was on a different level now. I was privy to confidential information, and I had to be professional about it. But every day I studied the newspaper waiting to see the player's name announced. It never was. We went to Denver for the game, I ran out on the field, and whoa! There was the player in warm-ups. I knew then that something was wrong with the new drug penalty system. Either the fix was in at the commissioner's office or some major legal roadblock had been thrown up.

I had already experienced the league's backpedaling. We had acquired a player who was step one for cocaine—meaning one more positive drug test and he was going to be suspended for a month. Two days after he put on the silver-and-black jersey, I got back one of his twice-weekly "reasonable cause" drug tests, given to everyone who is step one, and he had a level of cocaine of about fifty-five nanograms. So I called the player in, told him we'd found cocaine in his urine, and asked what was going on. He admitted that he was using cocaine and had desperately tried to get off for a couple of days so that the tests would come back negative, but was, for all practical purposes, in a high-use pattern of his cocaine addiction. So after discussing treatment options, I picked up the phone and called the coach and Al Davis to tell them that his drug test was positive and he was going to be suspended. To my shock, I got a call back from our front office telling me this player would *not* be suspended! I was outraged. Meeting after meeting with Tennant and NFL lawyer types to get the particulars of this program drilled into us, and now minutes after I make the phone call to the owner, our front office tells me it ain't so! I dialed Forrest Tennant to see what was going on.

I found out that based on legal challenges by players, the NFL had decided that for a player to be considered positive, his cocaine levels had to be over 300 nanograms on the usual test, or 150 on the much more sensitive GCMS machine. Okay. The player was considered negative. But he had already admitted he was positive. He got cut the next day. On the positive side, at least for the marginal players, the club was not tolerating drug use. On the negative side, so much for the ballyhooed rehabilitative focus of the new drug policy. The player was on a plane out of town before I could line up proper counseling.

"One thing, Rob," Tennant said. "Before you go, you know you've got work to do educating some of these team doctors."

"What do you mean?" I asked.

"Well, if you can believe it, we've got several club doctors who were mailed positive drug tests and didn't tell anyone on the team, the coaches or the owners. They didn't even tell the player, and we find out all of the sudden when the player gets the second positive drug test and is about to be suspended, and of course screams and yells because he's never even been told about the first drug test."

"What? How is that possible?"

I was horrified that any team doctor could be that negligent. Later, thinking about it, I wondered if those doctors had used this as a ruse to save players, or maybe been persuaded to do it by the team.

"Then," Forrest continued, "there are some doctors who tell the players that they're positive and don't lift a finger to get them counseling or treatment of any sort. We can't let that go on."

"Some doctors," I countered, "have been complaining that drug tests have been run in unaccredited laboratories and the chain of custody has been broken."

The chain of custody is that all-important link that makes sure the urine is not tampered with from the time it goes in the cup till it's tested in the lab.

"That's sheer unadulterated bunk," Forrest replied. "We test the samples as many as four or five times, in the best labs with the best equipment. Our main problem with the chain of custody is that at least one of the team doctors has been advising his players not to sign the chain-of-custody documents. That, of course, can then be an argument for them in court if they test positive. They can claim it wasn't their urine, because in fact they never signed the piece of paper saying that they had given the urine and that it had been witnessed by our drug collector."

"It's scary times," I responded. "You know, it might not be too far off when the money will be high enough that we open up the paper one morning and read that one of the doctors has been bribed to fix the drug tests."

"You're right," he acknowledged. "It could happen some day."

I was shocked. We were in New Orleans, standing in line for our Saturday-night buffet, and there was a new food choice! It was the first new course I had seen in the traditional pregame Saturday-night meal. Shrimp gumbo, and it was delicious. This soup happened to be the perfect meal for me, because I couldn't use my left hand for cutting or picking up food with a fork. The base of my thumb was swollen up to about five times normal size because of a stupid mistake I had made three days before. I hadn't learned from my previous wrestling attempt with Howie Long, and this time had somehow ended up baiting Linden King, one of my good friends on the team, a ferocious outside/inside linebacker. I stood in back of him, arms locked around his waist, kidding him that he couldn't get out. As a matter of fact, I have a pretty good hand grip, and in my college wrestling days the way I worked it, it was pretty much impossible for anybody to get out. As Linden tried unsuccessfully to free himself, I naturally ribbed him a little bit more. Then in walked more players, who started laughing and getting on him pretty good.

"What a wimp. You can't even get away from a lousy bookworm doctor!"

At that point something in him clicked; that animal instinct just took over. In an instant he isolated my thumb and grabbed it, a move flagrantly illegal in collegiate wrestling. I should have known he wouldn't abide by *those* rules. He yanked my thumb, ripping it a mile out of its socket. That definitely broke my grip. Instantly realizing what he had done, Linden turned bright red and started apologizing all over the place. I just laughed—Okay, a pained laugh—at how stupid I had been to egg him on. That instinctive aggression—that was why he was a first-team professional linebacker and I was an ex-athlete doctor.

During the meal the players were in a reflective mood, talking about how great football was, especially the boy's-club atmosphere, being able to get out and schmooze and laugh with the guys on a regular basis, how if there were no such game as football someone would have to invent some other way to get paid for hanging out together and playing games. Then talk turned to how much longer each player hoped to stay in the game. Vann McElroy talked about his investments in produce, specifically a lettuce-packaging plant. Charley Hannah talked about the car washes he was buying in his hometown of Tampa. Then Vann explained how the name of the game was to see if you could pay off your house and get $1 million in the bank. Then you had security. You could live on the interest, even if nothing else worked out for you the rest of your life.

"Assuming," said Terry Robiskie, one of the assistant coaches, "the f—-ing doctor bills don't get you. Those guys," he said, trying to razz me, "are the only guys with a chance to cut into that investment."

After each of the players said how many years he'd like to keep playing, Hannah summed it up by saying, "We're making too much money, we're having too much of a good time. No way—I'm not going to retire. They're going to have to drag me off the freaking field kicking and screaming."

The New Orleans game started with a flourish. Bo jetted right for eighteen yards. Then Bo scampered left for fifteen. But that was it for the highlight film. He felt a twang in the midportion of his hamstring. Not a pull, but a twang, the kind of sensation every sprinter knows and fears, because it more often than not heralds a full-blown tear.

As Bo sat down on the bench, Rosenfeld rushed over to examine him. He talked Bo into doing a three-quarter run on the sidelines. But something obviously didn't feel right to Bo, and that was it. Rosenfeld relayed his findings on the red phone.

Bo had set the tone the year before in one of the last season games in Kansas City. After a memorable opening kickoff, with our bench being bombarded with baseballs—not plastic facsimiles mind you, but actual hardballs—in honor of Bo's two-sport return to Kansas City, Bo went out on the field and on the very first play, he got the ball on a sweep only to tangle legs with pulling guard Dean Miraldi. He felt his right ankle pop and that was it for the last three games of the season. His autobiography was especially revealing in this regard when he recalled a severe ankle injury his junior year at Auburn.

He'd had a full complement of doctors and trainers evaluate him, but he'd gone back out and played against Texas on the twisted ankle. Well, he broke free on a long run and low and behold he got caught from behind. This was something that apparently hadn't happened before and certainly hadn't happened since. Worse, on that very tackle, he'd suffered a season-ending shoulder separation that took him out of the Heisman trophy race. So Bo knew firsthand the pitfalls of playing hurt.

Without Bo we struggled, and finally fell behind the New Orleans Saints. Jay Schroeder tried to pass us back into the game, but it was not to be. Then, in the third quarter, he threw an ill-advised pass that was picked off by a New Orleans defender. Charley Hannah, straining to pass-block out on the left end, got crushed underneath his teammates Bruce Wilkerson and Bill Lewis, who were attempting to hold off the charging noseguard. Charley was down banging on the turf in pain and trying to get our attention on the sideline. Meanwhile, after the interception players were running around in every direction. Poor Charley, immobile on the ground, was like a defenseless scrub bush in a cattle stampede. He knew something was terribly wrong and prepared himself for the possibility that when he looked down at the agonizingly throbbing ankle he might see a bone or something sticking out in the air. After the play, teammate Don Mosebar walked over and asked, "You okay? Don't worry. The docs and the trainers are on their way out. Oh, and by the way, don't try to get up."

When Charley heard that, he knew something very bad must have happened, and he slowly looked down. He wasn't prepared for what he saw. He had no foot! The shin had been snapped in two like a dry twig, with his ankle unhinged and torqued behind his calf. But from Charley's perspective, the whole foot was missing.

I arrived on the scene with the trainers. Distraught to see my friend screaming in pain, and mesmerized by the sight of his grotesque fracture, I mindlessly asked my usual opening question. "Charley, what's the matter?"

"You idiot! I don't have a freakin' foot!"

"Charley, I know that," I said quickly, recouping my wits. "I meant, do you have any knee or hip pain? I can see your ankle's broken."

We lifted him onto a stretcher, his helplessly dangling foot secured with a board from midcalf. Beads of sweat showered off his forehead as the Superdome paramedics scurried about for what seemed like hours trying to find the keys to get through the gates that separated us from the X-ray facilities.

"Doc," Charley said as he literally bit through his mouth guard, "I never thought it would end like this."

Once in the X-ray facility, I stripped off his uniform then placed an intravenous line after the paramedics failed on several attempts. As I injected morphine for pain, I heard the paramedics fighting over Charley's jersey in the back of the room.

"Do me two favors, doc," said Charley, now much more philosophical. "One, I'd like another pain shot, cuz that one just brought the pain down from hell to sheer agony. Number two, make sure you're taking good notes for workers' comp."

He cracked the first smile since the injury.

Charley boarded the plane that night with a full cast under a pair of gray sweats. He was just relaxing on the plane and had taken a couple of pain pills when I got nervous.

"When was your last pee?"

"I don't know. Before the game."

"No more pain medicines, no more beer; soup and water only until you pee."

One urination with clear urine would help rule out dehydration or kidney damage from a helmet to the flank, or from fat embolism related to his broken leg bones.

Unfortunately, it's hard to fit a six-foot-six, 280-pound guy with a full leg cast into a plane bathroom. So with me guarding the door, there he sat, leg out of the airplane bathroom, letting out some thunderclap gas up there in first class, turning red as a beet because he knew Mrs. Davis was sitting only a couple of yards away. Finally I looked in.

"Any luck?"

Charley pointed to a waterfall of drips sprayed over his gray pants.

"Good job," I complimented him.

We were up against the perennial NFC powerhouse San Francisco 49ers, the odds-on favorite for this year's Super Bowl crown. We had switched over from Schroeder to Beuerlein again, and he had pulled us back within striking distance of the division leaders. But this was the big game. Were we contenders or just pretenders? Beuerlein played well, but we just couldn't punch the ball into the end zone, settling for three field goals. We won the game, though, on the defensive line. Two kids stepped out from the shadow of Howie Long, who stood in street clothes on the sidelines. Mike Wise and "Tarzan" Scott Davis got up inside Joe Montana's helmet all day and held the All-World, first-in-line-for-the-Hall-of-Fame, quarterback to just three points.

It was a happy bunch that trotted down the stairs at the end zone of Candlestick Park and up the ramp toward the locker room. We were tied for first place in the division. We had beaten probably the best team in the league. We were for real. But in the locker room, Al Davis was moping.

He was coming to realize it had been a mistake to move to Los Angeles. His deal for a utopian Raiders complex in the Irwindale granite quarry was on the rocks. The L.A. Coliseum had reneged on many of its promises. Now he was trying to mend fences and either go back to Oakland or move to Sacramento, St. Louis, New York, or anyplace that would build him a stadium with luxury boxes so that he could make the income he needed to get the players he wanted.

He'd even had Tom Harmon, one of the guys who often ran interference for him, call up Merv Griffin about the feasibility of building a stadium in Hollywood Park, the large racetrack complex near the Forum where the Lakers played. Tom Harmon knew Merv had a lot of pull with his fellow Hollywood Park board members, so he asked Merv if he could get a majority to support a proposed Raiders stadium. Merv Griffin, who's got a wild sense of humor, told him straight-faced, "Absolutely I think I can get them behind you guys, *if* you agree to name it Rob Huizenga Stadium."

There was complete silence on the other end of the phone. I wonder if they ever figured out that Merv Griffin happened to be a patient who happened to know I was the doctor for the Raiders.

Another reason Al Davis was beside himself was that this team had potential, and he knew his trade for Schroeder had done nothing but hurt the team's chances. He had traded an All-Star lineman who could have given his quarterback that extra second of protection to find the open receiver for a quarterback who was sitting on the bench. He had admitted to close associates that he had hurt the team. Although it wasn't Al's style to publicly admit to screwing up, he would regularly criticize himself over real and perceived mistakes, beat himself up as badly as he beat up his staff. Mistakes made him more paranoid. He had already run out a cadre of his top coaches, front-office businessmen, PR personnel and scouts, anyone who had the nerve to get meaningfully involved in decisions, or, God forbid, take charge. Al had to make every decision, down to the patterns we could order for the Raider T-shirts and the color of the garbage cans.

Al was pacing, muttering to himself, almost distraught, when George Anderson came in and told him one of our key players had pulled a muscle.

"What? He played the whole game."

"No, it happened just now," George responded. "When he was taking off his uniform. He was just stepping out of his jock and he pulled his quad."

"Goddammit!" Al exploded as he stormed off.

"What does he expect from me?" George shrugged when Al was safely out of earshot. "You'd think he'd lighten up a little bit when we win."

"He pulled a muscle taking off his jock strap?" the other assistant trainer asked incredulously as he came out of the back of the locker room.

"Yeah," said George, a gleam in his eye. "I can only remember one injury wackier than this. Back in the early sixties, we had a big defensive tackle named Rex Mirich, and right before the coaches' locker room pep talk, as the whole team goes to kneel down for the Lord's Prayer—Mirich pulls a hamstring! That was it for religion that year. Next game we just went out and spat on the ground and cursed. I think we won too."

21

This Life Is Shallow

I smacked my alarm clock. The noise continued. It was the phone.

"This is Officer White. Your patient Stacey Toran is dead."

I looked at the digital clock. It was 1:22 in the morning. August 6, 1989.

I pulled my car into the crowded parking lot of the Maranatha Community Church. The stifling hot midday sun had driven four or five camera crews under the large eaves of the church entry for shade. But now they were back out jockeying for position to film Al Davis, who had arrived just ahead of me in his black suit, sunglasses, and Super Bowl rings. He strode through the doorway without stopping, then shook hands with Coach Shanahan inside the entry. It was about as close as they had been since the new coach was hired a year ago. I followed unnoticed, and sat in one of the few remaining seats in the back of the spacious but plain church.

The service started promptly. We all rose and bowed our heads. It was a crowd of dark suits interspersed with the jeans, bright shirts, and tennis shoes of Stacey's teammates, who had just arrived on three team buses from Oxnard wearing comfortable clothes that would be suitable for the local watering hole. The last thing the players had packed for when they left their homes for the six-week Raider camp was anything formal, much less a funeral. I looked around and saw teammates from the past: Mike Davis, Henry Lawrence, Cle Montgomery, Jim Plunkett, Bob Buczkowski, Lester Hayes. I saw players who had been traded to other teams but had flown in for the funeral, like Chris Bahr, now kicking for San Diego.

There were three or four cheerleaders who had been on the original squads when Stacey had broken into the big leagues. Tom Flores had flown in from Seattle, where he was now the Seahawks' general manager. Marcus Allen and Bill Lewis, both holding out for more money, were there.

Greg Bell, one of Stacey's close friends at Notre Dame, now himself in a contract dispute with the Los Angeles Rams, began by talking about the times he had spent with Stacey. How he regarded him as family. Tears poured down his cheeks. His football peers shifted uncomfortably in the stark wooden pews. Then Coach Shanahan followed with a message that was both inspirational and comforting. He acknowledged that what had happened wasn't fair, that we all felt terrible. But he told us it was okay to go back and play football, okay to continue to do what we did best, that if we died we would want that, and certainly, he assured us, that's what Stacey would have wanted.

The minister, who knew Stacey and his fiancée well, as they were regular members, was next, and he was not at all concerned with our comfort. He lit into the three or four hundred moneyed mourners, cutting past the superficial trappings of grief.

"This life is shallow. It's fleeting. Eternal life comes when you give your soul to Jesus. You people out there think that what you're doing means something, but you have nothing if you haven't found the Lord. Maybe this death was a message to get you to realize that this is your one chance to be saved. Stacey's okay. He has the Lord. But if any of you don't know the Lord, you're not okay, you're in trouble."

I was taken aback. Everyone was fidgeting and sneaking peaks at Al Davis, trying without being too obvious to see what his reaction was to that fire-and-brimstone, you-need-the-Lord sermon. He was stoic as usual. Nothing was going to get to that guy, not even a Higher Power, unless it came out of the heavens with a fist and grabbed him by the neck.

Several sobbing eulogies by family and friends followed before the audience got a reprieve with a soothing ballad backed by guitar. Through it all I couldn't help staring at a three-foot blowup of Stacey Toran's face with a wreath of flowers at the bottom.

He hadn't looked that way when he was found four nights ago. The front of his face had been nearly rubbed off, his skull cracked to pieces, when he was thrown thirty feet from his car onto the concrete street. Stacey had been an unbelievable specimen of a man. I got to know him the very first day he came to camp in 1984. He was a high draft pick and came into the Santa Rosa camp and just started busting his butt for the defensive coaches. They were really working him out. He was running as hard as he could. He finally had to leave practice at the very end because he was cramping up like a hot-wired frog in a lab experiment. He collapsed in the locker room and needed an IV. He didn't flinch when the needle pierced the skin. He never complained, never asked if maybe he should take a day off; he was right back out there the next day. He always worked harder than the next guy, a no-trouble, all-work kind of guy. He was on the quiet side but could hang with the jokes and clowning around. He didn't have enemies. About the only confrontational thing he had ever done was his relatively protracted contract holdout battle with Al Davis last summer.

According to the autopsy, he didn't feel any pain. He was probably out before he hit the pavement—there were no scrapes on his palms or forearms, indicating that he hadn't reflexively tried to protect himself. He had been drinking a lot, maybe more than twelve shots of hard liquor in the hours before his death.

Large, very muscular males tend to have lower blood alcohol levels than their fatter American counterparts, since alcohol is evenly distributed through muscles and blood but is excluded from fatty areas. Thus a 200-pound all-muscle athlete like Stacey might be able to drink almost twice as much as a chubby 200-pounder with 50 percent body fat and have the same blood alcohol level. But Stacey's blood alcohol level was in the severely disabled range. He failed to put on his seat belt, then failed to negotiate a curve less than a block from his home.

A very subdued group of mourners filed from the church to an adjacent function room where Al had paid for a large buffet catered by Aunt Kizzi's Soul Food. We grouped into small circles and commiserated. It was very comforting. We were family. We'd come back to rally around a fallen brother.

It seemed like only moments ago that he had been with the rest of the players and the coaches and trainers as Coach Shanahan individually introduced us to the three or four thousand fans on a high school field in Oxnard for Family Day that last Saturday. Family Day, when the natives from Oxnard come to meet the team, is a jovial Raider tradition. The team ran some demonstration plays, and then the fans came down on the field for pictures and autographs. At two o'clock that afternoon, everybody was off until early Monday morning. Stacey had driven back into L.A. and met with some friends at a Marina Del Rey restaurant. He never made it home.

The drinking was totally out of character. Nobody on the team could figure it out. We all knew who were the carousers and party guys on the team. He wasn't one of them. This was a churchgoing, in-control, moderation-at-most type of guy. Maybe that's why it seemed so unfair, so arbitrary, and hit so close to home. If he had a lapse, then it could happen to any one of us.

The newspapers drew parallels to John Matuszak. Matuszak was a Raider who had also died young, earlier in 1989, presumably due to drugs. But there any similarity ended. From all I had heard, Tooz had really lived to be over a hundred if you calculated it in party years. Matuszak had retired in 1982 just before I came on as the Raiders' doctor. Although he would occasionally turn up in the locker room, he was not one of Al Davis's "favorite son" veterans, the ones who would always get free invitations to go on the away trips, the ones who hung around a lot. I never did get introduced to him.

I did, however, hear of his pitiful but all too routine emergency room stops. Under the guise of back pain, he would come in demanding narcotics. My friends in the emergency rooms around town would sift word back that he was hooked on painkillers, but by then he had already prematurely stormed out of every rehab joint in town. He came out with his book *Cruisin' with the Tooz* in 1987 claiming he had gone straight, but the continuing stories the ER doctors told contradicted the book's happy ending.

He even got banned from the Raiders facility, banned from hanging around with the team that usually took in even the worst problem cases. In the spring of 1989, just a few months before his death, he was clowning around in front of a nearly jammed training room of players and coaches when a brain circuit snapped. Someone mentioned that the plan was to trade stalwart Todd Christensen and promote youngster Mike Dial for first-string tight end. Tooz flipped out. He madly rushed the tight end coach, Terry Robiskie, who was five or six inches shorter and seventy or eighty pounds lighter. He grabbed him by the throat, slammed him against the wall, and demanded to know how this could be true. The stunned coach, who had nothing to do with the decision, turned and tried to fend off the Tooz with a crutch that was leaning against a training wall behind the Jacuzzi. Tooz took a couple of fierce crutch hits to his chest and was finally restrained by five or six teammates. He was banned for life, and the badly bent metal crutch was bronzed and mounted by George Anderson. George's simple inscription below it read "Biskie's Tooz pick."

Matuszak had been in countless senseless scrapes with the law, involving guns, fights, and auto accidents. He usually insisted they were someone else's fault, but this time he took sole blame for the locker room fight, and begged to come back. But he had crossed the line once too often, and this time too close to the Raider heartland.

Matuszak, thirty-eight, finally stepped over the line of life on June 17, 1989. Cocaine and Darvocet had deadened his body, now defenseless against an enlarged heart and pneumonia. Al Davis and a handful of Raiders attended his burial in Oakcreek, Wisconsin. But bitterness surfaced when his parents, Marv and Audrey Matuszak, enraged to find out his doctor had renewed prescriptions for addicting pain medicines three times in the week before his death, were quoted in the *L.A. Times* attacking the "scoundrels in the medical profession who recklessly dispense prescription drugs." However, no charges were filed against Matuszak's doctor.

It must have been devastating for his parents. Not only losing a son, but also seeing the dark side of his life partially negate his football and show business accomplishments and dim the memory of his sensitive and kind side, his endless volunteer hours with sick kids.

The team dedicated the 1989 season to Stacey. Stacey's number 30 was Magic Markered on every loose piece of padding, and his picture stayed up in the locker room.

As I was leaving the funeral buffet, I ran into Lester Hayes. Lester had been dangled out in purgatory during the 1988 season. The feeling among the coaches was that he just didn't have it anymore, but Al Davis put him on injured reserve and—as he was known to do for veterans he felt a special debt to, like Cliff Branch, Dave Dalby, and Gene Upshaw—paid Lester an extra year's salary, although under ordinary circumstances a player would have been cut, left to finagle his last NFL dollars via workers' comp.

Lester had a major feud with his defensive backfield coach Willie Brown, who, in Lester's opinion, had lobbied to end his career prematurely. Turned out Willie Brown and Lester Hayes were tied with thirty-nine career interceptions. It was Lester's feeling that Willie would do anything to retain a portion of that record. To me, that was more than a little improbable. Willie's job depended on how many pics his guys got. An old record can't pay the mortgage.

But in that nonplaying frustration, tempers had flared and Lester had gotten into a vicious row with George Anderson. Maybe George called Lester a nasty name, maybe Lester threatened George. As a result, though, Lester was banned from the locker room, which was like telling him never to come home again. In 1989 he wasn't even asked to camp. He was out.

"Good seeing you, Lester."

"Likewise, good doctor," replied Lester.

"How are things going for you out in Houston?" I asked.

"I'm big in real estate, I'm big in oil and gas," Lester responded with his usual brashness. "I own that town, doc."

"I hear you're writing a 'tell-all' book," I said with a smile.

"Do tell, doc. It'll all be there in black and white on the printed page. So be it. I'm writing it every day. It's going to be the best thing since *Star Wars*."

He had the Raider staffers a little nervous. He'd been known to poke an opponent's eye during his playing days, and there was no reason to believe he'd lighten up now. People were holding their breath, half in humor and half in legitimate fear, wondering what was going to come out. Drugs, sex, and maybe some football. Given a street-smart alley cat like Lester, who had a backstreet poetic touch coupled with a take-no-prisoners literary objective, you assumed the book was going to be a barn-burner.

Later I mentioned to George Anderson that Lester's book sounded like a best-seller.

"What's the big deal?" George shrugged. "Hell, I could write a book about the old Raider team and sell a million copies too. It's just that there would be forty-five divorces and one murder. Mine."

I laughed. I'd heard that joke before. It probably had some truth to it, though. When Kenny Stabler came out with his book *Snake*, five divorces had followed. When he detailed the party days with his roommates he apparently was not concerned that many were already engaged or married to their current spouses.

In a sad postscript to a sad day, even Al Davis got dumped on. He picked up the bills for the funeral, the catered buffet for hundreds of guests afterward, and expenses for flying Stacey's body back to Indianapolis. The minister explicitly thanked Aunt Kizzi's at the end of the service. No one ever bothered to say thanks to Davis.

Stacey's death kept haunting us. We lost every exhibition game. We played hard, but something was missing. Maybe our killer instinct was gone. Or maybe it was just on holiday till the real season opener.

Several weeks into the exhibition season I got a jolting letter from the NFL office signed by Tennant, saying one of our starting players was suspended because of steroids detected in the urine drug tests taken in the beginning of the year.

There had been beginning-of-the-year testing for steroids in 1987 and 1988, but no penalties had been assessed. One reason was that although the anabolic steroid tests were technically quite accurate, there were few labs capable of doing these tests and returning the results in a timely manner. UCLA had one such lab and had done the 1984 Olympic testing, but Forrest Tennant and the NFL had political differences with that lab and chose to go elsewhere. In 1987 and 1988, the guys positive for steroids received a form letter in midseason declaring that they'd tested positive, that anabolic steroids were bad for their health and were illegal, and please don't do that. It did alert players that a legitimate, accurate test was available, so when the punitive phase began this year, only the very stupid or very unlucky got caught. The anabolic steroid guys were going underground.

Our player wasn't caught with one of the usual anabolic steroids, which are nonhuman artificial testosterone substances, easily detected in a urine test. He was caught with an abnormal ratio of testosterone (the good old "every male has it" hormone) to one of its breakdown products, epi-testosterone. There is a certain normal ratio of active testosterone to its breakdown product, and if you try to inject any additional testosterone you alter this delicate ratio. Obviously you can't suspend somebody for having testosterone in his bloodstream, but after much research, most of the drug test experts were very comfortable suspending athletes with high ratios of testosterone to epi-testosterone. Anything over a six-to-one ratio was a tip-off. Lots of players were using testosterone to get around the drug test system even though testosterone wasn't nearly as powerful as anabolic steroids in terms of muscle-building and had many more side effects. A standard muscle-building dose of it was probably more dangerous than other forms of anabolic steroids.

I'll admit I assumed our player was guilty, but something funny happened on the way to the hanging. After sitting down and talking to him for hours and listening to the persistent denials that he had ever taken testosterone or any anabolic steroids, after looking over his medical history, which revealed a medical condition that could easily affect the production of testosterone, after seeing his oversized family and learning of his huge size already in grade school, I began thinking maybe he was telling the truth. An extensive physical exam and esoteric blood tests seemed to bear out parts of his story, and I began to wonder if he was one of the rare individuals born with an abnormal way of breaking down his testosterone, giving him an abnormal ratio of testosterone to its breakdown product. I consulted with several other male-hormone experts in Los Angeles, and when they too expressed misgivings about the original urine test results, I fired off a letter to Forrest Tennant and Commissioner Rozelle requesting that the player's suspension be overturned. I also asked for the player's steroid and urine test results from as far back as 1988 as well as a direct comparison of his current urine with the urine said to be abnormal at the beginning of the year. I wanted to know if the player was telling the truth. Comparing the past urines with the current and following up his blood tests would clearly show whether he was legit, or was lying and had indeed been taking testosterone. Despite repeated requests, the NFL never sent me any of these crucial results. It did, however, reverse the player's suspension.

Of course, Al Davis loved this. I was hanging around with the big shots in the NFL's drug program and could spin out a fancy letter to the powers-that-be saying you can't suspend this player because you haven't done your homework. I was able to do it only because I really believed this player, but I knew Al just liked the results. Suddenly I suspected that I now had security clearance to go one step deeper into the Raider intelligence "ahgahnization." I took the opportunity to set up my third scheduled meeting in my six years as club physician with Al Davis in his office, ostensibly to talk about the steroid case.

After going over the case, I snuck in a second issue: my long-standing opinion that we were shooting ourselves in the foot every time we traveled to the East for an early-morning game. I pulled out a study I'd just completed that showed West Coast teams win fewer games in the East than would be predicted. I also showed him the huge drop-off in winning percentage when the San Francisco 49ers and the Los Angeles Rams had to fly across three time zones to play the Atlanta Falcons, and how it appeared other West Coast teams flying to the East also suffered. I was just starting to outline how we could combat this, how we could rearrange our practice and our travel times to gain an advantage no other team had, when he put up his hand and stopped me.

"I don't want to hear any more," he said in his Brooklyn/Boston twang. "I don't really fully understand it, but, you know, with all these statistics, I really don't think you've taken the great players into account."

And that was that. I'd been working on this project on and off for five or six years, the whole purpose being to try to give the Raiders an edge. I had factored in every variable I could, trying to get control groups that were statistically sound. Intuitively it made sense to me. We tended to practice from two to five in the afternoon, and if we suddenly relocated to the East Coast, it meant we'd be getting up for breakfast at about five in the morning West Coast time and playing that game at about ten in the morning our time. It didn't take many of these games for me to see that our players were dozing off on the bus rides before these games, and, more important, often playing as if they were still groggy during the first minutes of the game.

But that was just my impression. I wanted to prove it using a large number of games and a large number of teams. Rick Jehue, a student trainer in search of a thesis paper, was my victim. I got him to spend hundreds of hours entering the results of every game over the previous ten years into a statistical computer program. We then compared a team's performance when it flew to games within the same time zone to its performance when it flew for an away game three time zones away on the East Coast. The numbers seemed to support my impression. Just as interesting, we found one reason why the Raiders and all the other West Coast teams did so well in the Monday-night games. Remember, a Monday-night game is six to nine o'clock for the West Coast player, but nine o'clock to midnight or later for the East Coast player. It turns out the body isn't so proficient at catching touchdown passes when its inner clock says it should be in bed. This was data that could give us an advantage over all our football rivals. But it wasn't important to Davis. I submitted it the next day for publication in *Medicine and Science in Sports and Exercise*.

A little demoralized now, I continued with ideas I had about changing the pregame meals. Al didn't really agree to them, then again, he didn't say I couldn't make the changes. He said he'd think about them.

As I exited Mr. Davis's office, I couldn't help but notice stacks of newspaper articles neatly cut out with sections highlighted. There was a pile of New York papers, a pile of Los Angeles papers, and a pile from the San Francisco/Oakland area. You couldn't say something about Al and not have him find out about it. Later I found out Al had a library of news clippings, an entire room with black-bound three-inch-thick scrapbooks containing every word ever written about Al Davis.

With a pitiful record of nine wins and twenty-two losses, over a three-season stretch, now was a perfect time to make some bold moves. No one could claim that the players were eating steak and ice cream before games for good-luck reasons. Now was the time to move to pasta, potatoes, and plain bread, with no high-fat toppings, while the team was down. So I told our advance man to start giving our hotels a different menu. With the aid of a dietitian, we snuck in dishes prepared with far less fat and offered vegetarian pizza and a couple of Pritikin-like soups. We threw out the whole milk and added skim milk, we threw out the ice cream and substituted sherbet. I would stand by the food line and warn, "Unless you want to fade in the fourth quarter, don't take the steak, get the baked potato." The vets would give me incredible shit, but I'd pretty much given up on their diets. I was aiming my pitch at the young guys.

The football gods smiled on me, and we won the first couple of games after the food switch in mid-1988. So then I switched to the good-luck argument. "If you want to lose, be my guest, go back and eat the way you used to."

We played one of our last exhibition games in Oakland, as the home team. It was like stepping into a time tunnel. I'd heard all the old Oakland stories, but I honestly wasn't prepared for the experience. We showed up three hours before game time, as usual. The parking lots were overflowing, with entire barbecue setups seemingly next to every car or truck. When our bus finally came to a halt, it was rocked by about ten thousand cheering fans. It was ten times the attention we'd received at the Super Bowl.

By eleven-thirty the stadium was jammed. Standing room only. When we jogged out for pregame warm-ups just after twelve o'clock, we got an ovation such as I'd never heard. These fanatics, all wearing their Oakland Raiders T-shirts, were wildly cheering even practice field goals that happened to make it through the uprights.

When we ran out for the actual game, I got a chill. We didn't get an ovation, we got a thundering storm of heartfelt cheers. At that moment, I was certain that Al Davis would move the club back to Oakland when his deal with the L.A. Coliseum ended, or earlier if his lawyers could find a loophole. Crowds like this couldn't win a game for you, but there was no question they might inspire you to put a couple of extra points on the board. If, after the game, five thousand silver-and-black-painted fans shout encouragement and recite your key blocks and tackles through the chain-link fence as you walk to your car after the game, you'll want to excel that much more.

The deal with Irwindale had collapsed, and since Los Angeles didn't appear interested in kicking in the money for the all-important revenue-generating luxury boxes, it was back to Oakland to come up with a deal they should have done eight or nine years earlier. If they couldn't, Sacramento, another eager suitor, was right behind.

Moving back to Oakland not only seemed the right thing for the Raiders, but was going to work out the best for me personally. I could see that despite my putting pressure on Al Davis's close confidant Dr. Albo (Al's neighbor who had successfully resuscitated Carol Davis, an Oakland general surgeon and former Oakland A's and Golden State Warriors doctor who traveled to each of our games), the trainers, and the general manager whom I met with three separate times about how best to retire Rosenfeld, Rosenfeld's position with the team was still quite secure. Al Davis showed every indication of wanting to keep Rosenfeld indefinitely. He went out to dinner with him regularly. I had never been to dinner with him. He was openly distrustful of Rosenfeld's younger partners, who I felt should be awarded the job. He called Rosenfeld regularly, me irregularly, call frequency being the barometer of where you ranked on the close-to-Al scale. Rosenfeld lived for the Raider job. I suspected he would do whatever it took to keep Al Davis happy.

I saw a Raider move to Oakland as a perfect way to get a legitimate orthopedic doctor for the players in Oakland. Any move on my part was out of the question, since I now had a sixteen-hour-a-day practice in Los Angeles and no desire to move. But I assumed I could be an emeritus professor and hook up with the team charter for certain games, which would be the best of both worlds. The team would have great medical care, and I'd be in a position to chum around with the Raider family till it was my turn to get old and senile. But sometimes I wasn't sure I could hang on long enough for the Raiders to move to Oakland, and for my stint as president of the NFL Physicians Society to end.

An absurd event in the Kansas City locker room was a case in point. We had just lost a hard-fought battle to the Kansas City Chiefs, evening our 1989 season to 1–1. Our big offensive tackle Steve Wright trudged into the training room with blood dripping from his mouth.

"What happened?" I asked.

"One of those cheap motherf——ers caught me in the mouth with an uppercut and jammed my mouth guard up, which ripped my upper gum," he said with a dark scowl.

"All right, c'mon, get down on the table here."

I looked inside and saw that the entire gum line above his top front teeth had been sheared open. There was a big flap of gum just hanging. I began rinsing out his mouth and setting up the suture tray with absorbable catgut suture. I'd had a ton of experience suturing oral wounds from fights, auto accidents, and dog bites during my moonlighting years. But I'd never seen anything quite like this. Then in came Rosenfeld. Apparently there were no other injuries and he had time on his hands. He immediately started giving me orders on how to close the flap. When he put on a pair of sterile gloves and started grabbing away my suture material, I stood up and walked away. It was ludicrous. He had such a nasty tremor that I wasn't sure where the needle was going to come down—on Wright's nose, his teeth, or anywhere. As calmly as I could, I went out and persuaded a player in the locker room to develop some knee complaints. I then walked back into the training room and told Rosenfeld he was desperately needed outside. I removed the sutures Rosenfeld had placed, which had pulled the gash over to the left, and unbeknownst to Wright, whose mouth had been well numbed, started the process all over again.

We lost the next two games, for a grim 1–3 record. The next day, Coach Shanahan was gone. No departing talk, no handshakes. Just one fewer brand-new BMW 735i in the parking lot.

But the coaching change somehow invigorated the team. Newly appointed head coach Art Shell was a Raider guy from way back, and we had the feeling Al was going to stick with him for a while. Art would not suffer the constant uncertainty Shanahan faced with an office seeded with Al Davis moles, some of whom were feeding

Al minute-by-minute intelligence. Shanahan, only thirty-five when he arrived to try to turn the club's fortunes around, had set down more rules than Flores had. Probably one of his biggest mistakes had been taking players with a free-spirit tradition and trying to force them to sit in the same assigned seats for every meeting, to not sit on their helmets during practice, and to forsake other time-honored Raider Bill of Rights items. Then again, rumor had it that *Al* wanted tighter discipline and had made Shanahan front for the unpopular changes.

Shanahan worked hard and treated everyone fairly. No one questioned his smarts. But in changing the offense, he was somewhat handicapped from the start. Part of his deal with Al was that he couldn't change the whole complicated Raider play-calling number system. Why? Because Al didn't want to have to learn a whole new system of plays. So Shanahan had to rechart his system, resulting in a mishmash perhaps harder for the players to remember. But the biggest handcuffing was that Al Davis let him pick only three assistant coaches. A head coach needs a cooperative staff all working in one direction. And we were working in two or three directions. Some of the holdover Raider coaches rallied solidly behind Shanahan, but others got behind him to backstab.

For whatever reason, with Art Shell at the helm we started winning games. The pranks began to sprout like spring flowers. When you ordered room service you'd charge it to Bo's room and see what he did. Howie complained to someone grabbing his shirt collar that he was wrinkling it, and an iron and ironing board mysteriously appeared in his hotel room that night. Before the game with the division-leading Philadelphia Eagles, someone found out that our locker room was immediately adjacent to the locker room of the Eagles' cheerleaders. There was a near brawl as players jockeyed for position on the floor, trying to see under the door. It was quite a sight, just a few minutes before we went out for warm-ups—a pack of overgrown peeping toms in a scene out of *Porky's II*.

We played a damn good game against the top-rated Eagles but lost a heartbreaker when our field goal kicker missed two short chip shots. He hadn't been involved in the under-the-door adventure, and so there was no convincing evidence that women were bad for the legs.

We continued our newfound winning ways over the next several weeks, with Bo Jackson returning to Superman form and Steve Beuerlein holding his own as quarterback. The Raiders were definitely a hit against the Redskins, in our eighth game of the season, running up a two-touchdown lead against the perennial East Coast power. But the biggest hit came in the third quarter when an errant Mark Ripken pass was intercepted by outside linebacker Jerry Robinson. He pulled the ball out of the air and darted up the sideline toward Redskin territory. Suddenly our ex-teammate from 1988, the guy we'd traded away for Schroeder, 300-pound tackle Jim Lachey, creamed him from the left. The ball popped away as Jerry slumped to the ground. He remained limp for several agonizing seconds as we sprinted onto the field. By the time we arrived, he was up, moving everything, and had no complaints, just one persistent question.

"Did I fumble the ball?"

"Yes, Jerry, you fumbled it."

Five seconds later, "Did I fumble the ball, doc?"

"Yes, Jerry."

"Where am I?"

"You're at a football game."

"Did I fumble the ball?"

He was a little woozy, so we packed him in the cart and headed up toward the locker room for a better neurologic exam. It was hard to get through the exam, because he kept asking if he'd fumbled the ball. No matter how many times you gave the answer he couldn't remember it ten seconds later.

"What was the headline in this morning's newspaper?" I asked.

"The San Francisco earthquake."

"Right. Subtract seven from a hundred."

"Ninety-three."

"Seven from ninety-three."

"Eighty-six. Did I fumble the ball?"

"Who's president?"

"George Bush."

"Vice-president?"

"Quayle."

"Jerry, are you all right?"

One of the security guards had brought in his wife, who ran to him and wrapped her arms around him and gave him a reassuring hug.

"Honey, did I fumble the ball?"

* * *

"How are you feeling today, Jerry?" I asked. He stood next to me in street clothes as the opening kickoff against the Cincinnati Bengals, our next opponent, went up in the air. "Do you remember the play yet?"

"Well, I remember catching the ball, and putting a move on the first guy, y'know, and seeing the end zone in front of me, but geez, I have no idea what happened next," he said, shaking his head. "I didn't get a license plate number or anything."

Jerry had tried to go back out and run in the midweek defensive practice, but had gotten an instant headache with ringing in his ears. On top of that, he could barely remember anything from the defensive meetings. Things went blurry for him sometimes and he generally felt as if he were walking in a fog. A head magnetic resonance imaging scan obtained immediately after the game had been normal, and although he had had some postgame nausea and headache, no other worrisome signs had developed. But his postconcussive syndrome of altered memory and headaches was going to keep him out indefinitely.

Was there any risk of permanent brain damage? This was Jerry's second concussion. And what about several of our hari-kari special team players and quarterbacks who had been KO'd three or four times? What about former stars like Roger Staubach, who'd been knocked cold more than a dozen times? Many well-known professional boxers who'd rarely if ever been knocked out had nightmarish brain decay syndromes. From Sugar Ray Robinson's Alzheimer's-like dementia, to Muhammad Ali's Parkinson's, to Jake LaMotta's personality changes and loss of control, to Thomas Hearn's cerebellar slurring, multiple head hits can clearly ravage the brain. An additional sobering fact is that after the fighter retires, the neurologic deterioration continues unabated for several years. And amateur boxers, who have never fought without headgear, have been documented to risk trauma-induced intellectual decline.

Does the air-cushion-lined football helmet better protect the brain? Or do routine helmet hits up and down the line of scrimmage result in less brain trauma than a well-thrown boxer's punch? From what I could see, none of the returning Raider veterans had any of the aforementioned brain catastrophes. But were affected players too embarrassed to come back, or was damage more subtle? These were questions only a league-wide study could adequately address.

I marched into the head coach's office and explained to him a little bit about what Jerry was going through. Shell looked me straight in the eye and said, "Tell Jerry not to worry, I understand perfectly. I was a player. I'm not going to let him put one foot on the practice field until he's one hundred percent."

Later, I found out that Rosenfeld had told Davis there was no reason Jerry shouldn't be able to play, since the MRI was normal. The next day, Jerry came to me with a bottle of cortisone pills and said, "Rosenfeld told me to take these four times a day. Is that okay with you?"

It was such a time-honored treatment for other brain problems that I instantly had a few self-doubts, thinking, "Gee, did I miss something?"

High doses of cortisone are life-saving, especially when there's swelling around brain cancer, and extremely high doses are used when a spine injury causes paralysis. But in my fifteen years in medicine, I'd never heard of it for treating concussions. I took the pills away and headed down to the library. I learned this treatment had been used for postconcussive syndrome in the World War II era before falling out of favor decades ago. I called several local neurologists just to make sure. I was getting sick of World War II medicine, like giving a player plain penicillin for an infected skin cut, or for gonorrhea. Rosenfeld's prescription practices ignored the last twenty years of modern pharmacy.

"Doc, why do you even get concussions with these newfangled air-pressured helmets?" Jerry asked me on the sideline.

"Well, these more recent helmets, of course, are better than the old leather ones. The air cushion inside the helmet absorbs a lot more of the force of a blow to the head. But it seems like the better the helmet gets, the more the head is used as a weapon. The brain is suspended in a protective layer of fluid just inside the skull, so when the skull is hit suddenly, the brain matter slaps up against the inside of the skull and can be bruised. When a section of the brain gets banged like that, the result is often a brief loss of consciousness."

Just then, on Cincinnati's second series of plays, Boomer Esiason dropped back to pass and took a chest shot from one of our onrushing linemen.

Several minutes later, I got a message from the red phone to report to our locker room. A Cincinnati player needed help. It turned out the Bengals, in a money-saving maneuver, were just flying the orthopedic surgeon to away games, leaving them without an internist. And now their star quarterback was in the locker room coughing up blood and couldn't catch his breath.

Although the initial inspiration and expiration chest X-rays appeared perfectly normal, it didn't take a genius to come up with a list of potential lurking lung disasters. I recommended to their orthopedic surgeon that Boomer not play, and that if any deterioration or evidence of a partially collapsed lung was found, he be transported to Cedars-Sinai Medical Center. Fortunately, he stopped coughing up blood and stabilized sufficiently to allow the Cincinnati doctor to have him flown back on the team charter for the pulmonary studies he needed. So presumably he had just contused his lung, bounced it around a bit, and sprung open a tiny bronchial blood vessel.

The whole experience ordinarily would have been no big deal, but the following week we were sitting around our hotel in San Diego, watching the NFL pre-game shows while waiting for our night game. On came Boomer Esiason, who, when asked about his injury the previous week, said with what seemed to be a straight face that it was the result of a conspiracy between Al Davis and the Raider team doctor. He had been in the locker room getting X-rays, he told the TV commentator, and conveniently the Raider team doctor appeared to prescribe three quarters of rest. Boomer claimed if it had been up to him he would have stayed in with just one good lung. "I could imagine Al Davis giving the ole call downstairs, saying 'Ah, ya better not let him play.' "

"God, he's got a wacky sense of humor," laughed H. Rod Martin, who had spent time with Boomer in Maryland.

But other Raider officials, such as Al LoCasale, burst a gasket.

"He can't say that on national TV!"

Well, he had, and although LoCasale called and demanded an apology, we never got one. I didn't need one. I knew it was a gag. I can tell when a player has fear in his eyes. In person Boomer was courteous and very thankful to me for my help.

The end to our 1989 play-off hopes came several weeks later when we battled our archrival, the Seattle Seahawks, in the dome of Raider doom. The score was close and we just had to hold them. We had to get Bo the ball. The defense was attacking when, in a freak AstroTurf injury, Howie Long's shoe somehow stuck to the turf as he charged through their offensive line. He tried to shake off the pain in the foot, a jabbing pain that often disappears a minute or so after you get kicked, but this pain wouldn't go. He limped off the field, and when his shoe was removed, it was very obvious he had a foot dislocation. Rosenfeld shot the area full of a numbing solution, then pulled and popped the foot joint back in place.

The game ended with us on the short side, and we wheeled Howie over to the Seattle dressing room for X-rays. There was a tiny X-ray defect in the metatarsal bone. It was a questionable call. Either it was a nondisplaced new fracture, where the bone hadn't separated yet, or it was an unimportant old injury that had already healed. The way you usually tell the difference is to push on the skin over the bone about where you saw the abnormality on the X-ray. If it hurts a lot it's probably a new fracture. If it doesn't hurt at all, it's probably okay, just a blood vessel line or an old healed injury.

Rosenfeld went back to Howie's foot and jabbed his finger near the area where the possible fracture was located. Howie didn't react in pain.

"It's old," Rosenfeld concluded, muttering, "There's no new fracture."

"But Bob," I said, "you just numbed his entire foot."

22

Drugs and Politics

The damn phone was ringing. I'd just slammed shut my hotel door. I inserted my card key and hurried back in. It was Forrest Tennant.

"Where are you calling from?" I asked. "I thought you had a speaking engagement outside the country."

"That's the official NFL line. Actually, I was in Kansas City yesterday, ready to catch my flight to Indianapolis for your doctor meeting, when Tagliabue's office called and instructed me not to fly."

"But we've had you scheduled for over a month."

"They claim there might be a reporter there."

"Whaaat? There's just our sixty or seventy doctors who all know each other from way back when." It was obvious the NFL was about to ax him.

"Listen, Rob," Forrest continued, "I want you to get my message out to the doctors. In the last four years the drug positives have essentially gone away, and despite what you read in the press, there's not been one player, not one lawyer, who's challenged the validity of any of my tests. I need your support."

I glanced at my watch. I was just five minutes away from beginning my reign as president of the NFL Physicians Society and presiding over a combined meeting with the Professional Football Athletic Trainers Society (PFATS). Already I was mired knee-deep in politics.

"Well, Forrest, what the hell happened with that TV crew from Washington?" He had received blistering criticism from an investigative crew from Washington, D.C., and then in follow-up a biting review in *Sports Illustrated* that had placed his job in jeopardy.

"That TV crew claimed they wanted to talk to me about treating cocaine addiction in underprivileged children, then the minute the camera gets rolling they pull out a phony handwritten sheet with the names of three white quarterbacks who they said had all tested positive for cocaine, insinuating that I'd covered it up and played favorites. That's bullshit, an absolute fabrication. Hey, none of those quarterbacks were even in the confidential strike one phase."

"What about the story claiming urines were sitting out open in your lab with names on them?"

"Those were tests we had screened that were positive and subsequently sent for confirmation at outside labs. Just remember, the accuracy of the results was never questioned."

"Why do you think they won't let you talk at our meeting?"

"Who knows? Maybe that TV crew was a plant, paid for by some of the players I've gone after. Maybe the Colombian drug cartel. At this level, anything's possible. I'm the fall guy. You know, the majority of the cocaine positives have been in black players. Blacks make up about sixty-five percent of the league's players, and the innuendo, which is absolutely ludicrous, is that white doctors somehow are giving special consideration to the whites. That's why this thing about the white quarterbacks was so preposterous. I think the league is under some heavy pressure to have a commensurate number of black physicians in the drug program as players in the league."

"You think so?" I asked.

It was pretty obvious that minority doctors were pitifully underrepresented in the National Football League. There was one Hispanic team doctor and one black team doctor. Then again, that was about the same percentage minority representation as in the coaching ranks and infinitely higher than in the owners' ranks. That was an all-white group.

"Rob," Forrest ended, "I'd really appreciate it if you could have your doctor group issue a strong statement supporting the current drug program. We've got to keep politics out of this thing."

Unfortunately, a drug czar's job is nine-tenths political. Controlling drug use is an adversarial intervention. The NFL Players Association was openly hostile, and the NFL owners gave lukewarm support at best, many clinging to the our-players-are-not-going-to-get-screwed-worse-than-yours mentality. One owner openly told Tennant, "You only have to worry about twenty-seven teams—we do things differently here!" Of course, it soon became clear this team had more of a problem than most other teams.

But now, after he'd worked his butt off getting the twenty-eight-team, 2,500-man drug test program up and running, the unsubstantiated press charges were taking a nasty PR toll on Forrest's operation and on the NFL.

"I'll see what I can do, Forrest."

By the time I made it downstairs to the ballroom, I was already five minutes late. Fortunately I'd been farsighted enough to spend some money from the treasury for a table of hors d'oeuvres and a tub of iced drinks. Nothing like a nice cold beer to keep the members occupied.

"My name is Dr. Robert Huizenga," I said from the podium, surveying the turnout. "I'd like to welcome everyone here, the doctors as well as the National Football League trainers. I'd like to introduce, to my right, Dr. Peter Scranton from Seattle, our secretary/treasurer, and Dr. Michael Dillingham, our vice-president/president-elect. And on my left, of course, Dean Kleinschmidt from New Orleans, the president of PFATS. I'd like to thank you all for coming.

"Let's get right to the first point on the agenda. The drug counselor's report.

"Forrest Tennant was unable to attend tonight, but I'd like to pass along the distillate of his thoughts. The marijuana and cocaine problems have been controlled. In 1986, seventeen percent of the four hundred or so college athletes in the February combine tested positive for cocaine or marijuana. In 1989 the number is essentially zero. Positive tests in the announced preseason drug test for NFL vets have shown a similar drop-off. Tennant says we've got two remaining problems: alcohol and anabolic steroids.

"Alcohol is the number-one drug problem in the league. It's probably the number-one cause of deaths and drug-related problems with the law. I've seen it kill one of my players, and there are a number of you sitting out in the audience who have seen the same sort of alcohol-related tragedies. On the other hand, there is probably no legal basis for penalizing an athlete who comes in with high alcohol levels, assuming he's not driving.

"The second unresolved question, of course, is anabolic steroids. I don't think it's a secret that the current court-imposed once-a-year announced test for steroids is a joke."

Michael Dillingham then led a charged discussion about joint doctor/trainer malpractice issues related to the whopping $100 million Kenny Easley lawsuit against the Seattle trainers and doctors. Easley, a star defensive back, claimed the trainers, without proper doctor supervision, had made available large doses of an over-the-counter medication—Advil—which was sitting out in an open bin in the training room, as he was recovering from a shoulder surgery. Easley claimed the medication had resulted in the death of both of his kidneys.

The Seattle doctors had stormed into last year's meeting fit to be tied, with quite a different version. Apparently Easley's kidney problems had been identified years earlier in preseason testing, but Easley had sworn them to secrecy so as not to affect his contract negotiations with the Seattle club. He allegedly saw a kidney specialist at that time and was monitored by that doctor. A short time after the shoulder surgery he was traded to Phoenix, where the brand-new Cardinal doctor saw Easley as his first official duty. Easley looked great and outran the treadmill test, but when the blood tests returned it was clear he now had deteriorated to the point where his kidneys could barely sustain life. The trade was nixed, the $100 million lawsuit was born, and another name was added to the undersupplied national kidney transplant registry.

Easley's lawyers argued their case every day in the Seattle sports pages while the Seahawk doctors paced in their offices, unable to respond before their depositions were taken. The case had an immediate effect on the Raiders. I got a broom and swept the whole row of neatly marked canisters of over-the-counter drugs right into the trash. Thousands of brightly colored pills lay at the bottom of a dark green trash bag. Advil, Nuprin, Motrin, aspirin. Gone. The same for vitamin C (possible diarrhea or kidney stones), multivitamins (stomach upset), antacids (high calcium levels), Quinamm (low platelet counts with worse-case-scenario brain bleeding). Gone too was Tylenol, which when taken in excess has toxic effects on the liver.

Understandably, several players later stormed in, incensed that even their amino-protein packs were history. Even those amino acids can cause dehydration if taken in excess.

"Hey, what can I say—go to the drugstore and buy the stuff yourself," George said, shrugging. "Send the bill to Kenny Easley."

The keynote speaker for the doctors-only last session was a malpractice lawyer, really a sad commentary on the state of pro sports doctoring. A handful of the team doctors were currently being sued, and word was that in several NFL cities, top consultants were refusing to see players, fearing that the honor of seeing a pro athlete wasn't worth the risk of being frivolously sued for malpractice.

The lawyer monotoned through his defensive game plan for team doctors. Number one: obtain maximum insurance. That was a joke. Most insurance companies allowed only $3 million per incident. When you had players worth tens or hundreds of millions, $3 million didn't amount to a hill of beans.

Number two: seek indemnification from the team. Another joke. The Raiders had demanded indemnification from *me*. They'd made me sign a statement saying I was not a Raider employee, just a consultant. If a player sued, it was my tail, not theirs.

Number three: enter into a written contract with the team setting forth duties. That one kind of shook me. Doctors don't usually sign contracts. They know what their job is. I had always thought my handshake deal with Al Davis was a manly thing. Could Davis, in 1983, already have been shrewd enough to know that the less legally binding stuff there was between doctor and owner, the easier it would be for him to distance himself from me if there was a malpractice liability?

Number four: reduce the risk of malpractice by sending a registered letter to players after injuries, surgeries, or any significant health event, stating the consequences of that injury. That wasn't a bad idea. But there was supposedly already a case where a letter had been sent and the player sued anyway, claiming he didn't know how to read. So the lawyer suggested that team doctors videotape a speech in training camp describing the exact risks of playing professional football, the importance of the player's disclosing all his injuries to the doctor, and the importance of following the doctor's instructions. And then, showing how desperate the whole situation had become, he suggested that doctors tape the players signing in on a sheet and scan the room with the camera to prove the players were present during the talk.

I knew the Raiders would not allow this sort of risk-of-playing-pro-ball talk. The official Raider philosophy since day one was not to tell the players anything.

The lawyer also warned us about the draft physicals, the yearly exams we did on the four hundred college All-Americans. He said the prospective player should sign statements explaining that the physical was strictly for the benefit of the teams and at the expense of the teams, and not for the benefit of the prospective player. Otherwise doctors might start getting sued for not detecting illnesses, especially since illnesses were easy to miss—none of these players were giving us any history or hints of any ailments, hints that in a normal medical practice provide the initial clues leading a doctor to suspect and go after a certain disease.

Record-keeping, as in all malpractice situations, was stressed as the key to protecting oneself. Everybody admitted that record-keeping sometimes fell by the wayside when you went down to camp and were swarmed by a hundred players, twenty coaches, and twenty administrators, plus wives and kids. That was a dangerous trap.

The last legal point, number five: standard of care. We needed to get together and establish standards of care for professional sports. These guidelines would be invaluable when doctors who had never seen a professional sports game, much less cared for elite athletes, testified at malpractice trials involving pro athletes and their doctors. There aren't many situations in the real world where a worker gets liters of fluid pumped in over a fifteen-minute period because of stomach flu, or numbed up with Xylocaine and returned to the job. Maybe sports doctors should be certified; then if the question of competence came up at a malpractice trial, at least the experts who testified would be qualified in big-time athletics as well as in medicine.

"Thanks for a tremendously useful talk," I said as I replaced him at the podium. It was more constructive than what I'd heard from other lawyers, namely, "Resign your post. Being a professional team doctor is legal hari-kari."

It was getting late, and we had to be up at seven the next morning to finish the draft physicals. We hammered out a statement on the drug program for Commissioner Tagliabue that basically said, "The NFL Physicians Society continues to support the testing of athletes for alcohol, steroids, and illegal drugs." It stopped far short of personally supporting Forrest Tennant, who, as the middleman between the NFL hierarchy and the lowly team doctor, had picked up more than his share of enemies.

We battled about the transfer of medical records. When a player gets traded, some players, like Easley, demand confidentiality regarding certain medical problems. And what do you do if a player on his own goes into a drug rehab center and demands those records be kept secret? What are the ethics of sending those chart notes to his new team? This hot potato was tossed back to the league's legal department.

Finally I said, "The last agenda item is a study I'd like to propose to the membership on the long-term side effects of anabolic steroids."

I anxiously looked around the room to gauge by the expressions what their response would be. The night before, during our annual academic medical symposium, I had talked about anabolic steroids in the nineties and the need for some knowledge about possible long-term consequences. But that had been a theoretical "what ought to be done" review of the literature. This was an in-the-trenches, are-you-with-me proposal. It was hard enough to get doctors from twenty-eight teams to agree on the yearly dues. When it came to medical issues, mistrust and suspicion reigned supreme. But I needed the team doctors and trainers. Without their cooperation, going through the records of past steroid users would be technically impossible.

The initial comments from the floor were disheartening. Were we opening up a malpractice nightmare? If long-term complications were positively identified, would ex-users be able to come back and sue their respective teams? That had certainly been on my mind. Another even more immediate possibility was that past steroid users would sue the doctors. I was worried that some of the doctors may have prescribed steroids. Rosenfeld certainly had. It would be reasonable to assume that at least a few would be worried about their own rear ends. And doctors who had never prescribed steroids but had sat idly by without warning users of possible long-term effects might also be liable. Another comment from the floor touched on the confidentiality issues.

"You're tied to the Raiders—how could other teams be sure that this information wouldn't be leaked or used in a type of public relations blackmail attempt?"

Finally, just as the legal ramifications were starting to sour everyone on the study, a doctor from the Washington Redskins, seated in the rear, stood up.

"I think we all heard yesterday the magnitude of the steroid problem from high school kids on up. I personally feel we ought to step to the plate and, if we can, take a swing at this thing. We've got new leadership in our society, we've got a new commissioner, and I think it's time for a fresh wind to sweep through this league and for us to step forward and do the right thing. I support the study."

That was all it took. The entire membership subsequently endorsed the study in principle. I could barely contain myself. It was nearing midnight, but I was wide awake. I was positive that if I could get this group to agree, the NFL management and the Players Association endorsements would be a piece of cake.

"Okay, that brings the meeting to an end. I'd just like to reiterate that about half the members have not paid their fifty-dollar dues." I smiled. "And in a new twist this year, all nonpaying members will be on a list read by Al Michaels during Monday Night Football, so please avoid that national embarrassment and pay up now."

I was into something big. Really big. The new commissioner had invited me down to Washington, D.C., for a day of talks about ridding the NFL of steroids. Forrest Tennant had unceremoniously resigned weeks earlier, and the league was starting an anabolic steroid program from scratch. There had been a flurry of proposals faxed back and forth, and it appeared the new commissioner was willing to take some legal chances and propose a policy with teeth.

Tagliabue strode into the hotel restaurant punctually at eight in the morning. I was there with David Black, a toxicology expert from Vanderbilt, who'd assayed the urine steroid results the previous year. Tagliabue was a slender, well-conditioned six-feet-six and wore pale horn-rimmed glasses. He was relaxed and friendly. It wasn't too long ago that he had been dunking basketballs as a star on the Georgetown team. Now he had to guard a multibillion-dollar industry.

We spoke briefly of the March 4, 1990, on-court cardiac arrest of Hank Gathers, the NCAA's basketball scoring leader from Loyola Marymount. Unfortunately, exhaustive preparticipation cardiac work-ups of all players was not the answer for such tragedies. You might identify the rare individual who's going to die during strenuous activity, but you'll identify others with heart problems who'll be erroneously advised to stop competitive sports. Worst of all, because no test is perfect, you'll "falsely" identify athletes as having heart problems—when in fact their hearts are perfectly normal.

A team doctor's best tactic to ward off sudden cardiac death is to concentrate on high-risk players, those with exercise-related chest pain or fainting, hypertension, hypercholesterolemia, family history of sudden death, diabetes, cigarette use, a significant heart murmur, or Marfan's syndrome (characterized by a long, thin Abe Lincoln face, long arms and fingers, hyperflexible joints and, occasionally, a weak aorta prone to rupture).

Our recommendation for an internist trained in aggressive CPR—including defibrillation—at the Pro Bowl, submitted at our meeting just weeks before, showed we were thinking ahead. Previously only an orthopedist, who typically hadn't treated cardiac problems since med school, was present.

I wasn't sure how long I'd have Tagliabue's ear, so after Dr. Black got in a brief word, I went into a staccato summary of my view of the anabolic steroid problem in the NFL. I used a trick I had learned as a medical student—to repeat the spiel over and over until it's nearly memorized, so that you're able to fire the material back out in an organized, descriptive fashion that makes you sound ten times more intelligent than you really are.

"The problem's huge, Mr. Commissioner."

He smiled sheepishly at this form of address, as if someone barely in his fifties who had been on the job for only a few months felt much more comfortable being called Paul.

"There's probably a million users nationwide, half of them high school kids. Possibly three million Americans have used anabolic steroids over the last thirty or so years. When Americans smoke tobacco or use alcohol or cocaine, they're making an informed choice. They've been told what they're doing to their bodies. But we can't say that for anabolic steroids. There is zero information on the long-term consequences. We do know they work to make an athlete stronger, heavier, and maybe more aggressive. The NFL has decided they give an athlete an unfair competitive advantage, and it has banned them. Well, if we want to keep these drugs out of the hands of our athletes, we can try to decrease their availability by supporting Federal laws, such as the ones going into effect this year, making them controlled substances and making it a crime for doctors to prescribe them. But such laws have been ineffective in curtailing marijuana or cocaine use.

"The other alternative is to decrease the demand for the drugs. We've tried to do that with the beginning-of-the-year urine test for steroids, but that just encouraged players to go off for four to six weeks before the beginning of the season, enough time for the drugs to get out of the system. If we want to get anywhere with testing, we're going to have to test literally every month all year long, or, a cheaper alternative that might still keep the players honest, test a random sample of players every couple of weeks. This will work for the National Football League, which can afford the couple hundred dollars per test to go after the users, but if the NFL wants to be a leader it should do more. Testing can't help the other nine hundred and ninety-nine thousand-plus users in this country. Their only hope is education. Right now, education is laughable. You tell players that steroids work to make you bigger, stronger and maybe faster like Ben Johnson, but that we're not really sure of any permanent side effects. Hell, what would you do if you were a player? One study in Oregon actually showed that with the information now available on steroids, education actually increases use.

"But—and here, really, I think is the future—if accurate studies are done, indicating that anabolic steroids cause muscle and joint symptoms, that they actually make your athletic career shorter, like the circumstantial evidence we now have, if we can show steroids actually decrease the length of a life, increase heart disease and certain types of cancer, that will make a huge difference. Athletes would back off if such information was available. We have all the information we need right under our noses. If we study retired football players, and compare players who've used anabolic steroids with nonuser teammates who've played at the same position in the same number of games for the same number of years, if we compare their injury records, their blood tests, their heart tests, ten, twenty, thirty years down the line, we'll have the answer.

"I've talked with the other team doctors. They stand ready to cooperate. I've talked to endocrinology and statistical experts around the country. The study is doable. It would only cost about three hundred thousand dollars to complete. That's about twenty seconds of commercial time during a Super Bowl."

Tagliabue sipped his coffee.

"Very interesting," he said in a noncommittal tone.

He was being cautious. It was probably the last thing he wanted to get painted into a corner on. It was a real hot potato for the NFL. What if you showed that steroids were terrible and then proved that NFL employees had been suggesting athletes take them and NFL doctors had been writing the scripts?

From the restaurant we walked to the prestigious Covington and Burlington law offices just blocks from the White House lawn. I still have no idea how large that place is. It seemed like floor after floor, with a maze of long hallways with paintings on the walls and Persian runners down the middle of the hardwood floors. In a corner room with a view of several of the capital's historic landmarks, I was introduced to Jeff Pash, a lawyer who was Tagliabue's right-hand man and would be knocking out the legal mumbo-jumbo for this trend-setting random drug test program, a program above and beyond anything a professional sport had ever contemplated doing.

Tagliabue left, and Black and I battled Pash and several NFL lawyers over the pros and cons of who to test and when, what to test for, how to send it off, and lastly what lab with what credentials should test it. There were pitfalls at each step. We could test everybody. The money was there, but it was an organizational nightmare. Testing fifty guys with league security people watching as the urine left the body and getting all the proper seals and signatures so that the ownership of the urine would stand up in court could easily take five or more minutes per player. Multiply that times forty-five players and you're essentially disrupting a whole day's practice. The best compromise was testing a handful of players every couple of weeks.

We tossed around a couple of theoretical models, my favorite being to test about a sixth of the players every three weeks, which would statistically test every player an average of twice during the year, some as many as five or six times and only a rare few none. Testing a sixth or a seventh of the team would keep the testing manageable and would prevent disruption of practice, keeping coaching and front office complaints to a minimum. Another thorny issue was what lab to run the tests in. My opinion was that steroid drug tests should be run only at steroid testing labs certified by the International Olympic Committee. This would blunt one of the big criticisms leveled by the NFL Players Association and the press, against running tests in unapproved labs. But it turned out that only two labs in the country—UCLA and Indianapolis—were IOC-approved: politics plus hefty "certification" fees were effectively limiting competition. David Black claimed that his Vanderbilt lab was effectively disqualified from receiving IOC certification in this fashion.

I also pushed my education angle and got the NFL lawyers to include a special section in the policy stating that the NFL would fully cooperate with all appropriate research endeavors. I was pleasantly surprised when they agreed it was a good idea, that research needed to be done and that the NFL would do its share to clean up sports. My study was two-thirds of the way there.

The afternoon session proved to be a crash course in big-league law. In walked Gene Upshaw and his two lead National Football League Players Association lawyers, followed by Commissioner Tagliabue and a handful of his top legal aides. They were joined by Bill

Fralic, a star lineman from the Atlanta Falcons, who had admitted taking anabolic steroids earlier in his career and was now very vocal against them. Tagliabue and Upshaw seemed friendly, but the two sets of lawyers traded thinly veiled insults and snide remarks from the outset. And when we finished introducing ourselves, they really got ugly. There was no love lost here whatsoever. My read of the situation was that there were some deeply scarred egos. The NFL Players Association lawyers had gotten their asses kicked during the ill-conceived 1982 and 1987 strikes. But they had come back with a devious plan. They had disbanded and decertified their union so that they could attack in court with the A-bomb—antitrust. That strategy had the NFL lawyers on the defensive, which in turn had the NFL Players Association lawyers nervous as hell. They'd lost the last championship—in fact, the last several. They weren't going to lose three in a row.

The game plans seemed as follows. Tagliabue wanted Upshaw and the players to hear firsthand about his plans for random drug testing. He didn't want the players bringing the issue to court, where they could delay an effective antisteroid program for years. And for PR pressure purposes, the NFL brought along Fralic, who had been quoted in the paper saying that the NFL should test every player every day to make sure nobody was on steroids.

Upshaw and his lawyers, of course, wanted to be at this meeting. They wanted to hear what was going on, to interact with the new commissioner. They wanted to have a say. But they smelled a trap. They didn't want this meeting to be used as proof in a court of law that their union was still active. And so for what seemed like the first hour, the two sides of lawyers fought a bitter back-and-forth battle, throwing out a full complement of $400-an-hour legal terms that seemed to say that since the NFL Players Association had disbanded, it had no direct influence over the players. Since it had disbanded, this group of former employees for the NFL Players Association was not in fact the NFL Players Association. They didn't represent anybody, and they didn't have any influence. An hour into this legal quagmire, after more rounds of tense, nasty-toned negotiating it seemed that they all were agreeing to sign a waiver saying that in fact they were not in this room, and certainly not negotiating or representing the players. No way was this meeting going to backfire on the former NFL Players Association officials.

Weeks later, after the steroid program was essentially finalized, Dr. John Lombardo was appointed as the anabolic steroid adviser. A separate advisor for recreational drugs of abuse also was appointed. Forrest Tennant's job was essentially divided in two. Dr. Lombardo was an academic physician from the Cleveland Clinic who knew a lot about athletes from his association with the Cleveland Cavaliers. He had been on the top of my list when names were suggested for the position at the Washington meeting.

We first met in June 1990, when I attended the National Athletic Trainers Association meeting to give a talk on ergogenic aids, meaning anything that augments athletic potential. He was there to introduce himself to the National Football League trainers. I congratulated him on his appointment and briefly promoted my hope of a long-term study of anabolic steroids.

"Gee," he responded. "I'm filling out a grant right now to do just about that same study in local weight lifters."

"Really? Be my guest, read over my protocol. You'll see why testing former NFL players is a much better idea, and very frankly, as the perceived impartial steroid advisor, you're in a much better position than I to run the study."

I left feeling very secure. The NFL had stated their intent to cooperate with legitimate research. And their new medical advisor seemed right on my wavelength. Approval of the landmark anabolic steroid study, I figured, was now merely a formality.

23

Forty-eight Hours of Damage

In *Rocky II*, after suffering a retinal detachment, Rocky Balboa retires from the ring, but after a handful of demoralizing jobs and firings, realizes boxing is the only way he knows how to earn a living.

His wife discovers him in the basement, punching the speed bag in preparation for a comeback.

"What about your eye?" his wife asks nervously. "The doctor said you shouldn't fight anymore."

"No, no," Rocky quickly shoots back, "the doctor *recommended* I don't fight. And I recommend that I do. . . ."

"It's very good to see you, Wanda. I'm glad you could make the trip."

"Thank you for inviting the wives, Mr. Davis," she responded.

"Can I help you with one of your bags?" Davis asked, responding chivalrously to my eight-months-pregnant wife's protruding abdomen.

I nearly dropped the two bulging suitcases I was lugging through the LAX customs check-in. This was my eighth season with the Raiders and Al Davis had never, not once, spoken to me in that pleasant, casual tone. He'd seen Wanda only two or three times in the last seven years, but even though the conversations were brief he always gave her his undivided attention, and he somehow knew all the wives' names. Wanda thought he was the greatest.

This was the first time since the 1983–84 season's Super Bowl that wives and girlfriends had flown to one of our games. We were all flying to London, England, for the opening preseason game of

1990, to be played at the revered Wembley Stadium. In addition to the players and wives, Al had invited the minority owners and key sponsors and their spouses, along with the stable of former Raider greats. For them it would be an all-expense-paid vacation in the finest of London accommodations.

For three or four years now the NFL had flown the premier teams to Europe for a showcase preseason game. Al Davis had previously resisted these foreign trips because he felt the travel and associated fanfare caused practice intensity to drop off and detracted from preparations for the season opener. In fact, Al had never set foot in Europe. You couldn't learn much about football there, and besides, he wasn't into vacations. But after turning down the European game repeatedly, Al finally agreed to go. True, this exhibition game meant one extra game to risk injury in. The $1 million fee the NFL decided to kick in for each participating team may have helped ease some doubts.

On arrival, I got pulled over by the British customs officials. They rolled their eyes when they saw my fishing tackle box stuffed full of every prescription medicine in God's kingdom.

"What, pray tell, is this?" the customs agent asked as he pulled out the injectable narcotics along with a collection of knives, blades, and oversized tracheostomy needles.

"Anything can happen in American football," I said. "And I've got to be ready."

"Well, we've certainly got nothing like this on the sidelines of our football here," he said, shaking his head.

From there it was practicing five days in a row, the first three in an absolute jet-lag haze, in ninety-degree heat and humidity, the worst heat wave in England this decade had seen. We'd get up early every morning, have breakfast, then proceed to get taped. The entire team would load into five buses and head about thirty miles out of town to an Olympic development site. Instead of a locker room we used a large empty gymnastics room. No English locker room was set up to handle so many players and so much equipment. In Wembley Stadium, where we played the following Sunday, packing eighty players into a locker room constructed for twenty or thirty soccer players was like reenacting the seventies fad of stuffing as many people as you could into a phone booth.

After practice we were well taken care of. One night we attended an open-bar bash at a swank museum site, and the next night a reception at the U.S. embassy's palatial ten-acre estate; the embassy building was like the mansions you pay money to walk through in Newport, Rhode Island, now draped with Raiderettes, Saintettes, and literally tons of players. The ambassador's second-in-command stood at the front door and shook our hands, after our names were loudly and formally announced by a tall guy in a goofy hat standing by the door. Not a bad job if you can get it.

The next night Wanda and I went with a group of players, trainers, and wives on the Jack the Ripper walking tour. We strolled along gritty back streets of East London, our guide periodically halting us at the sites of Jack's grisly murders.

"In the fourth floor of that building," the guide said in her cockney accent, "the third victim was discovered, her abdomen slashed open in anatomically correct lines and her bowels neatly dissected. This led investigators to suspect that the perpetrator had formal medical training."

"Hey, wait a minute, what year did Rosie finish med school?" one of the players asked.

"Yeah, I guess it was probably in the late eighteen-forties or sometime around then," his roommate replied.

"Ma'am, we've got another suspect!"

The scariest medical moment of the preseason occurred the following week as we boarded our charter in San Francisco after one of our rare preseason victories over the San Francisco 49ers. One of our six-foot-eight, 300-pound-plus guys, was standing in the forward galley of the airplane with the usual assortment of players and coaches, eating and bantering. All of a sudden he collapsed dead away. He hit the floor with a thud, then just lay there motionless, half a cheeseburger still embedded in his mouth. I rushed over and, kneeling, shook his shoulder.

"Wake up! What's the matter? Talk to me."

Not a twitch of a response. By this time he was looking mighty white for a guy with four weeks of a summer camp tan. I cleaned out the cheeseburger remains, loosened his shirt, and got my ear right up next to his mouth and nose. There was a ton of commotion around me, but I could just barely make out breath sounds, and I could see his chest expanding. Meaning he wasn't choking on a chunk of cheeseburger. The Heimlich maneuver was not needed.

But I still had no idea what was going on, so I dug my knuckle into his sternum as hard as I could. I got an ever so slight groan and a head movement.

"Wake up! What the hell's going on?" I said, slapping his cheeks. "Who was with him when he came in?" I asked, looking up.

"He hit the bar pretty good, doc. Seventeen shots of tequila, a pain pill, and a muscle relaxant."

"You're kidding me," I groaned as I turned his head over to the side. Downing seventeen shots in such a short period of time was getting up near the lethal level of alcohol. And if alcohol in that range didn't kill you outright, it was definitely associated with vomiting. The head turn was an effort to prevent a Mama Cass or Jimi Hendrix inhale-the-vomit-and-suffocate scenario.

"We're thirty-five thousand feet in the air and this guy decides to OD! Beautiful!"

We cleared out a central row of five seats for a makeshift hospital bed. Getting him there was almost impossible. His shoulders were so broad they didn't fit down the aisle. Four or five of his teammates and I had to hoist him in the air up over the aisle seat tops, and then make the turn and deposit him facedown in the cleared seats.

I couldn't help but remember my conversations with Forrest Tennant about how best to deal with alcohol. There was just something about the stress of professional football that fostered the abuse of alcohol. The pressure on the young guys to beat out the old, the pressure on the vets to hang in there. Maybe stress reduction training should be part of an effective program attacking alcohol abuse.

Fortunately, he showed signs of life by the time we landed. He needed a wheelchair to make it through the airport, but he didn't need to be hospitalized.

On the other hand, the anabolic steroid problem seemed to be waning in the face of new random tests. Earlier in training camp, the long-term users had fretted, wondering whether they'd stopped their usage early enough to slip by the testing. Lyle Alzado hadn't been the least bit nervous, though. At least on the outside. He was making a highly publicized comeback five years after retiring and looked bigger and nastier than ever. I'd seen him on the Maria Shriver TV show working out under the watchful eye of some for-hire East German strength coach. It didn't take a rocket scientist to see that his bloated muscle mass was more than just extra meat and potatoes at dinnertime. I had given Lyle a somber speech in the spring when he announced his comeback, and then again at the start of summer camp, about how I had personally been down to Washington, helped formulate the new drug policy, and could guarantee that the testing for drugs and their various masking agents was going to be state-of-the-art. Alzado looked at me with one of his exasperated stares and gave me a patronizing pat on the back.

"I hope you know what you're doing," I said.

"Don't worry about me." He winked.

Several weeks later, the urine test results came in. Alzado had passed. That caused a buzz around training camp, since everybody knew he was juiced. But to my knowledge, nobody else dared to try and beat the test. Several of the previous users, guys who had stopped the steroids months ago, despite fearing the worst, noticed no weight change and no decline in their weight-lifting strength. These guys came to me amazed, almost embarrassed that they had taken steroids for so long and now, off the stuff for the first time in many years, had found out they really didn't need them.

Unfortunately, Pete Koch's story was more typical. Pete came to the Raiders in 1989 as a Plan B free agent. A former first-round draft pick with a perfectly muscled two hundred eighty-six-pound frame, he had coverboy looks and had already fought the Viet Cong in *Heartbreak Ridge* with Clint Eastwood. He looked like another wild, multitalented Raider. Another Al Davis find.

But when Pete came to the Raiders he wisely—and quietly—decided to stop steroids. He'd gotten started years before when one of his coaches pushed them—and sold them—to players. In the last year, though, the NFL had enacted stiff penalties, the government had passed legislation making possession a federal crime, and he began noticing side effects. He wanted off.

He slowly shrunk to two hundred seventy-three pounds, then two hundred sixty-five. He tried putting weights in his clothes for the weekly weigh-ins. His max bench press, previously a couple of reps at five hundred twenty-five pounds, was now down below four hundred. He started getting thrown around in practice, a humiliating experience for a guy used to doing the throwing. He still had an unbelievably sculpted build, but as his weight dropped near two hundred fifty, he got cut from the NFL.

The majority of players, the nonusers who managed to stay on the team, were thrilled. No more artificially inflated opponents, no more test-tube teammates trying to put them in the hospital or the unemployment line.

*   *   *

The big shock of the preseason was a string of acrimonious Davis/player run-ins. Since 1963, Al had openly mixed it up with only two or three players out of the thousand he had proudly dressed in the silver and black. But now, in the space of a few weeks, he had declared war on three of his stars who were holding out for more money.

"Don't they know I can crush them?" was Al's response, widely circulated among the players.

Steve Beuerlein, the upstart Notre Dame grad who had ended the 1989 season as first-string, was asking for $1.5 million over three years. Sure, a big jump from his 1989 salary of $120,000. But remember, Jay Schroeder, his backup, was making $1.1 million a year, so Steve was asking for less than 50 percent of that salary.

Still, Al was incensed. "He hasn't pissed a lick for us. He hasn't even played for a winning team."

Unbeknownst to Beuerlein, there was one other thing going against him. The guy on the bench, the guy Beuerlein had beat out for the job, was the guy Davis had gone after, trading away a franchise lineman and draft choices. Beuerlein, it turned out, was way too jumpy to stay at home, and after several weeks called in to accept Al's offer of $450,000 for one year.

"Unh-unh," said Al. "That offer's just been lowered to four hundred thousand."

Now it was Beuerlein's turn to fume, and he held out for the rest of the preseason. That drop in salary was shrewdly crafted by Davis. He apparently had decided he was going to try to shoot the moon. He would win his personal battle with Beuerlein, send a message to the rest of the team about holding out, and maybe redeem himself in the press for the Schroeder trade with one bold stroke. Without Beuerlein looking over his shoulder, Schroeder was playing with vastly improved confidence. So the plan was hatched. Have Beuerlein be the forty-sixth man, the guy who doesn't suit up, the guy who stands in his street clothes on the sideline for the entire year. Pay him his baseline amount, but, by not suiting him up, save yourself millions of dollars and lots of weeks of aggravation by making the rest of the team afraid to hold out in future years. Then, at the end of the year, if Schroeder played well, if he stayed healthy, the *coup de grâce* would be to trade Beuerlein to the team with the best and youngest quarterback. How about Dallas, with Troy Aikman? That way he'd be on the bench forever. A fitting punishment for a guy who'd crossed Al. And if he never played, he'd never get a chance to prove Al Davis wrong for dumping him.

Vann McElroy, our big-hitting safety, was the next player flattened under Al Davis's heel. McElroy was holding out for $800,000 a year, the going rate for the league's All-Pro safeties, a jump up from his previous $575,000. But in Al's mind, Vann, with his history of muscle pulls and assorted other war injuries, couldn't stay healthy. He decided to break Vann, then lower his contract so he'd be easier to trade. And here too, Al had a backup he believed in, Eddie Anderson, a standout from the 1987 scab football team. Al wanted Eddie to get some experience, again without being pressured from behind by some talented veteran.

Toward these goals, Davis pulled a variation of the Beuerlein scheme. The Raiders had initially offered Vann a raise to $625,000, but when McElroy held out, that offer was suddenly dropped to $450,000 just prior to training camp. This insult was shrewdly calculated to get Vann's Texas blood boiling—and keep him out of camp. Finally, just days before the season opener, Vann surrendered. He had no leverage. He just wanted to play. He'd still run through a brick wall—if asked—for the Raiders. He'd sign for the $450,000. Nope, it's now down to $400,000. Next phone call—down to $350,000. Vann signed. He had what was left of his heart ripped out by only being allowed to practice with the "Nugs" (the scrub team). He did not suit up for games. Finally, with his substantially below-market-value contract, he was traded to Seattle in the sixth week (only, of course, after we had already played both of our games with them). Surprise—after languishing on our third string, he played extensively and well that very week for the Seahawks.

Marcus Allen was the third star pitted against Davis. In the years I'd been with the team, Marcus had pretty much done it all. He was an inspirational team leader, a phenomenal player year after year, and probably one of the toughest two or three guys in terms of playing with injuries. His teammates had four times in the previous seven years voted him the player most valuable to the team, most representative of the "Commitment to Excellence" logo. But since his contract had run out in 1988, Al had refused to renegotiate it, leaving Marcus little choice but to protest via a training camp holdout year after year. No other team signed Marcus. The restrictive NFL rules stated that a team would have to surrender two first-round draft choices and give Marcus a hefty raise. If Marcus held out during the season, he would forfeit his salary. He realized it was pretty hard to complain in the newspaper when he was making $1 million a year, even though he would have been worth many times that on a free market. Marcus also knew that complaining in the press would only deepen the rift between him and Al Davis. Already Davis had stuck a finger in Marcus's face during a closed-door meeting and boasted, "I'll get you."

We won the first game of the year with Marcus Allen reporting days before the opener, then running brilliantly, though he'd spent no time preparing in training camp. Davis's ploy with quarterback Schroeder was paying early dividends: he had an error-free game as well. The coaching staff tried to accommodate Schroeder by running an offense where he would throw to a designated receiver, and if that receiver was covered, would immediately throw the ball away. Not exactly a Joe Montana offense, where the quarterback sequentially checks off the primary receiver, then, if he's covered, the secondary, and then the tertiary, and so on till you smell the defensive lineman's breath and have to scramble.

In the locker room after the game, Marcus took off his helmet, revealing a three-inch-long gash on his forehead, ripped by the front edge of the helmet, which had been jammed down by a head-popping lead block. It was a pretty deep cut, all the way down to the skull. I walked to my medical kit to get some salt water to cleanse it, but when I got back, Rosenfeld had already grabbed a suture set and was busily tacking the forehead together. The result was an uneven, buckled suture line. That could lead to a more visible scar, or worse yet, a keloid scar, one of those overgrown, bulging Frankenstein numbers.

I got Marcus alone by the locker room door as he was exiting.

"I want you to go to this address," I said, shoving a piece of paper into his hand. "I just called a top plastic surgeon and got him to agree to meet you in his office right now. The suture job you've got is okay—it's going to hold the thing together—but you've got a show-biz career after football. There's absolutely no reason for you to have any more of a scar than you need from this thing."

It was a brilliant sunny afternoon. The third game of the 1990 season, and we were in the driver's seat. We were shoving the

Pittsburgh team all over the field and were up 20–3 late in the game. We hadn't been ahead by this many points for nearly two years! The fans who had stayed until the fourth quarter were a little antsy, and fights seemed to be igniting everywhere between Raider partisans and the yellow-clad Steeler fans sprinkled throughout the crowd. One unlucky Steeler fan was carried out; we found out later that he'd suffered brain damage when a drunken high-school-aged Raider fan, apparently at the game with his father, decided to pop him for the crime of daring to cheer for his Steeler team in the Los Angeles Coliseum.

The afternoon shadows began creeping down the west side of the stadium, slowly at first, inching in through the end zone, then picking up speed as the leading edge of the shadow headed toward midfield. I was just beginning to relax. The game was now clearly in our column, and the evening breeze was bringing in some relief from the afternoon heat.

I was snapped out of my brief meditation by a helmet-knocking collision in midfield. When the pile cleared, one of our players remained on the ground, motionless. I sprinted out, not waiting for the injury whistle. It was Mike Harden, number 22, our hard-hitting free safety, who had just been acquired from the Denver Broncos to fill the void left by Stacey Toran's death. As I knelt down next to him on the field, he spontaneously moved his head right, then left.

"Keep your head perfectly still," I said, reaching down to secure his helmet and lower neck. "What happened?"

"My arms and legs went dead. They went dead."

He moved his toes and fingers.

"Then I got this burning from my neck out to my arms and feet. They're coming back now."

"Does your neck hurt now?" I asked.

"No, it's okay. The tingling's gone."

"Squeeze my fingers. Move your toes up, down. Does this feel normal?" I asked as I touched both forearms, both hands, and then his thighs and just above his ankles.

"I'm fine, doc."

Rosenfeld now arrived, and after he finished a miniature neurologic evaluation, it was obvious Harden was moving his neck on his own. He sat, then stood up and walked off the field on his own power. On the sideline, Rosenfeld repeated his neck evaluation and concluded there was no neck fracture. I rechecked his strength, his sensation, his balance, and his reflexes. He checked out fine.

"Can I go back in next series, doc?"

"No," I replied. "You're going to need some X-rays to make sure everything's all right."

Then, seeing Rosenfeld still talking on the red phone, I got up to tell his defensive position coach that the player was through for the day.

As I got to the coach, I could hear the cry go up—"Defense, get out on the field." We had apparently just punted the ball away. To my amazement, Mike Harden went whisking out on the field. I got a high-blood-pressure total-body-flush San Diego Kenny King neck injury *déjà vu* all over again. I stormed over and went ballistic in front of George Anderson.

"What the hell is he doing out there?"

"Don't look at me, doc. Doc Rosenfeld said he could play."

"Play! If you get nerve symptoms in your leg, if you get nerve symptoms on both sides, that's a spine injury. A spine injury means you're at risk for paralysis! Beautiful! Not only are we taking a chance with the kid's life, not only is he going out without being told of his risk of being a quad, he's risking it in the fourth quarter playing garbage minutes in a game we've already won!"

I stormed away and stood on the far end of the sideline and just stared at Harden. I couldn't blame him for wanting to play. He was a warrior in the truest sense of the word. He wanted to play desperately, we were undefeated, this was his last chance for a Super Bowl ring, and hell, he'd seen teammates go out with injuries only to be permanently replaced by a second-string guy who, when given playing time, performed brilliantly.

After what seemed like hours, the last minutes on the clock ticked off. Moments later in the locker room, I met face to face with Rosenfeld.

"Harden's exam is normal," I said. "But he's of course going to need flexion and extension films and a neck MRI tomorrow to work up his several seconds of complete paralysis."

"Ah, he doesn't need any studies," Rosenfeld scoffed. "He moved his legs right away. I saw him."

Fortunately Dr. Bob Albo, Davis's confidant, the doctor who had resuscitated Carol Davis, was standing right outside the training room door. I went for the submarine move.

"Dr. Albo," I called. "Come here a second."

In front of Rosenfeld, I repeated the story to Albo, including the newly discovered fact that two similar episodes had happened during Harden's Bronco days.

"Don't you think we ought to get some neck films on him?" I questioned.

"Absolutely," Albo replied.

It was a done deal. I'd trapped Rosenfeld. His associate, who'd agreed with me as we walked off the field that Harden needed these X-rays done, quickly added, "I'll schedule it, boss."

I finally got the X-ray report called to me on Tuesday.

"He's got a problem," the radiologist said. "There's a tight compression of the cervical spine between the sixth and seventh vertebrae. I wouldn't let this guy step out on the field unless a neurosurgeon cleared him."

"Did you call Rosenfeld with the report?"

"Yeah, I told him the same thing."

I phoned Mike Harden. But he was in Denver, his hometown, seeing his daughter. A lot of the players flew back to their homes after Monday practice. Tuesday was their off day, so they'd fly back just before practice on Wednesday. I left him a message saying I'd talk to him at Wednesday's practice.

Sunday's upcoming game was going to be a showdown of two undefeated teams, the Raiders and the Bears. Eighty thousand tickets had already been sold. So the Wednesday defensive day practice took on a bit more intensity than usual. The black-shirted first-team defense matched wits in noncontact scrimmage with the white-shirted second-team offense, which was running Chicago's plays. Beuerlein, back on the team but demoted to third string, would take on the maneuvers of each week's opposing quarterback, this time Jim Harbaugh. Beuerlein was just now realizing that he was not going to be allowed to suit up all year, punishment for his crossing Al. This drill was his only chance of getting back any self-respect. He was sharp today, threading passes through the defensive backs. Then the defensive line would start rushing him more realistically, or someone in the back, who knew what play was called, would signal it to the defense, and Beuerlein would get mad. Fortunately, no major fisticuffs erupted. Most fortunately, Harden stayed out of all the pushing matches.

After practice, Rosenfeld, the trainers George Anderson, H. Rod Martin, and Todd Sperber, and I were in the back area of the training room listening to Dr. Frank Shelloc, one of the Cedars-Sinai magnetic resonance imaging experts, talk about his experiments with MRI diagnosing of muscle pulls. In walked Harden.

"How'd my neck X-rays turn out?" he asked, looking at me and then back to Rosenfeld.

Without missing a beat, Rosenfeld replied, "You're OK. It's just a bruise."

"Good," said Harden, grinning broadly as he turned to exit the training room, still toweling off his hair.

I stared in disbelief at Rosenfeld. Where did he get the balls to tell this kid that he was fine? Rosenfeld hadn't done anything except roll Harden's neck around on the sideline. Then he'd gotten an X-ray report suggesting a severe spinal defect and recommending that a neurosurgeon be called. And without reexamining the kid, without even taking the time to go down to the X-ray facility to review the films personally, he had flat out lied to Harden.

Had he totally flipped his wig? He was speeding past bad medical judgment, past ethics, past malpractice. Way past. This was fraud, knowingly misrepresenting vital medical information to the patient.

I walked out of the room without saying anything and caught Mike Harden as he was leaving through the foyer.

"Listen, I've gotta tell you," I began. "I hope what Rosenfeld said is true, that it's just a bruise and you're going to be okay, but the X-ray wasn't normal. It showed a section of your spine right here"—I touched the lower midportion of his neck—"where the bony opening is too small for your spinal cord. That occasionally can be a risky thing, and very frankly, if it were my spinal cord, I'd get a second opinion and I'd get it from a neurosurgeon who works on this area of the body for a living."

He stopped and stared at me.

"Do you want me to set it up?" I asked.

"Yes," he stated in an unequivocal tone. "Those couple seconds lying on the ground, not being able to move my arms or legs but hearing the players around me, the crowd noise—it seemed like an eternity. I was really scared."

"I'll get you a consultation for tomorrow."

I got a call at about seven-thirty the next night.

"Has Rosenfeld totally lost it?" began Dr. Elliot Blinderman, a highly respected neurosurgeon who had seen numerous Raiders for other neurologic problems in years past. "He was screaming at me not to tell the patient anything derogatory or else I'd never get another case from him."

I found out later that Dr. Rosenfeld had gotten wind of the supposedly confidential referral. One of the secretaries had given Mike directions to Blinderman's office, and someone must have overheard the secretary and tipped off Dr. Rosenfeld.

"This kid Harden's got a real problem," Blinderman continued. "I'm worried about how smart it would be for him to return to football considering how much of a defect he's got in his neck and the fact that he's had two episodes of quadriplegia."

"What did you recommend to Harden?" I asked.

"Before I give him my final opinion I want to do a myelogram to double-check that this severe degree of blockage I saw on the MRI was not just some kind of artifactual blip."

"Thanks for your help," I said. "I'll arrange the myelogram with a CAT scan to follow first thing in the morning, and I hope you'll get a chance to review it right after you get out of surgery."

I hung up and flipped through an alphabetized computer print-out of my patients and their phone numbers. I slowly punched in Al Davis's phone number. The cat was definitely out of the bag. My underground system of second opinions was definitely exposed.

"Hello," Al said.

"Hello, Mr. Davis. This is Rob Huizenga. It looks like Mike Harden's got a bad medical problem."

"What are you talking about?" he said.

He had to have been filled in to the hilt by Rosenfeld, but I went on, "Well, you know that when Mike came out in the fourth quarter last Sunday, he complained of being paralyzed for a couple of seconds. The MRI of his neck on Monday showed a critical narrowing in the spinal column in his lower neck, and the neurosurgeon who he saw tonight thinks it could even conceivably be career-ending, but he wants to do a myelogram tomorrow before he renders his final opinion."

"Well, of course I want what's best for the kid," Davis began. "But how the f—— can you come to me at eight o'clock Thursday night and tell me I might not have a starting strong safety?"

"Well, Mr. Davis, I just found out about the neurosurgeon's opinion right now."

"It's Thursday! Why couldn't you have done all this Sunday night after the game?"

"The X-rays were set up for late Monday, and although they called Rosenfeld late Monday, I didn't hear until Tuesday. I called Harden on Tuesday, but he had flown to—"

"Why the f—— couldn't you have called me on Tuesday? I could have signed a new player. Aw, forget it."

Click.

It was high noon, Friday, September 8, 1990. I pulled back the drapes in the meticulously clean radiologic suite recovery room area. Mike Harden was lying comfortably in his bed with the drone of a cardiac monitor breaking the sterile silence.

"Hi, Mike. How you feeling?"

"Good, doc, good."

"No headache?"

A myelogram involves a spinal tap to inject dye into the layer around the spinal column, and post-spinal-tap headache is a common complication.

"No, I feel fine. I was worried because they said I might get a bad headache after this, but I don't feel a thing."

"Great. You're lucky."

"What do you think of the X-rays, doc?"

"Unfortunately, Mike, this study corroborates the original neck MRI. The compression of your spinal column—due to bony spurs and a herniated disc—is severe. The spinal cord is being pinched in a space only nine or ten millimeters wide. For most guys your size, if the opening is anything less than thirteen millimeters, many specialists think you're at too high a risk of nerve damage to let you play contact sports."

"What'd the neurosurgeon say, doc?"

"Well, he wants to come down and review the X-rays himself, of course. He's still in surgery. But he told me over the phone that if he agrees with this reading of the X-rays he'll recommend you retire."

A dejected look spread across Harden's face.

"If you really, really wanted to return to football, he'd recommend that you have a fusion of those two bones in your neck so that there'd be no chance of quadriplegia if you got hit the wrong way."

Mike shook his head. "That's funny, because Dr. Rosenfeld just called me on the phone and he told me the tests really didn't show anything new, and that he thought I was okay to play on Sunday."

"As in two days from now, Sunday?" I inquired incredulously. "Hold on, Mike, I've got to check something out." I turned around and stormed down the long corridor to the adjacent X-ray reading room.

Mike's scans were still on the board where I had reviewed them with Jerry Mink just moments before. Dr. Mink, the MRI world expert we'd page into the hospital not infrequently on Sunday nights after injury-marred home games, was dictating another scan into a hand-held tape recorder.

"What's going on here, Jerry?" I asked, interrupting him in midsentence. "Harden just told me Rosenfeld called up, he had a nurse bring over a telephone to the recovery room—to tell him the X-ray didn't show anything new and that he was OK to play in the game this Sunday. Did he come down here to look at the films?"

"He hasn't come down to personally review Harden's films with me."

"What did you tell him when you called him?"

"I told him the same thing I told you."

"What in the world is wrong with Rosenfeld?" I screamed.

I had four examining rooms full of patients when I returned to my office, but it was very hard to concentrate on their problems. The whole Mike Harden affair was becoming a soap opera. I couldn't get it out of my mind. I grabbed a chart and my stethoscope and headed into examining room number two. It was a straightforward recurrent kidney stone, and the pain was not too bad. As I was about to exit, the patient, still clutching the affected flank, asked, "Doc, are you all right?"

"I'm fine. Why?"

"You look terrible. Why don't you overbill my insurance and use the money to get away on a vacation down to Mexico or something?"

I tried to laugh, but I knew I had to make the phone call now.

"Sandy, get Mr. Davis on the phone . . . Hello, Mr. Davis?"

"Yeah."

"Rob Huizenga. The myelogram confirms the critical nine-to-ten-millimeter narrowing in the C-six-seven area. The kid's not going to be able to play this week."

There was silence on the other end. I continued talking to fill the void.

"I'm going to get another opinion from Rick Delamarter, the top orthopedic spine expert at UCLA, and we'll go from there."

"It's Friday, f——ing Friday! You're telling me now the kid can't play when you could have had this whole workup done on Monday?"

"I apologize," I said, trying to hold back my anger and eat a little crow. "You're right, I should have personally seen to it that this evaluation was done by the first of the week."

"Apologize! F——! You've done more damage to the Raiders in the last forty-eight hours than *anyone* else in the last twenty years!"

For some sick reason, my brain instantly locked on Pete Rozelle. As one of Al's soldiers for the last eight years, I'd had it drummed into me to hate Pete Rozelle. Now, in one short week, I had rocketed by the former NFL commissioner and taken my place at the head of the Raider enemy list.

"Gee, I'm sorry you feel that way," I said. "I'm just trying my best to do what's right."

"You're just covering your ass for malpractice."

"That's funny," I shot back, the word "malpractice" setting me off. "*You* leave me high and dry by forcing me to sign a statement saying I'm not an employee, only a consultant, thereby taking you off the hook if a player sues me. And you accuse *me* of being worried about malpractice?"

"Who gave you the power to circumvent Dr. Rosenfeld? The neck is his area."

"For your information, my job is to look after Harden. I'm getting him the best specialists, and then he can make his own decisions."

"Who gave you the power to request outside consultants?"

"I'm Mike Harden's doctor, and it's my job to do whatever I think is in his best interest."

"You don't care a rat's ass about Mike Harden's welfare. And you don't care one iota for the welfare of the Raider team. You're only interested in taking over for Rosenfeld as head team doctor, and calling all the medical shots."

"How dare you insult me!"

I knew I was screaming when I saw a look of alarm on Sandy's face as she closed my office door to keep the tirade from my patients' ears.

"You can't bully me around like one of your front office yes-men."

"You were nothing before I hired you," Al Davis responded cynically.

"I was never nothing," I shouted back. "You should be embarrassed, abusing your position of power by allowing a horror surgeon like Rosenfeld to take care of the guys that trust in you, that look up to you, that put their health, their lives, in your hands."

I was still screaming. I couldn't believe he hadn't hung up yet. After a pause, he came back on the line.

"You spend all this time, coming and meeting with me, about this bullshit jet-lag thing, trying to change our travel plans, our practice schedule, our pregame meals—why the f—— couldn't you take care of this *one* thing?"

"I apologize," I said, suddenly much cooler. "If you don't like what I did, if you don't think it's right, fine. I resign."

Click. This time I hung up on Al Davis.

That Sunday was perfect football weather. More than eighty thousand fans were jammed into the Coliseum to see the duel of the undefeated division titans, the Chicago Bears and the Los Angeles Raiders.

"These seats aren't half bad," Johnny Otten said to me, squinting into his end-zone camera. "You can really see the blocking lanes open up from here. You get a whole new perspective on football."

It was the first time in eight years—152 games—that I wasn't standing on the sideline. After my screaming tirade with Al Davis I'd gone into an unofficial limbo. I had walked Harden over to UCLA at six-thirty on Saturday morning to get a third opinion from Dr. Delamarter, the head of the spine division at UCLA. He'd told Mike that he was at increased risk of becoming a quadriplegic if he played football. What that risk was he didn't exactly know, although he admitted it could be as high as one in ten. He flatly stated that a neck roll or any other special protective equipment would be of no benefit.

Later that morning, Harden had a conference at the Raider facility with Dr. Rosenfeld and Al Davis. Rosenfeld was now backpedaling something fierce. I later found out that Dr. Martin Cooper, yet another highly respected neurosurgeon, had been summoned to Rosenfeld's Century City condominium for two hours on Friday night. Over and over they viewed the neck films. Over and over Dr. Cooper said the spinal narrowing put Harden at serious risk of paralysis should he return to football. Over and over Rosenfeld puffed on a cigarette and asked, "Are you sure?"

Cooper would respond, "Yes, I'm sure."

Then Rosenfeld would light another cigarette. He quickly filled an ashtray. And he had not smoked for ten years.

Now it was two top neurosurgeons, one world-authority orthopedic spine expert, two specialty bone radiologists, and I who felt football posed a potential risk, versus Rosenfeld's "It's just a bruise."

On Saturday, Rosenfeld for the first time recommended that Harden not play Sunday. He recommended Harden go on Monday to a neck specialist in Philadelphia, an acquaintance of Davis's confidant Dr. Bob Albo.

I'd talked to George Anderson and Steve Ortmayer and told them I couldn't in good faith return and continue working professionally with Dr. Rosenfeld. I was sure Al Davis would do the right thing and dismiss Rosenfeld. He always pissed and moaned, and usually stretched the limits, but I felt deep down inside he wouldn't tolerate incompetence.

"See what I mean, doc?" Johnny said as the kickoff flew high in the air and the parallel lanes each player ran in to protect his portion of the field were clearly evident.

"I'll tell you what this really has over the sideline," I said.

"What's that, doc?"

"You can sit down," I said.

We had three chairs cramped in a small concrete insert in the middle of the west end zone that served as the filming station. My seven-year-old daughter, Ashley, wasn't convinced these were good seats. She liked her usual thirty-yard-line seats behind the bench much better. She could see the cheerleaders. She could see the players. She could see her dad.

"You ready for a good game?" I asked her.

She nodded as she cracked open another peanut from Johnny's free stash piled up in front of the camera.

"Dad, why aren't you standing down there?" she asked, pointing to the Raiders' sideline.

"I wanted to watch a game with you, honey," I said.

"Are you still the doctor for the Raiders?" she persisted.

"No, not anymore," I replied.

"What's the matter?" she asked with a frown. "Don't they like you anymore?"

* * *

It was an eerie feeling—realizing that some day Mike Harden's neck could be sandbagged somewhere, and I'd have to testify in a courtroom. So I put down the facts as forcefully as I could.

October 1, 1990
Dear Mr. Davis:

This letter is intended to terminate our oral employment agreement and chronicle the disturbing events of the last week which I have previously laid out to you in our phone conversations on 9/7 and 9/8.

9/3: Mike Harden has quadriplegic episode. Dr. Rosenfeld okays Mike's return into the game after I tell him he is out for the remainder of the game.

9/4: Mike Harden's MRI result, namely a critical C6-7 canal narrowing, is called to Dr. Rosenfeld with the additional recommendation that a neurosurgeon be consulted.

9/5: I receive the above report. Mike Harden is in Denver and unavailable.

9/6: Dr. Rosenfeld tells Mike Harden (in front of the two senior trainers, a visiting MRI expert, and myself) that "the MRI is OK—nothing to worry about." This opinion is rendered without Dr. Rosenfeld examining the patient or ever personally reviewing the MRI pictures.

I speak with Mike in private and tell him the scan is not normal and suggest he get a second opinion from Dr. Blinderman, a neurosurgeon.

9/7: Dr. Rosenfeld finds out about the second opinion and calls Dr. Blinderman before the patient arrives and instructs him not to tell the patient anything—that Mike Harden is okay to play.

After examining Mike, the neurosurgeon calls Dr. Rosenfeld and myself, stating he is very worried about the severity of the problem, but suggests that I set up a myelogram before he renders his formal opinion.

9/8: The myelogram is performed. Mike Harden receives a phone call in the recovery room from Dr. Rosenfeld telling him that the myelogram reveals nothing new and that he is okay to play professional football. Dr. Rosenfeld calls Mike Harden again at six o'clock that evening and repeats he feels all the findings are old and Mike is okay to return to football.

Dr. Blinderman is in surgery all day but he reviews the films early that evening and tells Mike Harden he is at considerable risk of having permanent quadriplegia if he returns to football. He recommends Mike get additional opinions and consider surgery if he truly wants to return to football.

I discuss this with Mike and offer him a third opinion with the UCLA cervical spine expert, Dr. Delamarter.

9/9: Dr. Delamarter concludes after a thorough history, physical, and review of all films that Mike has a left C6 radiculopathy, old calcified and new soft disc herniations which are narrowing the cord to 10 mm. Because of the patient's *two* warning episodes of transient quadriplegia and more frequent transient episodes of bilateral neck, shoulder, and arm numbness, Dr. Delamarter concludes Mike is at substantial risk of permanent quadriplegia (as high as 1/10) should he elect to return to professional football. He discusses other possible consultants, surgery, and lack of benefit from special protective equipment with Mike should he elect to return to football and accept the above risks.

I believe Dr. Rosenfeld withheld urgent facts, rendered vital opinions without benefit of examining the data, and generally showed blatant disregard for standard accepted medical care in dealing with Mike Harden's problem.

I am deeply disappointed that you have seen fit to harshly chastise me for my handling of this matter in our phone conversation of 9/7 and 9/8. Since I refuse to work with Dr. Rosenfeld after this incident and since you do not support my actions, I am forced to resign.

As I have stated, I hope in the future you will see that it is in the best interests of the health of the players that you release Dr. Rosenfeld from his medical duties with the Raiders (replaced by his partners). Only you can guarantee that the players receive the quality of medical care they deserve.

Sincerely,

Robert Huizenga, M.D.

Assistant Clinical Professor of Medicine
University of California at Los Angeles
President, NFL Physicians Society
Member, NFL Anabolic Steroid Advisory Committee

I was sitting in my living room with my daughter weeks later, watching the Monday-night game, the Raiders away at Miami. It was an eerie feeling sitting at home and watching my friends go to war without me. I'd pretty much given up hope of going back. My ultimatum to Al Davis to get rid of Rosenfeld hadn't worked. I was genuinely surprised. The medical side of football could make or break a team. But in the end, Davis kept Rosenfeld, and he kept control.

The following Monday in Philadelphia, Dr. Joseph Torg "passed" Mike Harden's neck. That, in effect, sandbagged me. Torg was a well-respected national authority, like the Los Angeles doctors Harden had seen here, so I nearly fell off my chair when I heard Harden had been cleared to return to action—that Torg didn't believe Harden was predisposed to any catastrophic neurologic event if he returned to football.

It's okay for top medical experts to disagree—it happens all the time—but I was quite upset when I read his consultation letter and saw that he had not fully gotten the events of that day correct. His interpretation of the neck films was far more favorable than that of the radiologic neck specialists. He didn't call any of the previous doctors, neither me nor any of the five other experts who saw grave danger in Harden's returning to football. Furthermore, he appeared to be totally ignorant of the game of football. He had counseled Mike not to spear-tackle (that is, not to make initial contact with the top or crown of the helmet), saying if Mike avoided this, his risk of a catastrophic quadriplegia would be the same as anyone else's. But anyone who has ever sat through even one quarter of a football game knows that Harden's strong safety position involves more helmet-to-helmet and helmet-to-body collisions than any other position in the game. Expecting a strong safety never to ram an opponent with his helmet is like telling a running back with a sore elbow not to carry the ball with that arm. It's an instinctive reaction. You step on the field, it's bound to happen.

But none of the higher-ups on the Raider team seemed to care a hoot about the subtleties. There was a cry of relief. I was wrong. Harden agreed to play. Rosenfeld filled out a Lloyd's of London disability policy stating that Harden was fine, that there were no preexisting neck problems. The Raiders had their starter. Rosenfeld had played his medical Russian roulette and won again.

Suddenly, my eyes were glued to the TV.

"We've got a player down," Al Michaels intoned as the camera moved in on a motionless player. It was number 22.

"Oh, no. C'mon, *move*, Mike!"

"A time-out's been called, and we're gonna take a commercial break."

"Don't you dare!" I screamed.

Fortunately Harden was up and moving when live coverage resumed. Another day, another dollar, another bout of paralysis.

To replace me as team doctor, Ortmayer interviewed a list of Rosenfeld-recommended doctors. Ortmayer finally narrowed it down to three groups, the doctors Rosenfeld felt most comfortable dealing with. The only surprise came after the new doctor was announced. In the intensive selection process, apparently the Raiders had not had time to discuss salary. When they did I got a frantic phone call.

"What did you get paid when you were the team doctor?"

"Twenty-four thousand dollars . . . a year," I said.

"That's all?" he moaned. "I thought when I took the job I'd be getting a hundred and fifty, maybe two hundred—at the very least, a hundred thousand! They're offering me sixteen thousand!"

"It's not a money-making venture," I replied. "You've got to really love football. Good luck."

And I hung up quickly. I didn't want to keep the conversation going for too long—he might ask me for my four season tickets and the parking passes that came along with the job.

The finality of the situation hit. Now I knew how Coach Shanahan must have felt, leaving abruptly, with no goodbyes. It was also frustrating that because of patient-doctor confidentiality I couldn't tell anyone what had really happened. I figured the players would hear the truth in due time from locker room conversations, but I was in for quite a surprise.

"Doc, what's going on?" It was a former player calling me on the phone. "I ran into Plunkett the other day and he said he heard Davis fired your ass. Is that true?"

I also now wondered if I should resign my post as president of the National Football League Physicians Society. It would be awkward being the society's first lame duck president, presiding over my new replacement as Raider team doctor.

"Resign? Hell no," said one of the other officers I called. "You're president until next February. Hey, maybe just to piss Al Davis off we'll elect you for another two years."

My hardest decision was figuring out what to do about Rosenfeld. He could be a charming guy. When I started in 1983 he even seemed to be a good doctor. He got me the Raiders job, sent me a number of patients, and early on even tried to take me under his wing and teach me a thing or two.

After the first weekend of the Harden affair, he sent me a message through an intermediary—he had made a mistake, he was sorry, I was right, why didn't I come back on the team and we could just go on as before. For an instant I felt sorry for him. It was sad for a guy of his status to end up this way. But I finally relayed a reply that I couldn't go back to things the way they were before. I was tempted to let the whole affair rest. But did I have an obligation to file a complaint with the Board of Medical Quality Assurance of California?

It's not exactly a secret that doctors don't like to go after their own. I scheduled an appointment to talk to the head of Cedars-Sinai Medical Center, hoping for some advice. I sat down and spilled out the entire Rosenfeld tale.

"Some guys just don't know when to get out," the chief doctor said, sadly shaking his head.

"Should I report him to the California Quality Assurance Board?"

"No, there's no need for that," he replied. "We took away his operating privileges here several years ago."

"You what?"

"He was a bad surgeon—he had a very high complication rate, and he had a lot of malpractice cases. Rather than get into a lengthy court battle—they can be tough to win, because of laws favoring the doctors—we agreed not to kick him off the staff if he voluntarily agreed not to do surgery here."

I left the room happy and sad. I was happy that I didn't have to go any further, but I couldn't help but feel it was a pretty lousy system. Other doctors, and, more important, patients, were kept in the dark about incompetent doctors when such deals were made with the stipulation they be kept secret. I found out later that

Rosenfeld and/or his corporation had been sued over sixty times since 1963—most of these cases alleging malpractice. In one of these cases he allegedly operated on the wrong knee, and then supposedly had the nerve to tell the family that both knees were bad and he had decided to operate on both of them.

A couple of days after my chat with the head of the hospital, I got an interesting call from one of my patients. He had heard a rumor that Rosenfeld was going to sue me for libel. I had never thought I'd greet the news of a potential lawsuit with such joy. This would be an honorable forum to set the story straight, to clean up the Raiders' medical system, and maybe, by example, even help others too. But, surprise—the suit never materialized.

It didn't take long for me to realize I'd made the right decision in resigning. Suddenly I was getting phone calls with tips on other Raider medical problems past and present. I became a clearinghouse for Raider wrongs. I found out that back in 1983, our Super Bowl year, the year Marcus Allen had all the problems with numbness in his arm caused by his acrobatic goal-line dives, he had been sent for a CAT scan of his neck. It showed some problems that might have been serious and definitely indicated that he should be tested further to make sure he could safely play, but these results were never transmitted to him. Instead Rosenfeld checked the films out and deep-sixed them.

I was told that twenty-one-year-old Newt Harrell, the burly Texas offensive lineman who had been instructed to fake a neck injury in 1988, had, unbeknownst to me, been carted off to Cedars-Sinai via ambulance and actually admitted into the hospital by Rosenfeld for two days for what the discharge summary termed pain, numbness, and weakness in the upper and lower extremities. Newt was sitting up in his hospital bed feeling perfectly well, strapped into a Philadelphia neck brace, being carted off for neck X-rays and neck MRI scans and being given narcotic pain pills and Decadron, some of the strongest pills available in medicine. He was sitting in his room trying to be a model patient and cooperate with his doctor—so he could remain a Raider and have a chance to play pro ball in the NFL. But on the other hand, he was getting frantic phone calls from friends and family who were worried that he might be digging himself into a legal grave, being an accessory to insurance fraud. The nurses would come in like clockwork with his medication. No one had told him what to do with the medicines, and he had no idea what they were for. So he would hide the pills in his cheek until the nurse walked out of the room, then get up and flush them down the toilet.

The humiliation didn't end when he was finally discharged. He was told to wear the Philadelphia collar everywhere he went, his only relief being behind locked doors in his own apartment and during the closed-door Raider offensive line meetings. There he'd take the stupid collar off and throw it on the floor. Then, as the meeting was about to break up, and while his teammates laughed at him, he'd again have to put the collar on before he could step out into the outside world.

After the Miami game, Harden had two more temporary paralysis episodes while playing football. His nerve function returned after each incident, thank God—but the risk of permanent paralysis still remained. I phoned Dr. Torg, the physician who had cleared him, to relate my anxiety over what was happening and my dismay that he had interpreted Mike Harden's X-rays differently from the five experts Harden had seen here. Torg expressed concern and agreed that the situation definitely needed to be reevaluated. In a phone conversation he defended his interpretation of the CAT scan and MRI films by saying he hadn't gotten the originals but copies that were somewhat fuzzy and hard to read. I couldn't understand why he had not requested the originals or repeated his own in a case of this seriousness.

Also worrisome was the case of Chuckie Mullins from the Ole Miss football team. Like Harden, he was a defensive back. Like Harden, he had an episode of temporary paralysis after a hit. Like Harden, his neurological status promptly returned to normal and although X-rays showed he had spinal cord narrowing he returned to football. On Saturday, October 28, 1989, Chuckie Mullins spear-tackled an opponent—and became permanently quadriplegic. He died in 1991 from complications of the quadriplegia.

I turned on the Raiders–Buffalo Bills AFC championship game on January 20, 1991. Bo Jackson was walking up and down the sideline. God. Now I was *really* glad I wasn't the Raider doctor. I had heard through the grapevine that his MRI of a week ago had shown a hip fracture, not the mild muscle bruise the Raiders were claiming in the newspapers. Were they trying to get Bo up and walking without a limp, as a decoy for their next week's opponent should they win? Did they want that team to spend a lot of garbage time preparing a defense to stop Bo, when all the while they knew full well he was out for the duration, maybe longer? Would anybody dare sign onto a medical staff that was willing to give the world's greatest athlete the green light to walk and be a decoy with a broken hip? It might be okay from a strictly medical standpoint, but if by chance complications arose, good luck explaining it to a jury of twelve common folk.

24

The Mike Wise Suicide

I flipped through the August 22, 1992, *Los Angeles Times* as I angled forward against the kitchen counter to stretch my calves for my 5:00 A.M. run. Suddenly I stiffened. Deep inside the sports section, in the newswire column, was the heading "Former Raider Wise Found Dead at 28."

I had first met Mike, our number-four draft pick, in the summer camp of 1986 when he came up to me and offhandedly asked for a prescription of Accutane, an incredibly strong anti-acne medication, for his skin problems.

"Listen, doc, if I really wanted to I could get it from my dad—he's a pharmacist. I've used this stuff before, and it really works."

"Okay, hang on a second." I looked at his face, chest, and back. He had the deep, potentially scarring acne everywhere. He also had more of a receding hairline than you see in most twenty-one-year-olds.

"Do you take anabolic steroids?" I asked. After three years of battling Alzado, I was now at the top of my game in terms of suspecting steroid use.

"Aw, just a couple cycles in the past," he said.

I looked at the records from his initial physical exam, which had been just several weeks earlier. He had absolutely denied ever taking anabolic steroids.

"Do you know what steroids do to your skin?" I asked.

"I've taken the steroids before and they haven't affected my skin."

"Don't bullshit me," I continued. "Male hormones can make acne flare up so severely it can put you in the hospital. You've got to be nuts to take anabolic steroids, which sometimes affect your liver, and then take Accutane, which also can affect the liver. I'll prescribe Accutane if you stop the steroids."

He agreed to these terms, but since I had no control over his supply of anabolic steroids and we weren't testing for them at this juncture, I had to trust him, an iffy proposition at best.

I kept on him, though, reminding him every chance I had about possible consequences of mixing steroids and Accutane. After six weeks, the acne resolved. I could only hope part of the reason was his going off steroids. But I understood from the rumor mill that within a few months he went back to his other doctors and was again on the juice.

Mike Wise was the prototype of a small boy trapped inside a gargantuan six-foot-eight, 280-pound frame. Coddled through his high school and college years because of his sports skills, he wasn't well prepared for the cruel world of professional sports. He was generally unassuming, with a couple of mildly rough edges. He wasn't from a farm but somehow had a little of the country hick about him. He was not exactly erudite, and he was called Meathead by most of his teammates. Others claimed the "meat" portion of the nickname was too complimentary—it implied some life—so they called him Bonehead. Those monikers definitely irritated Mike, and he was forever trying to promote new nicknames for himself, such as Dr. Death, or the Grim Reaper. He tried to change his image by riding around on a motorcycle, growing a Fu Manchu mustache and a goatee, and getting a tattoo of the Grim Reaper on his ankle. He began seeing aggressive sports hypnotists who would continually drill him with combative autosuggestions, which he taped all over his apartment.

CHAMPIONS DON'T JUST HAPPEN, THEY'RE CREATED FROM WITHIN!
I AM PRECISION-HONED, MUSCULAR TEMPERED-STEEL . . .

Mike worked hard to improve. He showed promise in the preseason of 1987, when he recorded several quarterback sacks and a lot of "hurries," or near sacks. It definitely looked as if he was going to make an impact, even among All-Pro defensive linemen like Howie Long, Bill Pickel, and Greg Townsend. Then in September 1987 I got a call to see him late one night at the emergency room, the day after our last preseason game. He had noted the sudden onset of tea-colored urine and gray stools. It turned out he had a raging case of hepatitis A, which he had picked up either from another player or from some infected food.

I got a call from Al Davis, who was upset. He told me he had Mike Wise on the trading block and had actually traded him to San Francisco for draft choices. This six-week debilitating viral illness was going to nullify the trade.

For some reason, Mike never fit in with the other players. He was something of a loner, always a bit on the outside, never becoming one of the guys. But a new defense line coach, Bill Urbanik, seemed to bring out the best in him, and Mike prospered during the 1988 season. That was the season Howie Long got hurt, and Mike started fourteen of the sixteen games. His best moment was in the 49er game, when he repeatedly broke through their offensive line and got in Joe Montana's face.

MY LEGS, TORSO, AND ARMS ARE ENERGIZED POWER-THRUST DOMI-
NANCE WEAPONS . . .

We won 9–3, and Wise and fellow D-lineman Scott Davis were the heroes.

In that game, after several sacks, still searching for a more macho nickname, Mike went through different types of sack motions. One time, after standing over the downed Joe Montana, he crossed his forearms in a skull-and-crossbones sack dance. Then later he tried a Grim Reaper sack dance, curving his right arm into a sickle and then slicing the air with it. His unimpressed teammates, watching on the sideline, suggested he do the anabolic steroid sack dance, and they pantomimed a crab body pose such as you see those oiled body builders doing on ESPN, while pretending to inject a syringe into a forearm vein.

Mike hit the weights with renewed vigor in the off-season.

. . . CHANNELING THE FORCE OF CONQUEST WITH EVERY COMPELLING
MOVE . . .

But he was bothered by several significant shoulder injuries that lingered from the prior season. And despite his repeated denials, I heard through the rumor mill that he was still using steroids.

As his stock went up, so did his salary. He was now getting $25,000 game checks. I had a suspicion, however, that he was using some of that money to buy growth hormone, since his forehead began to protrude a little more. Excess growth hormone can make all the facial bones grow, eventually resulting in a Neanderthal look. Wise eventually went to a plastic surgeon to have his forehead chiseled back down.

. . . AND MY FACIAL EXPRESSION COMMUNICATES I TAKE NO PRISONERS.

In 1991, a year after I resigned as team doctor, Mike's world began to crack. He believed that since his playing time was equivalent to that of teammate Scott Davis, he should be paid an equivalent amount. But as a first-round draft pick, Scott Davis was making two or three times more than Wise. When Mike went to the Raiders with his request for $600,000, he was told categorically that he was not a $600,000 player. He tried to negotiate, but the Raiders stood firm. Mike really agonized over these negotiations. Should he sign for less money and keep the owner, his boyhood hero, Al Davis, happy and not jeopardize his job, or should he forget about all that and try to get the most money?

MY EYES PROJECT THE LASERED TORRENT OF MY CONVICTION TO PREVAIL.

Finally he worked things out and signed before the 1991 camp. But he was in camp no more than four hours before he went AWOL. The entire team was looking for him, and the press corps was asking head coach Art Shell every day what had happened. He rematerialized about a week later, claiming that his grandfather was dying and he just couldn't cope with camp anymore. We all knew he was extremely close to his grandfather, much closer than to his estranged father. However, since the urine drug screens were going to be done the second day of camp, the very day he left, the possibility also existed that he became leery about testing positive.

He stayed in camp no more than a few days before he went AWOL again. He returned just in time for the first preseason game in Japan. On one of the first days back from that game, he apparently was called Meathead in practice by fellow defensive end Emanuel King, who himself was trying to get into the clique. When Mike Wise objected vehemently, apparently Emanuel King taunted him, saying, "Sure, Meathead, I won't use that name Meathead again."

Later that night in one of the team meetings, King again called

Mike Meathead, and this time Mike jumped to his feet and punched Emanuel King, knocking him out cold.

I WILL USE MY THRUSTING EXTREMITIES TO DOMINATE.

When Emanuel King came to his senses, he stormed to his car, got a tire iron, and raced back into the clubhouse looking for Wise. The two faced off in the training room, but were restrained by worried teammates.

Further inflaming the situation, some outside the team tried to make it into a racial issue, since Mike was white and King was black, but none of the Raider players bought into that. In my eight years with the Raiders I never witnessed anything racial, although certainly events outside football, such as Marcus Allen's getting handcuffed in front of the schoolkids, reminded me that the same probably couldn't be said of the world in general.

In fact, the only story I had ever heard relating to race regarded George Anderson in the 1981 AFC championship game with San Diego. George had an uncanny knack of using humor—even when a player was down and hurting—to take his mind off the pain and get him thinking positively. One of George's better known motivational gimmicks was to humorously use the lowest ethnic slurs. He'd call the Italians wops, the Jews kikes, the Mormons f——ing wagon-train descendants, and the blacks niggers—a term that startled a lot of people, including me, even though we knew that the black players themselves would kiddingly refer to themselves as niggers, or to whites with speed as niggerlike. Everybody just called George himself Archie Bunker, kind of an early version of Howard Stern, who jived everyone separately but equally. Yet year in and year out, George continued to be the most genuinely loved Raider employee.

So in this critical play-off game in 1981, with the San Diego Chargers, we were driving down the field when suddenly Kenny King, who had a pretty wild sense of humor and was always pulling pranks back and forth with George, was groaning on the ground after taking a hit to his leg. George ran out there and in his usual inimitable way growled, "C'mon, Kenny, get your fat nigger ass off the ground."

Well, one of the defensive players for the San Diego Chargers standing just ten yards away overheard this and stormed forward angrily, gesturing at Kenny King, who was now beginning to get up on his own power, and saying, "Hey, man, that's racial. Don't take that shit."

Then Gene Upshaw, who even back then as a player had a Moses-like quality and commanded respect whenever he opened his mouth, grabbed the oncoming San Diego player and angrily retorted, "That's our trainer. And he can call us anything he goddamn wants. Now get your ass back on your side of the field."

After things settled down, Mike Wise was brought into Coach Art Shell's office.

"You know, Emanuel King is threatening to shoot you, Mike," Shell began. "I'm not so sure I want to stand in front of you to take that bullet. You can't go around and just hit people."

Mike Wise had clearly thrown the first punch, and he was told that he was being sent home for a period of days.

A couple of days came and went, the 1991 season opener was played (notably without Emanuel King, who had been released in the final cut), but Mike Wise stayed at home in Sacramento. The team did not contact him. Another game came, another game went. Mike Wise was sitting at home, the mortgage payments on his $600,000 home piling up on his desk, payments that he couldn't make, since he had not received a check in ten months.

He grew increasingly frustrated as the Raiders (1) refused to cut him so that he could see if he could pick up with another team, (2) refused to trade him so that he could then again be paid, and (3) refused to pay him, claiming he was on a "refuse to report" list and so they were not obliged to pay him a salary.

So finally, out of sheer frustration, Mike flew down and stormed into the Raiders office, demanding to talk to Al Davis.

I AM PRIMED FOR COMBAT, PRIMED FOR EXCELLENCE . . .

Al Davis didn't talk to him. George Karras, one of our scouts, saw him and told him to get the hell out of the building. So Wise flew back home. It was the last time he set foot on Raider soil.

Unbeknownst to him, the Los Angeles Rams, desperate that particular season for help on their defensive line, were offering the Raiders a fourth-round pick for him. (Remember, Mike Wise was a fourth-round pick himself. There were quite good players to be had at that round.) Al Davis refused that offer. The Rams would be playing the Raiders later in the season, actually the eighth game in the season, and Al had a standing policy never to trade a player to a team that he was going to play later that year. It might look bad in the local press if the player was doing well, and he never wanted to get in a position where a disgruntled former player could hurt the Raiders.

But after the Los Angeles Rams game, Al Davis released Wise outright. The Rams had taken care of their defensive needs, and no other team now wanted Wise in a trade. So Davis came away without a draft pick, but he sent Wise, and indirectly his teammates, a strong message by hurting him personally and financially. My way—or the highway.

Mike was picked up on waivers by Cleveland, which immediately put him into the lineup. He was in great shape. He impressed the coaches. In no time he was the Browns' starting defensive end.

I AM UNCHAINED DOMINANCE, FURY . . . I AM THE FORCE OF ACTION, CONQUEST, COMPULSION . . . I AM READY . . .

Then Wise suffered a knee injury and was put on injured reserve for the remainder of the 1991 season. He was doing well, rehabbing seven days a week, when he severely injured his back while lifting weights two weeks before the beginning of the 1992 season.

By now his story had a familiar ring to it. Maybe his use of anabolic steroids had something to do with his muscle and skeletal injuries. Maybe it was just football. He was cut in summer camp by the Cleveland Browns, who told him if he got healthy they'd certainly want to talk to him and take another look.

He went into a deep depression. Perhaps anabolic steroid withdrawal made it worse. Getting cut and unceremoniously tossed back into the real world with no means to pay his bills didn't help his moodiness. For five years he'd been a pro sports star, with every kind of medical attention available to him. Now he desperately needed medical help—and he either didn't know it or didn't know where to get it.

He put his house up for sale. His longtime girlfriend left him despite his pleas. He'd sit at home and tell friends, "God, I just can't get up today, my body hurts so much."

The Grim Reaper tattoo lurked on his ankle, a constant reminder that death was near.

Then he would tearfully add, "You just don't understand the pressure I'm under."

. . . NOW, RIGHT F——ING NOW!

On August 1, 1992, Mike Wise grabbed his 9mm Ruger, held it in front of his right ear, and pulled the trigger. He blew a two-inch-diameter hole between his right and left temples.

After twenty-eight years of life, most of them dedicated to just winning, Mike had lost. After only six years of living his dream in professional football, he had slipped into a nightmare. And there was no safety net. Had he heard the passionate message Lyle Alzado had urged on anyone who would listen twelve months earlier, he might never have needed one.

25

Lyle's Last Chapter

It was a mob scene. More than fifty people circled around the cordoned-off entrance to Lyle Alzado's newly opened West Hollywood sports bar. It was the spring of 1990, and Lyle's comeback at age forty-one, five years after his last NFL game, was netting him a ton of publicity. Wanda and I stood on the periphery.

"The prospects for getting in look kind of grim," I said.

"Hey, doc!"

We looked over to our left. It was Steve Wright, the handsome veteran offensive lineman whose gum line I had reattached.

"What are you doing standing out here?" he asked, a twentyish model draped over each arm. "All you have to do is show your Raider ID."

We followed his block through the crush of would-be patrons. Sure enough, my laminated NFL physician's picture ID was all it took. We inched our way around the packed central bar, the beautiful people elbowing by us. The twenty-foot-high walls were draped with Lyle Alzado football memorabilia. We grabbed a stand-up table and ordered some of the menu's stadiumlike items. No sooner had we gotten a beer than Lyle himself emerged out of the dense crowd.

"Doc, good to see you."

I was surprised he'd gone out of his way to greet me, and in such a friendly tone. I hadn't talked to him in five years. I could still vividly remember seeing his jugular veins rise in anger as I stood in his hospital room after his career-ending Achilles rupture.

It was our final steroid standoff. I laid out the tests he needed to have, and in no uncertain terms demanded he get off the juice. He blew up and blew me off. The next day he changed his mind and called me wanting to go through with the work-up. My staff spent days setting up his tests, making sure he would get VIP treatment, but he was a no-show.

"Lyle, this is my wife, Wanda. I don't know if you remember her."

"I don't forget a good-looking face. I remember seeing her at the Super Bowl ring dinner. I think you went out with my ex-wife Cindy a few times."

"Yeah, I did," replied Wanda. "Well! We're all excited about your comeback!"

"I'm the strongest I've ever been," Lyle boasted. "I'm working out six hours a day with my East German coach. I'm going to do this for every forty-year-old guy in the country. By the way, I want to pay for this," he said as he picked up our tab.

"Gee, thanks, Lyle."

"And I got to get over to your office, doc—I gotta get a physical."

"Anytime," I replied.

The "East German coach" line told me a lot about where he was on the steroid issue, though, and I doubted he'd be coming in to take a lecture from me.

"I'll talk to you later," he said. With a wave he was on his way to pump the crowd.

"That was very nice," said Wanda.

"Yeah." I shrugged. "But I'm still pissed at him for walking out on those tests and specialist consultations that I spent hours arranging for him. He just never showed up. I called looking for him, but his secretary said he was off shooting a movie in Mexico."

"That's the last you heard from him?"

"That's it."

As I'd expected, I didn't hear from Lyle until our three-day veteran camp in May. Several years before, we had switched our physical exams from the first day of summer camp in July to the May camp, because it gave me more time and better facilities for my player examinations. At the end of the day I happened to be exiting along with Lyle.

"Can I talk to you, Lyle?"

"Okay, but hurry up," he curtly replied. "I'm late."

His mood rainbow seemed to be on one of the darker colors.

"I just wanted to make sure you know about the new steroid testing," I said.

I was essentially positive he was on 'roids. His muscular development was as large as I'd ever seen it, and he was cut. He had the V-shaped upper body with the arm and leg muscles rippling in every direction. His hair was thinning and he had mild acne. He was moody as hell. His testicles on exam hadn't been that small, but his East German coach had probably thrown in beta-HCG, an injectable female hormone known to keep the testicles their normal size in steroid users.

"The league has a new drug policy," I continued, "and the testing is really accurate. We test for both steroids and the drugs that interfere with the urine tests for steroids. You know, like Lasix, Probenicid, and the like."

"Don't worry about me," he shot back confidently. "I know all about those tests, and I'm not going to test positive."

"Are you taking steroids right now?" I asked.

"Don't worry about me." He winked.

Three months later, toward the end of summer camp, the results of the preseason drug tests came in. Lyle was not on the list. He'd passed. I told him he'd passed, hoping he'd spill the beans and tell me what he was taking and how he'd beaten the test. But he just winked again and smirked, "I told you so!"

A week later, Lyle was starting as defensive end against the Bears in Chicago. It was our last preseason game. But something very strange was going on with Lyle. He had ripped a calf muscle on the second day of summer camp, then pulled multiple other muscles, and had essentially been unable to work out for the entire six-week preseason camp. He had also had a suspicious cough for the last five weeks. Other players on the team had come down with a cough too, but they seemed to shake it off after a week or so.

Finally Lyle made it through a couple of practice days uninjured and got a chance to play one more time in the big show. With our defense backed up to the goal line, Lyle made his last big splash. He muscled his offensive opponent to the side, then barreled toward the quarterback with arms screaming skyward. He swatted the quarterback's pass out of the air, collected the deflected ball in his arms, and steamed up the field. Sixty-seven thousand Chicago partisans, sensing they were seeing this great warrior for the last time, rose in a standing ovation. No matter that Lyle was able to run upfield only fifteen yards before being caught from behind. No matter that the play was called back because Lyle had jumped way offside. His hands were still stretched high in celebration. He could still kick ass.

The next day Lyle retired. That was how valued veterans with no chance of being picked up by another team were cut. Lyle had gotten his publicity, helped his bar and his show-biz career. The Raiders had been able to sell a few more preseason tickets. Lyle had lost a step. He couldn't quite keep up with teammates twenty years his junior. And even if he could, his injury pattern told a vivid tale. He looked like Tarzan, but the nonstop muscle pulls and strains made him play like Jane.

Unexpectedly, I saw Lyle again a week later. He lay before me on a hospital bed, with a large laceration on his nose and both eyes black and blue. The night before, while at an ice cream parlor with his ex-wife Cindy and son Justin, he had begun a violent coughing jag. Unable to get any air in, he turned blue then he fainted, landing flat on his face. The nose fractured for the sixth time.

"Doc, why the hell am I still coughing? It's been two months."

"It's a mystery, Lyle. Your chest X-ray is normal again today, your sinus CAT scans came back negative, you don't have asthma, and you've had two different courses of antibiotics without getting any help. You've probably got a very tenacious viral bronchitis, but sometimes it seems like your body is having an extra tough time fighting it off."

"What do you mean?"

"I don't know myself, Lyle. Um, tell me, what was that East German coach of yours giving you?"

"I was taking some injectable, but mostly oral steroids and growth hormone and Dexedrine before games and key practices."

"How'd you beat the drug test?"

"Since the spring I only took the short-acting oral steroids. I stopped them about six weeks before the preseason test and switched to human growth hormones—there's no test for them."

Growth hormone misuse was at epidemic levels. When I was team doctor, I'd never heard one player confess to using them. However, now that I'd resigned, players were freely admitting their use and telling of others who'd gotten them started. Besides Lyle and Mike Wise, at least five others were regularly injecting the genetically engineered hormone, and of note, four of the five were newly acquired from other teams.

"And after the preseason test, you went back to using steroids?"

"Yeah, we went back on some low cycles of steroids and backed off a little bit on the growth hormone."

"Well, what if you had made the team and your name came up for one of those random tests?"

"My guy said he had a blocking drug that never fails, and we were going to test it at a local lab if I made the team. And if that didn't work, I was just going to catheterize in some clean urine five minutes before I had to pee in front of the drug collector."

"Did you ever think that maybe some of that shit could mess with your immune system and prevent you from getting over a simple viral infection?"

"I'm off the stuff now, doc. My football career's over, so I'm getting off the stuff."

"Your mouth to God's ears, Lyle."

I didn't hear from Lyle again for another five months or so after he had ripped out his IVs and prematurely discharged himself from the hospital. He phoned my medical office late one January afternoon.

"Doc, I'm getting married."

"Congratulations, Lyle."

He then proceeded to ask me a medical question about his fiancée. It was hard concentrating on his question. I was wondering if she knew about his drug use—and resultant mood swings—that had on multiple occasions led to wife and girlfriend beating.

It didn't take disaster long to strike. But it hit Lyle, not his new wife. He came into the office several days after his marriage, admitting that he had had trouble walking down the aisle during his wedding ceremony. He somehow couldn't catch his balance. Now he had vertigo, double vision, slurred speech, and impossibly messy handwriting. Hours later, standing alone in the Cedars-Sinai MRI reading room, I found out why. It looked as if there were about eight large mothballs sitting in his brain substance.

"Hi, Lyle," I said in as upbeat a voice as I could manage under the circumstances.

"Doc, I want you to meet my agent, Lorraine Feinstone, and my accountant, Nicole Katz."

"Hi," I said, shaking their hands. "Um, would you all mind giving me a couple of minutes alone with Lyle?"

"It doesn't look good," I said after the others had left. "There's something very strange going on, and most probably, from the look of things, it's some kind of infection. I don't want to lie to you—rare infections in the brain make us think about AIDS. That's why I need to ask you—and don't bullshit me—have you ever had homosexual intercourse?"

"No."

"Have you ever been with prostitutes?"

"No."

"Have you ever done intravenous drugs?"

"No."

"Where did you get the needles that you used to inject the steroids?"

"I just got sterile needles and steroids from Dr. Jekot down here or Dr. Pearlzac up north."

"You never, ever shared needles when you were shooting the steroids?"

"No."

"When's the first time you ever used growth hormone?"

"I just used it for my comeback."

"You never used the cadaver growth hormone back in the early eighties?"

"No—well . . . maybe a time or two, but not enough to mention."

My heart stopped. Everybody knew the original growth hormone extracts had been taken from pooled cadaver brains. These human products could transmit deadly viruses, such as Creutzfeldt-Jacob or HIV.

Two days later, I was elated. The HIV antibody blood test was negative. Just to be sure, though, I sent back blood to be tested for traces of HIV genetic material and exterior markers that turn up even before the HIV antibody test turns positive. And I also had tests run for less common HIV-like viruses. They were all negative.

But the infectious disease and neurologic consultants were perplexed. A tap into Lyle's spinal fluid was negative—no evidence of any of the rare infections I was suspecting. His positional head spinning was worsening, and in a pitiful, ironic twist, he was prescribed a black eye patch just to be able to sit up in bed. Otherwise he'd pitch helplessly over to his side.

The brain biopsy was done on a Friday, and at eight in the morning on Saturday, I stood at his bedside and dropped the bombshell.

"It's cancer, Lyle. A rare type of lymphoma that's hopscotched from one part of your brain to another."

"What caused it?"

"Well, we see this type of brain lymphoma a lot in people with

AIDS. We know you don't have that. We also see it a lot in people who have a transplanted kidney. Their immune system gets battered by the years and years of chemotherapy-like drugs needed to keep the body from rejecting the transplant. A battered immune system may lead to lymphoma."

"What about the steroids and growth hormone?"

"I don't know, Lyle—I don't know."

"How do we get rid of it?"

"We've got a new form of treatment. Radiation therapy followed by high-dose chemo to the brain. Previous types of treatment haven't been all that successful, but we have every hope that this new approach will cure this lymphoma just as it can cure lymphoma that's outside the brain."

That was as close as I could come to telling him he had, on the average, less than six months to live.

"Doc, could you do me one favor?"

"Sure, Lyle."

"Could you call Al Davis for me? Let him know what I'm up against?"

Wanda and I stood outside the twentieth-floor open-air corridor of the Marina Center. The apartment complex was built in a very modernistic open arc, so that as you walked from the elevator to the various apartment doors on one side, on the other side there was only a thirty-inch railing separating you from a sheer drop. The corridor did give a beautiful view of the oceanfront community, but I was a little too height sensitive to venture near the edge. We knocked on the door again.

"It happened right here?" Wanda asked.

"Yup, I guess so," I said. "The female sheriff's deputy was standing right here. She knocked on their door at about five-thirty in the morning to serve a subpoena for some sort of bankruptcy hearing. Lyle stuck his head out the door and mothered her for waking him up. What happened next is in dispute, but the deputy responded by emptying a whole can of Mace at Lyle."

Lyle, with a tear-gas skin rash, eyes on fire, and a metallic taste in his mouth, had been arrested for battery on a police officer and hauled off and booked at the Marina del Rey station in his bathrobe. Lyle claimed he'd just stuck his head out the door, and obviously hanging on to the inside door handle to keep his balance, had thrown a few choice words at the deputy for waking him up at five-thirty in the morning. The deputy claimed Lyle had charged toward her, which based on my knowledge of Lyle's medical condition seemed close to impossible. Lyle couldn't walk, much less charge.

That was several days ago, but things hadn't settled down. Yesterday, Lyle's medical condition had been made public—his inoperable brain cancer was splashed across every newspaper in the country. Lyle and his wife had asked us over for dinner, and I hoped to get a few moments to check his progress with the radiation therapy over the last several weeks.

"Hi, you guys. You made it."

It was Lyle. He led us into the barren living room, where boxes had been stacked neatly against the walls in preparation for his move out of the expensive Marina complex into a modest one-bedroom house in the Beverlywood section of Los Angeles.

The jig was up on Lyle's wild financial dealings. He had missed the huge salaries of the mid-eighties when teammates made millions in salary. Still, even though his highest salary had been a comparatively low $350,000 per year, he did have fourteen years in the league. His heyday with a million-dollar Palos Verdes mansion and matching Rolls-Royce was over. Now he faced a bankrupt future. He owed $75,000 to his William Morris agents and $300,000 to the IRS for back taxes, not to mention various child support claims and business debts. He was hundreds of thousands of dollars down, and he had little or no chance of being able to go out and earn a living . . . ever.

The take-out Chinese food was spread out across the kitchen table, the only piece of furniture in view.

"Wanda, it's good to see you again," said Lyle in his Brooklyn drawl, spoken at about five-eighths speed.

He had already lost a chunk of weight and was down from his usual imposing 290 pounds to about 260. The biggest spot of cancer was in his cerebellum, the balance part of the brain, causing his faulty gait, double vision, and also nausea, which didn't do much for his appetite. Like most cancer patients, he may have had proteins in his blood that further decreased his appetite, and then there were the nauseating side effects of his cancer treatment. There was yet another contributing factor. For the first time in his life, he was scared to death—scared enough to stop his seventeen-year-long use of muscle-building cocktails. At first Lyle continued using, trying desperately to keep his weight up. But finally, with his neurologic deterioration painfully obvious, he was ready to quit.

Just to make sure, Lyle's new wife scoured the entire apartment when he was away for one of his brain radiation therapy treatments. What she found was beyond even my wildest imagination. She brought in an entire shopping bag chock full of every conceivable bulking concoction. There were thousands of dollars' worth of Genentech growth hormone vials, all interestingly enough marked "No Sale," meaning they were samples off some pediatric endocrinologist's shelf, or else stolen from an ongoing drug trial.

There were five types of oral anabolic steroids and sixteen types of injectable steroids, some of them veterinary with pictures of horses on the boxes. The labels were from West Germany, East Germany, France, Mexico, Italy, and the U.S.A. There was extract from pregnant women's urine that prevented the testicles from shrinking. There was an estrogen hormone blocker, tamoxifen, prescribed typically for women who have had breast cancer to help prevent a recurrence, but used by weight lifters to try to prevent "bitch tits"—the painful swellings and breast enlargement resulting from partial conversion of steroids into estrogen.

There was thyroid medicine. There was pain medicine. There was an asthma medicine from Canada, rumored to increase strength. There were boxes of syringes. There were pads of papers with various "stacking" schemes—schemes for taking handfuls of different steroids simultaneously, in hopes of more muscle and fewer side effects. About half the drugs had come from the refrigerator; the rest had been hidden under the kitchen sink, in the bathroom, under the bed, and behind Lyle's trophies. Some small-town pharmacies don't have this selection of drugs.

"I'd like to propose a toast to my gorgeous new wife, to my doc, his beautiful wife . . ."

Suddenly Lyle stiffened ever so slightly and his head tilted off to the right. I could see a faint tremor beginning in his left hand and slowly increasing.

"Lyle!" screamed Kathy. "This is what I told you I saw happen to him several times yesterday," she said as she began to cry.

In a moment he was in the midst of a full-blown herky-jerky seizure. His neck stiffened as foam formed around his lips, and a bluish hue crept across his strained face. I jumped around the table to cradle his head and slowly bring it down to the floor. He had bitten his tongue with one firm snap of the jaw, and there was some blood mixed with the foam from his mouth. Just as quickly as it began, it was over. And he opened his eyes.

"Lyle, where are you?"

He didn't respond, but instead peered from side to side as if to get his bearings.

"You're okay, Lyle, don't worry," I said. "It's normal to be confused for a couple of minutes after a seizure."

Just then, his head still in my hands, I noticed a small amount of whitish material in the back of his hairline.

"Where's his brain biopsy site?" I said, mystified that none of his incisions were in view.

"Ah, he's got his hairpiece on," said Kathy. "He refuses to ever take that off."

"Can you take it off for me?" I asked.

Lyle had always been very vain about his hair, despite the fact that he was probably about half bald on the top, at least in part because of the anabolic steroids he was taking. In his playing days, he'd always kept a brush in his back pocket.

Kathy pulled off the hairpiece. There was a column of pus coming from each one of his brain biopsy burr holes.

"When did this start?" I asked incredulously.

"I don't know," answered an equally surprised Kathy. "He just saw the neurosurgeons last week for a follow-up, but I don't think he took off his hairpiece for them."

The entire family was waiting for me outside the medical intensive care unit.

"He's got a raging staph infection in the brain. We're pouring in antibiotics, but somehow his own body's white blood cells just don't want to kick in. Antibiotics help knock down infection, but they often can't cure it all by themselves. Because of the infection that's irritating the brain, he's having almost nonstop seizures.

"Assuming you don't fall down and hit your head, a single seizure doesn't injure the brain. But when you have seizure after seizure, it can short out the brain and cause irreversible damage. So we've essentially anesthetized him into a coma on massive antiseizure medicines. Well, we finally got the seizures to stop. But then, wham! His platelets dropped from two hundred thousand to almost zero. Maybe from his seizure meds, maybe a complication of his infection. That's the last thing we wanted. The risk, of course, is spontaneous bleeding into the brain. He already has more than his share of trouble there.

"Of course, we're temporarily going to stop his brain radiation treatments. He needs all the immune function he can muster to fight off this infection."

"Can he hear me?" Kathy asked.

"Possibly," I said, "but don't expect him to acknowledge you just yet. Even after we take that tube out of his throat and he's able to talk, he'll still be very groggy and confused, and that will only get better when we get control of his problem—the infection, the cancer, the brain radiation, and the massive doses of seizure meds."

"Is he going to make it?" asked Peter, Lyle's older brother.

"He's critical. He's got inoperable brain cancer, life-threatening meningitis, status epilepticus, and a serious platelet absence. But if anyone can fight his way back, your brother can," I replied optimistically. "He's going to be very well taken care of here, with one-on-one nursing, so I suggest you all take a break, go home tonight, and get some sleep."

"No, I can't leave," said Kathy. "He needs me by his side."

It was a week later. After circling the drain for the first several days in the ICU, Lyle staged a dramatic recovery. His fever trickled downward, his platelet count bumped slowly upward, and his seizures finally came under control. We tapered the medicines. He awoke from his coma. We were able to take the tube out of his trachea, and he was soon up in a chair and eating. He was finally transferred back to a regular ward room, but he was still disoriented and confused because of his brain infection and megadoses of medication. He occasionally seemed to recognize family members, but for the most part, he really didn't know where he was or what was going on.

I arrived at the tenth-floor UCLA nurses' station at precisely six o'clock in the morning, right on schedule to begin seeing my office patients at seven. I pulled Lyle's chart out of the rack and began deciphering the handwritten consultant notes from the prior day. I flipped to the blood test section and was looking at his platelet counts as I backed through the door of his private hospital room. I looked up and stopped dead in my tracks. There lying next to Lyle, in the narrow hospital bed, was a stunning brunette. His wife was blond. For one of the few times in my medical career, I was speechless. She gave me a wink, which threw me even more off balance. I finally just decided to do the show-biz thing and get on with Lyle's examination.

"How do you feel this morning, Lyle?"

"Good, good, doc."

"Did you have any of the tremors or shaking in your left arm last night?"

"No, I was fine."

"He had two little episodes, each lasting about two or three minutes," his companion corrected, whispering as if Lyle wouldn't hear.

I listened to his heart and lungs, then looked at his scalp. The damn pus was still oozing from his brain biopsy site.

"Lyle, can you tell me where you are?" I asked.

"I'm at home," he said, looking over at his bed partner. "We're at home in the bedroom."

A few minutes later I went down the elevator, got in my car, and turned my key in the ignition. Finally my memory kicked in. I knew that woman. She had been with Lyle when I'd had my futile talk with him in 1985, before his last regular season. She was his post-Cindy, pre-Kathy wife.

I was about two hours into my office schedule when I got a frantic emergency call from Kathy.

"Dr. Huizenga! I want you to write an order not to let anyone but me in Lyle's room!" she demanded. "I can't believe what just happened to me! The first night I go home, the first night, and I come back at nine o'clock and ask the nurse where Lyle is, and the nurse tells me he's gone down on the gurney to the MRI suite with his wife! Janice and Peter, his brother and sister, lied to me last night. They told me to go home and get a good night's sleep—it was the first time I'd left Lyle's side. They told me she was his other sister. She's one of his ex-wives!" she said, sobbing.

He exited from the chauffeured limousine. We moved through the crowded entry of Spago's, a renowned celebrity eatery. The sight of the still powerfully built six-foot-three Alzado, wearing a bandanna, seemed to part the mass of humanity as if he were Moses heading through the Red Sea. This crowd usually didn't gawk at the face of fame, but something about Lyle's face, his proud cheekbones and exasperated eyes, attracted stares. Lyle's multicolored bandannas were fast becoming a fashion trademark.

Lyle had been complaining bitterly about the handfuls of hair he'd find on his pillow each morning. We had finally persuaded him to shave, to go for a bald Mr. T look, but although he actually looked quite good with a shaved head, everyone had to admit the bandanna was definitely a touch.

He was still very resistant to going anywhere public. He'd repeated over and over to me that he didn't want his teammates to see him this way. Lyle had a body image problem, a problem that definitely was part of his inability to come off anabolic steroids. He had visions of returning to his high school weight before he started steroids, or worse yet, going all the way down to the 170 pounds his brother weighed.

The maître d' brought us to the VIP table, the table front and center. I'd eaten at Spago's two or three times before. Of course, I'd come with family or friends and we'd been seated in the back room, the room usually reserved for tourists, locals not connected with the entertainment industry, or servants.

Greg Campbell was taking Lyle, Kathy, my wife, and me out to dinner to celebrate his reassociation with Lyle. Since Lyle's cancer was announced, and since his pronouncement to Maria Shriver that his steroid use was to blame, he'd gotten offers galore. The only problem was that his PR firm wanted thousands per month to deal with the flood of offers. Lyle was penniless. Enter Greg. He offered to handle things for free, *and* financially support him through the lean times. Greg had made a name for himself working for Muhammad Ali. He had become Lyle's agent when they met in Denver at the famous Muhammad Ali/Lyle Alzado exhibition boxing match. Lyle had pumped up for months, pushing the limits of his personal conditioning and whipping himself into the best shape of his life. He worked himself into a frenzy before stepping into the ring. Once the bell sounded, he hit Ali four or five times, then as Ali backpedaled into the ropes, slugged him two or three more times as hard as he could. The two then went into a clinch, and Ali said to Lyle, "Hey, ease up, buddy. This is only a charity event."

Lyle, always the aggressive warrior, didn't answer, but he was thinking to himself, "I got him."

Lyle hit Ali again with a powerful right and now began to get excited. "I can bring this guy down," he confidently told himself.

Then Muhammad Ali gave Lyle a look and hit him with both

hands about fifteen times in the mouth before Lyle could even react. All his pretensions faded. This was one of the few stories Lyle told me that included any self-deprecating humor.

Greg and Lyle had split up a number of years ago, in the midst of an argument over a five-figure sum that somehow didn't seem to be accounted for to either side's satisfaction.

But now he was back, with his chauffeured limo, his Century City staff, and his big ideas about how to get Lyle off his financial knees.

"Boy, it's great to get out with you, Lyle," said Kathy, giving him a big hug.

"Yeah, you just look great," said Wanda. "You're going to shock everybody and beat this thing!"

"Yeah, but I just can't keep my weight on. Still get tired so quick," Lyle said in his hoarse voice. His vocal chord nerves had been permanently damaged by the original cancer.

"You walked around the block the other day on your own—that's a huge step, Lyle," I replied. "And before you know it, we'll be letting you go back to Gold's Gym."

"Do you really think so?" he said.

"I know so. You know we have to take it easy at first, but you'll be back."

"Yeah, you got to get strong," Greg added, "cuz I got a lot of stuff planned for you. They're talking about a Lyle Alzado movie, a Lyle Alzado book, you got acting offers, we got possibilities for a sports talk radio show, all the evening talk shows, like Carson, Arsenio would like you to come back on . . . you've got tons of requests. It's just a question of when you're strong enough and the doc says you're ready to go."

That seemed to pick him up some, as did a personal visit by Wolfgang Puck, the chef of this pricey eatery. But by dessert, he was dragging pretty bad and asked to be taken home. He was barely able to balance his way up the sidewalk past the crush of photographers outside, and even this flash of attention was unable to recharge his energy store.

Greg's coming into the picture was a godsend for me. Despite being a tad on the flashy end of the spectrum, he seemed to be totally devoted to Lyle's needs, and they even seemed to pick up the close friendship that had abruptly ended several years before. Greg handled the hundreds of media requests coming in each week. It was a request from *Sports Illustrated*, coming on the heels of the

Maria Shriver television feature revelations, that changed the tenor of Lyle's last months on earth.

The July 4, 1991, cover was classic. There was Lyle's head shot, a wasted stare underneath his skull-and-crossbones bandanna. There was a large subtitle—I LIED—splashed below. Lyle wanted to come clean about his drug use. He knew firsthand the scope of the problem, and he wanted to do what he could to keep future generations of athletes off the juice. Lyle was convinced that the steroids and/or growth hormone had triggered his brain lymphoma. I told Lyle that no evidence existed to prove it or to disprove it, but that, in fact, twenty-two years of nonstop steroids, with growth hormone, thyroid hormone, and speed sprinkled in, could cause a lot of things, and there was some circumstantial evidence that years and years of various chemicals and drugs could induce this family of lymphomas.

So this issue of *Sports Illustrated*, the issue that went on to be a top seller, set off a media frenzy. Greg Campbell handled literally thousands of calls from every corner of the world. My office got hundreds of calls, which nearly paralyzed my already overworked staff.

I called Lyle to see if he really wanted me to say anything more about his condition to the media.

"Before I die, I'm going to get this thing off my chest, doc," he said slowly. "I *want* you to continue to talk freely to the media. You can help me get my message out. Help me make a difference. I wasn't honest with myself or my fans, and now I'm paying the price. No one else should ever have to feel the pain I feel."

I was curious to see how Al Davis would respond to Lyle's anti-anabolic-steroid crusade. From my first phone call, Davis had been very supportive. Of course, when he told me, through his secretary, "I don't care what it costs, I don't care what you have to do—make sure you get him the best cancer specialist," I was personally offended. How dare Davis give his entire team substandard medical care as a matter of policy and then get on his high horse in this sort of a situation? But I bit my tongue, and I'm glad I did, because his weekly calls to Lyle, following the updates he got from me via his secretary, meant a tremendous amount to Lyle. And as Lyle began getting national attention for his revelations of the darker side of football, Al Davis's support for him didn't appear to waver.

The Raiders did manage to get in a personal dig at me in the *Sports Illustrated* issue. There was a small insert in which I talked about the dangers of anabolic steroids, and in the italicized introduction, I was asked why I was no longer with the Raiders. I answered truthfully, but with some restraint, that I had resigned because of differences with the Raider organization about patient care. Al LoCasale, speaking for the Raiders, disagreed, saying I was "let go," which implied I'd been fired.

Lyle had been off steroids for three months. No more tantrums. No more out-of-control fits. He was turning into a nice guy. His desire to have me go on the front line of the battle against steroids was quite ironic. We hadn't really ever had a friendly conversation in the initial years I'd known him. Because of our arguments, though, I'd become obsessed with steroids. So now, after endless hours of research and thought, I knew as much about the problem as any doctor.

But there was something about a celebrity in distress that sent a message a thousandfold stronger than any well-meaning doctor could ever hope to deliver. Greg Campbell orchestrated a talk show blitz. Lyle beamed his message from the network news to Arsenio to the Roy Firestone show. As part of an educational video for athletes being developed at the time by Campbell, Lyle talked at length to the defending NCAA football champion University of Colorado football team.

"I always thought that I wanted to be a great football player," he began. "And I thought that using steroids would get me there. But I didn't know anything. What I face now, I face death right now."

The players pummeled him with questions.

"Why didn't you rely on your God-given talent?"

"I was confused," he said. "I thought I could take a short cut. I didn't know it would take my life."

"Wouldn't it mean more to you if you did it naturally?"

"I always thought I'd eventually stop," he said. "It was all right here," and he pointed to his head.

"When you were on the Arsenio Hall show," another said, "they took a poll. If you could play football for two years, make a million dollars, but die after that, eighty-five percent of the people said yeah."

"If they felt this pain, they would say no," Lyle responded. "If they could crawl inside of me . . . I hurt all the time."

"What would you say to a friend in the denial stage?" asked another young athlete.

"There's a right road, and a wrong road."

"I still have your autograph from when you were with the Broncos."

"Nice to see you again—ha ha ha." He smiled.

"How much did you spend a year on steroids?"

"Well, I spent around thirty thousand a year. Hey, that's why I don't have any money anymore. Why, do you want to take me to dinner?"

Another athlete said, "I'm not saying steroids are good or anything, but what about all the guys who are on steroids and making lots of money and are healthy?"

Lyle responded, "Would you trade your family and friends in this room for that? I wouldn't make that choice. I'd rather not play football, be All-Pro. I'd rather just live my life."

Finally as the session was wearing down, an interesting question came in.

"What could a friend have said to you?"

"I didn't want to believe anybody, or listen."

"I want to thank you for coming here tonight," the player said. "You might have saved one of our lives tonight."

"If anything positive can come from this, I hope I can save even just one life. This is the hardest battle I've ever fought. The doctors are not optimistic. But I've always loved a challenge. And this will be the greatest comeback I could ever achieve. And I hope that you will all help me in spreading this message. To stay off steroids. Believe in yourself, and do it naturally."

Lyle's message was hardly being embraced by the National Football League. Lyle estimated that on certain teams 80 percent of the interior linemen used anabolic steroids, a figure the NFL brass flatly denied.

My hope was that the NFL in its embarrassment, and possibly with some sympathy for Lyle and potential future cases, would look one step beyond the immediate public relations implications and do the right thing—allow former NFL football players who had used steroids to be studied, to see whether these players got more heart disease, more cancer, more divorces, more crippling orthopedic injuries, or more arrests than their nonuser "control" teammates.

Controls were, of course, desperately needed, because many people thought that 300-pound linemen didn't live much past their fifties anyway, steroids or not, given their notoriously fatty diets and higher-than-average alcohol intakes. You couldn't study weight lifters, because they didn't have the exceedingly careful medical attention that football players get from their team doctor and team trainers.

And while Olympic athletes also get very good medical attention, they're less likely to be honest, because if they admit steroid use they will have their medals taken away retroactively. And believe me, there'd be a lot of raised eyebrows if all the American athletes who have used enhancing drugs came clean.

One reason why football players were such an ideal group is that steroid use has been known in the NFL since at least 1963. It was the original San Diego Charger team, a team that coincidentally Al Davis helped coach from 1960 to 1963, that put the anabolic steroids on everyone's plate and even threatened fines for those players who didn't take the dinner pill.

Another reason to study the National Football League players was that a plethora of strange conditions was already known in steroid users. Without any formal study, I had already heard of three cases of cardiomyopathy, many cases of atrial fibrillation, three suicides, and a case of liver cancer in a Bronco lineman. This cancer, known to be associated with anabolic steroid use, is otherwise so rare in young American males that on a statistical basis not even one liver cancer would be expected to occur in a professional football player over the last several decades.

This was the study that John Lombardo, appointed to head up the anabolic steroid detection unit for the National Football League, had agreed was key. In fact, in 1990 Lombardo was trying to do an essentially similar study on weight lifters in his home state of Ohio, and agreed that much more information would come from a study on former National Football League players.

But talk of that study had occurred back when I was president of the National Football League Physicians Society. Now that I had been on the outside for nearly two years, all was quiet on the NFL's Park Avenue eastern front. It was obvious that they had problems with the potential public relations implications of any study that might reveal significant past use, or worse yet, the potential for future disaster. But I fired off letters to Lombardo and Gene Upshaw every so often anyway. I had applied for a government grant for the study and been told I couldn't get the needed money unless the government was assured that the Players Association and the NFL would cooperate with the study. Their silence killed the project.

Lyle by now was about five months into his monthly chemotherapy treatments. He was still edgy about his residual neurologic problems, specifically moderate balance problems, slurring of the speech, and episodic double vision. He got a massive outbreak of shingles with each chemo run, and probably most annoying to him was his nonstop weight loss. He could still curse a blue streak, and chose to do so every time he stepped on a scale in my office.

His spirits were buoyed, though, by the fact that the mothball-size brain cancers which had disappeared did not come back. All visible signs of cancer were gone. We were ecstatic, because brain lymphoma tended to laugh at the standard chemo. Maybe we had stumbled onto something good.

His gratifying response to treatment did not stop the constant barrage of letters with advice from well-meaning fans who themselves or whose friends had recovered from various brain ailments, as well as from faith healers and even a host of legitimate doctors, who appeared eager to have Lyle go to their facility to receive what they hoped would be the definitive treatment. Most of these were neurosurgeons who somehow had the mistaken impression that Lyle had one area of tumor. Of course, he initially had tumors spotted everywhere, and to remove them via brain surgery would have been essentially to remove his entire brain.

One of the most personally vexing bits of advice I was told that Lyle got was from Steven Seagal, known for his high-kicking action adventure movie roles. He had sent over a fabulous flower bouquet, then apparently followed up with a call to Lyle strongly suggesting Lyle stop chemotherapy and try an herbal remedy. I don't have a problem with people trying alternative treatments if state-of-the-art medical approaches aren't working. But in this case, Lyle's treatment was kicking ass.

Lyle had to deal with other fringe players as well. The *Globe* splashed a story indicating Lyle had a gay lover, with a picture of a weight-lifting acquaintance with his arm around Lyle. I was told the man later admitted giving the *Globe* the photo and "story" for $200.

I was getting weekly calls from *The New York Times*, *Sports Illustrated*, and TV news stations regarding the rampant rumor that Lyle had AIDS. One radio show, upset I didn't have time to return their call that day, threatened to "go on the air with the AIDS story" if I didn't call back by two that afternoon. I openly told the press that, true, Lyle's cancer was seen in increasing frequency in AIDS patients, but a wide range of HIV detecting tests had been repeatedly negative in Lyle. Of course the *National Enquirer* managed to twist these simple statements around. I guess you've really made it when the *National Enquirer* starts messing with your good name.

Lyle sat across from me at my littered desk, inside my office consultation room. He had been doing better little by little but today looked unusually lonely and subdued.

"Doc, I'm desperate," he said. "Can you help me out? I need a loan."

"Sure, Lyle," I said. "What, one thousand, two thousand, three thousand? What do you need?"

"Whatever you can spare, doc."

God, I hated those open-ended replies.

"I'm good for it, doc. The book deal and the movie deal, they'll add up to over a million dollars. But goddammit, the agents, the producers, the writers keep stringing it along—they're always negotiating. I need the money now. I got lawyers' bills, I got rent I can't pay, I got a car payment I can't pay."

After the *Sports Illustrated* article came out, Greg had set up what he called the Lyle Alzado Fund, to try to get Lyle and Kathy through on donations that fans around the country had sent in until the movie deal could click. It had all but dried up by now. There was not enough to pay for rent and food, and definitely not enough to pay for the bankruptcy lawyers and the other lawyers needed to fend off past lawsuits from people he'd slugged in various brawls. And that wasn't counting attorney fees for his upcoming day in court regarding battery on a police officer. Fortunately I ran into a friend, Bob Shapiro, one of LA's most prominent defense attorneys, who agreed to handle this for free when I appraised him of Lyle's desperate situation. Shapiro made a few key phone calls and presto, the case was indefinitely postponed.

And then there was ex-wife Cindy Alzado's overdue spousal support. Lyle was especially indignant about her claims because, by his accounting, he was ahead thousands of dollars, based on a house down payment he'd given her in the past. Cindy was indignant because Lyle was years behind in the $1,500 per month child support, but still managed to cover the $2,100 per month payment on his new wife's 500 SL Mercedes.

"I'll pay you back right after the benefit, doc."

The benefit was Greg's latest and grandest scheme. He was planning a gala $500-a-plate celebrity benefit for Lyle featuring, according to him, everyone from Muhammad Ali to Whitney Houston to John Madden to Jerry Lee Lewis. He was going to package it all up as a special and sell it to a major network. That fee plus the $500-per-head collection (Greg and some of the performers also were going to donate all fees ordinarily due them) would presumably pay off Lyle's after-bankruptcy debt of about $300,000 and give him an extra $100,000 or so to put in the bank.

I learned a bit of law when it was explained to me that even bankruptcy can't cancel out tax debts to Uncle Sam. Lyle had missed a few tax payments, including tax on the profits from the sale of his million-dollar Palos Verdes estate years earlier. All the bankruptcy would do is wipe out the $75,000 debt to William Morris, the bad investments, and the assorted bank loans. But he still had to ante up that $300,000 to get clear, and for the last couple of months, that had been his repeated preoccupation, to wipe out his debt and get back on his feet again working.

"Can you spare eight thousand?" he asked.

I gulped.

"Sure."

"Do you want me to sign a note?" he asked.

"Forget it," I said.

"Doc," he said, "I don't know how to thank you."

He looked embarrassed, humiliated, but relieved.

"Forget it," I said. "When your movie goes, we'll even up. Don't worry about it."

It was three o'clock Saturday afternoon, January 9, 1992. The midday sun shone down on me as I mindlessly rounded our back-yard bushes with my all-purpose hedge clipper.

"Rob, the phone's for you."

I picked up the backyard extension.

"Hello."

"Hello, Dr. Huizenga?" A woman's voice.

"Speaking."

"The Lyle Alzado benefit tonight at seven o'clock has been can-celed."

"Whaaaat? What happened to Lyle?"

"I don't know anything about it," she replied. "The producer of the show, Greg Campbell, was admitted to the hospital, and it's been decided to cancel the event."

I hung up the phone and dialed the Alzado residence as fast as I could. Lyle's cancer had just recurred after nine months in remission.

He had just resumed intensive chemotherapy, therapy that had numerous life-threatening side effects. I feared the worst.

"Kathy," I said as soon as she came on the line. "What's gong on?"

"They've canceled Lyle's benefit."

"Why? What happened?"

"The key sponsors all backed out on Greg. He's been taken to the Century City emergency room. He thinks he's having a heart attack."

"Oh my God. I'll call right over and check up on him. What about all your guests? Lyle's family, your family? All the football players that flew into town for this?"

"We don't know what to do," she said. "We're thinking of all going out to the Palm for dinner." She continued, "Something's wrong with this thing. I should have known after the first benefit fell through."

Greg had already canceled the previous benefit date, scheduled for early December several weeks before, claiming that a conflicting AIDS benefit with Elizabeth Taylor was drawing away a lot of his key sponsors.

"Hang on a second," I said. "Wanda, Lyle's benefit got canceled. Do you want to just have everybody come over here?"

"Sure, why not?"

"Kathy, let's have everybody come over here."

The house was jammed. Over two hundred and fifty people showed up. Our entire circular drive was blocked with limos. Traffic on our street was backed up for a couple of blocks—not exactly Woodstock, but much more than our neighborhood was accustomed to.

It was quite a crowd. It included Lyle's old college and high school coaches and many of his former teammates and former opponents, among them Franco Harris, who flew in from Pittsburgh, and Gene Upshaw, who flew in from Washington. Mickey Rourke, a good friend of Lyle's over the years, came in with his entourage of four or five other boxers. Mickey was taking the tribute's cancellation personally; if he'd found the person to blame, I think he would have punched his lights out.

Jerry Lee Lewis's people were there, fuming because they had been pulled to Los Angeles having paid all their own expenses, and now the hope of reimbursement seemed less than a faint glimmer.

"Jerry's gonna fire me!" his manager confided in me. "His motto's 'no pay, no play,' and I broke that trying to do Lyle a favor. We were going to play for free, but we're not paying for our expenses. If we do, I'm gonna be fired."

Rumors ran rampant among the guests as to the exact reasons the benefit had been called off at the last minute—a benefit so large that apparently many of the guests could not be notified. Some of the party guests had seen Maria Shriver walking up the ramp in a formal dress, only to be informed at eight o'clock that there was no event.

The bartender and the Price Club hors d'oeuvres we had rounded up with literally an hour to go before opening our doors were still holding up well at eleven o'clock when many of the guests circled in the living room and I read Lyle the proclamation from Mayor Tom Bradley that this was Lyle Alzado Day. But even that proclamation and the crush of faithful friends couldn't pull Lyle out of speechless disbelief. As he slowly bent his wasted 200-pound frame, clothed in black Armani tux and matching formal bandanna, into his limo to leave, for the first time I saw some quit in him.

"I can't walk, I can't see straight, you just told me my cancer's come back, I lost my house, I can't work, I lost all my money, I've got to beg for my rent, and now . . . this." He fell silent for a moment. Then:

"What's the use anymore?"

"Don't give up, Lyle. Look at all the people here that love you. Think about how important your steroid message is. We need you."

Five of us met at Lyle's house the next week. His balance and strength rapidly deteriorating in the face of the recurrent lymphoma, Lyle was still mute in anger and depression. He stayed in his bedroom while the rest of us did a postmortem on the canceled benefit.

"Greg tried to sell the benefit as a special to a network, but they weren't interested. He also tried to get sponsors to underwrite the whole affair—but only two wrote a check: Occidental for $30,000, and Al Davis for $75,000."

"What about the five hundred seats for five hundred dollars apiece?"

"Greg claimed no one was buying. So to ensure Lyle a room packed full of VIPs, he had to comp everyone."

The night before the benefit was supposed to go off, Greg still owed the Hilton $123,000. Then he had the chutzpah to go to Al Davis and other players he knew, who might remotely have that kind of money in a bank account, and asked them to fork it over with less than twenty-four hours to go before the event. Understandably, no one wanted to bail out a project this hopelessly screwed up at the last minute.

"Well, what about the $1 million movie and book deals?"

They were a cruel mirage. At the start, glowing financial numbers were tossed around. But when the book proposal went out, only rejection notices came in. The *Sports Illustrated* article was so revealing, publishers wondered if enough newsworthy material remained. The promotion people were worried that Lyle wouldn't be around to publicize his book. And at about the same time, a media backlash developed—an anti-sympathy-you-brought-this-on-yourself sort of coverage. Then Magic Johnson announced his retirement, and his positive HIV test. Interest in Alzado's plight dropped to zero. Even a last ditch effort to print Lyle's story in a "Christian publication" fell through when the publisher's research questioned Lyle's religious convictions. The TV deal suffered from the same woes, finally fizzling when several writers passed on the project.

"I don't get it," I said. "Here's a guy, Greg Campbell, who loved Lyle, who must have been spending fifty percent of his waking hours taking care of this thing, spending tens of thousands of his own money for the banquet room down payment, the oversize color invitations with silver imprinting that go for twenty-five dollars per—you can't tell me he was trying to scam anything out of this."

"His intentions may have been good, but he was in over his head. Hey, who on a network would buy a TV show with no experienced producer involved?"

"I don't know how much time we have to get together another benefit of this magnitude," I sighed. "I really think we should try to come up with something by the middle of February. After that, it may well be too late."

Lyle and I were driving to the restaurant Patina. I'd wanted to get him alone, so I had Kathy and Wanda drive ahead. When Greg had gotten out of the hospital, a day or two later, he had come back into Lyle's life and kind of shrugged off the benefit, explaining that he had gotten screwed by his various sponsors, who had backed off their promises. Kathy didn't want any part of him, and I could hardly blame her. But Greg was calling me, and claiming that Lyle was telling him in private that he still wanted Greg to represent him, and that Kathy was essentially holding him prisoner, and if she got her way, planned to further remove him by moving with him to Oregon.

"Lyle, who do you really want to represent you? Do you want to work with Greg? Or do you want to go with Jerry Katzman and the William Morris group?"

I had set up this dinner with Fred Westheimer, one of his former agents at William Morris years before, who had gotten him lots of work, only to be stiffed out of $75,000 in commissions. But that had all been forgiven now.

"I want to work with William Morris." Lyle's voice was a hoarse whisper, the nerves to his vocal cords now nearly chewed away by spreading cancer.

"What about Oregon?" I asked. "Do you really think it's a good idea to go up there, away from all your friends?"

"I've had too many bad things happen to me here. This isn't home anymore. I like Oregon."

"Well, as I told you before, Portland has one of the best teams of doctors, experts on brain lymphoma, so certainly from that standpoint you'll get equal care if not better."

"I appreciate what you've done, doc, but I just can't put up with L.A. anymore."

"We'll just have to figure out how we can get a little extra help for you on the plane flight up there. I'm sure you'll be fine. God willing, some of the experimental treatments they have available in Portland may be able to knock this thing back a little bit."

"I hope so, doc."

Lyle turned ever so slowly to get out of the car. I came around and assisted one of the parking attendants in helping him extend off the seat and onto the sidewalk. He had lost a hundred pounds of muscle. He walked with a slow, wide-based shuffle and was slightly hunched over at the shoulders. He was becoming progressively more off balance. I never let go of his arm.

We sat down with Fred Westheimer and his wife, Susie, and after an initial exchange of pleasantries, Lyle gave Fred the okay to see if anything could be salvaged of the TV movie and book projects. We all leaned back to relax, especially Kathy, who really hadn't been out of the house and had been functioning as a twenty-four-hour critical-care nurse for the last several months.

But Lyle's cancer also affected the nerves controlling swallowing, and with each bite of food, or even gulp of liquid, he would aspirate some the wrong way into the air tube, which would initiate a racking cough, and that alone wore him out. When the appetizer was done, it was clear he couldn't make it much longer, and he asked to be taken home.

I put him in my car. He wanted Kathy to stay. He wanted her to have a little more of the evening off. They'd just hired a nighttime LVN who could easily take care of him alone for the couple of hours till Kathy got home. I clicked in a seat belt as he leaned his patent-pending skull-and-crossbones bandanna back on the head rest and stared straight ahead. I clicked on the CD player, and we drove home, mostly in silence. We were just a few blocks from his home when I became aware of the haunting Jim Morrison lines:

> They're waiting to take us into the severed garden
> You know how pale and wanton, thrill full
> Comes death in the strange hour
> Unannounced, unplanned for
> Like a scaring, over-friendly guest
> You've brought to bed
> Death makes angels of us all
> And gives us wings
> where we had shoulders smooth as raven's claws.

Those lines, from "Albinoni Adagio," a poem toward the end of the soundtrack of the movie *The Doors* which I'd heard many times before, seemed to verbalize Lyle's unspeakable plight. I felt like crying. I nervously looked out of the corner of my eye to see if Lyle had similarly connected. I didn't know whether to turn off the CD or pretend nothing had happened. But Lyle, sitting bolt upright, just continued to stare straight ahead as if in a trance, a trance broken only by his shallow coughs.

Lyle finally had his day. His good buddies at Gold's Gym were the ones to come through for him. The benefit wasn't black-tie, and it wasn't $500 a plate, but there were tons of former football players and friends from all parts of his life, and instead of all the pomp and circumstance and big-name acts, there was moving speech after moving speech by those whose lives he'd touched. He was just able to move with someone else's assistance now, hardly a man you could imagine had only a year and a half before lined up in the trenches with the best that pro football had to offer. A guy who had boasted, "If me and King Kong went into an alley, only one of us would come out, and it wouldn't be the f——ing monkey!"

This was the guy who'd forced a change in the NFL rules when he ripped off an opponent's helmet and then hit him with it. The next year the Alzado Rule went into effect. You got fined if you removed an opponent's equipment and threw it back at him.

Now it was an effort to move an arm. While Marcus Allen, Carl Weathers, Nadia Comaneci, and Howie Long marched up to give their thoughts, I paced in the back of the ballroom wondering if the ideas I had jotted down earlier that day made any sense. Al Davis was in attendance, and I wanted to address some of the larger issues in sports as well.

"And now," said the host from Gold's Gym, "I'd like to introduce Lyle's doctor, Dr. Rob Huizenga, to say a few words."

April 3, 1949. Lyle Alzado was born. He was tough from the start. The doctor tried to slap him, but Lyle blocked it with a forearm, and slapped the doctor back. Then he got in a few punches to the doctor's midsection, for good measure.

I first met Lyle in the early 1980s when I was working in a prominent El Segundo outpatient psych ward .... I mean for the Los Angeles Raiders.

Lyle was intense, focused, and as intimidating off the field as on. I remember one Saturday-night meal, before the '84 Chicago game. I was sitting with Lyle, Mickey Marvin, Dave Casper, and several other linemen. Mickey, fully aware that Lyle was a fanatic when it came to having only A.1. sauce on his steak before games, pretended to be doing Lyle a favor and fakes like he's going to put ketchup on Lyle's steak. Then, when Lyle gave him one of his patented, menacing stares Mickey Marvin, our born-again Baptist, in his Southern good-ole-boy drawl, said "Ole Lyle, you know I love you, just kidding, good buddy."

Anyway, Lyle got up to get some A.1. sauce, and Dave Casper, the team jokester, took the entire ketchup bottle and emptied it out all over Lyle's plate.

I have never in my eight years of being around the NFL seen six two-hundred-and-eighty-pound men look so scared! Then the entire table jumped up, meals unfinished, and bolted for the door. And don't ask me what his reaction was, 'cause I sure as hell didn't stick around to find out. Room service was invented for nights like that.

Lyle, you were as mean and tough as they come.

Now, I know another side of Lyle. The real Lyle. The really tough Lyle. The Lyle that admitted he made a mistake and came out publicly against anabolic steroids and growth hormone. The Lyle that tackled over fifteen hospitalizations in the last year, including two brain surgeries, meningitis, seizures, pneumonia, paralysis, and horrible pain.

The Lyle that held his ground through two courses of radiation therapy, six months of IV chemotherapy, and most recently two months of chemotherapy injected directly into the base of his brain.

You know, on the way over here, I was telling my wife, Wanda, that this was going to be a difficult speech. I wondered if God was going to try to pay me back for an irreverent skit I wrote as a Harvard medical student for our year-end show called "The Lighter Side of Lymphoma." As I was trying to think what to say, the jokes I had written kept coming back. Now they seemed so crude and inappropriate. But I think I've got it in perspective now.

Lyle, you've shown me that there really is a light side to lymphoma.

Despite your hoarse speech, you've found your voice.

Despite your weight loss, you've gained inner strength.

Despite your troubled walk, you've discovered the path.

Many follow your footsteps. Athletes look to you, and are now reevaluating their use of potentially harmful performance aids. The rest of us, doctors, coaches, fans, and parents, look to you as we reevaluate our role in pushing athletes to unhealthy lifestyles.

Stay tough, Lyle . . . your life has just *begun*!

On May 14, 1992, Lyle died. Howie Long, Sean Jones, Marcus Allen, and many other of Lyle's teammates and friends, including Wanda and me, made plans to fly up for the funeral. But Lyle was buried the very next day. Kathy decided to have the funeral early. She had it in her mind that Lyle's former wives and other family members would disrupt the service if she gave them time to arrive. So only a handful of friends were able to attend. Worst of all, Justin—Lyle's only son—never got a chance to say goodbye to his dad.

"Rob," Kathy told me on the phone later that afternoon, "Lyle sent me a message. A white dove flew down and stood tall atop that casket. It chirped three times, and darted away. The woman in charge at the cemetery told me she'd never seen that before. I know it was a message. I know Lyle was telling me it's all right."

I wished I could see something positive. I was thankful that Lyle's day-in and day-out suffering was over. But I was upset that his message was in jeopardy of dying with him. On May 15, 1992, the NFL broke its silence about the long-term steroid study. Spokesman Greg Aiello stated, "We're not interested . . ."

26

The Last Raider Camaraderie

Under the shadow of the famed Coliseum arches, I shifted awkwardly in the slowly moving "will call" line. It was November 1, 1993, nearly three years since I'd walked away from football.

"Doc! Long time no see!" piped a voice from behind the ticket window. It was Louie. He'd been handling tickets for the Raiders for as long as I could remember. "It's good to see you!" He smiled as he handed me a sealed envelope.

I ripped the envelope open. Mother Dunn, the former Raider strength coach, who had been lured away by the Chargers, had left me a bench pass. Giving a bench pass to a friend was risky business. Each team was allowed a limited number of sideline personnel, and excesses could result in a sizable fine.

If I got caught and questioned, I'd have to take the Fifth. I showed my pass at the press gate.

"Dr. Huizenga, how are you?"

It was a woman's voice off to my right.

"Cheryl, good to see you."

Oh shit, I thought. It was Al's personal secretary. I hustled ahead without looking up. Wherever Cheryl was, Al couldn't be far away. I hurried through the tunnel, then finally strode into the light of a perfect football day in the newly renovated Los Angeles Coliseum. The east peristyle end had been roped off, with new bleachers constructed next to the end zone. The field had been lowered and the stands extended down to the playing field. Gone was the eight-lane tartan track separating the football game from spectators. I walked over to the visitors' sideline. I had timed it exactly right: 12:03 P.M. The players were just emerging for pregame warm-ups. I had forgotten that the visitors were always on the sun side; I needed a hat.

Across the field I saw Al Davis, in his signature baggy bells, Raiders sweater, and sunglasses. Windblown strands of hair flitted over his ear. He clapped encouragement to the drilling Raider team. Behind him, arms folded impassively, stood Jim Otto. For the first time since 1987, Dr. Rosenfeld wasn't on the Raiders sideline. He was recovering from a stomach ulcer and sat out of sight in the press box. Mother Dunn jogged over to chat with me as the teams headed toward the locker room promptly at twelve-forty.

"Good to see 'ya," he said, slapping my back. "Can you think far enough back to remember this game? A touchdown is six points. Got that?"

When all the players had disappeared into the tunnel, Al majestically turned and with security guards at his side strode off the field and up the stairs at the forty-yard line, reluctantly shaking hands with several fans on his way to the press box elevator.

As the teams reemerged from the tunnel, the crowd roared. I had an eerie flashback to Super Bowl XVIII, the addicting rush of gladiator neurotransmitters, the exhilarating burst of adrenal hormones that when filtered through the prism of pride and poise lifts the body till you swear you're walking on air.

"Hey, doc, I want to introduce you to our security chief. This is Doc Huizenga. He was the doctor for the Raiders when I was with the team."

The San Diego security chief eyed me up and down as if I were a plant from the enemy, and probably wired for sound.

"He's okay," Mother Dunn said, slapping my back again before darting back to the front lines.

The kickoff arced upward into the cloudless sky.

"I guess you know the drill, then," the security chief cautioned. "Stay over on the side of the bench here. Stand back behind the second line, on the carpet, and if any of the rent-a-cops hassle you, give me a holler."

Soon after he left, one of the local Coliseum security people walked up to me.

"Can I see your pass?"

I showed it to him.

"I'm sorry, you can't stand here. You're going to have to leave."

I looked at him incredulously. "I'm with the Chargers."

Then I realized I had drifted over the illegal grassy area behind the photographers to get a better view of the action. I quickly walked back into the safe zone.

Tim Brown knifed through the San Diego sideline after making an acrobatic catch of a Jeff Hostetler throw. I wanted to thump him on the back and scream, "Way to go, Timmy!" But I was a guest, bound by Charger sideline etiquette.

The San Diego doctors and trainers recognized me standing in the corner and one by one came over to schmooze between plays.

Whoa! Hostetler gunned a bomb fifty yards downfield to a wide-open Timmy Brown, who danced, ball held high, into the end zone. As the stadium erupted in celebration, the Charger team podiatrist kicked the ground in disgust. I felt a winning-the-lottery warmth stream to my fingertips. Maybe I was especially happy that one of the last bees in Al Davis's bonnet was doing so well this Sunday. I had seen Tim Brown about four months before at Marcus Allen's wedding; Marcus had joked that most of the guests were in Al Davis's doghouse. Marcus, of course, led the list, but also in attendance were Steve Beuerlein, Sean Jones (who provoked Al's wrath by leading the Raiders in the 1987 players' strike—"You ruined my team," Al said—and who was traded soon thereafter), Mike Ornstein (without question the most loyal front office guy ever, but he made the mistake of *listening* to a job offer from the Rams), and myself. Tim Brown was on the list because he was asking to be traded, in large part because he was incensed at Davis's treatment of Tim's good friend Marcus. Brown also questioned whether he wanted to sacrifice his body for a guy who had found a contractual loophole that kept Tim from becoming a free agent—and from the eight-figure salary a bidding war would generate.

"Excuse me, sir, can I see your pass?"

I looked over this time to see a uniformed Los Angeles policeman.

"I'm sorry," the policeman said, "you're going to have to leave."

"I'm with the Chargers," I insisted.

The San Diego security chief hustled over.

"He's with us."

It took a three-minute conference to convince the cop. I looked toward the owner's box. It had to be Al Davis. Or was it? I used to ridicule opposing teams who swore Al had bugged their locker room or somehow sabotaged the field. Was I slipping into the same pit of paranoia?

There was one more attempt to eject me from the sideline, but I was having too much fun. I decided they were going to have to carry me out. Preferably not on a stretcher.

Deep in the fourth quarter, the Raiders blew the game. Going in for a touchdown from the eight-yard line, Hostetler threw to an open receiver in the end zone only to have the ball intercepted and run back one hundred one yards for a San Diego Charger fourteen-point turnaround. The stadium fell silent, but the cheers were deafening in my immediate vicinity. My doctor counterparts waved their hands in the air. I wanted to curse. Once a Raider, always that loyalty.

"Hey, this is great!" screamed Dunny as the final gun sounded. "We beat the freaking Raiders! Come on, let's go over and shake some hands and rub it in their faces."

"Thanks for the ticket, Dunny," I said. "Looks like I'm your good-luck charm. Management will probably want me on the side-line for all your games."

He laughed as we shook hands, then he ran ahead to say hello to all his old Raider friends.

I slowly angled across the field, behind the swirling pack of players, photographers, sportswriters, and stadium security. As I turned to survey the Coliseum, maybe for my last time, I felt the power and exhilaration of professional football. The world's fastest, strongest, toughest men facing off in collision combat inside the country's largest stadiums, packed to the limit with rabid fans. This is one hell of a great sport. It will never die.

Sadly professional players do die—some at alarmingly young ages. In the last five years alone, five players from the 205-man regular 1982–92 Raider rosters, aged twenty-six, twenty-eight, thirty-two, thirty-eight, and forty-one have died. Is it football . . . or sheer coincidence?

There can be no doubt, football batters the body. Run into a wall full speed twenty or thirty times—then you'll know what an NFL game does to the body. A six-year NFL vet may absorb 100,000 of these full-speed hits. The starters play hurt nearly every game. True, injured players get a ton of respect from teammates, coaches, and owners for playing hurt, but when the cheers fade and their football careers are over, as many as seventy to eighty percent suffer from football-related permanent physical disability. Santa Ana attorney George Hill, the southern California maven in football-related work-ers' comp cases, has represented over eleven hundred ex-pros and never lost one case.

It's not that I'm such a great lawyer," he modestly shrugs, "these players are *really* crippled."

Football also batters the psyche. With the average NFL career dwindling to about three years, scores of twenty-something NFL veterans, many unprepared and untrained for life on the outside, are faced with an abrupt transition from idol to obscurity. The athlete who has focused his entire life between the hash marks, who has gained ungodly amounts of weight, used risky performance-enhancing drugs, removed protective equipment if it might interfere with performance, even hidden significant injuries from the medical staff . . . anything to make the team, is now forced to start over, many times from the bottom. His self-esteem is jolted. His bank account is often halved by divorce, rumored to be as high as seventy percent among players, and is further depleted by investments gone bad and the residue of free-spending playing days.

When the phone rings early on cut day, or retirement is announced, or worse, a career-ending injury occurs, the vast majority of NFL vets go into withdrawal. Symptoms range from brief periods of insomnia to despair and hopelessness to suicidal thoughts. Sports psychologist Tony Bober suggested there be a warning, stuck to the side of the players' helmets, like the one on cigarette packs— "Warning: Football has been found to be dangerous to your health."

Can we make America's most popular pastime safer? Less damaging to body and soul?

Yes, I believe we can. But it's going to mean changing the current NFL system of the dominating owner or coach selecting and paying for the team doctor—who is then magically expected to have the player's best interest at heart.

Imagine the pressure . . . the Super Bowl is a week away and your team's star is injured. Your boss—a win-at-all-costs business-man—has doled out over thirty-four million in salaries and expects a return on his investment. The player, mesmerized by the pregame hype, or subconsciously realizing that refusing to play hurt may damage his reputation as a macho tough guy (and eventually impact salary and endorsements), states openly that he's willing to take almost any risk to play. Enter you—the team doctor—perhaps also a little caught up in the pregame excitement. Remember, even medical professionals are human. They can occasionally succumb to pressure like *everyone else*.

Surprisingly, it appeared to me that many of the other NFL doctors successfully walked the tightrope between satisfying the owner and giving the player the best available care. However, too many times, the current system has failed. I'm witness to that. One way out of this bind would be to appoint the team doctor to a set term not unlike a judge, perhaps by a consensus of owners and players, but then supervised solely by an impartial medical board or state commission. California doctors who supervise boxing have such an arrangement. They report to a group of politically appointed commissioners, some of whom have no interest in boxing, so that if a doctor stops a fight in the first round he's not in immediate jeopardy of losing his job due to an angry fighter, upset managers, agents, or fight promoters.

Besides removing overt player and owner pressures, as well as unseen financial and malpractice conflicts, this arrangement would also be a step toward solving the player grievance dilemma. Not uncommonly a player files such a grievance when he feels he was cut from a club while still injured, in violation of the collective bargaining agreement which states an athlete cannot be released if he is "physically unable to perform the services required of him by his contract." Currently when a dispute arises, team orthopedists testify against the player—their patient. It's unheard of for a doctor in any other situation to testify against his own patient, unless that patient has literally committed murder.

One eye-opening grievance case illustrates just how far team doctors can go to please management. Joe McCall, a running back the Raiders originally drafted in 1984, moved on to another team and in 1986 suffered a knee injury requiring surgery. Following surgery Joe complained of persistent pain. His surgeon, the team doctor at the time, apparently felt Joe was faking the pain to prevent his new team from cutting him, thereby bilking the team out of the remainder of his 1986 salary. Because of the team doctor's suspicion, the team hired private investigators to videotape Joe after he left the training facility in the hopes of catching him dancing or riding a bike. When this surveillance proved inconclusive, the doctor persuaded Joe to be examined under sodium pentothal—truth serum. But this filmed exam also proved inconclusive. Two outside doctors disagreed with the team doctor's claims and countered that the athlete did indeed have pain—caused by a degenerative knee arthritis. The arbitrator awarded Joe $30,000—the unpaid portion of his 1986 salary. Small wonder that many players' lawyers and agents now instruct their player-clients to avoid team doctors at all costs

(unfortunately sometimes even in cities where the team doctor is acknowledged to be first-rate.)

Possibly the most difficult medical question is, What sorts of injuries should the team doctor allow back on the field? Should uniform standards be set? For instance, in California a boxer is prevented by state law from sparring for thirty days or competing for forty-five days after being knocked unconscious. Should a football player with injuries predicting a high chance of permanent joint or neurologic damage be similarly disqualified? Should we officially protect players from themselves—and from overzealous owners?

I feel the athlete can make the decision—when fully informed of the risks by a truly impartial doctor. Problem is, NFL medicine is still pretty much in the dark ages in terms of understanding risks. We have some understanding about the lasting effects of repeated concussions and the increased risk of playing on artificial turf. There are, however, no meaningful studies on the risks athletes face when exposed to numbing shots, corticosteroids, anabolic steroids, amphetamines, growth hormones, repeated collisions, excessive weight gains, or any of the other peculiarities of life in the NFL. So we really can't offer players accurate advice until the NFL gives independent researchers the green light to study these issues and the green light to have team doctors act on their findings.

Okay, maybe it's pie in the sky to expect a multibillion-dollar business to turn its back on its accountants and its Park Avenue PR wizards and do what I believe is in the best interests of the player's health. Then it's up to the NFL players to step forward and to take personal responsibility. Alone or together the players must pressure team owners for premier medical care—they must understand that in the past owners have treated players like pieces of meat if they so desired. No player would dream of hiring a team employee to negotiate a contract, yet I saw many Raiders unquestioningly accept the opinions of Rosenfeld in matters far more urgent than contract negotiations.

I thought I could be a team doctor and rise above the potential game-day pressures and conflict of interest. I took away the candy jar, explained risks, encouraged second opinions, talked openly about steroids, speed, and growth hormone, discouraged numbing shots, and preached priorities. I thought I could medically treat the Raider players like my other private patients and still please management. I was wrong.

* * *

I'd be a liar if I said I didn't miss the idle training meal chatter, the pranks, the sideline, and the Sunday urgency. I'll always have a silver-and-black hole inside. Replaying the glory days with many Raiders as I wrote this book over the last year has been therapeutic for me. I got lost family back. One player called last January, like a nervous aunt, to check up on me.

"Rob, what's up? I haven't heard from you in a couple of months. Is the book going to come out, or what? I keep looking in the newspaper to make sure they haven't found you in some lake with cement shoes."

"I'm fine." I laughed. "I did get kind of a scare the other day, though. My office got trashed. Books, charts, everything got thrown on the floor, pictures smashed down everywhere."

"No! You think he got somebody to break in?"

"Geez, don't you read the newspaper out there? We had a six-point-eight earthquake yesterday!"

I went to Johnny O's for his annual in-case-we-lose-in-the-play-offs 1994 Super Bowl party. Coaches, scouts, trainers, equipment guys, video crew, they were all there. I guess it was my last moment of Raider camaraderie. This book would be coming out in a few months, and I had to assume "Mr. Raider" would excommunicate me, or worse, when it hit the stands. I hadn't breathed a word about the book to Johnny or any of the rest of the Raider staff. But at the party I did have to bite my lip hard to keep it to myself. A couple of hours talking with Otten, George Anderson, H. Rod Martin, Art Shell, Tom Walsh, Terry Robiskie, or a few other coaches and I was sure I'd be able to write an entire second volume.

Johnny Otten grandly oversaw the eight-TV bash. One jokester had left a local newspaper out in plain view on the front table, open to an article speculating about which Raider coaches would get fired. *That* was also the Raiders. Camaraderie, but no sacred cows. (Okay, just one glaring exception.)

Over charcoal-grilled links, topped with special hot chili sauce, I said my coded last goodbyes to my Raider family.

"Well, you *said* you'd come back when Rosenfeld was gone, and he won't be back next year."

"No," I mumbled, shaking my head, still wondering what I

could have done differently, "I won't be coming back. I'm swamped with my practice now. I just can't go back."

"Oh, what's the matter?" the questioner shot back with feigned locker-room indignation. "Aren't we good enough for you anymore?"

Epilogue—Where Are They Now?

MARCUS ALLEN at the tender age of thirty-four was voted to yet another Pro Bowl in 1994 as a Kansas City Chief. Only one year before he had toiled as the third-string Raider running back, a player Al Davis called "a cancer to our team," and on another occasion "just a tired old veteran." Maybe Vann McElroy put it best when he said, "Marcus is living all of our dreams. He's playing great football, and showing up Al in a big way."

GEORGE ANDERSON entered his thirty-fifth year of service to the Raiders in 1994. He plans to retire at the end of this season. He is currently finishing a book of children's poems, tentatively titled *Grandpa George's Animal Primer-Rhymer*.

STEVE BEUERLEIN got his chance to shine as a Dallas Cowboy during the 1993 play-off stretch. Free agency brought him total freedom and a $7.5 million contract with Phoenix, five times more money than the amount Al absolutely turned down and tried to humiliate him over. To this day Beuerlein will not say the words A_ D____ in public.

DAVE CASPER is currently a hard-driving, very successful Northwestern Mutual agent in Minnesota. "Ghost" has calcific shoulder deposits and neck, back, and foot pain to show for his eleven mostly All-Pro years in football. He's proud to this day of going out on one leg (the other one was rubber-banded and shot up) and catching the key touchdown pass, his last as a pro, against the league-leading Dolphins. He's got no regrets. He figures he couldn't have played past his third year without the help of cortisone shots. The only thing he doesn't like about football today is the earrings.

DAVE DALBY is back going strong after a few rocky post-playing years. "I thought with my education I'd be able to handle retirement," he said. "I had no idea." The last bit of good news: a chunk of his $700,000 Technical Equities investment was salvaged in court.

AL DAVIS was voted into the Hall of Fame on January 25, 1992. As he stood at a Minnesota Super Bowl party several days after the announcement was made, he was overheard to say, "I'm in. Nobody can hurt me now."

BRUCE DAVIS, a Texas-based New York Life stockbroker, shakes his head as he recalls his six knee surgeries and countless weekly and eventually biweekly knee injections. Toward the end of his career as a Houston Oiler, where the orthopedists wisely refused to shoot up his knees, he'd have to line up in his tackle position standing up—his knees hurt too much to crouch into a three-point stance. Because of the pain, he couldn't even jog to the sideline, or to the locker room at halftime. He'd have to walk.

"Hey, I couldn't complain," he reminisced. "We had two guys playing next to me—Dean Steinkuler and Mike Munchak—who had much worse knees. Dean had thirteen knee surgeries, and Mike got cut nine times on his right knee alone!"

CHARLEY HANNAH is now a contractor on the eastern coast of Florida. His ankle never bent properly after surgery, but by that time he couldn't run anyway because of his knees. Charley has lost joint range of motion, but not his fabled storytelling ability. The same goes for Margaret-Ann Hannah: "You may as well write about the 1983 Escobar's restaurant after-game party. Almost everybody already knows about it anyway." She and Charley had just joined the Raiders weeks before and were chatting with the Guys and the Plunketts. Margaret-Ann had one drink too many and suddenly felt the urge to vomit. She had just managed to get up out of her chair and turn around when out it came, spraying all over Coach Flores's new $500 Italian boots.

MIKE HARDEN was forced to retire at the end of the 1990 season due to chronic neck pain, recurrent bouts of temporary paralysis, and a new fourth cervical hairline fracture. He still has neck pain everyday. DR. TORG, the Philadelphia neck specialist who cleared Harden to play after multiple other specialists had recommended he retire or be operated on, was just appointed the team doctor for the Philadelphia Eagles.

NEWT HARRELL, the rookie forced to wear the cumbersome Philadelphia neck collar when he was out in public after his rookie scholarship injury in 1988, now runs the Planet Car Wash and Quick Lube in Amarillo, Texas.

He had several bouts of atrial fibrillation (a heart rhythm problem) as a Raider, but his biggest medical scare came several years later just after he got traded. His new team checked him into a hospital to evaluate his heart before they'd sign him. When he was discharged, the team's *driver* informed him he'd failed his physical and was being taken to the airport, not back to the training facility. As Newt sat on the airplane and worried about what was wrong, a man dashed in just as the door was about to be sealed shut and breathlessly asked for Newt Harrell.

"You have to get off! You've got an important phone call!"

Newt was whisked off the plane and handed a phone at the airline check-in counter. On the line was a team executive. "We made a mistake. You're okay. You passed the physical!"

BO JACKSON is now a California Angel. The man who injured his hip on January 13, 1991, then paced behind the bench the ensuing week, is now the first professional athlete ever to play with a prosthetic hip. Doctors are worried that "impact loading" (jumping, landing hard, changing direction quickly) will shorten the life of the artificial joint given the everyday stresses of pro baseball. How much will it shorten the life of his hip replacement? No one can say.

DR. WALTER JEKOT was sentenced to five years in federal prison for distributing human growth hormone and/or steroids to Lyle Alzado, "Bay Watch" star David Hasselhof, many other L.A. stars, and numerous Olympic athletes. Dr. Jekot tried to get his sentence reduced by claiming he was studying anabolic steroids and their use in keeping weight on in AIDS patients. DR. JOHN PEARLZAC, another of Lyle's steroid "doctors," is in Lompoc Federal Reformatory serving a four-year term. Dr. Pearlzac attempted to get off the hook by saying that his services were vitally needed in an impoverished Pomo Indian clinic where he had worked for several months while he was awaiting sentencing.

SEAN JONES is a Beverly Hills-based stockbroker for Dean Witter. He appeared in the 1994 Pro Bowl for the Houston Oilers. In April 1994 he signed for $7.8 million over three years with the Green Bay Packers, now run by general manager RON WOLF, the ex-Raider head scout whose final head nod had convinced Al Davis to draft Sean in 1984.

SHELBY JORDAN is an entrepreneur in Los Angeles.

KENNY KING currently works for an overnight express company in the Midwest. He remembers pro football's good times, especially the will to win. But he adds, "Now that I'm retired, and suffer from chronic [football related] pain, I wonder if I should have followed my instincts in 1981 [after he was one of the heroes in the Raiders' Super Bowl victory over the Eagles] and retired and gone back to school."

LINDEN KING still apologizes every time I see him for jerking my thumb out of joint. He's been on the road for the last two years with his own country-and-western band. In 1994 he got his first opportunity to record an album. Stay tuned for a release date.

AL LoCASALE, Al Davis's perennial second-in-charge, now spends most of his time overseeing the Raiderettes. Al's right-hand woman is now his in-house legal expert, AMY TRASK.

HENRY LAWRENCE (aka KILLER) is active in the computer business in Los Angeles. His true love is singing and he occasionally gets the chance to sing professionally.

HOWIE LONG retired from the Raiders in 1994 after thirteen seasons. He has signed on to be one of Fox's featured announcers and is negotiating a major motion picture deal. He made it to his record-tying eighth Pro Bowl in 1994 despite a perplexing dig from Al Davis. Howie played defensive tackle, a position where sacks are few and far between. However, on the All-Star balloting, Al Davis insisted on listing him as a defensive end, a position where the league's stars average sacks in the double figures. Howie would have been a shoo-in as All-Pro if listed as a tackle, but for some reason, Davis didn't want it that way. Fortunately, even though he was a couple of votes shy of making the team outright, the Pro Bowl coach chose him as one of his discretionary picks.

CURT MARSH, after a seven-year pro career, found his real calling: helping kids. He now serves as the youth program coordinator for a large Northwestern city. In 1988, long before Alzado went public with his "I lied" steroid message, Curt wrote a newspaper article detailing the pressures that led him to use, and then launched an inspiring crusade to teach kids why they shouldn't. With his trademark humor and candor, he's talked eye-to-eye with nearly a quarter of a million kids—explaining that if you try your hardest, you're a winner. Drugs get you nowhere.

Tragically though, Curt now faces a possible foot amputation in the near future. Seven ankle surgeries and numerous joint infections have left him with few other options.

Curt has already visited the amputation clinic, and seen the artificial feet. Half laughing, half crying, he relates, "I'm not looking forward to waking up in the morning, turning to my wife and saying, "Honey, can you hand me my foot?" He chuckles, saying the only silver lining he can think of is getting a handicapped parking sticker. "I'll be able to park right next to the grocery store entrance . . . and that's an offensive lineman's dream."

VANN McELROY is a gentleman rancher deep in the heart of Texas. He also helps represent over fifty football players for Casterline, Vines, and McElroy Team Sports. He is contemplating major surgery on his larynx, which was fractured twice while absorbing forearms from ball carriers. The second fracture actually knocked things back closer to normal, but now the malpositioned vocal cords are weakening, and his voice is becoming hoarse.

MATT MILLEN has just signed a contract for $600,000 with Fox as a featured announcer. "Can you believe it?" he asked me. "First I get paid an outrageous amount of money to hang around and play a game. And now they're paying me to talk about it!" His past CBS job forced him to wear a suit and tie. Disbelieving ex-teammates never fail to razz him when they see him actually wearing a tie, or even carrying an overnight bag.

DEAN MIRALDI is down to a trim 235 pounds and is in the medical sales business in Southern California. Interestingly, he was recently diagnosed with dyslexia. His therapists were amazed he was able to play pro football with his degree of right-left confusion. Dyslexia doesn't explain Dean's muscle cramps or his "attacks," but if I were still in the league, I'd test for dyslexia before letting a player get labeled as a "head case."

DON MOSEBAR is still the anchor of the Raiders' line after ten seasons.

The NFL DRUG PROGRAM has been modified, perhaps to avoid the controversy that plagued former NFL drug czar Forrest Tennant. For starters, his replacements have been absolutely banned from speaking with the press. Additionally, the drug policy appears to be far more lenient than in Tennant's era. At least one recent athlete has tested positive for cocaine more than ten times with absolutely no action taken.

The NFL PHYSICIANS SOCIETY is currently trying to fight off an invasion from the big business hospital chains. Turns out some health companies are actually bidding for the right to be the official team doctor/team hospital for NFL teams. The hospitals have presumably calculated that getting their hospital logo right next to one of those stadium beer commercials is worth a lot of bucks. It's rumored the bidding may have reached $1 million.

JOHNNY OTTEN lives with his lovely wife and handsome son in his suburban home with a pool.

JIM PLUNKETT runs a beer distributorship but flies down from his San Francisco-area home to announce the Raider games along with ex-stars MIKE HAYNES and BOB CHANDLER.

JERRY ROBINSON is active in real estate in Las Vegas. Jerry, still a nonstop comedienne, remembers waking up from his 1989 concussion and thinking, "What the hell are all these white people doing standing over me?" Jerry's last few years in pro football were difficult. Whereas he'd typically come into camp knowing every defensive play, he now had to refresh his memory with the playbook. Whereas he used to be defensive captain, translating in the sideline signals to his teammates in the huddle, and calling audibles once the defense was set, he now informed the defensive coaches that he not only couldn't call signals, he was also sometimes forgetting what to do himself.

DR. ROBERT ROSENFELD died January 5, 1994, after a four-week battle with lung cancer. When Al Davis was notified of his passing, he shot back at the physician, "You just let him die?"

There was a minute of silence in his honor before the wild card play-off game with Denver the following Sunday. After the Raider victory, Coach Shell presented Rosenfeld's family with the game ball.

MARC WILSON is involved in real estate development in the Northwest. I'll always be able to picture him slumped over in front of his locker after he led us to a 16–6 division-clinching, nationally televised Monday-night thriller over the Rams in 1985.

He was all beat up—face, back, arms were bruised, he had ice on his separated shoulder (remember the "could-only-be-worse-if-the-bone-was-sticking-out" shoulder separation), and more ice on a banged-up knee and ankle. I watched in disbelief as one of his All-Star teammates walked in and began to scream, mothering Marc up and down: turned out, this athlete had a clause in his contract which promised him a huge bonus if he caught a certain number of passes, and he had ended up a couple catches shy. There was Marc, sitting exhausted, exasperated, and alone up against the cold, steel locker door. The victories, the verbal abuse, the injuries. That just about sums up Marc Wilson's career.